Cities of the
Biblical World

Cities of the Biblical World

An Introduction to the Archaeology, Geography, and History of Biblical Sites

LaMoine F. DeVries

Wipf & Stock
PUBLISHERS
Eugene, Oregon

Wipf and Stock Publishers
199 W 8th Ave, Suite 3
Eugene, OR 97401

Cities of the Biblical World
By DeVries, LaMoine F.
Copyright©1997 by DeVries, LaMoine F.
ISBN 13: 978-1-55635-120-4
ISBN 10: 1-55635-120-8
Publication date 11/29/2006
Previously published by Hendrickson Publishers, 1997

This book is dedicated to my parents,
Ferdinand and Velma† DeVries,
through whom I came to appreciate the Bible.

TABLE OF CONTENTS

PART I

CITIES OF THE OLD TESTAMENT WORLD

Unit 1: Cities of Mesopotamia

Unit 2: Cities of Aram/Syria and Phoenicia

PART II

CITIES OF THE NEW TESTAMENT WORLD

Unit 1: Cities of Palestine

Unit 2: Cities of the Roman World

ABBREVIATIONS

ABD	*Anchor Bible Dictionary.* Ed. D. N. Freedman. New York: Doubleday, 1992 (6 volumes)
BA	*Biblical Archaeologist*
BAF	K. N. Schoville, *Biblical Archaeology in Focus.* Grand Rapids: Baker, 1978
BAR	*Biblical Archaeology Review*
BASOR	*Bulletin of the American Schools of Oriental Research*
BCE	Before the Common Era
BEB	*Baker Encyclopedia of the Bible.* Ed. W. A. Elwell. Grand Rapids: Baker, 1988 (2 volumes)
BI	*Biblical Illustrator*
BW	*The Biblical World: A Dictionary of Biblical Archaeology.* Ed. C. F. Pfeiffer. Grand Rapids: Baker, 1966
ca.	circa (approximately)
CE	Common Era
EAEHL	*Encyclopedia of Archaeological Excavations in the Holy Land.* Ed. M. Avi-Yonah. Jerusalem: Israel Exploration Society and Massada Press, 1975 (4 volumes)
HBD	*Harper's Bible Dictionary.* Ed. P. J. Achtemeier. San Francisco: Harper & Row, 1985
HolBD	*Holman Bible Dictionary.* Ed. T. C. Butler. Nashville: Holman, 1991
IDB	*Interpreter's Dictionary of the Bible.* Ed. G. A. Buttrick. New York: Abingdon, 1962 (4 volumes)
IDBSup	*Interpreter's Dictionary of the Bible, Supplementary Volume.* Ed. K. Crim. Nashville: Abingdon, 1976
ISBE	*International Standard Bible Encyclopedia.* Ed. G. W. Bromiley. Grand Rapids: Eerdmans, 1979–88 (4 volumes)

MDB	*Mercer Dictionary of the Bible.* Ed. W. E. Mills. Macon, Ga.: Mercer University Press, 1990
NBD	*New Bible Dictionary.* Ed. J. D. Douglas. Grand Rapids: Eerdmans, 1962
NBD²	*New Bible Dictionary.* Ed. J. D. Douglas and N. Hillyer. 2d edition. Downers Grove, Ill.: InterVarsity, 1982
NEAEHL	*The New Encyclopedia of Archaeological Excavations in the Holy Land.* Ed. E. Stern. Jerusalem: Israel Exploration Society & Carta; New York: Simon and Schuster, 1993 (4 volumes)
NIDB	*The New International Dictionary of the Bible.* Ed. J. D. Douglas and M. C. Tenney. Grand Rapids: Zondervan, 1987
NIDBA	*New International Dictionary of Biblical Archaeology.* Ed. E. M. Blaiklock and R. K. Harrison. Grand Rapids: Zondervan, 1983
NT	New Testament
OEANE	*The Oxford Encyclopedia of Archaeology in the Near East.* Ed. E. M. Meyers. New York: Oxford University Press, 1997
OT	Old Testament
ZPEB	*Zondervan Pictorial Encyclopedia of the Bible.* Ed. M. C. Tenney. Grand Rapids: Zondervan, 1975 (5 volumes)

Biblical Books and Related Literature

Old Testament

Gen	Genesis
Exod	Exodus
Lev	Leviticus
Num	Numbers
Deut	Deuteronomy
Josh	Joshua
Judg	Judges
Ruth	Ruth
1–2 Sam	1–2 Samuel
1–2 Kgs	1–2 Kings
1–2 Chron	1–2 Chronicles
Ezra	Ezra

Neh	Nehemiah
Esth	Esther
Job	Job
Ps/Pss	Psalms
Prov	Proverbs
Eccl	Ecclesiastes
Song Sol	Song of Solomon
Isa	Isaiah
Jer	Jeremiah
Lam	Lamentations
Ezek	Ezekiel
Dan	Daniel
Hos	Hosea
Joel	Joel
Amos	Amos
Obad	Obadiah
Jonah	Jonah
Mic	Micah
Nah	Nahum
Hab	Habakkuk
Zeph	Zephaniah
Hag	Haggai
Zech	Zechariah
Mal	Malachi

New Testament

Matt	Matthew
Mark	Mark
Luke	Luke
John	John
Acts	Acts
Rom	Romans
1–2 Cor	1–2 Corinthians
Gal	Galatians
Eph	Ephesians
Phil	Philippians
Col	Colossians
1–2 Thess	1–2 Thessalonians

1–2 Tim	1–2 Timothy
Titus	Titus
Phlm	Philemon
Heb	Hebrews
Jas	James
1–2 Pet	1–2 Peter
1–2–3 John	1–2–3 John
Jude	Jude
Rev	Revelation

Other Early Writings

1 Macc	1 Maccabees
Ag. Ap.	Josephus, *Against Apion*
Ant.	Josephus, *The Jewish Antiquities*
Flaccus	Philo, *Against Flaccus*
Hist. eccl.	Eusebius, *Ecclesiastical History*
Life	Josephus, *The Life of Flavius Josephus*
War	Josephus, *The Jewish War*

PREFACE 🏺

The setting is still quite vivid in my mind, although I am not sure how old I was at the time. It was a typical summer evening in 1947 or 1948. In the driveway in front of our house on the grain and dairy farm where I grew up, my parents were visiting with neighbors, a tradition in that old German Lutheran and European Catholic community. They discussed current world events, particularly those in the Middle East and Palestine. As I listened to the conversation, it dawned on me that Jerusalem, the city I had heard about in Sunday school and church, was an actual city on the face of the earth. The story of the Bible suddenly took on new meaning. Jerusalem was not some ethereal city in the heavenly realm; it was a real city with real people who were involved in turmoil, like others in our world.

Though the story of this experience may seem insignificant, it is nevertheless through encounters of this nature that we grow and mature as persons. I still remember asking my parents that evening, "Jerusalem is a real town on earth?" What a breakthrough for a seven-year-old farm boy! That initial realization has led me, that simple farm boy from central Illinois, on an exciting, ever-expanding study of the biblical world and history.

Cities of the Biblical World is an introductory text. It is designed to introduce students of the Bible to the archaeology, geography, and history of several important sites of the OT and NT worlds. The text aims to be interesting, readable, and informational. It is designed with "handles." For instance, the title of each chapter includes a subtitle that highlights some important feature of the site's history, location, etc. In addition to the subtitles, the reader will find other "handles" which constitute important features of the story of the site. Because the text is intended for beginning students, numerous one-volume works have been cited in the bibliography for further reading. While the one-volume resources are limited in their treatment of a topic, they are often more accessible to the student and layperson. By presenting material in this way, it is my desire that *Cities of the Biblical World: An Introduction to the Archaeology, Geography, and History of Biblical Sites* will help expand the readers' understanding of the biblical world.

INTRODUCTION

Urban centers have always played an important role in the story of humankind and the shaping of history, including biblical history. The dynamic impact urban centers have had in shaping history is directly related to the factors that contributed to the establishment of the sites themselves. Villages, towns, and cities developed at precise locations for special reasons. In ancient times the location of a village, town, or city was often determined by the availability of water; by features of the terrain that made the site easy to defend; by the convergence of trade routes; or by other features that enhanced subsistence. Consequently, the village, town, or city became a dynamic part of society because its establishment, growth, and development came as a result of meeting the basic needs of the people.

Usually beginning as a small village, the city often became a center for trade and exchange, a melting pot for different cultural groups, a fortified defense center, the focal point for religious activities, the dwelling place of deities, a center for craftsmen and industry, and a seat of government or authority. In essence, it became a citadel for humans, a focal point for the settlement of people, a center of activity and change. This important role is reflected in the development of roads and highways, with the thoroughfares of the region, both primary and secondary, leading inward to the village, town, or city like spokes in the hub of a wheel.

Several terms appear in the text with which the reader may be unfamiliar. Two terms that appear frequently in reference to the geographical and archaeological features of sites in Palestine are tell (or tel) and wadi. The terms tell (Arabic) and tel (Hebrew), which mean hill or mound, are used in reference to ancient sites. In an archaeological context, the term tell/tel signifies an important feature of the ancient site, namely that it is a mound comprised of layers of debris with each stratum or layer representing a different period in the history of the site. Wadi, on the other hand, is an Arabic term used in reference to a stream or watercourse that is seasonal in nature. In other words, wadis have water in them during the rainy season but are usually dry during the summer months. Palestine has many wadis.

Many important villages, towns, and cities are mentioned in the Bible. They were a part of societies that formed the background for both OT and NT. Our purpose in this work is to provide a basis for the study of the cities that existed during the OT and NT periods. This study will concentrate on the cities in Mesopotamia, Aram/Syria and Phoenicia, Anatolia, Egypt, and Palestine during the OT period, and Palestine and the provinces of the Roman world during the NT period. Special attention will be given to the geographical setting of the city, the history of the development of the site and how it relates to the Bible, the major features of the city, and the significant archaeological discoveries at the site.

Bibliography: BONINE, M. E., "Cities: Cities of the Islamic Period," *OEANE*, 2:35–36; DRINKARD, J. F., Jr., "Cities," *HBD*, 171–73; idem, "Cities and Urban Life," *HolBD*, 264–66; ELWELL, W. A., "City," *BEB*, 1:468–73; FREYNE, S., "Cities: Cities of the Hellenistic and Roman Periods," *OEANE*, 2:29–35; FRICK, F. S., "Cities: An Overview," *OEANE*, 2:14–19; idem, *The City in Ancient Israel* (Missoula, Mont.: Scholars Press, 1977); FRITZ, V., "Cities: Cities of the Bronze and Iron Ages," *OEANE*, 2:19–25; idem, *The City in Ancient Israel* (Sheffield: Sheffield Academic Press, 1995); HAMMOND, M., *The City in the Ancient World*, assisted by L. J. Bartson (Cambridge: Harvard University Press, 1972); HERZOG, Z., and J. E. Stambaugh, "Cities," *ABD*, 1:1031–48; HOPKINS, D. C., "City/Cities," *MDB*, 157–58; HOUSTON, J. M., "City," *ZPEB*, 1:873–80; MCCOWN, C. C., "City," *IDB*, 1:632–38; MYERS, A. C., "City," *ISBE*, 1:705–13; PAUL, S. M., and W. G. Dever, eds., "Cities," *Biblical Archaeology* (Jerusalem: Keter, 1972) 3–26; STERN, E., "Cities: Cities of the Hellenistic and Roman Periods," *OEANE*, 2:25–29; STONE, E., "The Development of Cities in Ancient Mesopotamia," *Civilizations of the Ancient Near East*, ed. J. M. Sasson (New York: Scribners, 1995) 1:235–248; THOMPSON, J. A., and J. N. Birdsall, "City," *NBD*, 236–38; idem, "City," *NBD²*, 212–14; WESTENHOLZ, J. G., ed. *Royal Cities of the Biblical World* (Jerusalem: Bible Lands Museum, 1996); WHITE, W., Jr., "City," *BEB*, 1:468–73.

Part I

CITIES OF THE
OLD TESTAMENT
WORLD

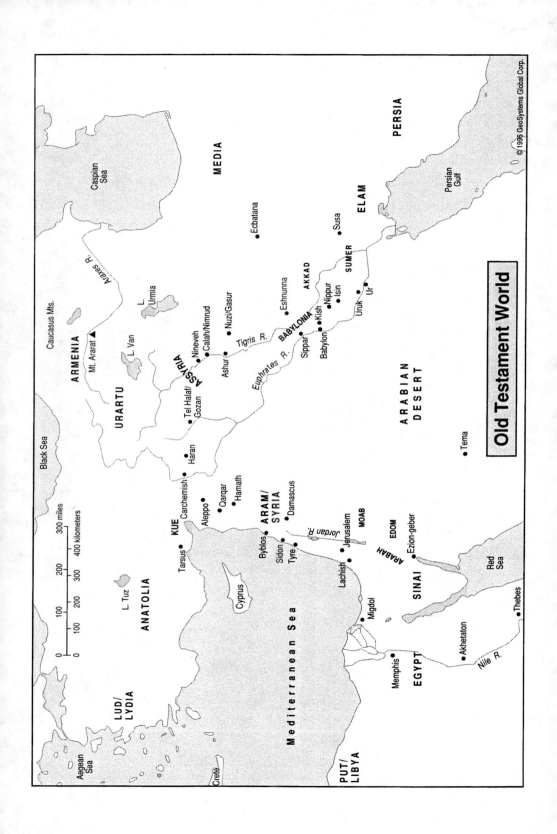

Old Testament World

Unit 1

CITIES OF
MESOPOTAMIA

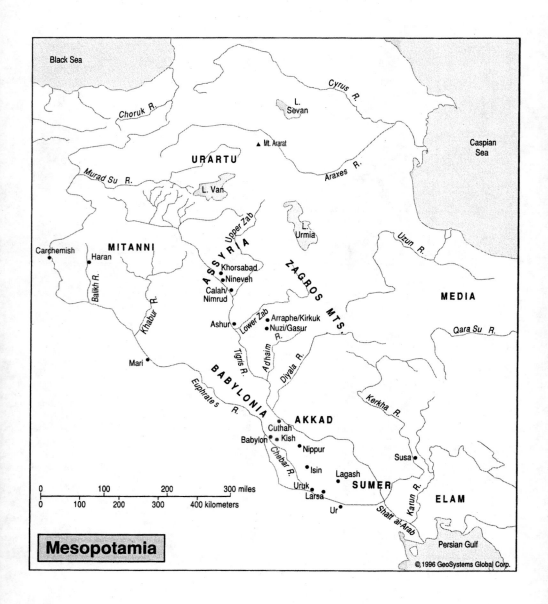

Mesopotamia

Black Sea

Choruk R.

Cyrus R.

L. Sevan

Caspian Sea

▲ Mt. Ararat

URARTU

Murad Su R.

Araxes R.

L. Van

L. Urmia

Carchemish

MITANNI

Haran

Upper Zab

A S S Y R I A

Z A G R O S   M T S.

MEDIA

Khorsabad

Nineveh

Uzun R.

Balikh R.

Khabur R.

Calah/ Nimrud

Ashur

Lower Zab R.

Arraphe/Kirkuk

Nuzi/Gasur

Qara Su R.

Mari

Tigris R.

Adhaim R.

B A B Y L O N I A

Diyala R.

Euphrates R.

Kerkha R.

AKKAD

Cuthah

Babylon

Kish

Nippur

Susa

Chebar R.

Isin

Larsa

Uruk

Lagash

SUMER

Karun R.

ELAM

Ur

Shatt al-Arab

Persian Gulf

| 0 | 100 | 200 | 300 miles |
| 0 | 100 | 200 | 300 | 400 kilometers |

© 1996 GeoSystems Global Corp.

MESOPOTAMIA 1

Land between the Rivers

Of all the regions that played a part in the OT story, the land of Mesopotamia was certainly one of the most important. Some of the earliest developments of civilization took place there. Mesopotamia was so named because of the presence of two important streams—the Euphrates River to the west and the Tigris River to the east. Because the two rivers formed a natural boundary on the east and on the west, the land between was identified as Aram-Naharayim in the Hebrew Bible and Mesopotamia, the name commonly used today; both names in essence mean "land between the rivers." Mesopotamia was the scene of perhaps the earliest developments in the ancient Near Eastern world. It was occupied by such notable groups as the Sumerians, a non-Semitic people, and the Akkadians and Amorites, both of which were Semitic. The southern part of early Mesopotamia was the region in which the great Sumerian culture developed. One of its most prominent cities was Ur, a city mentioned in the Bible. During the latter part of OT history, lower Mesopotamia was the homeland of the great Babylonian or Neo-Babylonian empire at the heart of which was the capital, the city of Babylon.

No less important was the region to the north, the land of Assyria, located on the upper end of the Tigris River. Important cities in that region included Nuzi, whose ruins shed light on the patriarchal period, though it is not mentioned in the Bible, and Ashur and Nineveh, major cities of the Assyrian empire. Two other cities of Mesopotamia also deserve mention. Mari, a rival of Babylon, was located in middle Mesopotamia upstream from Babylon on the Euphrates River. Haran, located on the Balikh River in extreme upper Mesopotamia, was the major home base of the patriarchs.

The geographical features of Mesopotamia played a vital role in the settlement and development of the land. The Tigris and Euphrates Rivers certainly influenced life in lower Mesopotamia. While rainfall was very limited in lower Mesopotamia, the area was abundantly watered by the annual flooding of the Tigris and Euphrates Rivers. For that reason lower Mesopotamia even in very early times was a key agricultural region, one of the most abundant food-producing areas in the ancient Near East.

Another unique feature that contributed to the life and development of lower Mesopotamia was an interlacing system of canals, streams, or rivers. This system of waterways was used for both inland irrigation and navigational purposes. But while lower Mesopotamia was fertile and productive, regions to the north included areas that were desertlike and unproductive and highland regions covered with forests.

Though Mesopotamia had its own unique geographical features, the land can never be completely understood apart from its people. Ancient Mesopotamia was the homeland of a variety of peoples who made important cultural contributions to the ancient world. They were among the earliest to domesticate cattle and cultivate crops. They developed a writing system comprised of wedge-shaped characters known as cuneiform. It was also among the peoples of lower Mesopotamia that the earliest law codes were written, including the famous Code of Hammurabi.

The OT reflects the influence that Mesopotamia, its people, and its empires had on biblical history. Mesopotamia was the original homeland of the patriarchs. Abraham's origin is associated with the cities of Ur (Gen 11:28; though the location has been debated) and Haran (Gen 11:31). Additional references to Haran in the patriarchal narratives suggest that the ancients had strong family ties to that part of upper Mesopotamia. It was to that region that Abraham sent his servant to find a wife for his son Isaac (Gen 24:10). And it was to Haran that Jacob fled from his brother Esau (Gen 28:10).

In addition to the accounts in the patriarchal narratives, other parts of the OT also show the influence of Mesopotamia. For instance, Joshua's admonition to forsake the gods of the fathers beyond the river (Josh 24:15) is generally considered to be a reference to the gods of Mesopotamia. During the period of the Judges, the Israelites experienced oppression for eight years as they were dominated by the

Mesopotamian king, Cushanrishathaim (Judg 3:8). Even David had to face horses and chariots from Mesopotamia as the Amorites fought against him (1 Chron 19:6). The most dramatic impact of the land of Mesopotamia in later OT history came through the Assyrians and Babylonians. After a period of political anarchy and decline, the northern kingdom and its capital, Samaria, fell to the Assyrians in 722 BCE. And in 587 BCE, the southern kingdom experienced a similar fate as the city of Jerusalem fell to the Babylonians. Since numerous Jews were transported from Jerusalem to Babylonia through a series of deportations, Babylonia became the home base for developments that helped reshape Jewish life and culture. For instance, trade and commerce began to replace agriculture and shepherding. And it was during the Babylonian exile that emphasis was placed on the Law and a new institution was born, the synagogue.

Bibliography: ADAMS, J. M., "Mesopotamia: Land of the Two Rivers," *Biblical Backgrounds,* revised by J. A. Callaway (Nashville: Broadman, 1965) 5–17; ALDEN, R. L., "Mesopotamia," *ZPEB,* 4:196; CHAPMAN, B. C., "Mesopotamia," *NIDBA,* 312–13; DeVRIES, C. E., "Mesopotamia," *NIDB,* 644; GORDON, C. H., "Mesopotamia," *IDB,* 3:359; GRAYSON, A. K., "Mesopotamia," *ABD,* 4:714; idem, "Mesopotamia, History of (Assyria)," *ABD,* 4:732–55; idem, "Mesopotamia, History of (Babylonia)," *ABD,* 4:755–77; HAYDEN, R. E., "Mesopotamia," *ISBE,* 3:329; HOOK, S. M., "Mesopotamia," *MDB,* 570; KNAPP, A. B., "Mesopotamia, History of," *ABD,* 4:714–20; NISSEN, H. J., "Mesopotamia: Ancient Mesopotamia," *OEANE,* 3:479–84; idem, "Mesopotamia: Prehistoric Mesopotamia," *OEANE,* 3:476–79; NORTHEDGE, A., "Mesopotamia: Mesopotamia in the Islamic Period," *OEANE,* 3:487–89; OPPENHEIM, A. L., *Ancient Mesopotamia,* revised by E. Reiner (Chicago: University of Chicago Press, 1977); PEARCE, L. E., "Mesopotamia," *HBD,* 629–30; SCHOVILLE, K. N., "Mesopotamia," *BAF,* 173–217; SIMPSON, St. J., "Mesopotamia: Mesopotamia from Alexander to the Rise of Islam," *OEANE,* 3:484–87; STEINKELLER, P., "Mesopotamia, History of (Third Millennium)," *ABD,* 4:724–32; WISEMAN, D. J., "Mesopotamia," *NBD,* 811; idem, "Mesopotamia," NBD^2, 763; WRIGHT, H. T., "Mesopotamia, History of (Prehistory)," *ABD,* 4:720–24.

ASHUR ☗

2

Fortified Citadel of Southern Assyria

In ancient times the name of a city was often ascribed to the territory around it, the city-state or empire as a whole. Such was the case with ancient Ashur (also spelled Asshur). With the passing of time the name of the city and the small city-state of Ashur became attached to the entire area of central Mesopotamia, the territory on the upper Tigris River, commonly called Assyria in the OT. While the name Ashur appears in the OT, it never refers to the city itself. It is used in reference to Ashur, the son of Shem, who is regarded as the founder of the nation of Assyria (Gen 10:22), and to the nation itself (Isa 10:5). Consequently, in ancient times the name Ashur was used in several different ways. It was the name of the capital city of the Assyrian empire; it was the name of the nation or people; and it was the name of the major god of the city and its territory.

Ashur was built on a bluff on the west bank of the Tigris River almost midway between the junctions of the Lower Zab and Upper Zab, rivers that entered the Tigris River from the east. The city lay approximately sixty miles south of Nineveh. Ashur was strategically located in relation to trade and exchange in lower, middle, and upper Mesopotamia in ancient times. Its location on the Tigris River made it an important center for river travel. But its location was also essential for land trade because the site was situated at a break in the Tigris River valley provided by the Hamrin Mountains, and it was through that pass that travel took place between lower Mesopotamia and the regions to the north. Because of the strategic location, the inhabitants of Ashur built a well-fortified city.

The site of ancient Ashur, known today as Qalat Sharqat, was first investigated by Henry Layard in 1847. But while Layard did a preliminary investigation of the ancient ruins, it was Hormuzd Rassam who later identified the site as the ancient city of Ashur. He did so on the basis of inscriptions he discovered that contained information from the reign of the Assyrian king, Tiglath-pileser I. The site was eventually excavated by a German team between 1903 and 1914. The excavations were directed by Walter Andrea and Robert Koldewey.

Excavations at the site revealed that the city's history extended back some five thousand years, beginning in approximately 3000 BCE and continuing to about 300 CE. During the first historical phase, ca. 3000–2000 BCE, Ashur was a colony of southern Mesopotamia. During the second phase, ca. 2000–1500 BCE (Middle Bronze Age), Ashur became an independent city-state. From about 1500–900 BCE Ashur became the leading city-state of the area and because of its position became the capital of the entire state and the Middle Assyrian empire. From about 900–614 BCE Ashur's role as capital and leading city was diminished as other Assyrian cities rose to prominence. Ashur became one of several centers of the enlarged, newly revitalized Assyrian empire, often referred to as the Neo-Assyrian empire.

Ashur's history as outlined above was shaped and molded by the major political and cultural developments that took place not only in Mesopotamia but in other parts of the ancient Near East as well. Initially, during the third millennium BCE Ashur was colonized by the Sumerians, a non-Semitic people whose kingdom and homeland were known as Sumer, located in southern Mesopotamia. During that era Ashur was one of the major northernmost satellites of the Sumerians. Following the Sumerian period, Ashur came under the control of Akkad, the kingdom that was located east of the Tigris River in lower Mesopotamia. During the period of Akkadian domination the city was controlled by the kings of the Sargonic dynasty.

By the nineteenth century BCE, the tide of Ashur's history began to turn. Ashur became a well-established city-state, and the early beginnings of the state of Assyria were underway. The kings of Ashur introduced a period of expansion and through a series of conquests increased their boundaries and the size of Ashur's territory. At the same time, the merchants of the state were actively involved in trade and exchange. Consequently they established new settlements and centers of trade, which in turn increased the wealth and economic base of Assyria. Assyria's prestige and status in the Mesopotamian world were especially enhanced during the reign of Shamshi-Adad I, 1812–1780 BCE, due to his many accomplishments, including the conquest of the city of Mari on the Euphrates River to the southwest. But perhaps the most critical development during his reign was the enhancement of trade through the establishment of caravan routes connecting the city of Ashur with other parts of the Fertile Crescent. Following Shamshi-Adad I's death, Ashur came under the domination of Hammurabi, the king of Babylon.

The most dramatic chapter in Assyrian history began during the fourteenth century and continued to the seventh century BCE, as the nation of Assyria became a major political power in the ancient Near East. The Assyrian kings of that era developed powerful armies, and their military expertise evoked fear in the surrounding nations. According to Assyrian records, the powerful Assyrian kings took great pride in using extremely cruel methods to deal with the prisoners of war taken captive from other territories. But the real burst of Assyrian power came during the mid-eighth century during the reign of Tiglath-pileser III, who came to the throne in 745 BCE. The Neo-Assyrian empire was underway, and Assyria began to play a dramatic role in biblical history. After he established his grasp on his homeland, Tiglath-pileser set in motion a strategy to achieve his major goal: to conquer all of the lands of the Fertile Crescent. Although Tiglath-pileser failed to realize his dream, he nevertheless set the process in motion. In 732 BCE he and his army conquered the city of Damascus, and in 722 BCE, Sargon II, one of his successors, conquered the city of Samaria, the capital of the kingdom of Israel, the northern kingdom. The empire of Assyria reached its zenith during the following century. In 701 BCE the Assyrian king Sennacherib moved into the kingdom of Judah and captured forty-six of the fortified cities of Judah; however, Sennacherib was apparently unable to capture the city of Jerusalem (2 Kgs 18:17–19:9). But the real climax to Assyrian power came near the middle of the seventh century in 664 BCE as Assyrian forces moved into Egypt and conquered the city of Thebes. Assyria reached its peak with the capture of Thebes; after that, however, the empire slowly declined. While the decline was due in large part to a series of weak leaders, it was hastened by external pressure by the newly formed Neo-Babylonian empire, a powerful force to the south that would eventually bring about the fall of the Assyrian empire. The events leading to that fall began in 614 BCE when Babylonian forces captured the city of Ashur, and they continued with the fall of Nineveh in 612 BCE, the fall of Haran in 610 BCE, and the fall of Carchemish in 605 BCE. While the fall of Nineveh was the straw that broke the camel's back, the battle of Carchemish in 605 BCE marked the end of one of the most powerful empires in the ancient Near East. Although Ashur is generally recognized as the capital of the ancient Assyrian empire, there were times when other Assyrian cities assumed that role, including Nineveh, Calah, and Khorsabad.

While excavations at Ashur have provided key information concerning its history, they have also provided valuable information about other substantial features of the city: its architectural remains, the gods worshiped there, and indispensable literary information in the form of inscriptions.

Ashur was a city of temples that were built for the numerous deities worshiped by the people of Ashur and its territory. The temple of Ashur, the chief god of the city of Ashur, was built during the Old Babylonian period. It was apparently built at a special location, the highest part of the city. Though parts of the temple have been found, its ruins have been damaged extensively due to erosion. The temple complex included several courts and a major courtyard. The temple of the god Anu-Adad is one of the most noteworthy because it attests to the excellent architectural skills of the Assyrian builders. The temple of Anu-Adad was in essence a large temple complex that was constructed during the twelfth century BCE; it included two ziggurats, or temple towers. Other temples discovered at Ashur include the temple of Enlil built by King Shamshi-Adad I and constructed in ziggurat form; the temple of Ishtar and Nabu, a complex that included both a temple and ziggurat; and the temple of Sin and Shamash, one of the earliest representatives of Assyrian temple architecture. The temple complex of Sin and Shamash included a large gateway designed like a house that led to a large rectangular central court. The inner part of the temple included two major rooms, one a large broad room, the other long and narrow.

The city of Ashur also had several palaces, and one can be dated to the Akkadian period. The palace was designed with a number of inner courtyards surrounded by rooms that formed the exterior of the palace. Another palace discovered at the site dates to the thirteenth century BCE and was built by King Adad-Nirari I. The palace complex had two major courtyards—the court of the gate and the court of the residents. Other parts of the city included residential areas and the commercial area, where merchants engaged in trade and exchange.

Excavations at the site have also produced several remarkable literary discoveries, including an Akkadian account of creation similar to the Babylonian *Enuma Elish.* The account dates to approximately 1000 BCE. The major difference in the two accounts is reflected in the heroes. In the Babylonian account the Babylonian god Marduk is the hero of the epic, while the hero in the Assyrian account is the god Ashur. A second important literary find was a copy of the Assyrian law code. This was comprised of two large tablets and several small fragments. The law code, which dates to the reign of Tiglath-pileser I, is the Assyrian equivalent of the Babylonian Code of Hammurabi; however, the former is only about one-fourth the length of the latter. A third document discovered at Ashur, in the ruins of a wall between the inner and outer wall on the south side, was the "king list." The list includes the names of Assyrian kings and the activities of those kings for each year of their reign, beginning about 1300 BCE.

Bibliography: GORDON, C. H., "Asshur," *IDB,* 1:261; GRAYSON, A. K., "Asshur," *ABD,* 1:500; idem, "Assyrians," *OEANE,* 1:228–33; JENNINGS, J. E., "Ashur," *NIDBA,* 76–77; LAMPRICKS, R. W., "Assur," *OEANE,* 1:225–28; MACHINIST, P. B., "Assur," *HBD,* 77; PFEIFFER, C. F., ed. "Ashur, Assyria," *BW,* 100–101; SCHOVILLE, K. N., "Ashur," *BAF,* 207–8; VOS, H. F., "Archaeology of Mesopotamia," *ISBE,* 1:267; WISEMAN, D. J., "Asshur," *ZPEB,* 1:369–70.

BABYLON    3

City of Marduk

The name Babylon evokes a variety of thoughts, ideas, and impressions. It is mentioned in the Bible and described in the accounts of ancient historians, especially Herodotus. The ancient city itself has come to light again through archaeological excavations at the site. Babylon is perhaps best known as the capital of the empire that brought about the fall of the southern kingdom of Judah and its capital, Jerusalem.

Southern Palace at Babylon

Ancient Babylon was located on the Euphrates River about fifty-five miles south of the modern city of Baghdad. This location possessed a number of features that contributed to the growth and development of what would become one of the largest cities in ancient Mesopotamia. The Euphrates River provided the means for navigation to the north and south. Through its location at the northern end of the Euphrates flood plain, Babylon became a thriving, major convergence of trade routes. It controlled the trade routes in that area and also became a flourishing center of trade and commerce. Further, the fertile valley of the Euphrates made this an important agricultural region, a feature that affected Babylon's history. Because of the region's rich agricultural resources, kings from other lands frequently attempted to control Babylon.

The name Babylon hints at another central feature of the site, that is, the site's identity as a center of religion. Even in its earliest stages, the site was called "the gate of the god(s)," a name that came from the Akkadian term *bab-ili*, the same idea reflected in the Hebrew name *babel*, which likewise means "gate of god." The accounts of Herodotus and the excavations at the site provide further evidence of Babylon's role as a major center of religion. Herodotus describes a city with many temples and their attendant gods; material evidence from excavations at the site have confirmed much of what Herodotus relates (*Histories* 1.178–186).

Babylon was one of the largest cities of Mesopotamia in ancient times, covering an area of approximately two thousand acres. The rediscovery of the site in more recent times is largely due to the efforts of Pietro della Valle who visited the town of Hillah in 1616 and learned from citizens that one of the mounds in the area was called Babil. The ruins of Babylon were later found south of the mound of Babil. The first excavations at Babylon were carried out by C. J. Rich in 1811 and 1817. In 1850 the site was revisited by A. H. Layard; however, a major excavation of the site did not get underway until 1899. In that year Robert Koldewey, sponsored by the German Oriental Society, began work at the site that continued until 1917. Material recovered during Koldewey's excavations forms the basis of our knowledge of the site today.

Though the early history of the site remains a mystery, both the Bible and the *Enuma Elish*, the major Babylonian account of creation, refer to the origin of the city. While the Bible attributes the founding of the city to Nimrod (Gen 10:9–10), who established other sites in the land of Shinar, the *Enuma Elish* attributes the establishment of the site to rebel Babylonian gods whom Marduk had defeated. The rebel gods built the city and a temple called Esagila for the victorious Marduk.

Excavations at the site have not been successful in recovering the remains of the earliest settlement because they lie below the present water table in the area; nevertheless, it is thought that the history of the site goes back to the sixth millennium BCE. Though the early stages of the development of Babylon are shrouded in mystery, the earliest reference to the city dates to about 2200 BCE. The reference appears in an ancient Akkadian text from the time of King Sharkali-sharri, who apparently constructed a number of buildings at the site, including a temple. At a later time near the end of the third millennium BCE Babylon was captured by Shulgi, the king of Ur, and the city remained under the control of Ur for some time. During that period Babylon was ruled by governors who were under the jurisdiction of and were accountable to Ur.

Early in the second millennium BCE Babylon was invaded by a wave of Semitic peoples called the Amorites, whose name means "the westerners" or "those from the west"; with them the first dynasty of Babylon was established. The sixth king of the dynasty, Hammurabi, who came to the throne about 1792 BCE, stands out in ancient history as a towering figure responsible for a number of notable achievements. Perhaps best known for the development of a law code, the so-called Code of Hammurabi, Hammurabi brought Babylon into its first golden age. Due to his capabilities as an administrator, a political and military expert, and a builder, Hammurabi beautified and brought about many improvements in the city of Babylon. Moreover, he unified many of the surrounding states, incorporating them into one large nation. The new nation came to be known as Babylonia, named after its capital city, Babylon. During that period, Hammurabi controlled southern Mesopotamia as well as the territory to the north as far as the city of Mari; he had representatives of his kingdom living as far away as Hazor, a city in northern Palestine. During that era, commonly referred to as the Old Babylonian period, the city of Babylon became a center of literature. Several great literary works were written by scribes who belonged to a large school of scribes. Using the cuneiform system, the scribes inscribed their literary works on clay tablets. Babylon's history as a major literary center was established early during the second millennium BCE, and it continued to the end of the first millennium BCE.

Babylon's history was marked by a golden age during the early part of the second millennium BCE, but Babylon reached its ebb during the period that followed. In 1595 BCE Babylon was invaded and fell to the Hittites, the inhabitants from the land of Anatolia, the region commonly known as Asia Minor. The Hittites controlled the city for only a brief period of time. About 1570 BCE Babylon was invaded by the Kassites, a people from the Zagros Mountains to the east. The city and its territory remained under Kassite control for several centuries. Although our knowledge of this period is limited, texts from both Babylon and Egypt indicate that Babylon maintained extensive trade with Egypt especially during the Amarna period in Egyptian history. By the latter part of the second millennium BCE, Babylon faced additional problems. The city was attacked by the Assyrians in 1250 BCE and by the Elamites in 1160 BCE.

Following the Elamite era a new dynasty was established in Babylon. Some degree of stability prevailed during the reign of Nebuchadnezzar I, the Babylonian king who came to the throne about 1100 BCE. However, for most of the next five centuries the history of Babylon was shaped by Assyria, the empire to the north. In 852 BCE the Assyrian king, Shalmaneser III, moved into Babylon and defeated a group of rebels responsible for causing an uprising. But the Assyrian king, Tiglath-pileser III, who came to the throne in 745 BCE, ultimately gained and maintained control of Babylon through a series of campaigns. Assyrian control of Babylon began during the mid-eighth century, continued during the latter half of the eighth century, and was reinforced in 710 BCE in a campaign by Sargon II.

But while the Assyrians dominated the scene during the last half of the eighth century and the first half of the seventh century, Babylon began to move into its second golden age near the end of the seventh century BCE, a dramatic change brought about by two significant developments. First, the powerful Assyrian empire that had dominated the ancient Near Eastern world since the middle of the eighth century BCE suddenly entered a period of decline beginning about 630 BCE. Second, Nabopolassar, the Chaldean, came to the throne in Babylon about 626 BCE, providing the city and its territory with stable leadership and initiating a period of reconstruction. The high point of the new age came later, during the reign of Nabopolassar's son, Nebuchadnezzar II. During his reign Babylon became one of the most magnificent cities of the ancient world as Nebuchadnezzar introduced a building program that included fortifications, public buildings, palaces, temples, and hanging gardens. Evidence of the city's magnificence has been confirmed by modern excavations. When Nebuchadnezzar defeated the

Assyrians in the battle of Carchemish in 605 BCE, he incorporated Assyrian territory into the Babylonian empire through an expansionist program that also included the land of Judah and the city of Jerusalem. The initial attack on Jerusalem took place in 597 BCE, and the final blow and the fall of the city came in 587 BCE as Nebuchadnezzar and his troops moved into Jerusalem and destroyed the city and the temple. In the process of his assault on Judah and Jerusalem, the Babylonian king carried out a series of deportations. Among the deported citizens was Judah's king, Jehoiachin. He was resettled in the city of Babylon or in one of the nearby communities such as those along the Chebar River.

But Babylon's glory was not to last. In 556 BCE the last of the Babylonian kings, Nabonidus, came to the throne, and a new dynasty was established. But by this time Babylonian power had weakened, and the empire as a whole faced a new threat: the development and advancement of the Medo-Persian empire to the east. The Medo-Persian empire reached its apex with the fall of the city of Babylon to Cyrus, the king of Persia, in 539 BCE. In 538 BCE the Persian king, more lenient than the Babylonian kings, issued an edict that granted those Jews living in exile in Babylonia permission to return to their homeland in order to rebuild it. During the years that followed, from 538 BCE to about 440 BCE, several groups took advantage of the edict and left Babylon. In 331 BCE Babylon was affected by yet another political change in the ancient Near East as Alexander the Great moved into Babylonia and made it a part of the vast Greek empire. Upon Alexander's death Babylonia was given to one of his major generals, Seleucus I, who in turn founded a new capital city for the province, Seleucia, locating it on the Tigris River. As time passed, the inhabitants of Babylon moved to Seleucia. The golden age was no more.

The history of the city of ancient Babylon ceases near the end of the first millennium BCE, but our knowledge of the physical features of the city is enhanced by both information from archaeological excavations and descriptions in the accounts of the ancient historian, Herodotus. We know of the major features of the ancient city, including its walls and defense system, its city gates, the city streets, palaces, the ziggurat, the temple of Marduk, and the bridge. The ancient city was nearly rectangular in shape and was bisected by the Euphrates River. One section of the city was west of the Euphrates, but the largest and oldest part of the city was east of the Euphrates.

The defense system of the city included surrounding double walls: the inner wall, a twenty-one-foot-wide wall named Imgur-Enlil, and the outer wall approximately twelve feet wide named Nimit-Enlil. The walls were constructed of sun-baked bricks and were fortified with towers approximately every sixty feet. The city's defense system was strengthened further by an encircling moat some sixty-five feet inside an outer wall of the city. Nebuchadnezzar's outer wall beyond the moat was a double wall constructed of baked bricks and was approximately twenty-five feet wide. The new wall was designed to prevent enemy projectiles from reaching the inner walls of the city. Nebuchadnezzar built a summer palace at the north end of the area just inside the outermost wall. The palace was on the banks of the Euphrates. Today the palace is covered by a mound called Babil, a name which preserves the ancient name Babylon.

The city's defense system also included a series of eight gates located at different points around the city, with each of the gates named for one of the chief Babylonian deities: Ishtar, Sin, Marduk, Ninurta, Enlil, Urash, Shamash, and Adad. Of the gates, the most famous and elaborately decorated was the Ishtar gate, located in the north wall of the city. The arched gateway was flanked by towers forty feet high and was decorated with bulls and dragons representing the gods Adad and Marduk respectively. The surface of the gate was made of glazed bricks and lapis lazuli tiles. The Marduk gate was located in the east wall of the city and was named after the patron deity of the city.

The city was segmented into rectangular areas by its major streets. Their location was determined by the location of the gates. The major thoroughfare, often referred to as the processional way or Sacred Procession, originated at the Ishtar gate and moved past the hanging gardens, the palace of Nebuchadnezzar, the temple of Ishtar, the ziggurat, the temple of Marduk, and the temple of Ninurta. It was approximately seventy feet wide. According to inscriptions on some of the limestone slabs that paved the surface, the street, or at least its final phase, was built by King Nebuchadnezzar as a processional way for the god Marduk to enter the city. The street was constructed in three layers: a layer of bricks and a layer of asphalt with a layer of square limestone slabs on the surface. The street was lined on each side by sidewalks made of square slabs of red breccia.

Excavations have produced the remains of the palace of King Nebuchadnezzar. The palace complex was located in the northwest corner of the eastern sector of Babylon between the Ishtar gate and processional way on the east and the Euphrates River on the west. The palace area contains perhaps two palaces or two major units often referred to as the southern citadel and northern citadel. The major palace, located on the southern citadel, was originally built by King Nabopolassar and was rebuilt and expanded by his son Nebuchadnezzar. It was located west-southwest of the Ishtar gate. This complex of buildings covered an area approximately two hundred by four hundred yards. It included several courtyards; quarters for mercenary soldiers who protected the king and the royal household; a throne room (approximately fifty-five by 170 feet); quarters for the king and family members; and quarters for the servants of the royal household. Some of the walls of the palace were finished with blue-glazed bricks. Other decorative motifs on the walls and pillars included garlands, rosettes, and lions, in yellow and white.

The northern citadel, located northwest of the Ishtar gate, included a large building approximately forty by 140 feet. The building, constructed at a level lower than the existing ground level, was walled off from the new palace to the south. In addition to being subterranean, the building had an unusual design comprised of fourteen long narrow rooms, all of which extended off a walkway. Clay tablets containing administrative information were found in some of the rooms. We may assume from the information on the tablets that the rooms were storerooms for palace supplies. Among the tablets discovered are those commonly referred to as the Jehoiachin tablets. These tablets contain information about the rations and supplies the Babylonian government provided for the former king of Judah, Jehoiachin, and his family. The tablets indicate that Jehoiachin, though living in exile, was treated like royalty and was still recognized as the king of Judah. Some have suggested that the hanging gardens of Babylon, described by Herodotus, were located in the area of the northern citadel. The hanging gardens, among the wonders of the ancient world, were in a massive terraced garden area built by Nebuchadnezzar for his bride Astyages. The hanging gardens were designed and constructed to remind Astyages of her mountainous homeland, Media.

Babylon was also a major center of religion and as such had a number of religious facilities. While temples and shrines were found throughout the city, the major sacred area was located between the processional way and the Euphrates River. Archaeological evidence is meager, but the most imposing structure of the sacred area appears to be the ziggurat or temple tower. The ziggurat, named Etemenanki, which means "House of the Foundation of Heaven and Earth," was surrounded by a large courtyard and wall. The wall's ten or twelve gates allowed worshipers to approach the ziggurat, which served as a type of holy mountain. The wall enclosed an area of approximately thirteen hundred square feet. The base of the ziggurat itself measured nearly three hundred square feet. In design, the ziggurat of Babylon was probably very similar to the one at Ur. The inner core of the ziggurat was constructed of mud brick and bitumen, while the outer layer was made of baked brick. According to Herodotus, a temple dedicated to the god Marduk stood on top of the ziggurat. The original date of the construction of the ziggurat may reach back to the third millennium BCE. The ziggurat of Babylon is of special interest because it is regarded by some as perhaps the inspiration for the story of the Tower of Babel in Genesis 11:1–9.

Dragon figure on Ishtar Gate (reconstruction)

Babylon had many temples, but the most important temple was the temple of Marduk, the patron deity of Babylon. The temple located south of the ziggurat was named Esagila, which means "House with the Uplifted Head." The temple itself was a long, narrow structure approximately thirty-five by 260 feet. According to Herodotus, the temple contained two gold statues of Marduk and was the scene of numerous festivals and countless animal sacrifices. Supposedly a thousand talents of incense were burned each year in temple rituals. In addition to the Marduk temple, Babylon had approximately fifty other temples dedicated to Babylonian deities. Inscriptions indicate that Nebuchadnezzar alone built fifteen temples in the city. While many of the temples have not been located, several of the more prominent ones have been discovered by archaeologists. These include the temple of Ishtar, goddess of fertility; the temple of Ninmah, goddess of the underworld; and the temple of Ninurta, the god of war. In addition to the temples, nearly two thousand shrines, niches, or other sacred spots dedicated to Mesopotamian deities were scattered throughout the city of Babylon.

Excavations have also uncovered the remains of family dwellings. The components of the houses generally included a central courtyard surrounded by rooms. The walls of the houses were made of mud bricks. The houses had roofs constructed of wooden beams covered with thatched mats. Some of the houses apparently had only one level, while others may have had two, three, or even four stories.

Bibliography: BROWNING, D., "Babylon, History and Religion of," *HolBD*, 141–44; HARRISON, R. K., "Babylon," *NIDB*, 116–20; JACOBSEN, T., "Babylon (OT)," *IDB*, 1:334–38; KLENGEL-BRANDT, E., "Babylon," *OEANE*, 1:251–56; idem, "Babylonians," *OEANE*, 1:256–62; LARUE, G. A., "Babylon," *BW*, 124–33; LONG, J. E., "Babylon, Babylonia," *BEB*, 1:243–50; MARGUERON, J. C., "Babylon," *ABD*, 1:563–65; PEARCE, L. E., "Babylon," *HBD*, 87–89; SAGGS, H. W. F., "Babylon," *Archaeology and Old Testament Study*, ed. D. Winton Thomas (Oxford: Clarendon, 1967) 39–56; SCHOVILLE, K. N., "Babylon," *BAF*, 188–92; WHITE, W., Jr., "Babylon," *NIDBA*, 85–86; WISEMAN, D. J., "Babylon," *ISBE*, 12:384–91; idem, "Babylon," *NBD*, 117–19; idem, "Babylon," *NBD²*, 111–13; idem, "Babylon," *ZPEB*, 1:439–48; YAMAUCHI, E., "Babylon," *Major Cities of the Biblical World*, ed. R. K. Harrison (Nashville: Nelson, 1985) 32–48.

HARAN 🏺   4

City at the Crossroads in Upper Mesopotamia

Like Ur, Haran was a major city during the patriarchal period and is mentioned in the patriarchal stories of the OT. However, the city's history and significance are not limited to that period. But our understanding of the city has been limited. The Bible does not describe Haran or include information about the features of the city. Archaeological information of the site is also extremely limited. The only major excavation or exploration of the site took place in 1951–52. Though the joint Anglo-Turkish excavation failed to produce a major historical profile of Haran, the information recovered suggests that the history of the site goes back to the third millennium BCE. The major discoveries at the site included three stelae from the later Neo-Babylonian period. Information about the features of the city itself is limited due to the very brief excavation of the site; nonetheless, our understanding of the life, history, and culture of Haran is enhanced by other sources, including biblical and extrabiblical sources. Based on that information, we may assume that the ancient city of Haran was a strategic city located at a principal intersection in upper Mesopotamia. Moreover, Haran was a city and a territory with which the patriarchs had strong ties. Ur was located in extreme lower Mesopotamia; Haran in extreme upper Mesopotamia, a part of modern Turkey. Haran was situated on the Balikh River, an important north-south tributary that entered the upper end of the Euphrates River approximately sixty miles to the south.

That Haran was a major city of upper Mesopotamia during the patriarchal period is suggested by the references to the city in the book of Genesis. According to the Bible, Terah, the father of Abraham, moved his family from Ur to Haran (Gen 11:31–32). We may assume that following that migration, Haran and the territory around it became the new homeland for Terah's family and descendants; however,

Abraham eventually left Haran and went to Canaan (Gen 12:4–6). Some suggest that the city of Haran was referred to as the "city of Nahor" (Gen 24:10), but the latter name may be that of a different city located in the territory of Haran. When Abraham moved to Canaan, he apparently maintained contact with Haran; consequently, it was to Haran that Abraham sent his servant in search of a wife for his son Isaac (Gen 24:10). And it was to Haran, the original home of Rebekah, that Jacob fled (Gen 27:43; 28:10), worked for his uncle Laban, and obtained his wives, Leah and Rachel (Gen 29).

In addition to its appearance in the Bible, the name Haran, along with other names found in the patriarchal narratives, also appears in the Mari tablets, but with one distinction. In the Mari tablets the names appear as place names, while in the biblical text they are primarily personal names, such as Terah, Haran, and Nahor.

In its position in upper Mesopotamia, Haran apparently had several attractive geographical features in relationship to the ancient Near East that attracted individuals like Terah and his family to the area. For instance, Haran was located on the major east-west trade route that ran from the Mediterranean Sea on the west to the Tigris River on the east. Furthermore, the major international trade route that extended from Ur northward along the Euphrates, up along the Balikh River to Haran, and northwestward to Anatolia, or southwestward to Egypt, passed through Haran. Even the Sumerian form of the name Haran, meaning "road," "route," or "journey," seems to reflect the city's association and identity with major trade routes. We may assume that by the end of the third millennium BCE and the beginning of the second millennium BCE Haran was already a major caravan center, an important center of trade and exchange. With caravans and traders coming from east, west, north and south, Haran was in all probability the chief commercial center in upper Mesopotamia during the patriarchal period. Its role as a commercial center is certainly reflected in the Bible. According to Ezekiel 27:23–24, Haran was the home of a major textile industry known for producing fine garments and carpets. The clothing produced was blue in color and decorated with embroidery. The carpets came in a variety of colors and were woven with cords that made them extremely durable. In all likelihood the textile industry is reflected in the story of Laban, who with his large flocks operated a lucrative business in a region supporting a textile industry.

Correspondence from the time of Zimri-Lim, king of Mari, indicates that the region around Haran was inhabited by a semi-nomadic group called the "Benjaminites." The letter speaks of an alliance between other local kings and the leaders of the Benjaminites. Apparently, the alliance or covenant-making ceremony was formalized in the temple of the moon god, Sin, the god of Haran.

Sin was essentially the same god as Nanna, the god of Ur. The name "Sin" was apparently a later form of the name "Nanna." The worship of the moon god started around 2000 BCE during the third dynasty of Ur and extended into the Babylonian period. The temple of Sin was called Ehulhul. According to inscriptions from the site, the temple was rebuilt twice, once by the Assyrians and once by the Babylonians.

Haran was also a part of the great Mitannian empire, which flourished in upper Mesopotamia during the mid-second millennium BCE, ca. 1600–1300 BCE. During that period the population of the region was comprised primarily of Hurrians, a non-Semitic people who apparently moved into Mesopotamia from the northeastern mountainous regions of Armenia and Urartu. During the latter part of the second millennium BCE, the Mitannian empire, and consequently Haran, was conquered by the Hittites of Anatolia. Hittite control ended about 1200 BCE with the arrival of the Sea People.

Haran also became the capital of a key Assyrian province. Since Haran was one of the more distant provinces of the Assyrian empire, the Assyrians attempted to maintain special ties with the city. As an important Assyrian provincial capital, Haran had a history that was certainly interwoven with and shaped by the events of Assyrian history. The relationship between Haran and the Assyrians is seen, for instance, in the position of governor of Haran. The provincial governor was appointed by the Assyrian king himself, and as the governor of the province he occupied a powerful administrative position. The governor not only was responsible for the administration of the province, but he also commanded the Assyrian forces in that area. Due to an uprising in the region, Haran was destroyed about 763 BCE by Assyrian forces (2 Kgs 19:12). The city was restored, and the temple of the moon god, Ehulhul, was rebuilt by the Assyrian king, Sargon II. One of the most significant roles that Haran played in Assyrian history came during the latter days of the Assyrian empire. With the fall of Nineveh in 612 BCE to the Babylonians, the Assyrian capital was moved to Haran. However, the city's status as the capital of the foundering empire was very brief. Pursued by Nineveh's conquerors, Haran fell to the Babylonians in 610 BCE. The Assyrian capital was moved to the city of Carchemish. Under Babylonian control, the city of Haran and the temple of the moon god were rebuilt.

While Haran had many different functions in ancient times, its most important role was related to its location. Located at a major intersection or crossroads on the international trade route in upper Mesopotamia, Haran contributed vitally in its capacity as an important caravan center—a major center of trade and exchange where people from the Fertile Crescent met and exchanged not only merchandise but cultural practices.

Bibliography: ANDREWS, S. J., "Haran," MDB, 357–58; BARABAS, S., "Haran (Place)," ZPEB, 3:32–33; GORDON, C. H., "Haran (Place)," IDB, 2:524; HALLO, W., "Haran, Harran," BW, 280–83; HARRINGTON, C. E., "Haran, Charran," NIDB, 418–19; HARRISON, R. K., and E. M. Blaiklock, "Haran," NIDBA, 228; HUGHES, R. J. III, "Haran," ISBE, 2:614; KOBAYASHI, Y., "Haran," ABD, 3:58–59; PEARCE, L. E., "Haran," HBD, 373; PRAG, K., "Haran (Place)," IDBSup, 387; WISEMAN, D. J., "Haran," NBD, 504; idem, "Haran," NBD², 453–54.

MARI 🏺 5

City of Zimri-Lim

While Mari is not mentioned in the OT, discoveries from the site of
Mari can enlighten students of the Bible because they provide information about upper Mesopotamia during the period of the patriarchs.
Ancient Mari was strategically located on the west side of the Euphrates
River in eastern Syria. It was an important center of trade and exchange
because it was located at the crossroads of several key trade routes.
Among the major routes that ran through Mari was the international
highway that extended along the Euphrates River valley, starting at the
city of Ur and extending northward through Babylon and Mari to Haran
in upper Mesopotamia. In addition to the main highway, other routes
branched off from the city of Mari and moved northward to Syrian
towns such as Ebla and Aleppo or westward to the cities of Damascus
and Hazor. The westward route connected Mari with the Mediterranean Sea.

The site of ancient Mari is in essence a large mound that first came
to the attention of W. F. Albright in 1925. Excavations sponsored by
the Louvre under the direction of A. Parrot began in the 1930s. Since
then the site has seen some thirty archaeological campaigns, with the
latest taking place in 1981. The excavations have provided insight into
the history of Mari, a history that started early in the third millennium
BCE and continued until about 1765 BCE when the city was destroyed by
Hammurabi, king of Babylon. The details of Mari's history are
somewhat complex; however, two periods of its history especially
stand out. The first was during the third millennium BCE when Mari was
one of the main cities of the Sumerian culture. From about 3000 to
about 2300 BCE, the city of Mari flourished and expanded; however,
that chapter in Mari's history came to an end about 2300 BCE when
Sargon, king of Akkad, conquered the city. The second major period of

Mari's history occurred from about 2000 to 1765 BCE. During that period, the Isin-Larsa and Old Babylonian periods, Mari again flourished and prospered. That era ended when Hammurabi conquered the site. Following Mari's defeat by Hammurabi, it never again rose to prominence. The latter period is especially important in OT studies because it formed part of the background of the patriarchal world.

One of the most noteworthy segments of the second major period of Mari's history concerns the Lim dynasty. This dynasty experienced its share of conflict and was led by two notable rulers, Yakhdun-Lim and his son Zimri-Lim. The Lim dynasty spanned a relatively brief period of time from about 1825 to 1765 BCE.

Though many discoveries were made at Mari, none surpass in significance the discovery of some twenty thousand cuneiform tablets commonly referred to as the Mari tablets or Mari letters. The tablets were found in the palace of Zimri-Lim, a massive building with approximately three hundred rooms. The letters constituted in essence the royal archives. They were inscribed on clay tablets by scribes from a school of scribes of the royal court. The letters include those of the king himself as well as correspondence from members of the king's family, public officials, and kings in other provinces in north Syria. The letters provide a wide variety of information from the twenty-year reign of Zimri-Lim, including information about Zimri-Lim's personal life, administrative matters, customs, and religion. Furthermore, the Mari letters afford valuable information about political matters and geographical features of upper Mesopotamia during that period. Information about Zimri-Lim's personal life touched on a number of topics. The king had two meals a day consisting of bread, produce, meat, and wine or beer. He took voyages up the Euphrates and other rivers to neighboring territories or provinces. In his leisure time, he enjoyed hunting lions. He had his own personal ballet corps of women which was also a part of his harem of wives. His many wives and concubines were housed in the four palaces located along the Euphrates and Khabur Rivers.

In political matters, Zimri-Lim was the chief administrator of the state; however, numerous other officials under his jurisdiction helped him administer the affairs of the provinces of the kingdom. Local administrators were in charge of a so-called *bitum*, or house. The *bitum* included work areas for craftsmen, storeroom facilities, and living quarters. The king carried out the administrative affairs in the provinces through administrators called *shapitums*. *Shapitums* were types of governors. Other officials of the kingdom were the *merkhum*, the military leaders, and the *suqaqum*, the king's emissaries to the local tribal units. The letters also inform us about military tactics, about weapons such as the battering ram, and about the fighting gear of individual soldiers. Further, among the letters are ecstatic or prophetic kinds of utterances that were relayed to the king about the threats he would encounter in the future. The letters also provide insight concerning the presence and customs of tribes of pastoral nomads in the regions. These groups, often referred to as Amorites, were a type of nomadic people who roamed the grasslands all the way from lower Mesopotamia to upper Mesopotamia, especially the area around Haran. Reference is also made to the Benjaminites, a name meaning the "sons of the south," and the Habiru, a stateless migrating people that roamed the ancient Near East.

Several of the names appearing in the Mari tablets hold special interest to students of the Bible because they are similar to names that appear in the patriarchal stories in the OT, names such as Terah, Haran, Nahor. However, while the names appear primarily as personal names in the patriarchal stories, they appear as place names in the Mari tablets. While the Mari tablets refer to numerous cities in upper Mesopotamia and northern Syria, only two cities of Palestine are mentioned—Hazor (Josh 11:10), located near Lake Huleh, and Laish (Judg 18:7), a site located at the headwaters of the Jordan that became biblical Dan.

Architectural remains found at Mari date to both the earlier and later periods of Mari's history. The most important remains are those of the palaces built for the rulers and the temples built for the gods of Mari. The major temples or shrines at Mari were built for Dagon, Ishtar, and Shamash. Apparently Dagon was the chief god of Mari and its provinces. Dagon, the grain god, recalls the god Dagon mentioned in the OT. Ishtar was a type of mother goddess or fertility goddess and as such probably had a function similar to the goddess Asherah in the OT. Shamash was worshiped as the sun-god. In addition to these gods, the pantheon of Mari included a number of other gods, such as Sin, the moon god; Beletekallim, goddess of the female attendants of the royal court; and Naru, the god of the river.

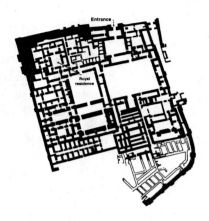

Royal Palace at Mari

Of all of the palaces or royal quarters found at Mari, the largest was the massive palace complex of Zimri-Lim. Built on the ruins of other palaces, the palace complex covered six to seven acres and was comprised of nearly three hundred rooms and a large courtyard. The palace contained elaborate decorations including fountains, sculptures, and large wall paintings. The wall paintings are the earliest Mesopotamian murals to be found. The wide variety of colorful scenes and topics provide insight into the different areas of life. Especially important are the multiregister worship scenes that feature worshipers approaching gods or goddesses with various offerings, including animal sacrifices, small fire offerings (including aromatics like incense) and libations. Many of the small altars or offering stands on which the offerings were made are of special interest because they are similar in style and design to offering stands that have been found in excavations at Canaanite and Israelite sites in Palestine. Other scenes include sacred or tree-of-life-like plants, royal processions and investiture scenes, palace and military personnel, weaponry, and clothing. One other feature of life in ancient Mari deserves mention. The residents of Mari had the means to make ice, store it, and have it available year-round. The ice was made and stored during the winter months. The ice-making facilities consisted of two parts, long rectangular ponds in which the freezing took place, and a large storage pit in which the ice was stored for usage throughout the year.

While the main part of Mari's history extended only from about 3000 BCE to 1765 BCE, its value for the study of ancient history in upper Mesopotamia only continues to expand. Though direct ties with the OT should not be pushed too far, the discoveries at Mari certainly provide rich insight, information, and background for a significant portion of the ancient Near Eastern world in which biblical history was born.

Bibliography: BEITZEL, B. J., "Mari," *HolBD*, 917–18; idem, "Mari," *Major Cities of the Biblical World*, ed. R. K. Harrison (Nashville: Nelson, 1985) 156–69; DURAND, J. M., "Mari (Texts)," *ABD*, 5:529–26; GAEBELEIN, P. W., Jr., "Mari," *ISBE*, 3:245–48; GATES, M. H., "The Palace of Zimri–Lim at Mari," *BA* 47 (1984) 70–87; HARRISON, R. K., "Mari," *NIDBA*, 299–300; HOFFNER, H. A., Jr., "Mari," *ZPEB*, 4:73–74; KECK, B. E., "Mari (Bibliography)," *ABD*, 5:536–38; LEMAIRE, A., "Mari, the Bible, and the Northwest Semitic World," *BA* 47 (1984) 101–8; LEWY, H., "Mari," *IDB*, 3:264–66; MARGUERON, J-Cl., "Mari (Archaeology)," *ABD*, 5:525–29; MARIOTTINI, C. F., "Mari," *MDB*, 548–49; MAUGERON, J. C., "Mari," *OEANE*, 3:413–17; MENDEN-HALL, G. E., "Mari," *Biblical Archaeologist Reader* 2 (1964) 3–20; PARDEE, D., and Jonathan T. Glass, "The Mari Archives," *BA* 47 (1984) 88–99; PARROT, A., "Mari," *Archaeology and Old Testament Study*, ed. D. Winton Thomas (Oxford: Clarendon, 1967) 136–44; SASSON, J. M., "Mari," *HBD*, 603–5; idem, "Mari," *IDBSup*, 567–71; SCHOVILLE, K. N., "Mari," *BAF*, 232–36; WISEMAN, D. J., "Archaeology," *NBD*, 68; idem, "Mari," *NBD*[2], 736–37.

City of Ashurbanipal

Nineveh was one of the oldest and most important cities in ancient Mesopotamia. The significant role it played in ancient Near Eastern history is substantiated by the OT, by other ancient Near Eastern writings, and by the impressive discoveries and excavations at the site.

The ruins of ancient Nineveh are located in upper Mesopotamia on the east side of the Tigris River about sixty miles north of the city of Ashur. Today the site stands opposite to the modern city of Mosul. The ancient city was comprised of two mounds: the mound on the north, called Kuyunjik, is a large mound twice the size of the small mound to the south called Tell Nebi Yunus, which means "the mound of the prophet Jonah." The two mounds are separated by the Khoser River, one of the many small rivers that flow into the Tigris from the east. In some regards ancient Nineveh was actually comprised of two parts, the city of Nineveh and greater Nineveh, the city's territorial holdings. Nineveh proper, comprised of the two mounds, was enclosed by a rectangular wall that was eight miles long and encompassed an area of about eighteen hundred acres. The statement in Jonah, that a "three day's journey" (Jonah 3:3) was required to cover Nineveh, suggests that greater Nineveh included a large area with the satellite towns or communities that were under Nineveh's jurisdiction, such as Nimrud, Khorsabad, and Karamles.

The name Nineveh apparently comes from the word Nina or Ninuwa. It appears in ancient cuneiform texts as well as in the Bible. The ancient cuneiform symbol for the word was comprised of a fish in an enclosure. The cuneiform symbols, or ideograms, indicate that the name was associated with not only the fish, but also Nina, the river goddess, an interesting association in light of the story of Jonah and the "great fish."

The OT testifies to Nineveh's prominence in the ancient world. For example, the table of nations attributes the founding of Nineveh as well as several other cities to Nimrod, the mighty hunter (Gen 10:11). The city is also mentioned in the story of Sennacherib's attack on Jerusalem and the fortified cities in Judah in 701 BCE (2 Kgs 19:35–36; Isa 37:37). The impending doom of Nineveh is recounted by the minor prophets Zephaniah (2:13–15) and Nahum. Perhaps the most familiar OT reference occurs in the story of Jonah.

The history of the exploration of the site dates back to 1820 when C. J. Rich initially investigated the site and made a map or a sketch of the ruins. Excavations began in 1842, when Paul Botta directed a small-scale excavation at the site. While the investigation of the site by Botta was rather limited, the latter half of the nineteenth century witnessed a series of excavations that revealed many of the important features of the ancient city. The excavations, sponsored by the British Museum, were directed by Henry Layard, H. Rassam, George Smith, and W. Budge. Additional excavations were conducted at Nineveh by R. C. Thompson (1927–32).

The excavations at Nineveh revealed not only many of the physical features of the ancient city but its long and important history as well. According to the archaeological evidence, occupation of the site dates back to about 5000–4500 BCE; however, it was not until later, during the third millennium BCE, that Nineveh developed into a major cultural center. During this period Nineveh was a province of the Akkadian empire, and a temple was built for Ishtar, the goddess of love and war. The construction of the temple led to the development of Nineveh as a great religious center. Later, during the reign of Shamshi-Adad I, king of Ashur, Nineveh became a province of Ashur. At this time the temple of Ishtar was rebuilt. Still later Nineveh came under the control of Babylon as Hammurabi, the king of Babylon, gained control of Assyria; however, Assyria regained its independent statehood shortly thereafter. Beginning in the fourteenth and thirteenth centuries BCE Nineveh reached a new status due to the extensive building programs of the Assyrian kings, especially Shalmaneser I and Tiglath-pileser I, building programs that included the construction of several new palaces as well as the restoration and renovation of the temple of Ishtar. Nineveh reached its height near the end of the eighth century and the beginning of the seventh century when a new round of building activities was initiated. The Assyrian king Sennacherib built a new palace at Nineveh and made the city the new capital of Assyria, replacing the old capital Ashur. During the following era Nineveh became a city of grandeur thanks to the building activities of the Assyrian kings Sennacherib, Esarhaddon, and Ashurbanipal, all of whom built monumental palaces for themselves in the city. However, shortly thereafter the fortunes of the city and the nation changed. Powerful Assyria went into a period of decline, and in 612 BCE the city of Nineveh fell as the nation began to crumble before the Babylonian forces.

While the Bible and other ancient records provide valuable literary information about ancient Nineveh, excavations at the site have recovered many of the magnificent features that made it a city of fame and importance in the ancient world. Of all these features, the temple of Ishtar, originally built by the Akkadian king Manistushu during the Akkadian period, was one of the most consequential. Built on the mound of Kuyunjik, the temple was perhaps the oldest building on the mound. It was maintained throughout the history of the site and was repaired or rebuilt many times. The continued maintenance of the temple suggests that the chief god of Nineveh was Ishtar, the goddess of war and love.

Sennacherib enhanced the city in several ways. He enlarged its size, surrounded it with a massive wall, improved its streets, and beautified it with expansive public gardens. The massive defense wall was constructed with large gateways that served not only as entrances to the city but also as fortified towers that protected the city against the approach of enemy forces. Sennacherib built an aqueduct designed to improve the water supply of the city. The aqueduct was thirty miles long and extended eastward from the city to the hills from which it brought fresh water into the city for its citizens.

In addition to the new defense wall and the aqueduct Sennacherib built a magnificent palace for himself, a palace constructed on a large elevated platform that was visible from any part of the city. The palace was approached by means of four marble stairways that led upward to the four entrances of the palace. The palace entrances were guarded by large lion-sphinxes and colossal winged bulls with human heads. The palace was designed with large courtyards, halls, and rooms. Its walls were decorated with large sculptured scenes depicting the achievements of

Sennacherib's reign, especially his military victories. Masses of clay tablets, about a foot and one-half in depth, were found on the floor of two rooms of the palace. The clay tablets and numerous clay cylinders or prisms found in the rooms were in essence the royal archives of Sennacherib's reign. The rooms were a part of a temple facility Sennacherib dedicated to the god Nabu, the god of wisdom and learning. One of the prisms, commonly referred to as the Taylor prism, relates the details of Sennacherib's attack on the city of Lachish in Judah in 701 BCE. The information from the prism was also depicted in relief form on one of the sculptured walls. Sennacherib built his palace on the northern mound (Kuyunjik), and his son Esarhaddon built a new palace on the southern mound (Nebi Yunus).

Like some of his predecessors, Ashurbanipal built a palace on the northern mound, a massive edifice known especially for its lion hunting gallery, a large hall with lion hunting scenes depicted in beautiful bas-relief, and the famous library of Ashurbanipal. The library, located in a room at the end of the gallery, had a high-vaulted ceiling and contained thousands of clay tablets with information and literature on a variety of topics. The tablets reflect Ashurbanipal's devotion to the god Nabu, the god of wisdom and learning. They provide valuable information about the political activities of Assyria, the study of language, Assyrian social laws and customs, history, religious writings, and scientific information dealing with such topics as botany, mathematics, and astronomy. Of all the writings discovered in the library, the religious writings constitute perhaps the most valuable because they include accounts of the *Gilgamesh Epic*, the Babylonian flood account, and the *Enuma Elish*, the Babylonian account of creation. The discovery of these stories provided some of the first examples of writings of this nature from the non-Hebrew people of the ancient Near East.

Bibliography: BLAIKLOCK, E. M., "Nineveh," *NIDBA*, 337–39; CHRISTENSEN, D. L., "Nineveh," *HBD*, 707–8; DEVRIES, C. E., "Nineveh (Nineve), Ninevite," *BEB*, 2:1553–55; FINLEY, H. E., "Nineveh," *BW*, 415–521; FOWLER, A. B., "Nineveh, Nineve," *NIDB*, 710–11; FRITSCH, C. T., "Nineveh," *ISBE*, 3:538–41; GRAYSON, A. K., "Nineveh," *ABD*, 4:1118–19; SCHOVILLE, K. N., "Nineveh," *BAF*, 198–200; SPEISER, E. A., "Nineveh," *IDB*, 3:551–53; STRONACH, D., and K. Codella, "Nineveh," *OEANE*, 4:144–48; WILSON, M. R., "Nineveh," *Major Cities of the Biblical World*, ed. R. K. Harrison (Nashville: Nelson, 1985) 180–89; WISEMAN, D. J., "Nineveh," *NBD*, 888–90; idem, "Nineveh," *NBD*[2], 836–37; idem, "Nineveh," *ZPEB*, 4:440–45; YAMAUCHI, E., "Nineveh," *HolBD*, 1024–25.

Community of Hurrian Customs and Traditions

While the town of Nuzi is not mentioned in the OT, discoveries at Nuzi have provided valuable information for the study of patriarchal customs mentioned in the Bible. These important discoveries were not buildings or architecture, but rather ancient writings, commonly referred to as the Nuzi tablets. As a city of the patriarchal world, Nuzi was a part of the kingdom of Arraphe, a small kingdom east of the Tigris River. It was located in the upper Tigris River valley about ten miles southwest of Kirkuk, the capital city of Arraphe. The modern name of the site of ancient Nuzi is Tepe Yoghlan.

While the discoveries at Nuzi have been unique, the site itself does not fit the typical archaeological profile of an ancient site because it is not comprised of a massive mound of ruins with multiple layers of debris. Nevertheless, the site was excavated as a joint project of the American Schools of Archaeological Research in Baghdad and the Semitic Museum of Harvard University, with excavations carried out from 1925 to 1931.

While the site of Nuzi is small compared to other ancient cities, Nuzi had a rather lengthy history, only a part of which is closely related to the Bible. The earliest remains at Nuzi go back to the fourth millennium BCE and extend to the Roman period. In that vast span of history there are two periods of special interest: the Old Akkadian period when the town was called Gasur, and the fifteenth and fourteenth centuries BCE, when the town was renamed Nuzi and was a part of the Mitannian kingdom. During the latter period, the period of our concern, the population of Nuzi, like the rest of the Mitannian kingdom, was primarily Hurrian.

Written documents found at Nuzi are of special interest for OT studies. Opinions vary concerning the value of these texts for biblical studies, but the information in the texts reflects the background of the ancient world, particularly the Hurrian population of Nuzi during the mid-second millennium BCE, and seems to have real potential for understanding the patriarchal period. The Nuzi tablets, comprised of some twenty thousand clay tablets, include administrative and written records that were in essence family archives.

The archives of the family of Tehiptilla, a wealthy resident of Nuzi, are especially interesting because they contain information about customs and practices of five generations of Tehiptilla's family, customs similar to those described in the patriarchal narratives in the OT. For example, the Nuzi tablets reflect the marriage customs of the day, particularly one in which the bride and family of the bride received a dowry or gifts at the time of marriage. The custom is similar to one mentioned in the patriarchal narratives in which Abraham sent his servant to Haran to find a wife for his son Isaac (Gen 24). After finding and selecting Rebekah, the servant prepared to return to Canaan with her. Before they left, the servant provided gifts for Rebekah and her family, such as gold and silver jewelry and garments (Gen 24:53). These gifts were perhaps recognized as a payment to the bride and her family.

The Nuzi tablets speak of the Hurrian custom in which a barren wife provided a female household servant to her husband to bear his child. The servant woman acted as a type of substitute wife. A similar custom is found in the OT stories of Sarah and Rachel. Because Sarah was childless, she provided Abraham with Hagar, her servant, to bear him an heir (Gen 16:3). In a similar story, Rachel provided Bilhah to bear a child for Jacob (Gen 30:3).

Another custom practiced at Nuzi was adoption. A husband and wife who were childless could select and adopt a servant as their heir. This custom may be reflected in the story of Abraham. After remaining childless for many years he apparently selected his chief servant Eliezer, originally from Damascus, as his adopted heir (Gen 15:2). The adoption apparently became void upon the birth of an heir.

Another Hurrian custom practiced at Nuzi was the sale of a birthright or inheritance from one brother to another. At Nuzi a brother traded his inheritance to another brother for three sheep, a transaction similar to Esau's trading of his birthright to Jacob for some red pottage (Gen 25:29–34).

The Hurrians at Nuzi recognized the validity of the oral last will or testament; a father could pronounce an oral last will or blessing upon an heir of his choice just prior to his death. In one instance a father gave an additional inheritance to his youngest son. This oral blessing was contested by the older brothers in court and was declared valid. In like manner Isaac pronounced an oral blessing upon Jacob, and though the blessing was intended for Esau, it was not revoked (Gen 27:27–35).

The Nuzi tablets relate information about women's inheritance rights. For instance the inheritance of land was not limited to sons alone. In Hurrian families daughters could inherit property. This was true as well in Israel; if a man died and had no sons, the family inheritance went to his daughter (Num 27:8).

The documents of the family archives are of special interest because of the information they provide about the customs of Hurrian families and the similarities they bear to patriarchal customs in the OT. Other types of useful documents found at Nuzi relate to the transfer of land, animals, and other essentials for daily life.

Bibliography: BUSH, F. W., "Nuzi," *ISBE,* 3:569–70; DEVRIES, C. E., "Nuzi," *BEB,* 2:1571–72; EICHLER, B. L., "Nuzi," *HBD,* 714; idem, "Nuzi," *IDBSup,* 635–36; FREDRICKS, D., "Nuzi," *HolBD,* 1032; GAEBELEIN, P. W., "Nuzi," *Major Cities of the Biblical World,* ed. R. K. Harrison (Nashville: Nelson, 1985) 190–97; MACRAE, A. A., "Nuzi," *ZPEB,* 4:470–73; MARIOTTINI, C. F., "Nuzi," *MDB,* 623–24; MORRISON, M. A., "Nuzi," *ABD,* 4:1156–62; PFEIFFER, C. F., "Nuzi," *BW,* 422–25; SCHOVILLE, K. N., "Nuzi," *BAF,* 192–95; SELMAN, M. J., "Nuzi," *NBD²,* 848–50; SPEISER, E. A., "Nuzi," *IDB,* 3:573–74; STEIN, D. L., Nuzi," *OEANE,* 4:171–75; THOMPSON, J. A., "Nuzi," *NIDBA,* 342; WEIR, C. J. M., "Nuzi," *Archaeology and Old Testament Study,* ed. D. Winton Thomas (Oxford: Clarendon, 1967) 73–86; WISEMAN, D. J., "Archaeology," *NBD,* 68–70.

UR 8

City of Ur-Nammu

Even though Ur is mentioned only a few times in the Bible, the city was important in Abraham's world. It is identified as Abraham's ancestral home (Gen 11:28, 31; 15:7). Though the Bible omits any description of the city, archaeological excavations have revealed features of the city that made it a great urban center. Ur functioned as a harbor city, a center of trade and industry, a center of government, and a center of religion.

While some prefer to locate biblical Ur in upper Mesopotamia near the city of Haran, it is more likely that it was in lower Mesopotamia. The city was located on the banks of the Euphrates in ancient times, but over the years the river changed course, cutting a new channel to the east. Consequently, the ruins of the ancient site are located approximately ten miles west of the river. It is quite probable that the upper end of the Persian Gulf extended up to or near the city in ancient times.

Ur's growth and development was due largely to its location on the Euphrates. Because of navigational travel on the river, Ur became a center of trade with one major harbor located on the west side of the city, and another on the north. Located on the east side of a bend in the river, Ur took on an oval shape.

The settlement of Ur dates back to prehistoric times, the Ubiad period (ca. 5500–4000 BCE) when a small village was apparently established at the site. Excavations at the site indicate that the site continued to be occupied during the prehistoric Uruk and Jemdet Nasr periods. During that time it experienced significant growth and witnessed major developments in both architecture and writing.

During the period that followed, the Sumerian period of the third millennium BCE, Ur developed into an important city and became the leading city-state in lower Mesopotamia. Known as Sumer, lower Mesopotamia and its city-states provided the setting for the development of the great Sumerian culture that included not only Ur but also Kish and Uruk, the biblical Erech.

During that period Ur was comprised of dynasties. The First Dynasty of Ur was established about 3000 BCE. Ur became the leading city-state in southern Mesopotamia during that period, even though there were times when it was controlled by kings of neighboring city-states, including Gilgamesh, the king of Uruk, and Gudea, the king of Lagash.

The Third Dynasty, established by Ur-Nammu, extended from about 2150 BCE to about 2000 BCE and was by far the most influential of the dynasties of the third millennium. Under the leadership of Ur-Nammu, an accomplished military leader and a capable administrator, Ur entered a new chapter in its history. Ur became the capital of a powerful, independent city-state that virtually dominated Mesopotamia. During the period of the Third Dynasty it reached a new plateau as a center of government, religion, culture, trade, and exchange, due in large part to the many achievements of Ur-Nammu and his son Shulgi.

Because of his expertise in military warfare, Ur-Nammu extended the borders of Ur's control to include other important city-states in Mesopotamia such as Lagash, Larsa, Nippur, and Uruk, while his son Shulgi extended the borders northward to include Ashur and eastward to include Elam. The one hundred thousand cuneiform tablets found in the cities of this period suggest that the Third Dynasty of Ur was the most literate period in all Sumerian history. The tablets provide valuable information not only about advancement in writing at that time but also about Ur-Nammu's many interests.

Among his accomplishments, Ur-Nammu brought about improvements in travel and irrigation by implementing a major renovation program of the canal system. He brought about advancements in religion by building or rebuilding worship centers such as the temples and ziggurats throughout the land. Ur-Nammu was interested in law and produced the first law code in history. The tablets inform us about other features of life and culture, such as family life, arts and crafts, religion, mathematical systems, and medicine.

Following the period of the Third Dynasty, the political status of Ur began to wane, though the city continued to be an important international trade center and center of worship of the moon god Nanna. The city was destroyed in 1740 BCE; it was rebuilt and continued to exist during the Old Babylonian, Assyrian, Neo-Babylonian, Persian, and Greek periods. During this span of time the city witnessed a number of building projects. The population remained sizable and stable until the Greek period, when a shifting of the Euphrates River sent the city into rapid decline. Eventually it was abandoned.

Some of the most valuable archaeological discoveries of the city are the sacred areas with the great ziggurat, the royal cemetery, and domestic houses. The site was excavated by Sir Leonard Wooley, in a joint expedition of the University of Pennsylvania and the British Museum. The sacred area provides insight into the religious life and practices at Ur. It consisted of a rectangular area enclosed by a wall and was located in the north half of the city. The most impressive feature of the sacred area was the ziggurat built by Ur-Nammu. The ziggurat had three levels or stages connected by stairways. The base of the ziggurat is approximately two hundred feet long and 170 feet wide. The inner core of the base was made of mud brick while the outer shell of the base, eight feet thick, was constructed of baked brick laid with a bitumen mortar. Three massive stairways of one hundred steps each led upward to a tower. Smaller stairways led from the tower to the second and third levels. A temple to the moon god Nanna was built on top of the third level. Apparently trees were planted on the terraces on the ziggurat. The sacred area also included other temples or shrines for the worship of Nanna and his consort, Ningal; a courtyard area surrounded by rooms, some used for worship rituals while others served as temple kitchens; and a temple storehouse comprised of long and narrow storerooms where supplies such as wool, cloth, and food were stored.

Nanna, the god of Ur, was also known as Sin, and as the moon god was responsible for the different phases of the moon from the full moon to the new moon. The worship of Nanna included festivals held on the first, seventh, and fifteenth days of the month. Devotees of Nanna believed that he was in the netherworld prior to the new moon, the day when the moon was not visible. Among his other roles, Nanna was the god of cowherders, cattle breeders, and orchardmen, all of which reflect Nanna's role as a god of fertility. Nanna's wife, Ningal, had a role similar to her husband's, as the goddess of cowherders. She was also recognized as the goddess of the marshes or the goddess of reeds.

Perhaps the most intriguing of the discoveries at Ur was the royal cemetery. The cemetery dates to the Early Dynastic III period, about 2600–2450 BCE, and was comprised of sixteen large vaulted tombs; its contents reveal the burial practices of the rulers of that period. The tombs contained the body of the deceased ruler; the attendants of the royal court, both males and females; and animals such as oxen harnessed to carts. The burial ritual included a procession into the tomb in which the attendants of the royal court entered the tomb voluntarily with the deceased ruler and drank a poisonous liquid in order to enter the netherworld with their leader. Their deaths were probably recognized as a type of human sacrifice. The investigation of the tombs and burials has produced a variety of unique artifacts that were a part of the royal court. These include the finely decorated ox carts of the attendants; the spears and daggers of the soldiers; musical instruments such as lyres and harps decorated with animal heads; statues of he-goats; a unique helmet of gold with wings; personal ornaments such as beads, earrings, and combs; gaming boards; and many other articles. Many of these stunning items were made of gold or lapis lazuli and demonstrate fine craftsmanship in their design and intricate details.

Ziggurat at Ur

Family houses were found in Ur in an area southwest of the sacred area. The houses dated to the Old Babylonian period, approximately 2000–1750 BCE. The houses were built of brick and were generally two stories high. These dwellings included a central courtyard or open area with a paved floor that was surrounded by rooms. A staircase at one end of the courtyard led to the upper story. The second floor of the house included a wooden balcony and rooms that surrounded the open area in the center. Wooden poles extended upward from the floor of the courtyard and provided support for both the second-floor balcony and the flat roof above. Some of the houses included a small worship room.

Apart from the many questions about the relationship between Ur and the biblical figure Abraham, Ur is still an important city in understanding the patriarchal world. Due to trade by both river navigation and caravan routes, Ur was a major cosmopolitan trade center. It was a center of religion that helped shape religious thought in the ancient world. As a major center of government, it benefitted from rulers who brought about domestic improvements in the city and the surrounding area. They were held in high esteem by the citizens of the region. It was a center of wealth and unique architecture. But it was also a city in which family life was important, as reflected in the family dwellings found within the city. All of these features have contributed to a fuller understanding of the biblical portrait of Abraham.

Bibliography: ANDREWS, S. J., "Ur," *MDB*, 944; CHAPMAN, B. C., "Ur," *NIDBA*, 462–63; FLEMING, D. M., "Ur," *HolBD*, 1385; GADD, C. J., "Ur," *Archaeology and Old Testament Study*, ed. D. Winton Thomas (Oxford: Clarendon, 1967) 87–101; JACOBSEN, T., "Ur," *IDB*, 4:735–38; LASOR, W. S., "Ur," *ISBE*, 4:950–55; MACHINIST, P. B., "Ur," *HBD*, 1105–7; MARGUERON, J. C., "Ur," *ABD*, 6:766–67; POLLOCK, S., "Ur," *OEANE*, 5:288–91; SCHOVILLE, K. N., "Ur," *BAF*, 181–86; SELMAN, M. J., "Ur," *Major Cities of the Biblical World*, ed. R. K. Harrison (Nashville: Nelson, 1985) 275–84; TENNEY, M. C., "Ur of the Chaldeans," *NIDB*, 1045–46; WISEMAN, D. J., "Ur of the Chaldees," *NBD*, 1304–5; idem, "Ur of the Chaldees," *NBD*[2], 1231; idem, "Ur of the Chaldees," *ZPEB*, 5:846–48; YATES, K. M., Jr., "Ur," *BW*, 596–603.

Unit 2

CITIES OF
ARAM/SYRIA
AND PHOENICIA

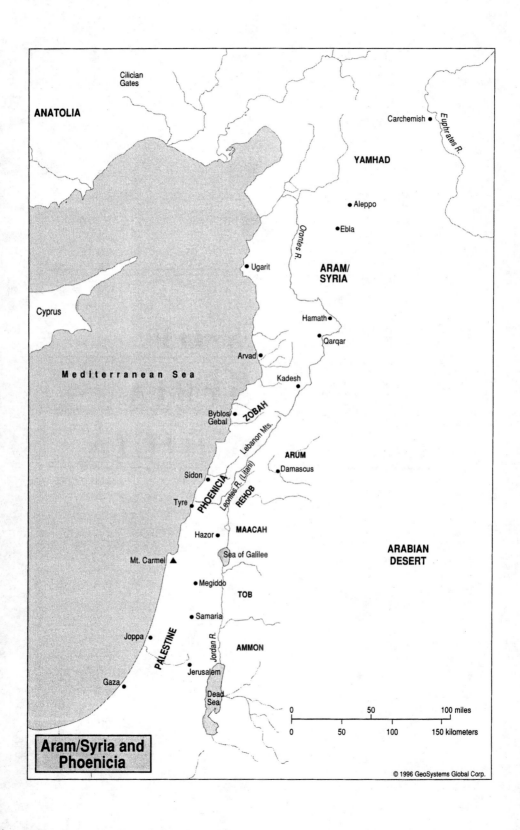

Aram/Syria and Phoenicia

© 1996 GeoSystems Global Corp.

ARAM/SYRIA & PHOENICIA   9

Israel's Neighbors to the North

Aram, commonly referred to as Syria, and Phoenicia played an important role in the OT story, at least in part because their territories and their inhabitants were located immediately to the north of Israel. The names Aram and Phoenicia, like Israel, were derived from the people who occupied the regions, namely, the Arameans or Syrians and the Phoenicians, though the inhabitants of Phoenicia for a time were also known as the Sidonians. The name Syria, which is commonly used in modern translations of the Bible, is a more recent designation derived from the term Aram, the name used in the Hebrew Bible for the territory occupied by the Arameans; however, the Arameans were not limited to the region traditionally known as Syria or Aram. Like Israel, both Syria/Aram and Phoenicia formed an important link in the Fertile Crescent, connecting the Mediterranean to the west, Egypt to the south, Anatolia to the northwest, and Mesopotamia to the east.

While the Greek historian Herodotus used Syria for the entire coastal region at the east end of the Mediterranean Sea, including the land of Palestine, the name is generally reserved for the territory located north-northeast of Palestine. Though it is difficult to outline the precise boundaries of Syria, the land of Syria is usually identified as the region located northeast of the Sea of Galilee, extending from the Arabian desert on the south to the Euphrates River valley on the northeast, to modern-day Turkey on the north, and to Phoenicia and the Mediterranean Sea on the west.

The land of Phoenicia was a narrow band of land approximately twenty miles wide and 120 miles long that extended from just north of the Mount Carmel mountain range northward along the Mediterranean coast. It was bounded by Israel on the south, Syria on the east and north, and the Mediterranean Sea on the west.

Both Syria and Phoenicia had distinctive physical features. Syrian territory included mountain ranges to the west along the Mediterranean, desert on the south, plains or steppes that were partially irrigated and used for agricultural purposes, and grazing lands with sparse grass and shrubs. Phoenician territory consisted primarily of mountain ranges, especially the Lebanon Mountains, with small plains located at intervals along the coast.

While the description of the physical and geographical features might seem to suggest that Syria and Phoenicia were unproductive regions, lacking in cultural development, such was not the case. In Syria even the desert regions provided seasonal grazing for the nomadic herdsmen, and the more fertile regions to the north supported an agricultural economy. Syria also had settlements that grew and developed into great urban centers. The development of these urban centers was facilitated by an adequate water supply provided by rivers such as the Orontes, Leontes, and Abana rivers, or by local springs. Damascus, for instance, was located in an oasis with mountains to the west and the desert to the east, its annual rainfall only eight to ten inches a year. However, tributaries from the Anti-Lebanon Mountains on the west, tributaries that formed the Abana River, provided Damascus with an ample water supply. This water supply, coupled with the location on the major trade route between Mesopotamia and Egypt, helped Damascus become a major caravan and trade center. Damascus is perhaps best known as the capital of Syria; however, Damascus was actually the most powerful and influential of several smaller states or city-states. Other major urban centers in Syria included the cities of Ugarit, Hamath, Carchemish, and Ebla. Although parts of Syria existed in isolation, many of the urban centers must have had a cosmopolitan atmosphere, since the major ancient Near Eastern trade route moved through Syria in the north and through Damascus in the south.

The Phoenicians had a distinctive culture. They were descendants of the Canaanites and like their forefathers engaged in harvesting, processing, and selling a purple dye they obtained from murex shells in the Mediterranean Sea. The prominent role the dye industry played among the Phoenicians is reflected in their name, which derived from the Greek term *phoinix,* "purple." The Phoenicians not only processed the dye but also had a major wool dying industry: they sold their purple wool to merchants from throughout the ancient world. The

Phoenicians had valuable timber resources, especially cedar and cypress, which they harvested from the Lebanon Mountains and used in their shipbuilding industry. Their expertise in shipbuilding was recognized throughout the ancient world. They also exported timber to other countries (1 Kgs 5:8–10).

The land of Phoenicia had several major cities, all of which were located on the coast. These included Tyre, Sidon, Byblos (also known as Gebal), and Arvad. Because of their presence on the Mediterranean coast, the Phoenicians operated fleets of ships engaged in sea trade in the Mediterranean and perhaps in the Red Sea (1 Kgs 9:26–28).

Among the important groups in Phoenician society was the merchant class. Located in major cities on the coast, the merchants traded by sea and by land. Merchant ships from throughout the Mediterranean docked at Phoenician ports, and caravans passed through the major Phoenician cities as they traveled up and down the coastal plain route. In addition to purple dye, dyed wool, and cedar and cyprus, the merchants sold expensive ivory carvings that were used as ivory inlays in the construction of furniture for the wealthy classes throughout the ancient Near East.

Bibliography: BALY, D., "Syria," *HBD*, 1009–10; BLAIKLOCK, E. M., "Phoenicia, Phenicia," *NIDB*, 786–88; BOWMAN, R. A., "Arameans," *IDB*, 1:190–93; BROWNING, D. C., Jr., "Syria," *HolBD*, 1313–14; CAUVIN, J., "Syria (Pre-history)," *ABD*, 6:271–74; DEVER, W. G., "Syria-Palestine," *OEANE*, 5:147; DORNEMANN, R. H., "Syria (Bronze Age and Iron Age Syria)," *ABD*, 6:274–81; GUZZO, M. G. A., "Phoenician-Punic," *OEANE*, 4:317–24; HARRISON, R. K., "Phoenicia," *NIDBA*, 363–64; HOFFNER, H. A., Jr., "Phoenicia," *ZPEB*, 4:778–82; HOOKS, S. M., "Aram/Arameans," *MDB*, 52–53; HUNT, H. B., Jr., "Phoenicia," *MDB*, 689–90; KAPELRUD, A. S., "Phoenicia," *IDB*, 3:800–805; KITCHEN, K. A., "Syria, Syrians," *NBD*, 1229–30; idem, "Syria, Syrians," *NBD*[2], 1155–56; LASOR, W. S., "Syria," *ISBE*, 4:686–94; LIVERANI, M., "Phoenicia; Phoenicians," *ISBE*, 3:853–62; MARKOE, G., "Phoenicians," *OEANE*, 4:324–31; MCCLELLAN, T. L., "Phoenicia," *HBD*, 791–94; PECKHAM, B., "Phoenicia, History of," *ABD*, 5:349–57; PITARD, W. T., "Arameans," *OEANE*, 1:184–87; SCHOVILLE, K. N., "Syria and Lebanon," *BAF*, 231–32; SCHUMACHER, F. T., "Aram," *IDB*, 1:185; THOMPSON, J. A., "Aram, Arameans," *NIDBA*, 37–38; idem, "Syria, Syrians," *BEB*, 2:2009–13; TRAMMEL, T., "Phoenicia," *HolBD*, 1110; WALKER, L. L., "Aram, Arameans," *ZPEB*, 1:246–49; WARD, W. A., "Phoenicia," *OEANE*, 4:313–17; WESSEL, W. W., "Syria," *NIDB*, 975–77; WISEMAN, D. J., "Phoenicia, Phoenicians," *NBD*, 992–94.

Phoenician Timber and Shipbuilding Center

Like Tyre and Sidon to the south and Ugarit to the north, Byblos became an important center of trade and industry on the Syrian-Phoenician coast in ancient times. This was largely due to two features unique to the site's location: an abundant supply of high quality timber from the Lebanon Mountains and a small inlet on the Mediterranean coast that could function as a shipping harbor. These two features combined with a location at the eastern end of the Mediterranean Sea to make Byblos an ideal seaport town.

Byblos was midway between Egypt and Anatolia. Its central location on the coast made it an ideal port for transporting goods to other parts of the Mediterranean world as well as an ideal location for ships coming from other parts of the Mediterranean world to dock. The city was located on a slope just above the harbor. The city, known as Gebal in the OT, was named Byblos ("book") by the Greeks because of the large quantities of papyrus transported to the port by the Egyptians. The most important natural resource of Byblos was the cedar and cyprus timber harvested from the Lebanon Mountains to the east. Because of the abundant supply of high-quality timber, Byblos became famous for its shipbuilding industry and the highly skilled craftsmanship of its carpenters, masons, and shipbuilders. According to an ancient tradition Byblos/Gebal was built by the god El, the head of the Canaanite pantheon, the god who was in essence the father of the gods. Because the city was founded by the father god, the inhabitants of the city believed that Byblos was the oldest city in the world.

References to Byblos in the OT reflect interactions between the people of Gebal and the Israelites and provide valuable information about the skills of its people. The "land of the Gebalites" mentioned in Joshua (Josh 13:5) probably referred to the city of Gebal and its

territory. Since the Gebalites harvested timber from the Lebanon
Mountains, we may assume that the area east of the city was a part of
Gebal's territory. Although the Israelites may have wanted to take
control of the territory of Gebal during the conquest, they failed to do
so (Josh 13:1–5). The OT also informs us that Solomon was assisted in
the building of the temple by artisans from Gebal (1 Kgs 5:18),
particularly those who were skilled as masons and carpenters. Ezekiel
refers to the fame Gebal achieved in the ancient world because of its
skilled shipbuilders and its shipbuilding industry (Ezek 27:9). This
industry would have had a valuable market among the seaport cities of
the Mediterranean Sea.

Archaeological evidence from excavations directed by Pierre Mon-
tet, 1921–24, and Maurice Dunand beginning in 1925 indicates that the
history of Byblos/Gebal extended from the Neolithic period to the
Crusader period. According to the archaeological evidence Byblos was
originally settled during the Neolithic period, perhaps as early as 8000
to 7000 BCE. While the precise nature of that early settlement still
remains somewhat obscure, the site continued in existence into the
Chalcolithic period, when it was inhabited by a people, small in stature,
who lived in small circular or rectangular huts. Among the discernible
customs of this period was their practice of burying their dead in
pottery.

Near the end of the Chalcolithic period and the beginning of the
Early Bronze Age, the city of Byblos experienced a dramatic change.
Byblos became an important urban center on the Phoenician coast and
acquired several new features including a city wall and several new
temples dedicated to the gods of Byblos. Of these temples perhaps the
most important was the temple of Baalat Gebal, the goddess recognized
as the Lady of Gebal. But in addition to the new construction, trade
made Byblos an increasingly consequential city. The inhabitants of
Byblos exported significant quantities of lumber, leather, oil, wine, and
spices to other parts of the Fertile Crescent including the lands of
Mesopotamia, Anatolia, and Syria.

Because of the limitless supply of wood the inhabitants of Byblos
had at their disposal, the Egyptians tried to maintain control of the city
and its territory whenever possible. Wood was essential for shipbuilding,
and Egypt had no forests. For that reason Byblos was virtually an
Egyptian colony during much of the period of the Old Kingdom in

Egyptian history. The Egyptians recognized the gods of the city by sending votive offerings to the temple of the goddess Baalat. Evidence of the shipment of cedar from Byblos to Egypt is found in the text of the Palermo stone, an account that dates to the period of the Fourth Dynasty about 2500 BCE. The text refers to one such shipment that included forty ships loaded with cedar logs, a sizable shipment of timber to say the least.

A new chapter in the story of Byblos began to unfold near the end of the third millennium BCE as a new wave of people, most likely the Amorites, moved into the area, destroyed the city, and subsequently rebuilt it. The population of Byblos at that time was predominantly Amorite, but the population base of the city also included other groups such as the Hurrians and Hittites. During this period, near end of the Early Bronze Age and the beginning of the Middle Bronze Age, new cultural elements were introduced to the city. Bronze became increasingly important in the production of tools and weapons, and a metalworking industry apparently began to flourish at Byblos. More extensive cultural exchanges took place between Byblos and other areas, including the Aegean islands. During the Middle Kingdom period in Egypt, Byblos was once again dominated by the Egyptians. This is seen in the inclusion of the name of the city in the cursing rituals of Egypt's Execration texts from that era. During the Middle Bronze Age yet another temple was constructed in the city, a temple built for Resheph, the god of plagues and destruction.

With the decline of the Middle Kingdom (ca. 1800–1750 BCE), the Egyptian delta and the cities of Palestine and Phoenicia, including Gebal, apparently came under the control of the Hyksos. Following the expulsion of the Hyksos (ca. 1600–1500 BCE), however, Egyptian control of the Phoenician coast was apparently reestablished, though it was perhaps limited in comparison to that of the preceding periods.

Information from the Amarna letters suggests that Gebal remained faithful to Egypt during the Amarna Age and that the city-state of Gebal repeatedly requested assistance from Egypt during that troubled era in an attempt to withstand the Habiru. According to the letters, Rib-Addi, the king of Gebal, wrote to Akhenaton more than fifty times in order to assure the Egyptian pharaoh of his faithfulness and to remind the pharaoh of his need for assistance as he faced the threat of the Habiru. After the relatively weak Egyptian presence during the Amarna period, a revival of Egyptian power came during the reign of Ramses II. The city was destroyed ca. 1195 BCE by the Sea Peoples. During the following period Egypt went into decline, and the land of Phoenicia and its cities experienced a period of independence. The independent spirit of Byblos is reflected in an account of its rude reception of Wen-Amon, an Egyptian official, when he went to Byblos and attempted to buy lumber.

Perhaps the most important discovery from Byblos was the inscriptional evidence that came from the period of King Ahiram, ca. 1000 BCE, particularly the inscription on the sarcophagus of Ahiram. It was written in the Phoenician alphabetic characters, the same alphabet of consonants used in early Hebrew. The inscriptional evidence is especially valuable because it provides insight concerning the early stages in the history of the development of the Hebrew alphabet, an alphabet consisting of twenty-two characters and written from right to left.

During the period that followed, the role of Byblos as the leading city of Phoenicia began to wane, and Tyre became the dominant city of the Phoenician coast. While Byblos was overshadowed by the prestige of Tyre, Byblos nevertheless remained an important center of shipping and trade.

Yehimilk inscription

During the period of Assyrian imperialism Byblos supplied forces for the anti-Assyrian coalition at Qarqar in 853 BCE. Like many other cities, Byblos became a vassal of the Assyrians and during the ninth to seventh centuries BCE paid tribute to the Assyrian kings. During the centuries that followed Byblos was a part of the empires that prevailed in the ancient world including those of the Babylonians, Persians, Greeks, and Romans. The city continued to function as a significant center of trade until the Byzantine era. The history of Byblos eventually came to an end during the Crusader period. Evidence of the city's important past is present at the site in the remains of an eleventh-century crusader castle and ruins from the Greek and Roman periods.

Bibliography: ARMERDING, C. E., "Gebal," *NIDBA,* 208–9; BALY, D., "Gebal," *HBD,* 334; DEVRIES, L. F., "Byblos/Gebal," *MDB,* 124; HUEY, F. B., Jr., "Gebal," *ZPEB,* 2:666–68; JOUKOWSKY, M. S., "Byblos," *OEANE,* 1:390–94; KAPELRUD, A. S., "Gebal," *IDB,* 2:359–60; KAUFMAN, P. L., "Gebal," *BEB,* 1:842; MILLARD, A. R., "Gebal," *NBD²,* 407; REA, J., "Gebal," *NBD,* 455; ROTH, R. L., "Gebal," *ABD,* 2:922–23; SCHOVILLE, K. N., "Byblos," *BAF,* 247–51; TENNEY, M. C., "Gebal," *NIDB,* 375–76; VOS, H. F., "Gebal," *ISBE,* 2:420–21.

CARCHEMISH   11

City of Decisive Battles

The battle of Carchemish in 605 BCE was, for the kingdom of Judah, one of the most consequential battles in ancient times. That battle marked the end of an era and signaled a major change on the political scene of the ancient Near East, a change that drastically altered the course of history for the kingdom of Judah. But the battle of 605 BCE was not the first battle fought at Carchemish, nor was it the first time the site of Carchemish played a major role in ancient Near Eastern history. The city of Carchemish witnessed many battles during its lengthy history and as a result experienced many political changes.

The history of Carchemish is a history interspersed with battles and political change, due at least in part to the strategic location of the site. It was located on the west bank of the Euphrates River in north Syria at the north end of a plain that ran along the Euphrates. The site was originally settled during the Chalcolithic period, the copper-stone age, just prior to the Bronze Age. As time passed, Carchemish became one of the major cities of north Syria. But it was the features of the location more than anything else that contributed to the growth and development of the site over the years. Carchemish was located at the major crossing on the upper Euphrates River, which meant that trade from both east and west was funneled through Carchemish. Consequently, Carchemish became the major trade center on the upper Euphrates River, entertaining merchants and travelers from lower and upper Mesopotamia, Anatolia, Syria-Palestine, and Egypt. But the city's location on the upper Euphrates had other implications. Because of its close proximity to the crossing, the city of Carchemish was in a position to guard and control the river crossing. Whoever controlled Carchemish controlled the crossing on the Euphrates and the flow of trade in that area. From early times Carchemish was not only a major center of trade and exchange but also a major military center. But the city's location at the major crossing on the upper Euphrates was enhanced by yet another feature, namely, the city's position at the north end of an important plain. This plain contained the major thoroughfare for travelers from the east and south to enter Anatolia to the west and also valuable timber resources and fertile soil, both of which contributed to the economic base of the city.

Some of the earliest information concerning the history of Carchemish comes from the Mari letters, ancient records discovered at the site of Mari on the Euphrates River. According to the Mari texts, Carchemish was already recognized as a significant independent city-state in north Syria during the eighteenth century BCE. The texts indicate that Carchemish had already developed into a major trade center by that time. During the centuries that followed, Carchemish drew the attention of other ancient Near Eastern peoples. From the seventeenth century BCE through the thirteenth century BCE the history of Carchemish was shaped and influenced by the Hurrians, the Egyptians, and the Hittites.

During the seventeenth century BCE Carchemish found itself sandwiched between two growing powers: the Hurrians on the east and the Hittites on the west. Carchemish apparently aligned itself with the Hurrian state of Mitanni in an attempt to stop the encroachment of the Hittites of Anatolia. However, the Hittite king Mursilis I was successful in destroying the north Syrian town of Aleppo approximately sixty miles southwest of Carchemish as well as the city of Babylon. Carchemish apparently continued as an ally of the Mitannian empire during the sixteenth and fifteenth centuries, when the Egyptians demonstrated their interest in Carchemish and other sites and territories to the south through annual campaigns. According to Egyptian records one such campaign to Carchemish was carried out by Ahmosis, the Egyptian king following the expulsion of the Hyksos from Egypt. However, the most significant campaign of this type occurred during the fifteenth century when the imperialistic Egyptian king, Thutmose III, traveled through north Syria during his eighth campaign, and conquered the city of Carchemish. Amenhotep III (fourteenth century) and Ramses III (twelfth century) made similar claims, though the validity of their claims has been questioned.

One of the most dramatic chapters in the history of Carchemish took place during the fourteenth century, when the Hittite empire was revitalized through the efforts of Suppiluliumas. According to Hittite sources Suppiluliumas conquered the city of Carchemish in approximately 1350 BCE. Following the conquest Carchemish became the major Hittite center in north Syria and continued as such for several decades. However, that phase was interrupted during the latter part of the thirteenth century by the arrival of the Sea Peoples, a wave of people comprised of several tribes or clans who moved from their homeland on the island of Crete and the Aegean through the lands of Anatolia, Syria, and Palestine as far as Egypt, destroying what lay in their path, including the Hittite empire and the cities of Ugarit and Carchemish.

Following the fall of the Hittite empire with its capital in Anatolia, Carchemish became the capital of the Neo-Hittite culture, a culture that combined features of both the Hittite and Syrian cultures during the twelfth and eleventh centuries BCE. The new kingdom, like the old, was referred to as the "land of Hatti," and its records were inscribed in a type of script commonly called hieroglyphic Hittite. According to inscriptions from the Neo-Hittite culture as well as Assyrian inscriptions, the kings of Carchemish and the kingdom of Hatti were powerful figures who maintained control over north Syria. During that period Carchemish was certainly the most important center of the Neo-Hittite culture in north Syria.

In the eleventh century BCE yet another chapter in the history of Carchemish began to unfold as the Assyrians made their first major attempt to gain control of Carchemish, an attempt initiated by Tiglath-pileser I, who moved westward seeking to conquer not only Carchemish but also the entire land of Hatti. As the Assyrian king and his army approached, the forces of Carchemish met him east of the Euphrates River and engaged in battle with the Assyrian king. While the threat posed by the Assyrians was substantial, Carchemish was able to withstand the Assyrian encroachment for approximately three centuries, though both Ashurbanipal II and Shalmaneser III were able to attack the city and take tribute from it. During that three-hundred-year period Carchemish might best be described as the hub of an independent city-state ruled by local dynasties.

Ruled by Pisiris, last of the independent kings, Carchemish faced a new threat as Tiglath-pileser III, the most powerful Assyrian king in OT history, came to the Assyrian throne in 745 BCE. Interested in gaining control of the lands west of Assyria, Tiglath-pileser III brought about a revival of Assyrian power and attacked the city of Carchemish in 743 BCE. He engaged in battle with Pisiris and defeated him and his army. As a result Pisiris and the people of Carchemish had to pay a heavy tribute to Assyria. But a more devastating blow was delivered to Carchemish during the reign of Sargon II, who came to the Assyrian throne in 722 BCE. With a new king at the helm in Assyria, Carchemish, like other states, tried to break away from Assyrian control. King Pisiris demonstrated his rebellion against Assyria by withholding the tribute. In 717 BCE Sargon II responded by attacking and destroying the city. Isaiah the prophet refers to this event, noting that Carchemish was one of many cities in Syria and Palestine that experienced defeat at the hand of Assyria (Isa 10:5–11; esp. v. 9). Following the capture of the city, Sargon deported the citizens of Carchemish to other parts of his empire, repopulated Carchemish with Assyrians, and appointed an Assyrian governor over Carchemish. According to brick inscriptions found in Carchemish, Sargon rebuilt the city and made it the Assyrian provincial capital of the upper Euphrates.

But the important role of Carchemish in history was not yet at an end. Carchemish was the site of one of the most decisive battles in ancient Near Eastern history. The Assyrians, assisted by the Egyptians, made one final effort to withstand the Babylonians in a climactic power struggle. The Assyrian empire reached its height in 664 BCE with the conquest of Thebes, but the great empire began to face some serious problems during the latter half of the seventh century BCE: an internal struggle and decline beginning about 630 BCE as well as an external threat from the newly formed Neo-Babylonian empire to the south. The Assyrian domination of the Fertile Crescent was being challenged by the Babylonians. In 614 BCE the Babylonians moved into Assyria and took the city of Ashur. Two years later they conquered Nineveh and yet two years later invaded the city of Haran.

The Assyrians had little hope of surviving this kind of aggression; nevertheless, one final attempt to withstand the new world power took place at the site of Carchemish. As the final confrontation drew near, the Assyrian forces tried to regroup. In 609 BCE Neco II, the king of Egypt, grew fearful of the increasing threat of the Babylonians and moved up the coast of Palestine and Syria toward the site of Carchemish to assist the Assyrians. With the Egyptians moving to join the confrontation, Josiah, the pro-Babylonian king of Judah, attempted to intercept Neco at Megiddo and was killed in the ensuing battle (2 Chron 35:20–27). For all practical purposes the struggle for power was between Egypt and Babylonia. The forces were in place for the final confrontation at Carchemish. Neco, knowing the importance of the battle, had rallied the very best of his forces. According to Jeremiah (Jer 46:9), Neco's army included a large contingent of mercenary soldiers made up of Ethiopians (men of Ethiopia), Libyans (Put), and Lydians (men of Lud). But Neco's efforts were not enough. In May of 605 BCE Nebuchadnezzar, the crown prince of the Neo-Babylonian empire, advanced his army to Carchemish, defeated Neco II, and established Babylonia as the major empire in the ancient Near Eastern world.

Following the battle the city of Carchemish went into decline. A new city was built on the site approximately three centuries later during the early part of the Seleucid period in Syria. The new city, built during the reign of Seleucus I, was named Europos.

The rediscovery of the site of Carchemish in modern times began in the late nineteenth century, when the large mound of ruins was identified as Carchemish by George Smith in 1876. These ancient ruins, located near the modern village of Jerablus, were investigated in 1878 by a team sponsored by the British Museum; however, a major excavation of the site was not undertaken until 1912, when D. G. Horgarth began an excavation project that continued for several seasons. In 1920 Sir Leonard Wooley became the director of the project. The excavations have confirmed the identification of the site and have discovered many important features of the ancient city.

Archaeological evidence indicates that Carchemish was constructed at a bend on the west side of the Euphrates River. The city was enclosed by a wall and had walls dividing it into three basic parts—the citadel, the town proper, and the outer city—making up a large city complex. The citadel was located in the bend of the river on the west bank of the Euphrates. Excavations in the citadel have uncovered a fortress or palace built by Sargon II. The city proper was oval in shape and was located to the west of the citadel. It included a processional way, a temple, and a lower palace. Two gates were located in the western wall of the inner city. The gates led from the inner city to the outer city to the west. Excavations at the site itself have been especially valuable because they have produced buildings and artifacts that date to the time of Sargon's and later Neco's occupation of the site. Our understanding of ancient Carchemish and its role in ancient history has also been enhanced by discoveries at other sites and in other lands, including those in Hittite Anatolia, Ebla (the Ebla tablets), Mari (the Mari tablets), Babylon (the Babylonian Chronicle), and Egypt (the Egyptian king records).

Bibliography: COCHRAN, B. H., "Carchemish," *MDB,* 136–37; COLESON, J., "Carchemish," *HolBD,* 235; GORDON, C. H., "Carchemish," *IDB,* 1:536; HALLO, W., "Carchemish," *BW,* 165–69; HARRISON, R. K., and E. M. Blaiklock, "Carchemish," *NIDBA,* 119; HAWKINS, J. D., "Carchemish," *OEANE,* 1:423–24; HOFFNER, H. A., Jr., "Carchemish," *ZPEB,* 1:752–54; PEARCE, L. E., "Carchemish," *HBD,* 156; TENNEY, C. M., "Carchemish, Charchemish," *NIDB,* 195; WISEMAN, D. J., "Carchemish," *NBD,* 200; idem, "Carchemish," *NBD*^{2}, 179; YOUNGBLOOD, R., "Carchemish," *ISBE,* 1:616–17.

DAMASCUS

Caravan Center in the Oasis

Nowhere have environmental factors, especially the presence of water, played a more important role in the life and development of a site than at ancient Damascus. The significance and the quality of the water supply are reflected even in the Bible, in Naaman's question, "Are not Abana and Pharpar, the rivers of Damascus, better than all the waters of Israel?" (2 Kgs 5:12).

Damascus is located east of the Anti-Lebanon Mountains in southern Syria. It is approximately fifty-five miles east of the Phoenician city, Sidon, twenty-five miles east-northeast of Mount Hermon, and fifty-five miles northeast of the site of ancient Hazor. Today Damascus is the capital and largest city in Syria.

A casual survey of the physical features of its location might prompt one to question why Damascus developed as it did in ancient times. Damascus is sandwiched between two natural barriers, the Lebanon and Anti-Lebanon Mountains on the west and the Syrian desert on the east. However, other physical features of the immediate area offset the limitations of the location and make it ideal for settlement. Damascus has fertile soil and a plentiful water supply. Damascus is west of the Syrian desert, located on the west edge of a fertile basin; its water supply comes not from rainfall but from the Barada River, a perennial stream, which originates in the tributaries of the Anti-Lebanon Mountains. The Barada River, the biblical Abana, runs through Damascus and then eastward through the fertile basin. The el-Awaj River, the biblical Pharpar, runs somewhat parallel to the Barada but several miles south of Damascus.

The combination of fertile soil and clear cool water from the mountains created an oasis. The oasis itself was called the Ghuta, the semi-arid region beyond the Ghuta was called the Merj, and the entire area was called the Damascene. The gardenlike atmosphere of the fertile basin was so well known in antiquity that it gave rise to a tradition that Damascus was the location of the Garden of Eden. This combination of features attracted the earliest inhabitants to settle at the site and created a mainstream for life in Damascus and the nearby area. During very early times the residents of the area developed irrigation systems to distribute the water of the mountain streams throughout the fertile basin and created a productive agricultural area. The inhabitants of the area engaged in gardening, farming, the cultivation of fruit orchards, and cattle raising.

But the economy of Damascus was not limited to the local agricultural and cattle industries. With the development of trade routes Damascus became a major caravan center and perhaps the most vital link in the whole trade route system. It was at Damascus that the major trade routes of the ancient Near East converged. Damascus entertained caravans and merchants from Egypt and Arabia to the south, Anatolia and north Syria to the north, and Mesopotamia to the east. Because of its location and the important role it played in trade and exchange during the OT period, Damascus became a major center of communication and religion. But the location of Damascus also had political implications. As the connecting hub for major trade routes that ran north, south, and east, Damascus was sure to be affected by the political changes in the ancient Near East; consequently the history of Damascus, like that of many other cities in the Fertile Crescent, was shaped dramatically by political change. During its lengthy history Damascus and its territory were controlled or their history shaped through the influence of the Egyptians, Hittites, Israelites, Arameans, Assyrians, Babylonians, Persians, Seleucids, Romans, and Nabateans.

While Damascus played a vital role in ancient Near Eastern affairs, a detailed history of the city has not been written due in part to two major problems. First, ancient Near Eastern records currently available are inadequate. While the Bible and other ancient texts refer to Damascus or its territory, they do not provide detailed historical information. Rather, these accounts make reference to isolated events about Damascus, its territory, or its kings. Second, archaeological information from the site itself is extremely limited. A major systematic excavation of the site has never been carried out since the site has been occupied continuously from ancient times to the present.

Excavations have been limited to very small areas in the city or outlying communities. Wayne Pitard has admirably overcome these limitations in researching Damascus and has provided a masterful treatment to which I am deeply indebted. His work is a must for anyone interested in Damascus.

Just exactly when the site was settled has not been determined; however, excavations at nearby sites indicate that Damascus originated during prehistoric times. Neighboring sites have produced evidence from the Paleolithic, Neolithic, Chalcolithic, and Early Bronze periods. The early beginnings of Damascus are shrouded in mystery, but we may reasonably assume that Damascus became a thriving trade center during the Middle Bronze Age (the patriarchal period in the Bible) during which the international trade route system apparently developed, and many of the sites of Palestine and southern Syria became major cities or tells (successive levels of settlement forming a mound). Based on information from the Execration texts in Egypt, texts that date to the Middle Bronze Age, Damascus was in the land of Apum. While the meaning of this name is still open to discussion, it perhaps meant thicket of canebrakes or reeds, a name derived from the cane-filled marshes east of Damascus. Archaeological evidence from both the Twelfth Dynasty in Egypt and the Old Babylonian period in southern Mesopotamia further suggests that Damascus was involved in trade activities with both Egypt and Mesopotamia. Consequently, we may assume that during the Middle Bronze Age Damascus became a major hub for trade routes from Egypt and Mesopotamia, a major caravan center and center of trade, a major cosmopolitan center for foreign merchants, and (though the evidence is not conclusive) a city under Egyptian control during a part of the Twelfth Dynasty. The Bible tells us that Abraham's chief servant, Eliezer, came from Damascus (Gen 15:2).

Though information is limited, the history of Damascus, like that of other cities in Syria, was certainly shaped by the political contacts between the Egyptians, Hurrians, and Hittites during the Late Bronze Age. While the territory of Damascus was known as Apum during the Middle Bronze Age, this name was replaced by the names Apu, Api, Opu, or Upi during the Late Bronze Age. During the early part of the Late Bronze Age, Damascus and the land of Upi were most likely under the control of the Hurrian empire of Mitanni. Because it was located on the southern fringes of Hurrian-controlled territory, the land of Upi was always subject to the expansionist tactics of the Egyptians, especially during the Eighteenth Dynasty, when the Egyptian king Thutmose III conducted annual campaigns to sites and territories in Palestine and southern Syria as he attempted to push his border as far north as possible. An account of one such campaign includes a list of 119 towns whose rulers, including the ruler of the city of Damascus, were captured by Thutmose III and his army. This indicates that during the reign of Thutmose III, Damascus and the land of Upi, like many other cities and regions in Palestine and southern Syria, were under Egyptian control.

Additional references to Damascus and the territory in which it was located are found in the Amarna letters and the Hittite suzerainty treaties. These references provide limited insight about Damascus during the Amarna Age, that period in Egyptian history when the capital of Egypt was located at Akhetaton (Tell el-Amarna) and the concurrent period of Hittite aggression in Syria. According to the Amarna letters, a series of letters written by the vassal city-state kings or administrators in Palestine and Syria to the king of Egypt, Damascus was most likely under Egyptian control during the early part of the Amarna period, the period of Amenhotep III; his name appears in an inscription from the period of his reign. Egypt apparently lost control of Damascus and the land of Upi during the latter part of the Amarna Age, when the Egyptian control of Amenhotep IV and Akhenaton was challenged by the Hittite king Suppiluliumas. The Amarna letters tell us that an Egyptian official named Biriawaza attempted to defend the area against the threat from the north. However, information from one of the Hittite suzerainty treaties indicates that Suppiluliumas moved into southern Syria and defeated Ariwana, king of the territory of Apina, the Hittite name for the land of Upi. Following a period of Hittite control Damascus and the land of Upi once again came under Egyptian control during the Nineteenth Dynasty during the reign of Seti I and Ramses II.

With the arrival of the Early Iron Age, Damascus again witnessed a series of new developments, and the city was on its way to becoming a major Aramean city-state. During that period a number of small kingdoms or city-states, occupied in part by Arameans, formed in the areas east of the Jordan River and north and northeast of the Sea of Galilee. These included the kingdoms of Ammon, Tob, Geshur, Maacah, Rehob, and Zobah. Whether the Arameans who occupied these regions were newcomers or descendants of an earlier population is still debated. The OT is the major source of information for this period; it tells us that the development of these small kingdoms resulted in conflict as the larger states attempted to increase their territory and gain control of neighboring states. Especially significant was the power struggle between Israel and Zobah that may have originated during the reign of Saul (1 Sam 14:47). This conflict intensified during the reign of David, and David ultimately defeated Hadadezer, the king of Zobah (2 Sam 8:3–8). This victory gave David control not only of Zobah but also of Damascus (2 Sam 8:5–6) and several states in the area east-northeast of the Sea of Galilee including Maacah, Geshur, and Tob. But perhaps most significant was the final chapter in the lingering conflict between the two kingdoms, which took place during the reign of Solomon. Tired of oppression at the hands of the Israelites, Rezon, originally of the royal court of Hadadezer, rebelled against Solomon and became king of Damascus (1 Kgs 11:24), introducing a new era in the history of Damascus. With Rezon as king, Damascus was on its way to becoming the capital of a major Aramean state and a political entity that would play an important role in the political affairs of the ancient Near East during the ninth and eighth centuries BCE. The OT refers to this kingdom as Syria. The political activities of Damascus especially involved Israel and Judah to the south and Assyria to the northeast. Rezon established the kingdom and its independence from Israelite control; Rezon's successors, Hezion and Tabrimmon, devoted their efforts to helping the new state become more firmly established.

The role of Damascus in the affairs of the kingdoms of Judah and Israel is clearly seen in the OT (though the chronology and details of some of the events are still debated). For example, King Asa of Judah established an alliance with Benhadad I, the king of Damascus and successor to Tabrimmon, in a power play against King Baasha of Israel (1 Kgs 15:18–19), who posed a threat to Judah's security (1 Kgs 15:16–17). Benhadad took advantage of the opportunity, invaded the kingdom of Israel, and conquered several of its cities (1 Kgs 15:20). But Damascus's aggressive policies against Israel came to a halt during the reign of Omri. Known for his genius and power (1 Kgs 16:27), Omri most likely established a treaty with the Assyrians, thus neutralizing Damascus and the Syrian forces located between the two nations.

The warfare that often characterized relations between Israel and Damascus is reflected in the stories of Ahab (1 Kgs 20:1–19; 23–34;

22:1–40). Although the two nations were often bitter opponents, they became allies during the period of Assyrian aggression during the reign of Shalmaneser III. According to the Monolith Inscription of Shalmaneser III, Ahab and Benhadad (probably Benhadad II), along with others, joined forces and halted the Assyrian king in the famous battle of Qarqar in 853 BCE. Ultimately, Ahab met his death in battle with the Syrians (1 Kgs 22:1–40).

During the period following the reign of Ahab, Israel was at the mercy of Damascus and its king, Hazael. According to the OT, Hazael, whom the Assyrians referred to as the "son of nobody," gained control of Syria by killing its former king, Benhadad (2 Kgs 8:7–15). During this period, Israel, weakened by the policies of Jehu, not only lost most of its territory east of the Jordan, especially Gilead and Bashan (2 Kgs 10:32), but eventually lost its independence and became a vassal of the Syrian king (2 Kgs 13:1–9). But Hazael's aggressive activities were not limited to Israel. He also moved into Judah, especially the cities of Gath and Jerusalem, and received tribute from Judah's king, Jehoash (2 Kgs 12:17–18).

While Damascus maintained political supremacy during the latter half of the ninth century, the tide turned during the reign of Benhadad III, the son of Hazael, in the early part of the eighth century, when Jeroboam II was king of Israel. Apparently inspired by the foreign policy of Solomon, Jeroboam II introduced a period of expansion and extended the border of Israel north toward Hamath (2 Kgs 14:25), consequently exercising control over Damascus and its territory.

The latter half of the eighth century saw another change in the relationship between Israel and Damascus. Threatened by the imperialistic strategy of Tiglath-pileser III who sought to incorporate all the lands of the Fertile Crescent from Mesopotamia to Egypt into the Assyrian empire, Rezin, the king of Damascus, and Pekah, the king of Israel, formed an anti-Assyrian coalition and attempted to stop his westward movement. Realizing the magnitude of the threat, Rezin and Pekah invited other neighboring kingdoms, including Judah and its king Ahaz, to join the coalition. The refusal of Ahaz to join the coalition resulted in an immediate full-blown crisis, the Syro-Ephraimitic crisis of 734 BCE, in which Syria and Israel waged war against Judah in an attempt to force Judah to comply with their demands (2 Kgs 16:5; Amos 1:5). The war had dire consequences: Ahaz became a vassal of Assyria to escape Rezin and Pekah (2 Kgs 16:8); Damascus was captured by the Assyrian forces in 732 BCE and its people carried into captivity; and Rezin was killed, and his kingdom became in essence an Assyrian vassal state (2 Kgs 16:9). The fall of Damascus in 732 BCE brought to an end the once powerful Aramean kingdom. According to the biblical account the Assyrians deported the inhabitants of the city to the land of Kir (2 Kgs 16:9). Assyrian records provide additional information indicating that the Assyrian forces moved into Syria destroying its towns like the waters of a flood destroy ancient mounds. According to the Assyrian texts, 591 towns were destroyed. Damascus unsuccessfully attempted to break away from Assyrian domination in 727 and 720 BCE. Damascus continued to be an important trade center, but its political future was controlled by others such as the Babylonians, Persians, Greeks, Seleucids, and Romans, except for a brief period from 85 to 65 BCE, just prior to the Roman period, when Damascus was the capital of a Nabatean kingdom.

Because Damascus was a major international trade center, foreign influences certainly affected and shaped many aspects of life and culture in the ancient city. This was especially true in the area of religion. Among the deities worshiped in Damascus were those of the Canaanites, Hittites, Hurrians, and Assyrians. The story of Naaman, the Syrian army officer who came to the Israelite prophet Elisha seeking a cure for his leprosy, even reflects the influence of Israelite religion (2 Kgs 5:1–14). The chief god worshiped in Damascus was Hadad, the Semitic storm god, for whom several of the kings had been named. Ahaz, the king of Judah, was impressed by the altar he saw in Damascus and sent a model of the altar to Jerusalem where Uriah the priest had such an altar constructed for the king's personal use (2 Kgs 16:10–16). While this passage does not inform us about the god or gods served at the altar in Damascus, we may assume that it was an Assyrian altar used in the worship of the Assyrian astral deities, an assumption based on the fact that Damascus was under Assyrian control at the time.

Bibliography: BORAAS, R. S., "Damascus," *HBD,* 203; BOWLING, A., "Damascus," *ZPEB,* 2:7–9; BUTLER, T. C., "Damascus," *HolBD,* 330–32; FREEMAN, J. D., "Damascus," *NIDB,* 248–50; HALDAR, A., "Damascus," *IDB,* 1:757–59; LIVINGSTON, G. H., "Damascus," *Major Cities of the Biblical World,* ed. R. K. Harrison (Nashville: Nelson, 1985) 96–106; MARE, W. H., "Damascus," *NIDBA,* 147–48; MCRAY, J., "Damascus (The Greco-Roman Period)," *ABD,* 2:7–8; PERKIN, H. W., "Damascus.

Damascenes," *BEB,* 1:567–68; Pitard, W. T., *Ancient Damascus* (Winona Lake, Ind.: Eisenbrauns, 1987); idem, "Damascus," *OEANE,* 2:103–6; idem, "Damascus (Pre-Hellenistic History)," *ABD,* 2:5–7; Unger, M. F., "Damascus," *ISBE,* 1:852–55; Unger, M. F., "Damascus," *BW,* 179–84; Wiseman, D. J., "Damascus," *NBD,* 288–89; idem, "Damascus," *NBD*², 260.

EBLA 🏺   13

Monumental City-State of North Syria during the Third Millennium BCE

Ebla was the hub of a major city-state in north Syria in ancient times, an important center of government, trade and commerce, industry, and religion; its location, size, and archaeological remains bear witness to its prominence in ancient history. While references to Ebla do not appear in the Bible, they are found in other ancient Near Eastern writings including texts from Mesopotamia and Egypt. Ancient Akkadian inscriptions indicate that both Sargon and his grandson Naram-Sin at one time controlled the city and its territory.

Ebla is located in north Syria about thirty-five miles south of Aleppo and approximately midway between the Mediterranean Sea and the Euphrates River, near the village of Mardikh (the ancient site Tell Mardikh), which is unoccupied. In ancient times the site lay near the major north-south trade route that ran through Damascus and Hamath. Today the mound of ruins is the largest of its kind in that part of Syria—approximately fifty feet high and covering about 140 acres.

The discovery of ancient Ebla is certainly one of the most important of its kind during the latter half of the twentieth century. When excavations at Tell Mardikh began in the mid 1960s, the ancient name of the site was not known. It was identified as ancient Ebla in 1968, based on inscriptional evidence discovered by an archaeological team from the University of Rome under the direction of Paolo Matthiae. The inscription, located on the statue of King Ibbit-Lim, stated that the work of art was dedicated to the goddess Ishtar and that the name of the ancient city in which it stood was Ebla. Excavations at Tell Mardikh produced yet another dramatic breakthrough during the seasons of 1974, 1975, and 1976, when the royal archives of Ebla were excavated.

The archives, labeled palace G, contained thousands of clay tablets with valuable information about the government, life, and culture of Ebla as well as evidence that Ebla was the capital of a major city-state. It was the largest and most influential city in north Syria during the latter half of the third millennium and first half of the second millennium BCE.

The ancient city of Ebla was comprised of two parts—an acropolis and a large surrounding city below. Excavations have produced evidence of occupation from ca. 3500 BCE to ca. 600 CE; the major period of occupation was during the Early Bronze and Middle Bronze ages, ca. 2600–1600 BCE.

Archaeological evidence indicates Ebla's earliest inhabitants established a small village in the area of the acropolis (ca. 3500 BCE). At about 2900 BCE the community increased dramatically and expanded to occupy the lower city. During the next three centuries, ca. 2900–2600 BCE, Ebla moved well beyond its early beginnings as a village and became a major town.

The period that followed, ca. 2600–2250 BCE, was Ebla's golden age. The town experienced massive growth and became a major city, the largest city in north Syria, and the capital of a major city-state. It was during this period that the large, elaborately decorated palace G, in which the archives of clay tablets were stored, was constructed on the southwest slope of the acropolis. The palace was designed and functioned as the administrative headquarters of the kingdom. It included a large audience hall and storerooms in which the tablets of the archives of the kingdom were kept. The audience hall apparently served as a reception area for the king or governmental officials to greet and carry out business transactions with dignitaries from other areas. The hall contained a raised platform for the royal throne. A stairway extended from the audience hall up the slope to the acropolis, which included the royal palace, the king's stables, quarters for the servants, and the city's main hall or municipal building. The city was destroyed ca. 2250 BCE; this was probably the destruction of Ebla of which Naram-Sin of Akkad had boasted.

The city regained its importance following the destruction of 2250 BCE, but it did not reach its former level of influence in Syria. Palace G, which had been destroyed, was not rebuilt. In 2000 BCE the city experienced yet another destruction, which may have been related to the appearance of the Amorites.

Shortly after being destroyed, the city of Ebla was again rebuilt. Archaeological evidence indicates that the new occupation beginning ca. 2000 BCE bears signs of a new culture, perhaps the Amorites whose presence in Mesopotamia, Palestine, and Syria is noted in ancient texts. For all practical purposes the new inhabitants used the city plan of the earlier city as they built the city of that period. Features of the city that have been discovered from the period include a new fortification system comprised of a major rampart wall, four monumental city gates and watch towers, a fortress, four temples or sanctuaries, private dwellings, and two new palaces—one on the acropolis, the other in the lower city west of the acropolis.

About 1800 BCE the fortunes of Ebla changed again as the city-state was absorbed by the kingdom of Yamhad, a major kingdom north of Ebla. While this development affected Ebla's political status, Ebla nevertheless continued to prosper economically and to be an important cultural center in north Syria. During this period yet another palace, often referred to as the western palace or Q, was built. Under the palace was a royal cemetery comprised of caves. Three of the nine royal tombs have been excavated: the tomb of the princess, the tomb of the lord of the goats, and the tomb of the cisterns. The Hittites from Anatolia invaded north Syria ca. 1600 BCE and brought with them the final destruction of Ebla under the leadership of either Hattusilis I or Mursilis I. Following that destruction Ebla never again rose to prominence.

While the discoveries at Ebla have no direct tie to the OT, they are nevertheless important because they provide valuable information about the city-state itself and north Syria in general from ca. 2600 BCE to ca. 1600 BCE, a period for which new information is always welcomed. The discoveries may be divided more precisely into two categories: those that pertain to the Early Dynastic III period, ca. 2600–2000 BCE, and those that pertain to the so-called Amorite period, roughly 2000–1600 BCE. Royal palace G and the royal quarters on the acropolis belong to the former period, whereas the ramparts, city gates, watch towers, sanctuaries, dwellings, western palace, and royal cemetery belong to the latter period.

While the architectural remains discovered at the site are important, the most valuable of the discoveries at Ebla are the thousands of clay tablets discovered in the royal archives, palace G, that had been organized in categories and placed on shelves. When palace G was destroyed, the wooden shelves burned and the rows of tablets fell one on top of the other, preserving the original organization. This feature of the ruins of the archives proved to be extremely beneficial to the excavation team. But even more helpful has been the information the tablets provide, information about the system of government at Ebla, its trade, industry, professions, and religion. The ancient records were written in the type of cuneiform script used by scribes, especially in Mesopotamia. Among the written materials scholars have distinguished two different languages that were used at Ebla in ancient times—the old Sumerian language used by the inhabitants of lower Mesopotamia in the land of Sumer, and a formerly unknown language distinctive to Ebla itself and consequently called the Eblaite language. The tablets reveal that at its height Ebla developed into perhaps the most powerful city-state in north Syria with a population of approximately 260,000 people and a system of government that included a king and a body of elders. Originally the king was an elected official who did not necessarily come from the royal family. An election for king was held every seven years. Other important figures in the government included members of the royal family (the queen and princess) and public officials (governors, commissioners, and supervisors), as well as others.

The tablets also contain information about the rations and supplies purchased for approximately eleven thousand members of the royal household, other governmental personnel, state officials, and servants. Supplies for the group included metals like silver and gold, fabrics of flax and wool for garments, cereal grains like barley and wheat for bread, oil, beer and wine, fruits, cattle, and weapons.

The tablets also provide insight into Ebla's economy, an economy that was based largely on agriculture, shepherding and herding, industry, and trade. The farmers of the city-state produced a wide variety of agricultural products including cereal crops like wheat and barley, figs, pomegranates, olives for olive oil, grapes for wine, and malt for beer. Herdsmen produced an annual supply of stock including sheep, goats, and cattle, which were all valuable for meat, wool, and religious offerings and sacrifices. But while agriculture, shepherding, and herding formed an important foundation for Ebla's economy, the city-state apparently gained much of its wealth from industrial enterprises including the manufacture of textiles, metals, and furniture. The manufacture of these products established Ebla as a major center of international trade.

Some of the tablets in the royal archives suggest that a school was located in royal palace G; numerous fragments contain lengthy lists of vocabulary words used in Ebla. The words are written in both Sumerian and Eblaite. On the tablets are basic terms or vocabulary words, as well as lists of geographical place names, personal names, different kinds of professions, and the names of birds, fish, and animals. The lists were apparently used by instructors and copied by students who were being trained to function as the scribes or record keepers of the kingdom.

The archives also contained tablets that provide information about the relationship Ebla had to other cities or city-states. For instance, some of the tablets contain the names of those cities over which Ebla exercised control, while other tablets contain information about treaties, such as the important treaty established between Ebla and the city of Ashur. The treaty was comprised of several parts including the stipulations for trade upon which both parties agreed, taxation guide-lines designed to prevent the double taxation of merchants, as well as other political matters pertaining to the two parties involved. The historical documents also record political alliances that were sealed in marriage.

Ebla was a major center of religion, and this affected the life and culture in the city. Numerous tablets contain references to the many gods worshiped in Ebla and the offerings and sacrifices made to them. Several temples and sanctuaries were discovered in the city, and structures such as the major city gates were named for the deities of the city. That the city was one in which numerous gods were worshiped is further reflected in the fact that over five hundred gods are mentioned in the texts; these include non-Semitic deities, that is, Sumerian gods, and Semitic deities or Canaanite gods. The chief god of the city was the god Dagon, who was worshiped as the "Lord of the Land," an agricultural deity. Like many other ancient Near Eastern deities Dagon was worshiped by several different groups. Dagon was a Canaanite god and is also identified with the Philistines in the Bible (Judg 16:23; 1 Sam 5:2). At Ebla one of the four city gates was named for Dagon. Other prominent gods of the city included Resheph, the Canaanite god of plagues; Hadad, the god of storms; Ishtar, the goddess of love and war;

Kamish, the biblical Chemosh and god of Moab; and Baal, the Canaanite god of fertility.

Bibliography: ARCHI, A., "Ebla Texts," *OEANE,* 2:184–86; BIGGS, R. D., "Ebla Texts," *ABD,* 2:263–70; BIGGS, R., "The Ebla Tablets: An Interim Perspective," *BA* 43 (1980) 76–87; HOOKS, S. M., "Ebla," *MDB,* 225–27; HORSNELL, M. J., "Ebla," *Major Cities of the Biblical World,* ed. R. K. Harrison (Nashville: Nelson, 1985) 108–18; LASOR, W. S., "Ebla," *BEB,* 1:648–50; MACHINIST, P. B., "Ebla," *HBD,* 234–36; MATTHIAE, P., "Ebla," *OEANE,* 2:180–83; idem, *Ebla: An Empire Rediscovered* (New York: Doubleday, 1980); idem, "New Discoveries at Ebla," *BA* 47 (1984) 18–32; MOYER, J. C., "Ebla," *HolBD,* 387–88; PERKIN, H. W., "Tell Mardikh," *NIDBA,* 440–42; RENDSBURG, G. A., "Eblaites," *OEANE,* 2:183–84; SCHOVILLE, K. N., "Ebla (Tell Mardikh)," *BAF,* 242–46; VIGANO, L., "Literary Sources for the History of Palestine and Syria: The Ebla Tablets," *BA* 47 (1984) 6–16 (rev. and ed. Dennis Pardee); WISEMAN, D. J., "Ebla," *NBD²,* 295.

SIDON    14

Phoenician Seaport with Dual Harbors

The city of Sidon had certain features in common with its sister cities Byblos and Tyre, features that made it an important city of the OT world. Like its sister cities, Sidon was a major seaport town on the Phoenician coast, which helped shape the history of the site and the destiny of its seafaring citizens. The city had its own identity as the hub of a small independent city-state in the OT world. Because the NT always refers to "Tyre and Sidon," Sidon's identity is frequently tied to that of Tyre to the south.

Sidon was located on the Phoenician coast approximately twenty-five miles north of Tyre and forty-five miles south of Byblos. The city was about fifty-five miles due west of the Syrian capital of Damascus. It was situated on a small hill that extended into the Mediterranean Sea and had one harbor to the south of the promontory-like projection and one to the north. The site was enhanced even more by a series of small islandlike formations that extended from the promontory into the sea and provided a type of breakwater for the harbors. These gave Sidon the advantage of offering options to ships seeking to dock in all sorts of wind and water current conditions. Of Sidon's two harbor areas, the one on the north was the more favorable and served as the major port. It had two pools (an inner pool and an outer pool) that formed an inner and an outer harbor. A fertile plain east of the city and the nearby mountains with valuable cedar and cyprus timber were other important features that contributed to the development of the city and the community as a whole.

Like many other cities of the ancient Near Eastern world, Sidon benefitted from its geography, which played an indispensable role in its growth and development by providing an economic base for the area. The sea provided the city with many opportunities for trade and commerce, and the fertile plain was valuable for agricultural purposes. Its resources of cedar and cypress were sought by many nations. The city of Sidon was famous for yet another industry—the production of purple dye that its inhabitants, like other Phoenicians, procured from the murex shell harvested from the Mediterranean Sea. Today a large mound of murex shells near the harbor serves as a reminder of the purple dye industry in the ancient city.

Other significant factors in Sidon's economy included fishing, metal-working, and glassblowing. The role of fishing in the economy of Sidon is perhaps reflected in the name Sidon itself; it may derive from the term "fish" or "to fish." Even today the harbor at Saida, the modern-day city of fifty thousand people that stands on the ancient ruins, is used by Mediterranean fishing fleets.

The area of Phoenicia was comprised of a number of separate city-states such as Sidon, but Phoenicia was never a kingdom within itself. Of the city-states of Phoenicia, however, Sidon and its people had one unique privilege; in ancient times the names Sidon and Sidonians seem to have been used synonymously with Phoenicia and the Phoenicians (e.g., 1 Kgs 5:6).

While archaeological excavations often produce information that provides a portrait of an ancient site, such is not the case with Sidon because the modern Lebanese town of Saida stands on the ruins of the ancient town. However, the limited excavations that are possible in the area, together with the Bible and other ancient texts, do provide valuable insight. Just exactly when the site was settled cannot be dated, but excavations near the city have produced discoveries that date to the Chalcolithic period. On that basis we may assume that the site, like other Phoenician sites, was settled quite early. Its antiquity is probably reflected in the table of nations in which Sidon is identified as the firstborn son of Canaan (Gen 10:15). According to the Bible and ancient Assyrian texts, ancient Sidon was comprised of two parts: "Great Sidon" and "Little Sidon" (Josh 11:8; 19:28). However, the most ancient parts of Sidon's history will remain a mystery until more excavations are done at the site.

The earliest reference we have to Sidon in extrabiblical literature is found in the Amarna letters from the fourteenth century BCE. According to the Amarna letters, although Zimrida, the king of Sidon, had assured the Egyptian pharaoh of his allegiance, he aligned himself with the rebel forces in the area, particularly the Amorite king Aziru. During this period Sidon was probably a substantially strong city-state seeking to gain control of the Phoenician coast, including the cities of Tyre and Byblos. By joining forces with the Amurru or Amorites, Zimrida increased his chances to gain that control. Near the end of the thirteenth century Sidon experienced a time of turmoil occasioned by the arrival of the Sea Peoples. The newcomers plundered the city, causing many of Sidon's citizenry to flee to Tyre, its sister city to the south.

Following the incursion by the Sea Peoples, Sidon apparently rebounded and became the leading city of the Phoenician coastal cities during the early part of Iron Age I (ca. 1200–1000 BCE). During that period Egyptian influence on the coast was weak, and Sidon took advantage of the situation. Assyrian texts from the period also reflect Sidon's supremacy at that time. They include references to Sidon, while references to Tyre are conspicuously absent. Wen-Amon's reference to the fifty ships in the harbor of Sidon also suggests that Sidon was an important seaport town at that time. The tide apparently changed about 1000 BCE as Tyre gained supremacy and Sidon slipped into a secondary position.

Like other coastal towns, Sidon had its encounter with the kings of Assyria and paid tribute to several of them, including Tiglath-pileser I, Ashurbanipal II, and Shalmaneser III. As Sennacherib approached the city in 701 BCE, Luli, the king of Sidon, escaped to the island of Cyprus and never returned. Perhaps the most devastating blow came in 677 BCE as King Abdi Milkutti of Sidon withheld Assyrian tribute. The Assyrian king Esarhaddon attacked and destroyed the city.

Esarhaddon then rebuilt the city on a new location and named it Kar-Esarhaddon. The new city was designed as an Assyrian commercial center. Its purpose was to provide an Assyrian port on the Mediterranean Sea through which the Assyrians could engage in sea trade with the Mediterranean. With the decline of Assyria, Sidon regained its independence. Near the end of the seventh century and the beginning of the sixth century, Sidon got caught in an international struggle between Egypt and Babylon and, like many other cities, was conquered by Nebuchadnezzar, the Babylonian king.

During the Persian period Sidon once again became an important city on the Phoenician coast, this time as a major royal center of the

Persian empire. Perhaps the most valuable contribution Sidon made to the Persian cause was in the area of naval resources. The majority of the ships in the Persian navy during the reign of Xerxes I were from Sidon. The Sidonians contributed three hundred triremes to the Persian navy. The triremes were designed for intense sea battles and were equipped with three banks of oars. One of the darkest hours in Sidon's history came ca. 350 BCE during the reign of Artaxerxes III. Tabnit II, the king of Sidon, formed a coalition with Egypt and rebelled against the Persian king. But the Egyptians betrayed Tabnit and provided no help as Artaxerxes approached. The city was burned, and more than forty thousand Sidonians perished. In 333 BCE Sidon surrendered to the forces of Alexander the Great. Following the death of Alexander, Sidon became a part of the kingdom of the Ptolemies and in 197 BCE the kingdom of the Seleucids. In 64 BCE Pompey claimed the city for the Roman Empire, and Sidon became a city in the Roman province of Syria.

Inscriptions on the sarcophagus of Eshmunazar II provide information about the religion of Sidon. According to the inscriptions the citizens of Sidon worshiped the gods Eshmun, Astarte, and Baal. King Tabnit, the father of Eshmunazar II, was a priest of Astarte. The royal family had several temples built for the worship of Astarte. Temples were also built for Eshmun, the chief god of Sidon and Baal, the god of healing.

Sidon is frequently mentioned in the Old and New Testaments. The Bible notes that the city and its territory were in close proximity to Israel's northern border (Judg 1:31). The turmoil and destruction Sidon experienced during its later history is described in the prophetic literature (Isa 23; Jer 25:22; 27:3; Ezek 28:20–23). Based on the NT references, we may assume that Sidon was an important city during the NT period (Matt 11:21; Luke 10:14): the gospels refer to Jesus' visit to the area of Sidon (Matt 15:21–28; Mark 7:24–30); the book of Acts mentions the ship on which Paul was transported from Caesarea to Rome and the stop it made at Sidon (Acts 27:3), a reference that reflects the city's role as an important seaport city.

Bibliography: BLAIKLOCK, E. M., "Sidon," *NIDBA*, 414; idem, "Sidon," *NIDB*, 942–43; CRAIGIE, P. C., "Tyre and Sidon," *Major Cities of the Biblical World*, ed. R. K. Harrison (Nashville: Nelson, 1985) 266–74; HUNT, H. B., Jr., "Tyre and Sidon," *MDB*, 938–39; KAPELRUD, A. S., "Sidon," *IDB*, 4:343–45; KHALIFEH, I.

A., "Sidon," *OEANE,* 5:38–41; LANGSTON, S., "Sidon and Tyre," *HolBD,* 1277; LIVERANI, M., "Sidon," *ISBE,* 4:500–502; MCCLELLAN, T. L., "Sidon," *HBD,* 949–50; SCHMITY, P. C., "Sidon," *ABD,* 6:17–18; VAN ELDEREN, B., "Sidon," *ZPEB,* 5:426–28; WISEMAN, D. J., "Sidon," *NBD,* 1184–85; idem, "Sidon," *NBD*[2], 1110–11.

TYRE 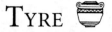 15

Citadel in the Sea

Tyre is perhaps best described as "the citadel in the sea." Like Sidon and Byblos, it was a key seaport on the Phoenician coast. But Tyre had its own distinctive character and features as well. It was a citadel both physically and culturally. It was Tyre, the citadel of Phoenician culture, that Solomon included in his foreign policy program, a program that resulted in the establishment of strong ties and trade relations between Solomon and Hiram, the king of Tyre.

Tyre was located on the Mediterranean coast approximately twenty-five miles south of Sidon, near the mouth of the Litani River. The site was unique because it was comprised of an island that lay approximately one-half mile off a promontory-like formation on the coast. The rocky island apparently inspired the ancient inhabitants to adopt the name Tyre, which means "rock." Today the island is connected to the coastline by a sandy beach that formed over the years along a ramp or causeway Alexander the Great built from the mainland to the island.

The ancient city actually had two parts, one on the island and the other on the coast. The community on the coast was referred to as Ushur or Old Tyre. But it was the island in the sea that provided the unique setting for the development of a seaport town that was an almost impregnable citadel. Perhaps the most important feature of the site was the sea itself, the barrier of water that surrounded the perimeter of the island (Ezek 27:4), defending against any attack by land. To this natural barrier the citizens added walls and towers (Ezek 26:4), making it a well-fortified city (Josh 19:29). Springs on the island provided a limited supply of water. The island had two natural covelike pool formations that were developed and used as docking ports for ships, the Sidonian harbor on the north and the Egyptian harbor on the south. But the island also had its limitations. Food as well as other essential supplies had to be transported to the island, and the water supply had to be supplemented from the mainland.

Tyrian life and culture cannot be understood apart from the sea because the sea itself provided many unique opportunities for the inhabitants of Tyre. Fishing was one of the earliest industries to develop at Tyre. According to ancient texts the fish around Tyre were as numerous as the sand of the sea, and we may assume that fishing fleets operated in the waters of Tyre in ancient times as they still do today. The rocky surface of the island was ideal for spreading the nets to dry (Ezek 26:5). Tyre was also known for the production of purple dye, a costly dye that was obtained by processing a fluid found in the shell of the murex, a mollusk the Tyrians harvested from the waters of the Mediterranean. The dye industry of Tyre was so well known throughout the ancient world that the dye was often referred to as "Tyrian purple."

Shekel of Tyre

The Tyrian people probably gained their greatest fame as a seafaring people and merchants. Tyre was called "the entrance to the sea," and the "merchant of the peoples on many coastlands" (Ezek 27:3). It was that expertise and fame that prompted Solomon to engage in shipping operations with Hiram the king of Tyre. With the assistance of Hiram and perhaps using Tyrian shipbuilders, Solomon built a fleet of ships at Ezion-geber and together with Hiram's skilled navigators operated the fleet in the Red Sea (1 Kgs 9:26–28). Solomon participated jointly with Hiram in a number of shipping enterprises (1 Kgs 9:27–28; 10:11–12, 22), through which gold, almug wood, precious stones, silver, ivory, apes, and peacocks were imported. Hiram and Solomon also traded other commodities. Hiram supplied cedar and cyprus wood for Solomon's temple, and Solomon paid the Tyrian king with wheat and olive oil (1 Kgs 5:10–11) as well as twenty cities in the area of Galilee (1 Kgs 9:10–11). According to the prophet Ezekiel (Ezek 27), merchants of Tyre carried on trade with many lands and in turn received payment in goods and livestock—fir from Senir (v. 5); oak from Bashan (v. 6); pine from Cyprus (v. 6); linen from Egypt (v. 7); silver, iron, tin, and lead from Tarshish (v. 12); bronze from Javan, Tubal, and Meshech (v. 13); horses and mules from Bethtogar-mah (v. 14); ivory and ebony from Rhodes (v. 15); emeralds, linen, coral, and agate from Edom (v. 16); wheat, olives, figs, honey, oil, and balm from Judah and Israel (v. 17); wine, white wool, iron, cassia, and calamus from Damascus (vv. 18–19); lambs, rams, goats, spices, precious stones, and gold from Arabia (vv. 21–22); and garments and carpets from areas in Mesopotamia (vv. 23–24). As Tyre became a citadel of wealth, the Tyrian people gained a reputation for pride and arrogance that was addressed by the Israelite prophets (Isa 23; Jer 27:1–7; Ezek 26–28; esp. 26:1–6 and 28:1–10).

In addition to amassing wealth through trade, Tyre initiated colonizing activities in other lands. From the eleventh century to the ninth century BCE Tyre established colonies on the island of Cypress, at Carthage in North Africa, and perhaps in the mining areas of north Greece.

Tyre was also the home of many artisans and skilled tradesmen. Tyrian carpenters and masons assisted in the building of David's house (2 Sam 5:11) and the temple in Jerusalem (1 Kgs 5:18). In fact, much of the work of constructing the temple was done under the direction of Hiram, a Tyrian craftsman, who was skilled at working with bronze, gold, silver, iron, stone, wood, and fine fabrics and linens (1 Kgs 7:13–47; 2 Chron 2:13–14; 4:11–17). Ezekiel mentions other occupations or skills including oarsmen or rowers, pilots and those who caulked the seams of ships, some of which the Tyrians obviously enlisted from other Phoenician city-states such as Sidon, Arvad, and Byblos (Ezek 27:8, 9, 27). Like many other countries, the city-state of Tyre had a mercenary army comprised of foreigners to protect it—"men of war" from Persia, Lud, and Put; guards from Arvad on the city wall; and watchmen from Gamad in the watchtowers (Ezek 27:10–11).

The origin of the site of Tyre has never been clearly established. According to the Greek historian Herodotus, the city of Tyre was established in the twenty-eighth century BCE. The Jewish historian

Josephus dated its origin to the thirteenth century BCE (*Ant.* 8.62).
However, the occupation of the site probably reaches back to the third
millennium BCE and perhaps even earlier. The most important literary
information available concerning the antiquity of Tyre is the appearance of the name in the Execration texts that date to the period of the
Middle Kingdom in Egypt. Information from the Amarna letters
indicates that Tyre like many other city-states was a vassal of the
Egyptians during the Amarna period and that the king of Tyre,
Abdi-Milki, appealed to the Egyptian king for assistance as he tried to
withstand the influx of the Habiru. During the twelfth and eleventh
centuries BCE, Sidon, Tyre's sister city to the north, was the predominant
Phoenician city-state on the coast; however, Tyre began to emerge as the
major Phoenician seaport about 1000 BCE, and during the period that
followed Tyre became the great citadel of Phoenician trade and culture.
The emergence of Tyre was due especially to the efforts of Hiram, the
king of Tyre and friend of David and Solomon. He made many
improvements during his reign, including a breakwater for the harbor.
He also constructed temples in the city for the worship of the Tyrian
Baal, Melqart, and the goddess Astarte. During this period Tyre began
colonization efforts in other lands, efforts that continued from the tenth
to the ninth century BCE.

During the ninth and eighth centuries Tyre tried to maintain its
independence in the face of the Assyrian threat. However, the city had
to pay tribute to several Assyrian kings, including Tiglath-pileser III and
Shalmaneser V. The city was also besieged during the Assyrian period by
Shalmaneser V, Esarhaddon, and Ashurbanipal. Though Esarhaddon
conquered Ushur on the mainland, he never succeeded in conquering
Tyre. At the end of the Assyrian period the citadel in the sea continued
to maintain its autonomy.

The fate of the city changed during the Babylonian period. In 585
BCE the Babylonian king Nebuchadnezzar laid siege to the citadel in the
sea and for thirteen years continued his attack. Finally exhausted in 572,
Tyre yielded to the Babylonian king and became a Babylonian province.
The thirteen-year siege probably provided the inspiration for the
oracles of Jeremiah and Ezekiel against Tyre (Jer 25:22; 27:3–11; Ezek
26–28). During the latter part of the Babylonian period Tyre was ruled by
"judges," Babylonian governors who had limited power. Tyre continued
to be a vital seaport town and center of trade and industry during the

Persian period; however, Sidon surpassed Tyre and became the predominant seaport city of the coast.

A new chapter in the history of Tyre unfolded with the arrival of Alexander the Great in 332 BCE. While the other cities of the Phoenician coast opened their gates and surrendered to the Macedonian, the citizens of Tyre, confident the island could not be conquered, took sanctuary in the citadel. Unwilling to either leave Tyre unconquered or engage in years of battle, Alexander built an isthmus or causeway from the promontory on the coast to the island. After a seven-month siege Tyre was conquered for the first time in its history.

Tyre again became a major seaport and center of trade and industry during the Hellenistic and Roman periods when it acquired Greco-Roman features such as colonnaded streets with shops and a theater. Tyre is mentioned along with its sister city Sidon in the NT. According to the gospels, citizens of Tyre were among those who were interested in the ministry of Jesus (Mark 3:8; Luke 6:17), and at some point during his ministry Jesus visited the territory of Tyre (Matt 15:21–28; Mark 7:24–30). Jesus' familiarity with the city is obviously reflected in his comparison of the coastal Tyre and Sidon to the towns of Chorazin and Bethsaida north of the Sea of Galilee (Matt 11:20–22; Luke 10:13–14). As Paul returned from his third journey, he stopped off at Tyre and for seven days met with Christians in the community while the cargo was unloaded from his ships (Acts 21:3–4). Tyre apparently became an important center in the early Christian movement. The early church father Origen was buried at Tyre. The site continued to function as a major seaport and center of trade during the Byzantine period and into the Crusader period, when it was destroyed. Today the ruins are still visible, and there is a small town named Sur at the site, population about six thousand people.

Bibliography: BLAIKLOCK, E. M., "Tyre," *NIDBA*, 459; idem, "Tyre," *NIDB*, 1040–41; idem, "Tyre," *ZPEB*, 5:832–35; CRAIGIE, P. C., "Tyre and Sidon," *Major Cities of the Biblical World*, ed. R. K. Harrison (Nashville: Nelson, 1985) 266–74; HUNT, H. B., Jr., "Tyre and Sidon," *MDB*, 938–39; KAPELRUD, A. S., "Tyre," *IDB*, 4:721–23; KATZENSTEIN, H. J., *The History of Tyre* (Jerusalem: Schocken Institute for Jewish Research, 1973); idem, "Tyre in the Early Persian Period (539–486 B.C.E.)," *BA* 42 (1979) 23–34; KATZENSTEIN, H. J., and D. R. Edwards, "Tyre," *ABD*, 6:686–92; LANGSTON, S., "Sidon and Tyre," *HolBD*, 1277; LIVERANI, M., "Tyre," *ISBE*, 4:932–34; MCCLELLAN, T. L., "Tyre," *HBD*, 1101–2; WARD, W. A., "Tyre," *OEANE*, 5:247–50; WISEMAN, D. J., "Tyre, Tyrus," *NBD*, 1302–3; idem, "Tyre, Tyrus," *NBD²*, 1227–29.

UGARIT 🏺 16

City of Baal and Center of Canaanite Religion

Ugarit was the administrative center of a kingdom on the Syrian coast. Due to its location, Ugarit was a major cosmopolitan center—a center of trade, government, and religion. Ugarit's role as a major center of the Canaanite culture has been illuminated by thousands of clay tablets containing information about the culture, government, and religion at Ugarit.

Ancient Ugarit was located on the Syrian coast directly east of the island of Cyprus, approximately twenty-five miles south of the Orontes River. It was a seaport town that lay about a half-mile southeast of a cove. The inlet that the ancient Greeks referred to as the white harbor is today known as Minet el-Beida. During its golden age Ugarit was the capital of a kingdom with approximately two hundred towns and villages in its territory. The ruins of ancient Ugarit are located at the present-day site of Ras Shamra.

While several features contributed to Ugarit's growth and development, perhaps none contributed more than the site's strategic location. Located on the Mediterranean Sea, Ugarit became a major center of sea trade. The merchants of the city engaged in trade not only with other cities along the coast to the south, such as Byblos, Tyre, Sidon, and Ashkelon, but also with other lands such as Egypt, Anatolia, Cyprus, and Crete. Ugarit was also a major center of land trade with several important trade routes converging at the site. The coastal plain route moved south through Phoenicia and Canaan to the land of Egypt, and north to the land of Anatolia. Ugarit also had contact with north Syria and Mesopotamia by means of a major trade route to the east connecting it with the cities of Mari, Babylon, and Ur on the Euphrates River.

The discovery of ancient Ugarit began in 1928 when a Syrian peasant farmer plowing his field struck some stones that turned out to be a fourteenth century Mycenean tomb. Excavations under the direction of Claude F.-A. Schaeffer began in April 1929. While the investigation initially began in the field located near the harbor, it soon turned to the mound of ruins southeast of the harbor, the site of Ras Shamra. The excavations produced valuable returns: tablets known today as the Ugaritic texts and inscriptions that identified the site as Ugarit, a site also mentioned in the Amarna tablets. The ancient name Ugarit means "field." The modern name Ras Shamra means "hill of fennel" and is derived from the fennel commonly raised in this area. The trapezoid-shaped mound of ruins is approximately 3,300 feet long, 1,650 feet wide, and sixty-five feet high.

Alphabetic cuneiform tablet from Ugarit

Excavations at the site have provided valuable information about its history. The earliest settlement, level V, dates back to the prepottery Neolithic period, approximately 6000– 5000 BCE, when the inhabitants of the site did not use pottery, at least during the early phases. Tools and other implements used for daily living were made of bones and flint.

The second major period of occupation, level IV, occurred during the Chalcolithic period, approximately 4000–3500 BCE, the period during which the inhabitants of the site established a well-developed culture and used a type of painted pottery associated with Tell Halaf in north Syria. This pottery has also been found at other sites in Syria and Palestine.

The third period of occupation, represented by level III, began about 3500 BCE and continued until about 2100 BCE. During this period Ubaid pottery appears, indicating that Ugarit was influenced by the Ubaid culture of Mesopotamia. It was during this period that Ugarit began to develop into a major trade center. Around 3000 BCE the town was destroyed and resettled by outsiders. A new city, often referred to as the Early Bronze city, was established at the site; the new settlement was characterized by a poorer quality of pottery and by a decline in culture generally. The Kerak type pottery used at Ugarit during the latter part of the period has also been found at sites in Palestine. Like many other communities in the ancient Near East, Ugarit was invaded and came under the influence of the Amorites during the latter part of the third millennium BCE.

The Middle Bronze city at Ugarit, level II, began ca. 2100 BCE and continued until ca. 1500 BCE. During this period Ugarit became a prosperous city-state with an increase in trade and exchange with other countries, as is evidenced by archaeological remains that are heavily influenced by cultures such as that of Egypt. During this period Ugarit became a major religious center, as can be seen in the city temples that were built for the worship of the Canaanite gods Baal and Dagon. But while the Middle Bronze city experienced significant development and expansion, it also experienced conflict with such groups as the Hittites, Hurrians, Mitannians, and Hyksos.

During the Late Bronze period, represented by level I, dating to ca. 1500–1200 BCE, Ugarit experienced a golden age. Two discoveries from the Late Bronze city have been of special interest for OT studies—the large royal palace and a significant cache of texts, commonly referred to as the Ugaritic texts. Ugarit also faced a number of problems during the Late Bronze era. Egypt's attempts to maintain control over Syria-Palestine certainly affected Ugarit. The city and the harbor suffered a devastating earthquake during the fourteenth century, but the inhabitants of Ugarit rebuilt both. The ultimate blow came ca. 1200 BCE when the Sea Peoples invaded Ugarit and destroyed the city so thoroughly that it was never rebuilt.

Perhaps the most valuable discovery at Ugarit is a large collection of ancient texts, most of which were found in the royal palace and the library of the priests. The texts, written on clay tablets, provide crucial information about the language, historical and administrative matters, and the religion of Ugarit. While most of the tablets were written in the well-known Akkadian cuneiform, others were inscribed with a cuneiform script previously unknown. This script, recognized as an alphabetic script in contrast to traditional Akkadian syllabic script, was deciphered by Hans Bauer, Edouard Dhorme, and Charles Virolleaud. It was named Ugaritic. Tablets written in other ancient Near Eastern languages, including Sumerian, Hurrian, Hittite, and Egyptian, were also found. The presence of these languages provides further proof that Ugarit was a cosmopolitan center with strong international ties.

In addition to the tablets, excavations have revealed features of the city, including the royal palace, the religious precinct, private houses, and tombs. The royal palace was located on the west side of the city. Apparently the original palace, consisting of several rooms around two courtyards, grew into a massive complex as the kings from the fifteenth to the thirteenth century built additions. Ultimately the palace covered approximately two and one-half acres. Built of stone, it had ninety rooms, five or six large courtyards, an elaborate pool, several stairways that led to an upper story, and an interior garden area. The water for the palace was supplied by a well, located away from the palace. Apparently servants dipped the water from the well and poured it in a trough leading to an elaborate aqueduct system to the palace. A fortress, located on the west side of the palace, protected the royal palace. Two smaller palaces and a royal stable were located near the palace complex. The most significant discovery in the palace complex was the royal archives comprised of several units located in different parts of the palace. The palace had five different archives—a central archive, a western archive, an eastern archive, a southern archive, and a southwestern archive. Each archive contained different types of documents; for instance, the eastern archive contained documents concerning the city of Ugarit, the central archive contained legal texts, and the western archive contained documents pertaining to the royal family.

The religious precinct was located in the northeast part of the city. It was comprised of the house of the high priest, a temple library, the temple of Baal, and the temple of Dagon. The house of the high priest, situated between the two temples, consisted of a central court surrounded by rooms. This priestly complex had several functions. It provided living quarters for the priestly officials. It also included a religious library—rooms in which the religious texts containing stories about the

Canaanite gods and goddesses were stored. Further, the house of the high priest had rooms in which scribes made copies of the religious texts and students were educated to be scribes.

The temple of Baal was located northwest of the house of the high priest. The Baal sanctuary had features similar to the temple of Solomon, with an inner sanctuary, an outer room, an entrance way, and an outer courtyard with an altar. The temple area was surrounded by a wall. A number of artifacts were found in the temple, including bronze weapons and tools used in religious rituals. A large stele of Baal was also found near the temple. It featured Baal dressed in a kilt, with a horned helmet, a club in his right hand, and a bolt of lightning in his left hand. The design of the temple of Dagon, located southeast of the high priest's house, is similar to that of the Baal temple.

Private homes have also been found at Ugarit. The houses generally had two levels. The ground level was comprised of rooms around an open courtyard with a stairway leading up to the main living level. Many of the houses included features that reflect the wealth of the citizens of Ugarit. The houses were large, sometimes having thirty rooms or more, with some rooms that were quite expansive. Some households had their own family archives. The houses were equipped with bathrooms and a flush system: water from the household well was poured into a channel which in turn carried the waste to a catch pit.

Family tombs were usually located under the floor of the courtyard, effecting a close relationship between the family dwelling and the dwelling place of the dead. The stone tombs were similar to tombs found at Crete. The tomb was entered by a stairway that led from the ground level to the tomb below. The deceased were buried with pottery containers, tools, and weapons. The tombs were also designed with a channel by which living family members could provide water to the deceased family member below. The tomb was equipped with a container that caught the water and a cup for the deceased to drink with.

The discoveries at Ugarit provide valuable information about other features of life and culture in Ugarit during the golden age. The economy of the city-state was based upon agriculture, industry, and trade. Since much of the population of the city-state lived in outlying towns and villages, Ugarit had a thriving agricultural industry that included the cultivation of cereal crops and the production of wine and olive oil. Livestock production was also important. One of Ugarit's most valuable natural resources was timber. It was used in local industries including shipbuilding and bow making and was traded to other countries. Local merchants processed and sold purple dye obtained from the murex shells harvested from the Mediterranean Sea. The city of Ugarit prospered from a metal industry that produced bronze weapons and a textile industry that produced fabrics made of wool and other natural materials.

The literary texts discovered at Ugarit are especially important because they provide the most valuable information to date on Canaanite religion. These texts contain the major religious stories of the Canaanites, stories that introduce the gods and goddesses of the Canaanite pantheon and their roles. The literary texts include the legend of King Keret, the legend of Aqhat, the story of Baal and Yam, the story of Baal's palace, and the story of Baal and Mot. The legend of King Keret describes the experiences of Keret who loses everything through a series of disasters and is later blessed by the god El. In the legend of Aqhat, a young warrior who possesses a special bow loses his life because Anath, the goddess of war, wants the bow for herself. The story of the conflict between Baal and Yam details the struggle between the two gods, in which Baal is ultimately victorious. The story of Baal's palace describes the events leading up to its construction. Building the house was important because it demonstrated the recognition of Baal's authority. The story of Baal and Mot (death) describes the cycles of conflict between the two gods.

Among the gods, El was recognized as the chief god of the pantheon at Ugarit. He was the father of the other gods except Baal, whose father was Dagon. As the father of the gods, El presided over the pantheon. According to the texts, he was the source of authority; therefore, the activities of the other gods required his approval. El was referred to as "the bull," a title that highlighted his role as a fertility god and the source of life. He was described as the creator and the father of humanity.

El's companion was Astarte, also known as Asherah. Astarte was the wife of El and mother of the gods. Her primary role was that of a fertility or mother goddess.

While El was recognized as the head of the Canaanite pantheon, Baal was the most prominent figure in the pantheon. Known also as

Hadad, Baal was a storm god, the god of the rains and fertility. As the son of Dagon, he was perhaps an outsider in the pantheon. This may be the reason that Baal experienced conflict with figures like Yam (sea) and Mot (death). Baal had many titles and roles: the rider of the clouds, the king, the prince, the most high, to name a few. His primary role was that of a fertility god. He was an agricultural deity. He was responsible for the fertility of the soil, the herds, and the flocks. His sacred animal was the bull, the symbol of fertility.

Baal's companion was the goddess Anath, who appeared sometimes as Baal's sister and other times as his wife. Anath was the goddess of love, fertility, and warfare. As the goddess of war and Baal's companion, she is portrayed as the one looking out for Baal's welfare and at times going to battle on his behalf. On the battlefield she is described as standing knee-deep in blood.

Among the other gods mentioned in the Ugaritic texts are Dagon, the god of grain; Mot, the god of death; Yam, the god of the sea; Shamash, the sun goddess; and the twin gods Shahar and Shalim, the gods of dawn and dusk respectively.

Bibliography: CRAIGIE, P. C., *Ugarit and the Old Testament* (Grand Rapids: Eerdmans, 1983); CURTIS, A., *Ugarit* (Grand Rapids: Eerdmans, 1985); DEMOOR, J. C., "Ugarit," *IDBSup*, 928–31; DEVRIES, C. E., "Ras Shamra," *NIDB*, 846–47; GOOD, R. M., "Ras Shamra," *HBD*, 853–54; GRAY, J., "Ugarit," *Archaeology and the Old Testament*, ed. D. Winton Thomas (Oxford: Clarendon, 1967) 145–67; HARRISON, R. K., "Ugarit," *NIDBA*, 460–61; KAPELRUD, A. S., "Ugarit," *IDB*, 4:724–32; LIVERANI, M., "Ugarit," *ISBE*, 4:937–41; PARDEE, D., "Ugaritic," *OEANE*, 5:262–64; idem, "Ugaritic Inscriptions," 5:264–66; PARDEE, D., and P. Bordreuil, "Ugarit, Texts and Literature," *ABD*, 6:706–721; PFEIFFER, C. F., "Ugarit." *ZPEB*, 5:837–42; SCHOVILLE, K. N., "Ugarit," *BAF*, 236–42; SMOTHERS, T., "Ugarit," *HolBD*, 1380–82; WISEMAN, D. J., "Archaeology," *NBD*, 70–71; idem, "Ugarit, Ras Shamra," *NBD*[2], 1229–30; YON, M. "Ugarit," *ABD*, 6:695–706; idem, "Ugarit," *OEANE*, 5:255–62.

Unit 3

CITIES OF
ANATOLIA

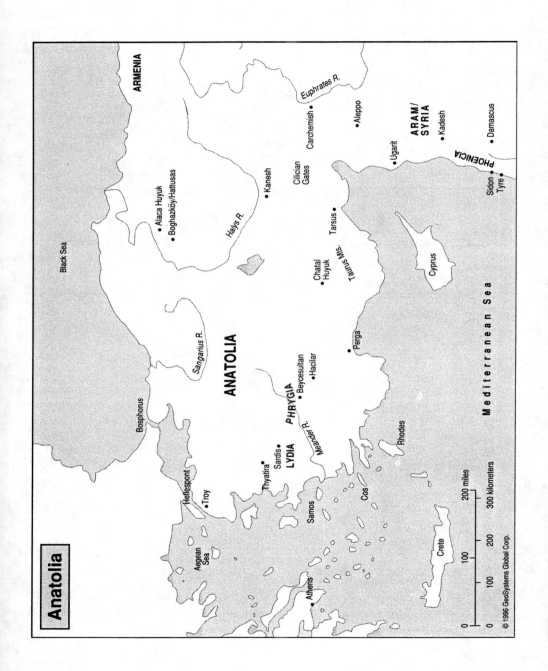

Anatolia

© 1996 GeoSystems Global Corp.

ANATOLIA 🏺 17

Land Bridge between the Fertile Crescent and the West

The land of Anatolia was an important and unique part of the ancient world, even though it is not always familiar to beginning students of the Bible. It may be described not only as a backwater land but also as a land of surprises—a description that is appropriate from a geographical and historical perspective as well as from modern exploration and historical research.

Geographically, Anatolia does not appear to have been in the mainstream of life in the ancient world. It was not a part of the Fertile Crescent that stretched from Mesopotamia to Syria-Palestine. Rather, Anatolia was like an appendage that extended from the northwest corner of the Fertile Crescent. It was a peninsula of western Asia surrounded by the Mediterranean Sea on the south, the Aegean Sea on the west, the waters of the Hellespont pass, the Sea of Marmara and the waters of the Bosphorus pass on the northwest, and the Black Sea on the north. In some ways Anatolia was isolated, but its close proximity to Europe at the Hellespont and Bosphorus passes made it a unique land bridge between Europe and the Fertile Crescent.

During the course of its history it has had three different names: Asia Minor, Anatolia, and Asia. Asia Minor is probably the most familiar of the three. The designation "Asia Minor" was used by the Romans to distinguish the small appendage of Asia from the rest of Asia. Since the Greeks did not have a name that distinguished the small peninsula from the rest of the continent, the name "Asia" was used for the appendage as well as the continent. NT writers followed the Greek tradition and referred to the area as "Asia." The name "Anatolia," often used in reference to the land and its earlier periods, is Greek in origin and means "the land of the sunrise" or "the land to the east." During the Byzantine period, the term referred only to the area of Asia Minor directly east of the Hellespont and Bosphorus passes; however, during the Turkish period it designated the whole of Asia Minor. Today Anatolia is a part of western Turkey.

The peninsula-like land of Anatolia has striking physical features including an extensive coastline, mountains, rivers, and a major central plateau. The coastlines lie along the Black Sea, the Aegean Sea, and the Mediterranean Sea. The major mountain ranges of Anatolia are located in the north and south, along the Mediterranean Sea and the Black Sea. In the west, several ranges extend westward from the interior out toward the Aegean Sea. The mountain ranges along the Black Sea and Mediterranean Sea are actually extensions of the Caucasus Mountains to the east and Armenia or eastern Turkey. The Taurus Mountains in southeastern Anatolia are the largest of the Anatolian ranges. Though the Taurus Mountains constitute a major barrier to travel along the southern coast, a pass known as the Cilician Gates, located at the north end of the range, has provided passage for east-west travel throughout the history of Anatolia.

The rivers of Anatolia flow from the interior through the mountain ranges along the coast outward and empty into one of the three major bodies of water that surround Anatolia. Few rivers are found along the southern coast, owing to the height of the southern ranges, but several larger streams flow into the Black Sea. The major river of Anatolia is the Halys, which forms a major loop in central Anatolia. The Halys River begins its journey in the northeastern part of Anatolia, flows southwestward through central Anatolia, loops around to the north, and flows into the Black Sea. Since the Halys River is located in central Anatolia, it has functioned as the major geographical division between eastern and western Anatolia. Several rivers are found in western Anatolia including the Meander, the Hermus, and the Sangarius.

One of Anatolia's most unique features is the large central plateau of the interior. Surrounded by the mountain ranges of the coastal areas, the plateau has fertile soil and reaches a height of approximately four thousand feet. The terrain of the central plateau is hilly with some small mountain ranges scattered throughout. Perhaps more than any other area, the central plateau has had a definite bearing on the development of life and culture in Anatolia. The plateau is dry and often experiences long, hard winters. Consequently, it was conducive to agriculture, shepherding, herding, and the development of rural life in general—lifestyles that are still found in Turkey today. While the weather in the central plateau area can be harsh, the western part of Anatolia enjoys a milder Mediterranean climate.

Because of the rural lifestyle of the central plateau and a lack of knowledge about its history, Anatolia has often been seen simply as a backwater land off the mainstream of life and development in ancient times. For those reasons early explorers visited sites in the more popular lands of the biblical world like Mesopotamia and Palestine rather than Anatolia. However, archaeological research during this century has demonstrated that Anatolia is a land of surprises. Among the discoveries that have stimulated interest in the land two especially stand out—the 1906 discovery by Winckler of the capital of the Hittite empire, and in more recent times the discovery of Neolithic remains at several sites in Anatolia.

Archaeological research gives us a much better understanding of the major segments of Anatolian history. The early beginnings of life and culture in Anatolia reach back to at least the Neolithic period. Neolithic material has been found throughout central Anatolia, but three sites have provided particularly valuable discoveries: Chayonu Tepesi, Chatal Huyuk, and Hacilar. According to the archaeological data, small towns or villages appeared in Anatolia during the Neolithic period prior to 7000 BCE. The villages had an agricultural economy in which the inhabitants cultivated cereal crops, domesticated animals, and engaged in hunting. Among the buildings found in the villages were mud-brick houses comprised of a courtyard, kitchen, and several rooms. Mud-brick worship centers were decorated with paintings or figurines of bulls, rams, and deities. Similar to the practice of the Neolithic community at Jericho, special attention was given to the skulls of the deceased. They were usually deposited in the house or worship center and preserved apart from the rest of the body. The Neolithic people made pottery, jewelry, and weapons, and they engaged in trade with other areas. During the Neolithic period Anatolia witnessed the development of village life, agriculture, crafts, art, trade, and religion.

The cultural developments that began during the Neolithic period continued throughout the Chalcolithic period and Bronze Ages without any major break. Especially important have been the discoveries at Troy, on the Aegean coast, Alaca Huyuk, just north of Boghazköy, and Beycesultan, a site located on the Meander River in western Anatolia.

During the Bronze Age massive defense centers were constructed, especially at major sites like Troy, and trade increased significantly. Troy apparently functioned as a major trade center between the Aegean Sea and the Black Sea. The contents of Bronze Age tombs at Alaca Huyuk indicate the citizens of that area carried on trade with such areas as central Asia, Mesopotamia, Canaan, Egypt, and the Aegean. Among the discoveries at Beycesultan were a palace and worship center. In general, trade and commercial activities increased significantly in Anatolia during the Bronze Age especially in relationship to major centers. During the latter part of the Early Bronze Age and the early part of the Middle Bronze Age, Anatolia was comprised of several small kingdoms ruled by kings, with centers such as those mentioned. At that time Anatolia was generally inhabited by non-Indo-European peoples. The name Hatti, a designation for one of the larger population groups in Anatolia at that time, came to be ascribed to all the inhabitants of the land.

The period from about 2300 to 1900 BCE was a time of turmoil. The land was invaded by several waves of people, and many sites were destroyed by fire. The earliest written records from Anatolia date to about 1900 BCE. The writings indicate that Assyrian traders established *karum*s, or trade centers, in Anatolia during that period. One such center and the hub of Assyrian activities in Anatolia was Kanesh, the site at which the Assyrian records were found. Assyrian traders were especially active in the exploitation of metals found in central Anatolia. As time passed, however, newcomers brought an end to the small Hattian kingdoms and Assyrian trading outposts in the land. The newcomers were Indo-European peoples who probably moved into Anatolia by crossing the Hellespont. By 1700 BCE or shortly thereafter, a new kingdom was beginning to take shape. The newcomers, who assumed the name of their predecessors the Hattians, were known as the Hittites. For all practical purposes, the Hittites were probably a mixture of different peoples present in the land at the time, including Hattians, Hurrians, and Indo-Europeans. They established a capital at Hattusas, modern Boghazköy, and shaped the history of Anatolia for the next several hundred years. The period from 1600 to 1400 BCE was known as the Old Kingdom, and the period from 1400 to 1200 BCE, the New Kingdom or the Empire. In addition to shaping the history of Anatolia, they left an indelible mark on the entire ancient Near East through establishing one of the most powerful empires in the ancient world. During the Hittite empire the land of Anatolia was the homeland of one of the two major forces in the ancient Near East—the other being Egypt.

But the Hittite empire was not to last. Near the end of the thirteenth century, Anatolia, the land bridge between east and west, became the thoroughfare for the movement of the Sea Peoples from their homeland in the Aegean through Anatolia and Syria to Canaan and Egypt. Consequently, the Hittite empire, like many other kingdoms or city-states in the path of these military and seafaring aggressors, was destroyed; Hattusas was destroyed in 1200 BCE.

During the period that followed, Anatolia became the homeland of migrant groups. Hittite influence continued in the city-states of north Syria, and the focal center of the new age and its culture (the Neo-Hittite period) was Carchemish. Because of the Neo-Hittite influence, the Assyrians ascribed the name "Hatti" to the territory of north Syria and at a later time to southern Syria and Palestine. During the first millennium some minor kingdoms of Anatolia developed—the kingdom of Phrygia in the eighth century and the kingdom of Lydia in the seventh (until the Persians conquered the Lydian capital, Sardis, in 546 BCE). With the arrival of Alexander the Great, Anatolia functioned as a major thoroughfare for the conqueror's march eastward as he crossed the Hellespont, moved through Anatolia, and proceeded onward to the Fertile Crescent and the lands beyond. During the latter part of the first millennium BCE Anatolia was the homeland of small provinces that were under the control of the Greeks, then the Seleucids, and finally the Romans. It functioned as a major thoroughfare for exchange between west and east. It was the homeland of a number of towns and cities prominent in the history of early Christianity including Tarsus, Derbe, Lystra, Iconium, Antioch, Miletus, Ephesus, Sardis, Pergamum, and Troas. Most of these cities were located along the southern and western fringes of the land and were centers of cosmopolitan populations.

Bibliography: BALY, D., and A. D. Tushingham, *Atlas of the Biblical World* (New York: World, 1971) 18, 24–26, 34–36, 40, 43, 44, 48, 50, 51, 74, 78, 117, 139; BRUCE, F. F., "Hittites," *ISBE*, 2:720–23; CERAM, C. W., *The Secret of the Hittites* (New York: Schocken, 1973); GORNY, R. L., "Anatolia: Prehistoric Anatolia," *OEANE*, 1:122–27; idem, "Anatolia (Prehistory of Anatolia)," *ABD*, 1:228–33; idem, "Environment,

Archaeology, and History in Hittite Anatolia," *BA* 52 (1989) 78–96; GUNTER, A. C., "Anatolia: Ancient Anatolia," *OEANE*, 1:127–31; GURNEY, O. R., *The Hittites* (Middlesex: Penguin, 1952); HAMMOND, M., "Anatolia," *The City in the Ancient World* (Cambridge: Harvard University Press, 1972) 92–104; HARRISON, R. K., "Asia Minor," *NIDBA*, 78–79; HEMER, C. J., "Asia Minor," *ISBE*, 1:322–29; MACQUEEN, J. G., *The Hittites* (London: Thames & Hudson, 1986); MALTSBERGER, D. C., "Asia Minor, Cities of," *HolBD*, 114–16; McMAHON, G., "Anatolia (History of Ancient Anatolia)," *ABD*, 1:233–36; idem, "The History of the Hittites," *BA* 52 (1989) 62–77; SCHOVILLE, K. N., "Asia Minor and the Hittites," *BAF*, 219–29; SCOTT, J. A., "Anatolia: Anatolia from Alexander to the Rise of Islam," *OEANE*, 1:131–35; VAN ELDEREN, B., "Archaeology of Asia Minor," *ISBE*, 1:246–48; VOS, H. F., "Anatolia," *BEB*, 1:85–86; idem, "Asia Minor," *Archaeology in Bible Lands* (Chicago: Moody, 1977) 305–40.

Hattusas 18

Citadel of Hittite Culture, Government, and Religion

Of all Anatolian discoveries that relate to OT times, Hattusas especially stands out because it constitutes the major surprise in Anatolian archaeology. It was not just another city but the capital of a major empire in the OT world, a capital that was located in the upper central plateau of Anatolia. Hattusas was the capital of the Hittite empire, an empire that at its peak from 1400 to 1200 BCE stood equal to Egypt, which often controlled Syria-Palestine and commanded the attention of the rest of the Fertile Crescent.

The site of Hattusas is located on a tributary of the Halys River in the upper central plateau of Anatolia near the present-day town of Boghazköy, approximately one hundred miles east of Ankara, Turkey. The site, which covers approximately four hundred acres, has a number of unique features. Located on a ridge surrounded by valleys on three sides, it was easily fortified and defended. Other features that contributed to its growth and development include an available water supply, tillable land in the nearby valleys, and the site's location at the intersection of two important trade routes—the north-south route that ran from the Black Sea through the Cilician Gates and the east-west route that connected the Aegean area with Urartu and upper Mesopotamia.

Hattusas was discovered through a series of investigations that began with a visit by Charles Texier, a Frenchman, in 1834. He noted the remains of massive defenses at Boghazköy, but the antiquity of the site and its real significance were not evident until 1893–94 when Ernest Chantre, another Frenchman, discovered fragments of clay tablets inscribed in cuneiform, in a language that was unknown at the time. So as to engage in a more systematic study of the remains of the ancient site, Hugo Winckler initiated an excavation at the site in 1906. The excavations, which continued for several seasons between 1906 and 1912, resulted in the discovery of some ten thousand fragments of clay tablets. Much to the surprise of those involved, the tablets turned out to be the records of the royal archives of the kings of the Hittite empire. The site discovered was Hattusas, the capital of the kingdom. Through the efforts of B. Hrozny, a Czech scholar, the tablets were deciphered, and the previously unknown language was identified as Hittite. Excavations since carried out at the site have produced additional information about the Hittites, their capital city, Hattusas, their empire, and their culture.

The Hittites of central Anatolia responsible for establishing the Hittite empire and their capital Hattusas were actually a mixed group. They were called Hittites, a name inherited from the earlier, original inhabitants of Anatolia, the Hattians. However, the Hittite population was comprised of people from different backgrounds, including Indo-Europeans, Hattians, and Hurrians. In the OT, the name "Hittite" also refers to Canaanites and the people and territory of north Syria, that is, the Neo-Hittite city-states in north Syria.

Excavations at Hattusas have provided valuable information about the features of the capital city itself. Hattusas was a large fortified city of over four hundred acres comprised of two major sections, a lower city and an upper city, and a large royal citadel. The city's fortifications consisted of a massive wall system with towers and numerous gates. The impressive stone gates were designed in the shape of an arch flanked by large sculptured lions or sphinxes. Among the major buildings discovered at Hattusas were the great temple, temple I, in the lower city, temples II, III, IV, and V, and the southern citadel in the upper city; and the enclosed royal residence and citadel, or the great fortress, between the upper and lower city. The five different levels identified in excavations at Hattusas correspond to the different time periods—level V, the pre-Hittite period or era of the Assyrian trading post; level IV, the Old Hittite Kingdom period; level III, the period of the Hittite empire; and levels I and II, the post-Hittite period.

The written texts from the archives and inscriptions from other sites in Anatolia and north Syria indicate that the Hittites used several different languages. The predominant and presumably official language of the empire was cuneiform Hittite. The cuneiform script was borrowed from the Mesopotamian area perhaps from the Akkadians. The language itself was Indo-European in background. Hieroglyphic Hittite inscriptions that have been found at other sites in Anatolia and north Syria are inscribed with hieroglyphic characters rather than the wedge-shaped characters of cuneiform. Other languages used by the Hittites were Akkadian, Sumerian, Hurrian, Hattic, Luwain, and Palaic.

The texts from the archives are valuable not only because of the insight they provide about the Hittite language but also because of the information they provide about the Hittites and their culture. The cuneiform Hittite texts have provided information about the development of the kingdom and the kingship. Hittite history can be divided into three or four periods—the Old Kingdom, the New Kingdom or the period of the Hittite empire, and the Neo-Hittite Kingdom. The Hittite kingship began with Labarnas I, the founder of the Old Kingdom, with several important developments taking place during that period. Hattusilis I, son of Labarnas, was responsible for establishing Hattusas as the capital and expanding territorial holdings of the newly-formed kingdom by crossing the Taurus Mountains and carrying out military campaigns in north Syria. Mursilis I, successor of Hattusilis, intensified campaigning activities and in the process conquered Aleppo in north Syria as well as Mari on the Euphrates and Babylon in lower Mesopotamia. Telipinus played an important role in stabilizing the kingship by establishing an official document outlining guidelines for royal succession and establishing a Hittite law code.

The period of the New Kingdom began with Tudhaliyas II, who renewed the use of expansionist campaigns. The high point of the empire came during the reign of Suppiluliumas, who secured the kingdom at home and also moved into north Syria, subduing the Hurrian kingdom of Mitanni in upper Mesopotamia. While Suppiluliumas established Hittite supremacy over the Hurrian kingdom politically, much of the Hurrian culture was absorbed by the Hittites. A new threat was posed by Egyptian aggression that developed to the south along the coastal regions of Syria-Palestine. Initially the two powers engaged in battle at Kadesh on the Orontes River. This struggle was later resolved as Hattusilis III, the Hittite king, and Ramses II, the king of Egypt, established a treaty between the two kingdoms in 1269 BCE. The Hittites encountered a more serious threat during the latter part of the thirteenth century, as the Sea Peoples, known to us from Egyptian record, moved into Anatolia from the Aegean area, ended the Hittite empire, and destroyed the capital city, Hattusas, about 1200 BCE.

While the Hittite empire came to an end as such, Hittite influence continued in several major city-states in north Syria. Consequently, the following era of the empire is known as the Neo-Hittite period. Among the Neo-Hittite city-states in north Syria, Carchemish became the most prominent. With the end of the empire the use of cuneiform Hittite also came to an end. Hieroglyphic Hittite continued to be used in the Neo-Hittite city-states of north Syria.

The Hittite state was basically feudal in character. The supreme official of the state was the king, whose authority and power were limited by a council or assembly of nobles, a type of ruling class. The king was the head of the army and also functioned as the high priest of the religion. Officers of the provinces who were under the domination of the Hittite state were actually local princes who functioned as vassal kings.

Texts from the archives also provide insight into Hittite law, the legal code of the empire. According to these laws, Hittite society was basically patriarchal. In contrast to the legal codes of other ancient Near Eastern societies, Hittite law allowed Hittite women more privileges and a much better standing in general. Hittite law did not propose retaliation in civil matters in instances where loss was incurred, that is, the principle of an eye for an eye. Rather, Hittite law proposed compensation as the means by which to resolve the situation.

Also among the tablets of the royal archives were accounts of treaties or covenants that the Hittites made with other nations. The treaties fall into two basic categories—Hittite suzerainty treaties and parity treaties. The Hittite suzerainty treaty was a treaty established between a superior power and a lesser power, a treaty between the Hittite king (the suzerain) and a vassal state. The parity treaty was established between two equal powers. Hittite treaties had a form or outline comprised of several parts, including: (1) a preamble; (2) a historical prologue; (3) the stipulations of the treaty; (4) a statement about depositing the treaty in the temple; (5) a list of witnesses; (6) a section of curses and blessings. The treaties have been of interest to students of the Bible because the treaty form is similar to covenant forms found in the OT. For instance, the covenant in Exodus 20 includes: (1) a preamble, "I am the LORD your God"; (2) a historical prologue, "the one who brought you out of your bondage in Egypt"; and (3) stipulations, the Decalogue or Ten Commandments.

The archives also contained religious texts and information about Hittite gods and religious practices of the people. Since the Hittites were a people comprised of mixed backgrounds, it is not surprising that they had a pantheon of many gods. The Hittites themselves referred to their homeland as the land of a thousand gods. In addition to the gods of the original Hattian population, the Hittite pantheon probably came largely from the Hurrians as well as other Mesopotamian cultures such as the ancient Sumerians. The major god of the Hittites was the Hurrian storm god Teshub, called Taru by the Hittites. Since the sacred animal of Teshub was the bull, the god himself was at times represented in the form of a bull. Other gods of the pantheon included Hebat, the wife of Teshub; Sharruma, the son of Teshub and Hebat; the sun goddess of Arinna; and Ishtanu, a solar god. The religious texts of the Hittites included prayers, instructions for religious rituals, and accounts of divination procedures.

The Hittite economy was based primarily on agriculture, iron production, the manufacture of weapons, and trade. The fertile valleys of central Anatolia enabled the Hittites to engage in agricultural pursuits and pastoral activities of shepherding and herding. The Anatolian highlands had valuable deposits of iron ore, and the Hittites operated mines, processed the ore, and manufactured weapons and implements. The Hittites also carried on trade with major areas of the Fertile Crescent including Egypt, Syria-Palestine, and Mesopotamia. The art and architecture of Hattusas display the skilled craftwork of builders, stone masons, and sculptors.

The precise role that the Hittites played in Israelite history is still open to debate. To be sure, the name "Hittite" appears with significant frequency in the OT, and individual Hittites appear in several important narratives: Abraham purchased the cave of Machpelah from Ephron the Hittite (Gen 23); Judith and Basemath, both identified as having Hittite origins, became wives of Esau (Gen 26:34); Bathsheba, the wife of Uriah the Hittite, became David's wife (2 Sam 11); and Solomon not only traded in horses and chariots with the Hittites (1 Kgs 10:29) but also married Hittite women (1 Kgs 11:1). In one of the most interesting statements in the OT, the prophet Ezekiel says about the origin of Jerusalem that "your father was an Amorite, and your mother a Hittite" (Ezek 16:3). So what can we conclude about the Hittites and the role they played in OT history? First, scholars have recognized that the term "Hittite" seems to be used in different ways, not always reflecting an ethnic origin. In some instances it seems to be used interchangeably with Canaanite; in others it may refer to Horites or Hurrians; and in still others it may refer to individuals from the Neo-Hittite city-state kingdoms in north Syria. Second, it seems plausible that in some instances the Hittite references must be to the Anatolian Hittites. This influence may or may not have come by means of the Neo-Hittite city-state kingdoms of north Syria, areas with which David and Solomon would have had contact. Perhaps our best evidence of that influence comes from archaeological research from the period of the settlement in which influences from Anatolia and north Syria seem to be present at sites like Ai, Raddana, and Hazor. While the literary sources fail to paint a clear picture concerning the influence of the Hittite empire in Anatolia, perhaps archaeological research in the future will provide the necessary information.

Bibliography: BRUCE, F. F., "Hittites," *ISBE*, 2:720–23; DEVER, W. G., "Hittites," *MDB*, 382–83; DeVries, C. E., "Hittites," *BEB*, 980–82; GELB, I. J., "Hittites," *IDB*, 2:612–15; GURNEY, O. R., "Bogazkoy," *Archaeology and Old Testament Study*, ed. D. Winton Thomas (Oxford: Clarendon Press, 1967) 105–16; GUTERBOCK, H. G., "Bogazkoy," *OEANE*, 1:333–35; HARRISON, R. K., "Boghazkoy," *NIDBA*, 103–4; HOFFNER, H. A., Jr., "Hittite," *OEANE*, 3:81–84; idem, "Hittites," *OEANE*, 3:84–88; idem, "Hittites," *ZPEB*, 3:165–72; HOUWINKTENCATE, P. H. J., "Hittite History," *ABD*, 3:219–25; MCMAHON, G., "The History of the Hittites," *BA* 52 (1989) 62–77; PAYNE, J. B., "Hittites," *NIDB*, 442–44; ROBERTS, J. J. M., "Hittites," *HBD*, 399; SCHOVILLE, K. N., "Asia Minor and the Hittites," *BAF*, 219–29.

Unit 4

CITIES OF
EGYPT

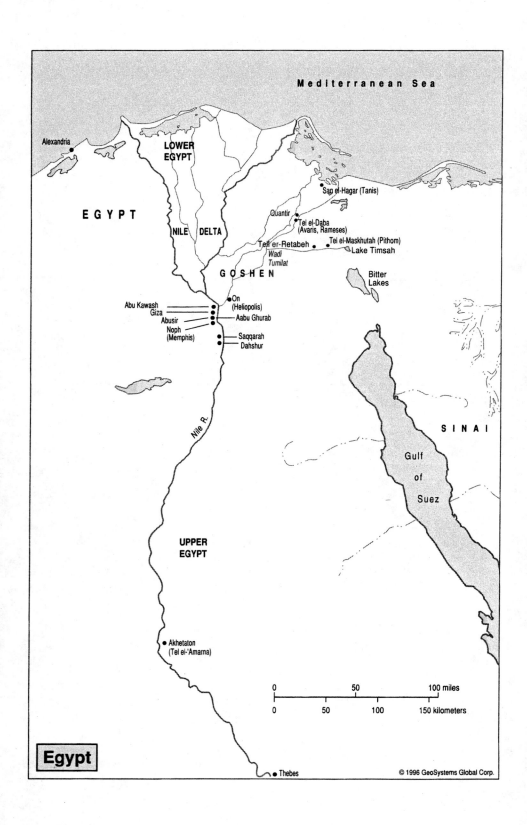

Mediterranean Sea

Alexandria

LOWER
EGYPT

EGYPT

NILE DELTA

San el-Hagar (Tanis)

Quantir
Tel el-Daba
(Avaris, Rameses)

Tell er-Retabeh
Wadi
Tumilat

Tel el-Maskhutah (Pithom)
Lake Timsah

GOSHEN

Bitter
Lakes

Abu Kawash
Giza
Abusir
Noph
(Memphis)

On
(Heliopolis)

Aabu Ghurab

Saqqarah
Dahshur

SINAI

Nile R.

Gulf
of
Suez

UPPER
EGYPT

Akhetaton
(Tel el-'Amarna)

0   50   100 miles

0   50   100   150 kilometers

Egypt

Thebes

© 1996 GeoSystems Global Corp.

Gift of the Nile

While Mesopotamia, the "land between the rivers," comprised the eastern end of the Fertile Crescent, Egypt, "the gift of the Nile," formed the western end. Though the two lands have their distinct differences, they also have some interesting parallels. Egypt and Mesopotamia were homelands of the two major civilizations in the ancient Near East. The development of life and culture in both was largely dependent on rivers, the Tigris and Euphrates rivers in Mesopotamia, and the Nile River in Egypt.

The land of Egypt is located in North Africa, and like other lands of the Fertile Crescent, the land itself holds its own unique surprises and special characteristics. Egypt is basically a desert, receiving little or no rainfall. The greatest rainfall occurs in the delta where up to eight inches fall annually, but in the region south of the delta the rainfall tapers off to nothing. Nevertheless, ancient Egyptian civilization blossomed and grew in this area because early on the inhabitants of the land realized that the annual Nile River flood provided two important essentials for life—water and fertile soil. For that reason life in Egypt developed in the fertile regions along the Nile River and in the delta region. Consequently, the Egyptians even in ancient times had an agricultural economy. The Nile River valley, which varies from one to twenty-five miles in width, was like a fertile garden. The ancient Egyptians excelled in land reclamation projects that increased their agricultural productivity. Realizing that the marsh lands of the delta were rich and fertile, some of the pharaohs of the Twelfth Dynasty developed land reclamation programs that built levies in parts of the delta, pumped the water out of those areas, and reclaimed the rich, fertile land for agricultural use. The Egyptians excelled in the production of cereal crops like wheat and barley, fruits and vegetables, and flax for linen. They also engaged in animal husbandry, primarily raising cattle rather than sheep and goats.

No other physical feature in the land of Egypt had as much impact on Egyptian life as the Nile River and its annual flooding. The Nile originated some four thousand miles to the south of Egypt in the waters of the White Nile. In the Sudan the waters of the White Nile were joined by those of the Blue Nile. Seasonal rains south of Egypt raised the Nile to flood levels in Egypt from about July to September. Because the Nile flooded annually and provided food for the Egyptians, it also took on religious significance for the Egyptians. It was seen as the gift of the gods and therefore sacred. Consequently, many of the Egyptian gods were associated with the Nile.

Geographically, Egypt was a land isolated by several natural barriers—the Libyan desert on the west, the Sinai and the Red Sea on the east, the Mediterranean Sea on the north, and the cataracts of the Nile on the south. These barriers provided protection from outside attack and also provided isolation for cultural development within the land. Nonetheless, the Egyptians established communication and trade relations with other lands. A land trade route moved along the coast through the Sinai and Syria-Palestine, and there were sea trade routes on the Mediterranean and Red seas. While Egypt's production of cereal grains made it a type of bread basket, it was dependent on other lands for other commodities—olive oil from Palestine for food; cedar and cypress wood from the Phoenician seacoast for houses and ships; and incense and myrrh and other spices from Arabia on the Red Sea. The Egyptians obtained copper and turquoise from the Sinai through mining operations in that area.

Of all the Egyptians' contributions to the ancient world, writing was certainly one of the most important. The ancient Egyptians developed a type of written communication known as hieroglyphics, a writing system consisting of picturelike symbols. They also developed a process that turned papyrus into a paperlike writing material. Using the pith of the plant, the Egyptians interlaced the papyrus strips and formed a mat or page. After a gluelike substance was painted on the mat, pressure was applied and the mat was allowed to dry.

In spite of the important role the ancient Egyptians played in the ancient Near Eastern world, the early beginnings of life and culture in Egypt are still shrouded in mystery. During the very early stages of that history Egypt was possibly divided into two areas, Lower Egypt along with the delta and its immediate surroundings, and Upper Egypt, the southern part of the land. The mainstream of Egyptian history began ca. 3100 BCE when Egypt came under the control of one leader. In the third century BCE, the ancient historian Manetho, seeking to categorize the scores of rulers and pharaohs that comprise Egypt's lengthy history, divided them into dynasties, that is, into their ruling families or houses. Dynastic rule began with Menes, the first pharaoh of Dynasty I, who united Upper and Lower Egypt. Egyptian history is also divided into major periods of strength and decline, such as the Old Kingdom Period and the First Intermediate Period.

Both the OT and archaeological data from Egypt and Palestine reflect the exchange and interaction that took place between the two lands and their people. In the Bible this is expressed in numerous prophetic oracles (Isa 19:20; Jer 46:1–12; Ezek 29–32; Hos 8:13; 11:1; 13:4; Nah 3:8) and stories: the patriarchal visits during times of famine (Gen 12:10; 42:1–5; 43:1–15); the sale of Joseph (Gen 37:25–28); the Hebrew oppression (Exod 1:8–22); the exodus (Exod 12:37–14:30); Solomon's marriage alliance (1 Kgs 3:1); Solomon's trade relations (1 Kgs 10:28–29); the invasion of Judah and perhaps Israel by Shishak king of Egypt (1 Kgs 14:25–28); Egypt's involvement in international affairs at the time of the decline and fall of Judah (2 Kgs 23:29, 31–35); and the resettlement of refugees from Judah in Egypt (Jer 43:1–7; 44:1). In archaeological materials the exchange and interaction between the two lands and their people is witnessed in the Execration texts, the accounts of the campaigns of Thutmose III, the Amarna letters, the Merneptah victory stele, and the Karnak inscription of Shishak's invasion of Palestine. As in other ancient Near Eastern countries, several cities, towns, and settlements in Egypt played an important role in some phase of the OT story, whether directly or indirectly. These include Akhetaton/Tell el-Amarna, Avaris, Elephantine, Memphis, Pithom, Rameses, and Thebes. Alexandria, which developed on the coast west of the delta during the later OT period, was an important Jewish center as well as a major center of early Christianity.

Bibliography: ABD AL-MALIK, B., "Egypt," *BW,* 207–18; BAINES, J., and J. Malik, *Atlas of Ancient Egypt* (New York: Facts On File Publications, 1980); BIANCHI, R. A., "Egypt: Postdynastic Egypt," *OEANE,* 2:201–5; BROWNING, D. C., Jr., "Egypt," *HolBD,* 399–403; CRAPPS, R. W., "Egypt," *MDB,* 236–38; DEVRIES, C. E., "Egypt,"

NIDB, 293–98; HUFFMON, H. B., "Egypt," *HBD,* 248–51; KITCHEN, K. A., "Egypt," *NIDBA,* 171–73; idem, "Egypt," *NBD²,* 301–10; idem, "Egypt, History of (Chronology)," *ABD,* 2:321–31; LACOVARA, P., "Egypt: Predynastic Egypt," *OEANE,* 2:191–95; LASOR, W. S., "Egypt," *ISBE,* 2:29–47; SCHOVILLE, K. N., "Egypt," *BAF,* 253–58; VOS, H. F., "Egypt, Egyptians," *BEB,* 1:662–75; WEINSTEIN, J. M., "Egypt: Dynastic Egypt," *OEANE,* 2:196–201; WILSON, J. A., "Egypt," *IDB,* 2:39–66.

AKHETATON   20

Capital of the Amarna Age

Tell el-Amarna, the site of ancient Akhetaton, and Avaris (ch. 21) played similar roles in Egyptian history. Each was an Egyptian capital for a brief period of time. The circumstances surrounding the establishment of each capital were unusual. Avaris was the capital city founded by outsiders who gained control of the land. Tell el-Amarna was the site at which an Egyptian heretic king attempted to distinguish himself from the status quo. Avaris was the capital of Egypt during the Second Intermediate period (the so-called Hyksos period during the latter part of the Middle Bronze Age), and Tell el-Amarna was briefly the capital during the period of the New Kingdom (Late Bronze Age, the so-called Amarna Age). For students of the Bible the discoveries at Tell el-Amarna have been especially valuable because they provide important information about the political situation in Palestine and Egypt during the period of oppression.

The ruins at Tell el-Amarna were discovered in 1887 when a peasant woman dug for fertile soil at the site. The soil, a combination of decayed matter intermingled with deteriorated mud-brick structures at the site, was used as fertilizer by the peasants. But the woman's efforts turned up more than fertile soil; she unearthed clay tablets, a part of the royal archives of Amenhotep IV also known as Akhenaton, Egypt's famed heretic king. Unaware of the significance of her find, the woman sold the tablets for bakery goods. Initial scholarly examination of the tablets concluded that the tablets were fakes, but the antiquity of the tablets was eventually recognized, and excavations at the site began. Tell el-Amarna was first excavated by Flinders Petrie in 1891. Further excavations were conducted by a German archaeological team and the Egyptian Exploration Society. The modern name, Tell el-Amarna, is derived from local inhabitants, the Beni Amran.

The ruins at Tell el-Amarna are those of Akhetaton, the royal capital of the Egyptian pharaoh Akhenaton. Amenhotep IV (Akhenaton) built the new capital as a part of a new era he attempted to introduce in the land. The pharaohs of the preceding era, including such notables as Thutmose III, Amenhotep II, and Thutmose IV, had built and attempted to maintain a powerful empire. Through military campaigns they extended their control into Syria-Palestine. Eventually the imperialistic spirit waned, and the Egyptian grasp of Syro-Palestinian city-states weakened. When Amenhotep IV succeeded his father, Amenhotep III, he introduced a revolutionary change to Egypt's religion by replacing Amon with Aton, the sun god, as the god of the state. Abandoning the priesthood and worship of the god Amon in the capital city Thebes, Amenhotep IV changed his name from Amenhotep to Akhenaton and built an entirely new capital city approximately two hundred miles down the Nile. He named this city Akhetaton, meaning "the horizon of Aton." Because the modern name of the site is Tell el-Amarna, the period during which the Egyptian capital was located at the site is often referred to as the Amarna period.

The new god needed a new capital city and so Akhetaton was constructed. Excavations at the site have revealed mud-brick structures of poor quality caused by the haste in which they were built. But the inferior quality was generally hidden beneath plastered surfaces and elaborate decorations that reflected tremendous wealth. Akhetaton was built on a flat plain on the east side of the Nile just beyond the fertile band of soil on the bank of the river. The city was approximately five miles long and one-half mile wide and was comprised of several sections including the north city, the north suburb, the central city, the south suburb, and the royal garden called Maruaton. Additional features of the community included those outside the city proper—the village of the tomb cutters, and the tomb areas, the north tombs, the south tombs, and the royal valley. The major part of the city was connected by the royal road.

The north city contained facilities for the royal family, including the north riverside palace and the north palace. The north riverside palace was a fortified structure in which the king apparently resided. The north palace most likely provided living quarters for other members of the royal family. It was comprised of living quarters, a temple, gardens, and courtyards. The north suburb, a residential area, was an area in which the private houses of nobles and middle-class citizens were built. The houses generally included a central reception room, bedrooms, toilets, and in some instances a second floor. The houses usually had a well, a garden area, a grain storage area, and a shrine for Aton.

The central city included the great palace, the king's house, the office of records and correspondence, the royal stables, and the great temple. The great palace, comprised of large courtyards, halls, and statues of Akhenaton, was designed for royal ceremonies and receptions. It was perhaps the facility in which coronation ceremonies were held. Additional state functions, such as promotions, probably took place in the so-called king's house across the royal road from the great palace. The office of records and correspondence, the administrative quarters located behind the king's house, has provided the most valuable discoveries, namely, clay tablets with cuneiform writing. The tablets, commonly known as the Amarna letters, contain correspondence from city-state kings in Syria-Palestine as well as correspondence from kings in other parts of the Fertile Crescent. The long, narrow building behind the office of records and correspondence apparently served as the royal stables. The central city also included the great temple dedicated to Aton. The temple was comprised of large courts equipped with hundreds of stone altars for food and libation offerings to Aton. Similar to the great temple was a smaller temple located near the king's house.

The south suburb comprised the major residential area of the city. The houses in this section apparently were those of the common people or the lower classes. No temples or shrines have been found here, indicating that provisions for worship were not afforded the lower classes.

Another feature of the city was the royal garden called Maruaton. It included shallow pools or lakes, garden areas, shrines, altars, and a moat.

The village of the tomb cutters and the tombs themselves were located east of the city. The village was built on the plateau area between the city and the rock cliffs to the east. The purpose of the village was to provide housing for the craftsmen who hewed the tombs as well as the artisans who decorated the tombs. The tombs hewed in the cliffs to the east of the village are clustered in two groups, the north tombs and the south tombs. The tombs were used to bury officials of the royal court. The tombs are particularly valuable because they are decorated with wall carvings of scenes from the life and experiences of the royal household as well as scenes that reflect official functions of the royal family. The royal valley, apparently a new project that was designed to be a royal necropolis (cemetery), was located several miles east of the original tomb area. Only one tomb was completed, that of Akhenaton.

The religious revolution of Akhenaton was short-lived, the Amarna period lasting approximately only twenty-five years, from ca. 1375 to 1350 BCE. Upon his death, Akhenaton was succeeded by Tutankhaton, the half-brother of Queen Nefertiti. During his reign he abandoned Akhetaton and moved the capital back to Thebes. He reinstated the worship of Amon and changed his own name to Tutankhamon. Shortly thereafter, during the reign of the army general Horemhab, a concerted effort was made to remove all the evidence of the Akhenaton era.

The discoveries at Akhetaton reflect advancements that took place in art during this period. The artwork that decorated the walls and hallways of the buildings in the city as well as the tomb walls represents new artistic styles. The artists attempted to produce realistic scenes, a definite departure from earlier Egyptian art. Some of the finest artwork was that of plaster relief figures such as the bust of Akhenaton's beautiful wife, Nefertiti.

Over 350 clay tablets discovered in the complex of rooms, apparently the office of records and correspondence or royal archives, have provided the most valuable information. These tablets are often referred to as the Amarna tablets or Amarna letters. They were inscribed in Akkadian cuneiform, the international language of diplomatic correspondence of that day. They contain correspondence to Egyptian officials from the leaders of other major powers in the ancient Near East such as the Hittites, the Mitannians, and the Assyrians. The vast majority of tablets contain correspondence from kings of Egypt's vassal city-states in Syria-Palestine. These letters are especially valuable because they reflect the political situation in Canaan at that time. The letters indicate that Canaan was in turmoil and that Akhenaton was neglecting that area. During the Amarna period Canaan was comprised of a number of small city-states. The letters written by the vassal city-state kings in that region to Akhenaton addressed a number of problems including the Habiru, conflict between neighboring city-state kings, and dishonest Egyptian commissioners. The letters came not only from city-states in Canaan such as Jerusalem, Hebron, Shechem, Hazor,

Megiddo, and Gezer, but also from the territory of Phoenicia and Syria. Often the letters included pleas for military assistance because the city-states faced imminent danger at the hands of the Habiru, also called the SA.GAZ. For instance, Abdi-Heba, king of Jerusalem, made an urgent plea for archers because the Habiru were not only plundering the area but also threatening to take control of it. Rib-Addi, the king of Byblos, wrote more than fifty letters to Akhenaton assuring the Egyptian king of his faithfulness, reporting territories that had been lost to the Habiru, and repeatedly requesting military assistance. The repeated requests and the absence of any acknowledgment that assistance was received suggest that Akhenaton did not respond.

The Habiru or SA.GAZ are mentioned not only in the Amarna letters but also in other ancient Near Eastern texts from Mesopotamia to Egypt that date from the Early Bronze to the Late Bronze Age. In spite of the many references, the Habiru are difficult to define or identify precisely. They cannot be equated with any one particular ethnic group. They seem to be a homeless, stateless, semi-nomadic group comprised of foreigners who moved through regions of the ancient Near East. They cannot be equated with the Hebrews, although the Hebrews at some point may have been among them or may have comprised a similar social class.

The Habiru threat combined with the lack of interest on the part of Akhenaton affected the morale of the city-state kings and resulted in heated conflicts between the local leaders. The local leaders were primarily interested in the welfare of their own territory and at times engaged in alliances for personal gain. For instance, Labayu, city-state king of Shechem, aligned himself with the Habiru in an attempt to gain control of more territory in the central hill country, a move that brought protests from neighboring city-state kings, including Abdi-Heba of Jerusalem and Biridiya of Megiddo.

The morale of the city-state kings was affected further by the presence of corrupt Egyptian commissioners in the land. The Egyptian presence in vassal territories was represented by local commissioners stationed at administrative centers in the land. The commissioners, known as the *rabu*, were responsible for protecting Egyptian interests in the vassal states and administrative functions such as collecting tribute money and sending it to Akhenaton. The Amarna letters indicate that the commissioners were generally corrupt, often gave in to bribes, and probably in most cases kept the tribute money for themselves.

In general, the Amarna letters indicate that during the Amarna period Egyptian interest focused on the homeland rather than the vassal city-states of Syria-Palestine, and Egyptian control of the area continued to slip. Consequently, the vassal regions were in turmoil and facing a state of anarchy.

Bibliography: BOWLING, A., "Tell El-Amarna," *ZPEB*, 5:615–21; BRUCE, F. F., "Amarna," *NIDBA*, 22–23; idem, "Tell el-Amarna," *Archaeology and Old Testament Study*, ed. D. Winton Thomas (Oxford: Clarendon, 1967) 3–20; BRYAN, B. M., "Amarna, Tell El-," *OEANE*, 1:81–86; HUFFMON, H. B., "Amarna," *HBD*, 25; IZRE'EL, S., "Amarna Tablets," *OEANE*, 1:86–87; KEMP, B. J., "Tell El-Amarna," *Ancient Centres of Egyptian Civilization*, ed. H. S. Smith and Rosalind Hall (Windsor Forest: Kensal, 1983) 57–72; LAMBDIN, T. O., "Tell El-Amarna," *IDB*, 4:529–33; LONG, J. E., "Amarna Tablets," *BEB*, 1:65–68; RAINEY, A. F., "Tell El-Amarna," *IDBSup*, 869; REDFORD, D. B., "Amarna, Tell El-," *ABD*, 1:181–82; SCHOVILLE, K. N., "Tell el-Amarna," *BAF*, 258–61; SELMAN, M. J., "Amarna," *NBD*^{2}, 28–29; TENNEY, M. C., "Amarna, Tell El," *NIDB*, 39; TOBIAS, H., "Amarna, Tell El," *HolBD*, 41; WILES, J. K., "Amarna," *MDB*, 22–23; WISEMAN, D. J., "Archaeology," *NBD*, 67–68; YOUNGBLOOD, R. F., "Amarna Tablets," *ISBE*, 1:105–8.

Capital during the Hyksos Period

Avaris is certainly not a name well known to students of the Bible; in fact, the name does not even appear in the biblical text. Yet Avaris occupied an important place in Egyptian history. It was one of Egypt's capital cities for approximately one to two hundred years. The historical events of that era comprise a unique chapter in Egyptian history.

Avaris was the capital of Egypt during the Hyksos period, when the traditional line of Egyptian pharaohs lost control to an outside force. The events that led to the establishment of the Hyksos kings came in the aftermath of the Twelfth Dynasty. While the pharaohs of the Twelfth Dynasty were powerful figures who maintained control of Egypt and also improved it, such was not the case during the Thirteenth Dynasty. A series of weak kings led Egypt into decline. Near the end of the Thirteenth Dynasty and the beginning of the Fourteenth Dynasty, governmental control of the land was taken over by the so-called Hyksos rulers, and Egypt entered its Second Intermediate period.

Hyksos control of Egypt began about 1750 BCE and continued until about 1550 BCE. The Hyksos were presumably Asiatics who moved into the delta area of Egypt, took advantage of the demise of the government, established control over the delta, and built a capital at Avaris. Consequently, the rulers of the Fifteenth and Sixteenth dynasties were Hyksos, rather than representing a traditional pharaonic line.

The identity and background of the Hyksos are still subject to debate. The third-century Egyptian priest, Manetho, translated the term Hyksos as "shepherd kings," but the Old Egyptian terminology for the rulers probably meant "rulers of foreign countries." Some have suggested that the Hyksos were disgruntled Egyptians rather than outsiders who entered the land. Though the ethnic origins of the Hyksos cannot be determined with any great certainty, they do appear to be Asiatic.

Because many of the Hyksos names are Semitic, we may assume that there was a substantial Semitic element among them. There were Indo-Europeans and Hurrians among them as well.

While we know that Avaris was located in the eastern part of the delta, its exact location is still open to debate. The most likely candidate for the site of the ancient Hyksos capital is Tell el-Dabah; however, some would identify it with San el-Hagar, ancient Egyptian Tanis or biblical Zoan, approximately ten miles to the north. Both sites have significant Hyksos remains, but the best evidence seems to come from Tell el-Dabah, which includes temples and tombs.

As the Hyksos rulers attempted to govern Egypt from the capital at Avaris, they probably never gained control of the entire country. According to ancient Egyptian texts, lower and middle Egypt were under the control of Apophis, one of the most powerful Hyksos kings. The Hyksos did succeed in capturing the Egyptian capital in Memphis in 1667 BCE, but Hyksos control of middle Egypt is questionable. After Memphis was captured, the traditional line of pharaonic leaders moved to the city of Thebes. In addition to exercising control over the Egyptian delta, the Hyksos dominated the southwest part of Palestine and there established a major center named Sharuhen, Tell el-Farah (south).

While the Hyksos period was brief and Hyksos control of Egypt was limited, they surely left their mark on Egyptian history. (Hyksos influence on the Egyptian culture was minimal. In fact, the Hyksos culture was largely shaped and influenced by the Egyptians. An example of this is Hyksos religion. The major god of the Hyksos was the Egyptian god Seth.) They are credited with introducing the use of the horse and chariot and the composite bow in military campaigns. They perhaps also introduced new designs in hand weapons such as swords and scimitar daggers. The Hyksos may have also been instrumental in the introduction of new skills in metallurgy, the processing and use of bronze.

The Hyksos period was for the most part a time of peace and prosperity in Egypt. Egyptian borders were open to trade and exchange. Traders moved freely between Egypt and Anatolia as well as other parts of the Fertile Crescent. Hyksos scarabs (seals in the form of beetles) have been found at sites as far away as Anatolia. Scarabs inscribed with the names of Hyksos kings have been commonly found at sites in

Palestine and Egypt. Some propose that it was during this period of open borders, when traders moved freely in and out of Egypt, that Joseph was taken into Egypt by Ishmaelite traders.

But Hyksos control of Egypt was not to last. Egyptian unrest over foreign domination grew until Kamose, the last king of the Seventeenth Dynasty of the old line of Egyptian rulers in Thebes, made his move. He apparently succeeded in driving the Hyksos out of whatever part of middle Egypt they had occupied. The final expulsion of the Hyksos from Egypt came with Ahmose, the brother of Kamose and first king of the Eighteenth Dynasty, who (ca. 1545 BCE) destroyed the Hyksos capital at Avaris and drove them back into Palestine and their stronghold at Sharuhen.

Bibliography: BROWNING, D. C., Jr., "Hyksos," *HolBD,* 679–81; DEVRIES, C. E., "Hyksos," *ISBE,* 2:787–88; KITCHEN, K. A., "Hyksos," *NIDBA,* 245–46; idem, "Hyksos," *ZPEB,* 3:232–33; idem, "Rameses (Raamses), City of," *NIDBA,* 384; REDFORD, D. B., "Hyksos (History)," *ABD,* 3:341–44; REDFORD, D. B., and J. M. Weinstein, "Hyksos (Archaeology)," *ABD,* 3:344–48; TRAVIS, W. "Hyksos," *BEB,* 1:1010–12; VAN SETERS, J., "Hyksos," *IDBSup,* 424–25; WEINSTEIN, J. M., "Hyksos," *HBD,* 412–13.

Royal Necropolis of Ancient Egypt

Memphis might well be named "the monumental capital of ancient Egypt." Not only did it produce literal monuments, but it also had a monumental effect on Egyptian life. No other Egyptian city enjoyed the long and continuous prosperity—culturally, politically, and economically—that Memphis did. The city's fame and importance continued even after Thebes displaced it as the capital of Egypt and did not diminish until Alexandria became the major cultural center.

Memphis was located on the west bank of the Nile River approximately thirteen miles south of the present capital of Cairo. According to Herodotus (*Histories* 2.98), Egyptian tradition held that the city of Memphis was founded and established by Menes, the first pharaoh of Egypt's First Dynasty. Menes, who was responsible for uniting Lower and Upper Egypt, apparently selected the site because of its location near the junction of the Nile valley and the Nile delta, the point at which Lower Egypt and Upper Egypt met. Originally the new city, which remained the capital through the Pyramid Age, the period of the Old Kingdom, was called *Inb-hd*, or White Wall. Later, it assumed the name *Mennufer*, the pyramid of Pepi I, pharaoh of the Sixth Dynasty. The new name perhaps conveyed the idea of "the goodness of Pepi." When Menes founded the city as the new political center he also, according to tradition, erected a temple dedicated to the Egyptian god Ptah. As a result he set the course of the city as a major religious center. Later, perhaps during the period of the New Kingdom, the city assumed yet another name, *Hikuptah*, meaning "the temple of the ka (spirit) of Ptah." The new name, which in Greek was *Aigyptos*, came to signify the entire land.

Memphis remained the capital during the period of the Old Kingdom, but it was replaced by Thebes about 2200 BCE during the First

Intermediate period and never again played an important role as a political center. According to Josephus, Memphis may have served as the Hyksos capital under the king Salatis prior to the establishment of Avaris (*Ag. Ap.* 1.77–78). The city continued to be an important city and in many regards the real center of Egypt. During the height of the Assyrian era, Memphis was captured by Esarhaddon and for a brief time was a part of that empire. In 332 BCE Alexander moved into the city and took it without opposition. Memphis lost its position as the cultural center of Egypt to Alexandria during the Greek period. During that era Alexandria surpassed Memphis as Egypt's largest city. Eventually the population of Memphis dwindled to nothing, and the city lay in ruins. During the seventh century CE the site was plundered by the incoming Arabs who used its materials to build old Cairo.

Pyramid and sphinx at Giza

The monumental role Memphis played as the first major capital city and the major cultural and cosmopolitan center of the land is attested today by the many monuments that are a part of the landscape of Memphis and the greater Memphis area. Memphis was the major center of pyramids, tombs, and temples—the monumental center of Egypt's pharaohs and their gods. Memphis was the major pharaonic necropolis (cemetery) in the land. While the original city was probably constructed in the area of the modern village, Mit Rahinah, throughout the course of its history the greater Memphis area encompassed an area of some fifteen or twenty miles in length running from Dahshur on the south to Abu Rawash in the north. The extent of the city itself remains a mystery because only limited excavations have been conducted at the ruins. Archaeological investigations have concentrated on the necropolis, the major pyramid areas and the tombs and temples that surrounded them. The greater Memphis necropolis includes sites at Dahshur, Saqqarah, Abusir, Abu Ghurab, Zawyet el-Aryan, Giza, and Abu Rawash. Of the major components of each site only a few can be mentioned—the temple enclosure of the god Ptah, the temple of Ramses II, and palace of Merneptah at Mit Rahinah; the Bent and Red Pyramids of Snofru at Dahshur; the step pyramid of Djoser, and the Serapeum, the name given to the complex of tombs of the Apis bull cult at Saqqarah; and the great pyramid of Khufu and great sphinx at Giza. The necropolis also yielded discoveries, including many statues or fragments of statues, such as the colossal statues of Ramses II; the pyramid texts inscribed on the chamber walls inside the pyramids; the boats and boat chambers that accompanied pharaonic burials; and the thousands of facades and panels of accompanying tombs and temples that depict the many facets of Egyptian life.

The chief god of Memphis was Ptah, recognized as the creator god and great craftsman. To the ancient Egyptians, Ptah was the oldest god and was responsible for the creation of the other gods and humankind. Ptah's wife was Sekhmet, and their son was Nefertem. The Apis bull worshiped by the ancient Egyptians was regarded as Ptah's sacred animal. As the divine craftsman, Ptah was also the god of the arts, crafts, and craftsmen.

Memphis is mentioned in the prophetic literature of the OT. Hosea must have been well aware of Memphis, the great royal necropolis, as he proclaimed that Israel would soon fall and "Memphis shall bury them" (Hos 9:6). In his oracle concerning the doom of Egypt, Isaiah labeled the princes of Memphis as "deluded" (Isa 19:13). Jeremiah also made reference to Memphis (2:16; 46:19), indicating that it was one of several sites in Egypt to which Jews fled following the fall of Judah and

Jerusalem (44:1; 46:14). And Ezekiel, probably knowledgeable of the greater Memphis area with its many temples and statues, proclaimed "I will destroy the idols, and put an end to the images, in Memphis" (Ezek 30:13).

Bibliography: BAINES, J., and J. Malek, "Memphis," *Atlas of Ancient Egypt* (New York: Facts On File Publications, 1980) 134–65; DEVRIES, C. E., "Memphis," *NIDB,* 639–40; idem, "Memphis," *ZPEB,* 4:179–83; DEWIT, C., "Memphis," *NBD,* 807; idem, "Memphis," *NBD²,* 759; HUFFMON, H. B., "Memphis," *HBD,* 625; KITCHEN, K. A., "Memphis," *NIDBA,* 310; LAMBDIN, T. O., "Memphis," *IDB,* 3:346–47; MALEK, J., "Giza," *Ancient Centres of Egyptian Civilization,* ed. H. S. Smith and Rosalind Hall (Windsor Forest: Kensal, 1983) 25–36; MARTIN, G. T., "Saqqara," *Ancient Centres of Egyptian Civilizations,* ed. H. S. Smith and Rosalind Hall (Windsor Forest: Kensal, 1983) 37–44; PATCH, D. C., "Memphis," *OEANE,* 3:470–71; REDFORD, D. B., "Memphis," *ABD,* 4:689–91; THOMPSON, J. A., "Memphis," *ISBE,* 3:315–17; VOS, H. F., "Memphis," *BEB,* 2:1435–36.

Store Cities and Border Fortresses in the Eastern Delta

Though important to the biblical story of Hebrew oppression in Egypt, the location of Pithom and Rameses is still uncertain. Pithom and Rameses are mentioned in Exod 1:11 as the two store cities the Hebrew slaves were engaged to build for the Egyptian king. No other reference to Pithom is found in the Bible. Rameses is further identified as the site from which the journey of the exodus started (Exod 12:37; Num 33:3, 5). There is little doubt among scholars that the two store cities were located in the eastern part of the Nile River delta.

Scholars generally associate Rameses of the biblical story with the city of Per-Ramesses built by Ramses II and mentioned in a number of Egyptian texts. Today it is commonly held that Ramses II was the pharaoh of Egypt at the time of the exodus. During the Ramesside period, when members of the Ramses dynasty occupied the throne, the delta area received special attention. Extensive building projects were carried out in the eastern part of the delta. Per-Ramesses, built by Ramses II, became the capital city in the delta (Lower Egypt), and Thebes (Upper Egypt) was the southern capital.

With the information at hand we may assume that Pithom and Rameses served several purposes. The Bible indicates the cities were store cities, centers at which facilities for grain storage were constructed. Since the cities were located in the eastern delta, which was subject to invasion from the east, we may also assume they were fortified and part of the border fortress system of that region. In addition, the city of Rameses functioned as a northern "White House." According to the Bible the cities were constructed of mud brick, which was used extensively in building projects throughout Egypt, including Akhetaton, at Tell el-Amarna. Eighteenth Dynasty tomb paintings from Thebes depict brickmaking scenes and the process involved.

While the precise location of Pithom and Rameses awaits further excavations, most scholars agree on their general location. Two sites in the wadi Tumilat, a fertile valley in the eastern delta, are considered likely candidates for the location of Pithom—Tell er-Retabeh and Tell el-Maskhutah nine miles east of Tell er-Retabeh. Both sites have been excavated and have yielded ruins from the time of Ramses II, but the evidence is inconclusive. Currently Tell er-Retabeh seems to be the most likely location for Pithom. Likewise, two sites have been proposed as possible locations for Rameses—San el-Hagar, which some also identify as ancient Tanis, and Tell el-Dabah also named Qantir, approximately twelve miles south of Tanis. Currently the evidence from the two sites seems to favor Qantir, the Tell el-Dabah location.

Bibliography: Brisco, T. V., "Pithom," *ISBE*, 3:875–76; DeVries, C. E., "Rameses, Raamses," *NIDB*, 845; Dewit, C., "Pithom," *NBD²*, 943; Elwell, W. A., "Rameses (Place)," *BEB*, 2:1820; Huckabay, G. C., "Pithom," *HolBD*, 1115; Huffmon, H. B., "Pithom," *HBD*, 801; Kitchen, K. A., "Pithom," *NIDBA*, 365–66; idem, "Pithom," *ZPEB*, 4:803–4; idem, "Ra'amses, Rameses," *NBD²*, 1006; idem, "Raamses, Rameses (City)," *ZPEB*, 5:14; idem, "Rameses (Raamses), City of," *NIDBA*, 384; Lambdin, T. O., "Pithom," *IDB*, 3:821; Pierce, R. W., "Rameses," *ISBE*, 4:39; Schoville, K. N., "Pe-Rameses and Pithom," *BAF*, 262–64; Wei, T. F., "Pithom," *ABD*, 5:376–77; Weinstein, J. M., "Raamses, Rameses," *HBD*, 848; Wente, E. F., "Rameses," *ABD*, 5:617–18; Wilson, J. A., "Rameses (City)," *IDB*, 4:9.

THEBES 🏺 24

City of Temples, Palaces, and Tombs

If Memphis was the monumental capital of Egypt during the Old Kingdom, Thebes was the monumental capital during the Middle Kingdom, the New Kingdom, and the period that followed. While the monumental building projects of the Memphis area consisted of pyramids surrounded and accompanied by temples and tombs, those at Thebes were comprised of massive temple and palace complexes. Each site was, for a major period of time, the capital and royal necropolis (cemetery) of the land.

Thebes was the southernmost capital of Egypt. While Memphis was located at the point where Upper and Lower Egypt met near the junction of the Nile and the delta, Thebes was located some 330 miles up the Nile in Upper Egypt. The city, known in ancient Egyptian as *waset*, "city," in Hebrew as *no'*, "city," or *no' 'āmôn*, "City of Amon," and in Greek as "Thebes," had a strategic location. It was close to Nubia to the south and Egypt's mineral-rich eastern desert to the east. The city also had command of the trade routes in southern Egypt and was far from Lower Egypt, which at times provided valuable insulation for the Theban kings. Though the early beginnings of Thebes go back to the predynastic era, the city did not become prominent until the First Intermediate period (Eleventh Dynasty) and the Middle Kingdom (Twelfth and Thirteenth dynasties) when it replaced Memphis as the capital city. The history of the new capital was briefly interrupted during the Second Intermediate period, as the Hyksos gained control of the delta and established a capital at Avaris. Due to the efforts of a new line of Theban pharaohs at the end of the Seventeenth Dynasty and the beginning of the Eighteenth Dynasty, the Hyksos rulers were driven out of Egypt, and Thebes once again became the major political center in the land. During the era that followed, the period of the New Kingdom, which extended from the Eighteenth to Twentieth dynasties,

Thebes entered its heyday. The new era, often called the period of the Empire, was characterized by imperialistic pharaohs such as Thutmose III, who extended Egyptian control into the territory of Syria-Palestine and built an empire that extended from Egypt to the Euphrates. Several pharaohs of the New Kingdom conducted annual campaigns to the city-states of Syria and Palestine and through these campaigns not only maintained control over the vassal kingdoms to the northeast but also accumulated tremendous wealth from them, wealth that is reflected in the monumental building projects—the temples, palaces, and tombs—built at Thebes by the pharaohs of that era.

But the period of New Kingdom was not without problems. Akhenaton, who initiated a religious revolution in Egypt, rejected the Theban god Amon and moved the capital from Thebes to the city of Akhetaton, which he built and dedicated to the god Aton. After Akhenaton's death, Thebes became the capital of Egypt once again. While Thebes remained a southern capital and an important religious center for the god Amon, the city never regained the prestige of the preceding era. In 663 BCE Thebes was conquered and destroyed by the Assyrians and receded from the history of Egypt.

Colossal remains in western Thebes

The spectacular ruins of ancient Thebes are located on both sides of the Nile. Since the royal necropolis with its mortuary temples and burial sites are located west of the river, the ruins on the east bank are often referred to as the city of the living and those on the west as the city of the dead. The ancient ruins are actually located in several different areas, in sectors or at sites that bear different names—at Luxor and Karnak on the east side of the Nile, and at Medinet Habu, Deir el-Medina, and Deir el-Bahri on the west. Among the impressive ruins at Thebes are the temple at Luxor, the temple complex at Karnak, the mortuary temple of Ramses III at Medinet Habu, the mortuary temple of Ramses II, the Valley of the Queens and village of the workmen at Deir el-Medina, and the mortuary temple of Hatshepsut and Valley of the Kings at Deir el-Bahri.

The earliest part of the city apparently developed on the east bank of the Nile, the area occupied today by the city of Luxor. The most impressive ruins at Luxor are those of an ancient temple built and dedicated to Amon, the god of Thebes. The temple itself was built primarily by Amenhotep III and Ramses II, and other minor structures and reliefs were added by other kings. The temple, a massive complex of courts and halls, is approximately 850 feet long. The many columns and walls are decorated with relief carvings and inscriptions. Those at the entrance to the court of Ramses II provide details of the battle between the Egyptians and Hittites at Qadesh in Syria. The most impressive of the many architectural features at Thebes include the colossal statues of Ramses II at the entrance to the court of Ramses II, the peristyle court of Ramses II with seventy-four relief decorated papyrus columns featuring Ramses II and a variety of Egyptian gods, the processional colonnade of Amenhotep III with fourteen massive columns, the peristyle forecourt of Amenhotep III with sixty-four columns, and the hypostyle hall with thirty-two columns.

The ruins at Karnak lie almost two miles northeast of those at Luxor. The two areas are connected by an alley lined with human-headed sphinxes. The many temples at Karnak are located in or near one of three courts or precincts—the court of Amon, the largest of the courtyards located between the court of Mut to the south, and the court of Montu to the north. The many walls, reliefs, columns, statues, and stelae of the temples at Karnak are perhaps the most impressive in the entire land. The temple complex at Karnak is dominated by temples constructed by pharaohs of the New Kingdom. The earliest structures at the site, however, probably date to the time of Sesostris I, pharaoh of the Middle Kingdom. The most impressive part of the court of Amon is the hypostyle hall of Seti I and his son Ramses II. The hypostyle hall features 134 papyrus columns and wall reliefs depicting military battles the two kings fought in Syria-Palestine. Like the temple at Luxor, the reliefs and inscriptions at Karnak provide valuable historical data including details of Shishak's invasion of Palestine (1 Kgs 14:25–28). The Karnak inscription indicates that Shishak captured dozens of towns from Ezion-geber in the Arabah to Megiddo. The precinct of Amon also contains inscriptions of the military campaigns Thutmose III made into Palestine and Syria.

Mortuary temple of Hatshepsut (Deir el-Bahri)

The temples on the west side of the Nile are generally classified as mortuary temples that were designed to honor the deceased king rather than a god. While the temples at Luxor and Karnak were freestanding, some of the mortuary temples west of the Nile were partly freestanding and partly cut into the rock cliffs behind them. Among the mortuary temples are those of Hatshepsut, Thutmose III, Ramses II, Merneptah, and Ramses III. Like the reliefs and inscriptions of the temples east of the Nile, those of the mortuary temples west of the Nile also provide valuable historical data. An excellent example is the mortuary temple of Ramses III at Medinet Habu in which reliefs and inscriptions provide valuable details of the king's encounters with the

Sea Peoples, an invading group from the Aegean area comprised of smaller groups or tribes including the Pelesti, the biblical Philistines. The members of the royal family were generally buried in the rock cut tombs beyond the mortuary temples—the kings themselves in the tombs in the Valley of the Kings, and the queen and other members of the family in tombs in the Valley of the Queens. Also among the ruins west of the Nile were those of a walled community which was inhabited by the workers who constructed the royal tombs.

Though Thebes is mentioned only a few times in the OT (solely in the prophetic books), the city must have played a vital role shaping Egyptian history especially during the period of the New Kingdom, in biblical history the period of the sojourn in Egypt, the period of the exodus, the period of the conquest, and the period of the judges as well as others. The references to Thebes in the prophetic books reflect the demise of the city. Nahum was aware of the destruction of the city (Nah 3:8–10) at the hands of the Assyrians in 663 BCE, and Jeremiah and Ezekiel spoke of the trying times Thebes would experience during later periods (Jer 46:25; Ezek 30:15–16).

Bibliography: ANDERSON, R. D., "Thebes," *Ancient Centres of Egyptian Civilization,* ed. H. S. Smith and Rosalind Hall (Windsor Forest: Kensal, 1983) 45–56; BAINES, J., and J. Malek, "Thebes," *Atlas of Ancient Egypt* (New York: Facts on File Publications, 1980) 84–107; BUTLER, T. C., "Thebes," *HolBD,* 1336–37; DORSEY, D. A., "No," *HBD,* 709; HOFFMEIER, J. K., "Thebes," *Major Cities of the Biblical World,* ed. R. K. Harrison (Nashville: Nelson, 1985) 249–57; KITCHEN, K. A., "Thebes," *NIDBA,* 449; idem, "Thebes," *NBD*[2], 1192; idem, "Thebes," *ZPEB,* 5:714–17; LAMBDIN, T. O., "Thebes," *IDB,* 4:615–17; NOTH, M., "Thebes," *Archaeology and Old Testament Study,* ed. D. Winton Thomas (Oxford: Clarendon, 1967) 21–35; REDFORD, D. B., "Thebes," *ABD,* 6:442–43; SCHOVILLE, K. N., "Thebes," *BAF,* 264–68; YOUNGBLOOD, R. F., "Thebes," *ISBE,* 4:824.

Unit 5

CITIES OF

PALESTINE

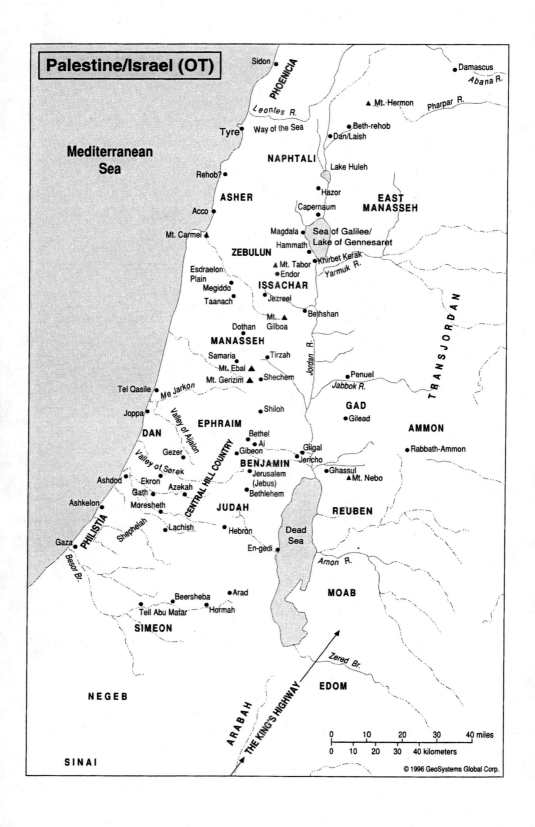

Palestine/Israel (OT)

Mediterranean
Sea

Sidon

PHOENICIA

Damascus

Abana R.

▲ Mt. Hermon

Pharpar R.

Tyre

Way of the Sea

Beth-rehob
Dan/Laish

Leontes R.

NAPHTALI

Lake Huleh

Rehob?

ASHER

Hazor

EAST
MANASSEH

Acco

Capernaum

Mt. Carmel ▲

Magdala
Hammath

Sea of Galilee/
Lake of Gennesaret

ZEBULUN

Khirbet Kerak

Esdraelon
Plain

▲ Mt. Tabor
Endor

Yarmuk R.

Megiddo

ISSACHAR

Taanach

Jezreel

Dothan

Mt. ▲
Gilboa

Bethshan

MANASSEH

Samaria

Tirzah

Mt. Ebal ▲
Mt. Gerizim ▲

Shechem

Penuel

Tel Qasile

Me Jarkon

Jabbok R.

Joppa

Valley of Aijalon

Shiloh

GAD

DAN

Gilead

AMMON

Gezer

EPHRAIM

Bethel
Ai

Gibeon

Gilgal
Jericho

Rabbath-Ammon

Valley of Sorek

BENJAMIN

Ashdod

Ekron

Jerusalem
(Jebus)

Ghassul

▲Mt. Nebo

Gath

Azekah

Bethlehem

Ashkelon

Moresheth

JUDAH

REUBEN

Shephelah

Lachish

Hebron

Dead
Sea

Gaza

PHILISTIA

En-gedi

Arnon R.

Besor Br.

MOAB

Beersheba

Arad

Tell Abu Matar

Hormah

SIMEON

NEGEB

Zered Br.

EDOM

ARABAH

THE KING'S HIGHWAY

TRANSJORDAN

CENTRAL HILL COUNTRY

Jordan R.

SINAI

| 0 | 10 | 20 | 30 | 40 miles |
| 0 | 10 | 20 | 30 | 40 kilometers |

© 1996 GeoSystems Global Corp.

PALESTINE 🏺   25

Homeland of Israel

Of all the lands involved in OT history, tiny Palestine played the most important role because it was the homeland of ancient Israel, where many important OT events took place. Ancient Palestine was located on the west end of the Fertile Crescent and the east end of the Mediterranean Sea. The land was surrounded by the Mediterranean Sea on the west, Phoenicia and Syria on the north, the Arabian desert on the east and southeast, and Sinai and Egypt on the south and southwest.

Palestine's boundaries fluctuated during the course of OT history, the traditional northern boundary being located near Dan and the southern boundary near Beersheba, leading to the expression "from Dan to Beersheba" (Judg 20:1). It was a long and slender land approximately 150 miles long, about thirty to forty miles wide in the north and fifty to sixty miles wide in the south. It was both a homeland and a land bridge: a land bridge connecting Egypt and Arabia with the rest of the Fertile Crescent; a connecting link between the lands of the Fertile Crescent and the Mediterranean world; a land sometimes in the mainstream, sometimes in the backwater; a land with limited resources, but also a land that experienced unparalleled development; and a land that witnessed and was affected by numerous political changes, both local and international.

During the course of history the land was known by different names including Canaan, Israel, and Palestine. The first two are found in the Bible and the latter in the Greek historian Herodotus. All three designations are derived from a group that in biblical times occupied the land or some part of it—Canaan, from the Canaanites, one of the earliest groups to inhabit the land (Gen 12:5–6); Israel, from the Israelites (2 Kgs 5:2); and Palestine, from the Philistines who occupied the southwest part of the land known as Philistia.

Palestine has several distinct geographical regions of special interest, five narrow bands of land running north and south, each with its own unique characteristics. The westernmost coastal plain is a gentle rolling plain that extends the length of the land, interrupted only by the Mount Carmel mountain range. The shephelah, though generally not mentioned among the major geographical divisions of Palestine, was nevertheless a region of strategic importance, a very slender wedge-shaped area, for all practical purposes the foothills, located between the central hill country of Judah and the coastal plain. Many of the important passes connecting the coastal plain with the central hill country went through the shephelah. The central hill country, often called the backbone of the land, and the area the Israelites originally settled following the conquest, is the third and largest of the geographical regions. The Jordan River valley, the fourth of the geographical regions, also known as the Rift valley, is perhaps the most unusual of the regions, reaching a depth of 1295 feet below sea level at the Dead Sea. The Transjordan, the fifth of the geographical regions, is the highland plateau east of the Jordan River and the Dead Sea.

In recent times archaeological research has provided valuable information concerning the beginnings of life and culture in the land: discoveries in the caves along the Mount Carmel mountain range; the evidence of the Natufian culture in the wadi Natuf, which subsisted by hunting and gathering wild grain; the Neolithic prepottery and pottery cultures at Jericho which introduced early agricultural practices including the cultivation of wheat and barley and the domestication of small animals including goats and sheep; the Chalcolithic remains at En-gedi and Ghassul; and the development of urban life in the land during the Early Bronze Age. These early developments provide a backdrop for the OT period, which began with the Middle Bronze Age and continued through Late Bronze, Iron Age I, Iron Age II, Persian, Hellenistic, and Roman periods.

During the course of OT history Palestine was the homeland of several different groups including the Canaanites, Amorites, Hittites, Jebusites, Horites, Philistines, and Israelites. Some of these groups are difficult to define clearly. Both the Philistines and Israelites, two groups that supposedly arrived in the land near the end of the thirteenth century, fought for supremacy of Palestine. According to the Bible, around 1000 BCE David united the land into one kingdom, the kingdom of Israel, and put the Philistine threat to rest. However, the united kingdom of Israel was short-lived. Following the death of Solomon in 922 BCE, the united kingdom of Israel divided into the kingdom of Israel and the kingdom of Judah. During the eighth century BCE, the kingdom of Israel entered a period of decline and in 722 BCE fell to the Assyrians. The kingdom of Judah came to an end in 587 BCE with the destruction of Jerusalem by the Babylonians. During the periods that followed, Palestine came successively under the control of the Persians, the Greeks under Alexander the Great, the Ptolemies of Egypt, the Seleucids of Syria, the Hasmoneans of Judah, and the Romans.

Palestine's relationship to the rest of the Fertile Crescent during the OT period was a unique one. It formed an important land bridge through which the major trade routes from Egypt to Mesopotamia passed. Palestine itself had two major highways that traversed its territory, the coastal plain highway, often called the Via Maris or Way of the Sea, and the King's Highway in the Transjordan. The location of the highways made them a part of the international trade route system; caravans and merchants from every direction passed through Palestine—from Egypt to the southwest, Arabia to the south, Syria and Anatolia to the north, and Mesopotamia to the east. Consequently, many imperialistic powers during the course of OT history attempted to control Palestine.

The villages, towns, and cities of Palestine played an important role in the OT story. Jericho was founded around 8000 BCE, possibly making it the oldest city in the world. Abraham worshiped and in many instances built altars at a number of sites, including Shechem, Jerusalem, and Beersheba. The books of Joshua and Judges refer to numerous cities, many apparently functioning as hubs of city-states of the Canaanites, whom the Israelites encountered during the period of the conquest and settlement (Josh 6–11; Judg 1). The cities of the Philistine pentapolis (1 Sam 6:17) were also significant centers during that same period. After David established Jerusalem as the capital of all the tribes (2 Sam 5:6–12), both David and Solomon, apparently through the use of corvée labor, refortified many of the cities (1 Kgs 9:15–19) throughout the land. Jerusalem became the major center of worship with the construction of the temple (1 Kgs 5–7; 9:15). During the period of the divided monarchy, Rehoboam attempted to secure the southern kingdom by refortifying its major cities (2 Chron 11:5–12), and Jeroboam attempted to establish a new capital (1 Kgs 12:25; 14:17) and new worship centers in the north (1 Kgs 12:26–29). The problem of a new capital in the north was resolved when King Omri built Samaria (1 Kgs 16:24). The kings of both kingdoms experienced attacks by invaders such as Shishak, the king of Egypt (1 Kgs 14:25–28), and Sennacherib, the king of Assyria (2 Kgs 18:13). Ultimately both kingdoms fell to imperialistic powers, and the capital city of each kingdom was either captured or destroyed. Samaria, the capital of the northern kingdom, was captured by the Assyrians in 722 BCE (2 Kgs 17:6), and Jerusalem, capital of the southern kingdom, was destroyed by the Babylonians in 587 BCE (2 Kgs 25:8–17).

While many of the cities throughout the land apparently lay in ruins during the Babylonian period, the temple (Ezra 3:8–13; 5:1–2; 6:13–15) and walls of Jerusalem (Neh 3:1–32) were rebuilt during the Persian period. During the periods that followed, especially the Hellenistic and Roman periods, many old cities of Palestine were rebuilt and new cities were constructed. Herod the Great was especially instrumental in giving the land a new appearance.

Bibliography: AHARONI, Y., *The Land of the Bible: A Historical Geography,* rev. and enl. (Philadelphia: Westminster, 1979); AHARONI, Y., and M. Avi–Yonah, *The Macmillan Bible Atlas* (New York: Macmillan, 1968); BALY, D., *Basic Biblical Geography* (Philadelphia: Fortress, 1987); idem, *The Geography of the Bible* (New York: Harper & Row, 1957); BALY, D., and A. D. Tushingham, *Atlas of the Biblical World* (New York: World, 1971); BAR-YOSEF, O., "Palestine: Prehistoric Palestine," *OEANE,* 4:207–12; BEITZEL, B. J., *The Moody Atlas of Bible Lands* (Chicago: Moody, 1985); BLAIKLOCK, E. M., "Palestine," *NIDB,* 742–48; DEVER, W. G., "Syria-Palestine," *OEANE,* 5:147; DORSEY, D. A., *The Roads and Highways of Ancient Israel* (Baltimore and London: The Johns Hopkins University Press, 1991); ELWELL, W. A., "Palestine," *BEB,* 2:1598–1604; FRANK, H. T., ed., *Hammond's Atlas of the Bible Lands,* new ed. (Maplewood: Hammond, 1984); idem, "Holy Land Horizons," *Discovering the Biblical World,* rev. ed.; ed. James F. Strange (Maplewood: Hammond, 1988) 18–30; GRAF, D. F., "Palestine: Palestine in the Persian through Roman Periods," *OEANE,* 4:222–28; HOPKINS, D. C., "Palestine, Geography of," *MDB,* 637–42; HOUSTON, J. M., "Palestine," *NBD²,* 865–71; JOFFE, A. H., "Palestine: Palestine in the Bronze Age," *OEANE,* 4:212–17; KING, P. J., "Palestine," *HBD,* 740–46; LASOR, W. S., "Palestine," *ISBE,* 3:632–49; MAY, H. G., ed., *Oxford Bible Atlas,* 3d ed. (New York: Oxford University Press, 1984); MAZAR, A., "Palestine: Palestine in the Iron Age," *OEANE,* 4:217–22; MCCOWN, C. C., "Palestine, Geography of," *IDB,* 3:626–39; ORNI, E., and E. Efrat, *Geography of Israel* (Jerusalem: Israel Universities Press, 1973); PATERSON, J. H., "Palestine," *ZPEB,* 4:564–86; PFEIFFER, C. F., ed., *Baker's Bible Atlas,* rev. ed. (Grand Rapids: Baker, 1973); PRITCHARD, J. B., ed., *The*

Harper's Atlas of the Bible (New York: Harper & Row, 1987); RAPHAEL, C. N., "Geography and the Bible (Geography of Palestine)," *ABD*, 2:964–77; RASMUSSEN, C. G., *NIV Atlas of the Bible* (Grand Rapids: Zondervan, 1989); ROGERSON, J., *Atlas of the Bible* (New York: Facts On File Publications, 1985); TRAMMEL, T., "Palestine," *HolBD*, 1063–69; TURNER, G. A., *Historical Geography of the Holy Land* (Washington, D.C.: Canon, 1973).

AI

Citadel of Terrace Farming during the Iron Age

Ai's greatest fame in biblical history comes from the role it played in the Israelite conquest of the land of Canaan described in the book of Joshua. The stories in Joshua 6-11 seem to provide insight concerning the military campaigns, battles, and skirmishes connected with the conquest. The Israelites crossed the Jordan (Josh 3–4), set up their base of operation at Gilgal (Josh 5), and engaged in what appears to be roughly three major military campaigns—a central campaign (Josh 6–8), a southern campaign (Josh 9–10), and a northern campaign (Josh 11). Ai was the second major site the Israelites encountered in the central campaign (Josh 7–8).

Ai was located in the central hill country, according to the biblical account "near Bethaven, east of Bethel" (Josh 7:2). Today Ai, which means "ruin" in Hebrew, is generally identified with the site of et-Tell, which means "ruin" or "mound of ruins" in Arabic. Though some question this identification, et-Tell seems to be the most viable of all the sites in the region based on both the biblical description of the location and the archaeological remains of an Iron Age I village at the site. The site also fits well the location of Ai mentioned in the patriarchal narratives in which Abraham upon entering the land of Canaan came to an area east of Bethel where he "pitched his tent, with Bethel on the west and Ai on the east" (Gen 12:8), and later returned "to the place where his tent had been at the beginning, between Bethel and Ai" (Gen 13:3). The investigation of et-Tell began with John Garstang, who in 1928 conducted soundings at the site. Judith Marquet-Krause conducted the 1933–35 Rothschild expedition that discovered the ruins of both an Early Bronze city and an Iron Age I village. But Marquet-Krause died, and the excavations in 1936 came under the direction of Samuel Yeivin. Joseph Callaway led major excavations at the site from 1964 to 1972.

Under his direction the joint expedition to Ai attempted to continue the work interrupted by the death of Marquet-Krause, to clarify the chronology of the site, and to look for new evidence regarding the role of the site in the conquest.

The excavations of Marquet-Krause and Callaway indicate that Ai, et-Tell, was occupied during two major periods, the Early Bronze Age (ca. 3100–2350 BCE) and the Iron Age I (ca. 1220–1050 BCE) with an eleven-hundred-year gap in between. The original occupation of Ai began ca. 3100 BCE when a small unwalled village was established at the site. During its Early Bronze history Ai grew from a small village to a sizable city or town and in the process experienced several significant changes. The first major change came ca. 3000 BCE as newcomers arrived and built a new walled city at Ai. These newcomers from north Syria and Anatolia were responsible for establishing Ai as a major urban center. The new city covered some twenty-seven acres and included a temple, a royal palace, and sizable private dwellings. Already at this point trade and commerce played an important role in supplementing agriculture, shepherding, and herding as the foundation for the local economy. About 2850 BCE Ai's defense system was strengthened, perhaps due to some threat. The inhabitants of the city increased the width of its walls. Egyptian influence at Ai was already evident during this period.

Iron Age pillar buildings at Ai

About 2700 BCE the city experienced a major destruction, the cause of which is still undetermined, and a new city was built. The new city reflects strong Egyptian influence. It included a large rectangular temple with pillar bases down the center of the temple court, all of which are Egyptian. The temple had many Egyptian architectural features and was apparently built by either Egyptian masons or builders who were skilled in the use of Egyptian building techniques. A large community reservoir was also constructed at Ai during this period. The new earthen reservoir was lined with stones and had a capacity of almost one-half million gallons. Many of the people who moved into Ai ca. 2550 BCE brought with them influences from Khirbet Kerak. The Early Bronze city of Ai was destroyed ca. 2350 BCE, and the site lay in ruins until 1220 BCE.

About 1220 BCE the site was inhabited again, but this time on a much smaller scale. According to archaeological evidence newcomers came from the north—they may have been Hittites from north Syria—and established the first Iron Age I settlement at Ai when they built a small village approximately three acres in size (in contrast to the twenty-seven acre Early Bronze city). The new village atop the ruins of the earlier city was an unwalled agricultural village that had cobble-stone-paved streets. The newcomers lived in pillar houses, in which stone pillars or piers were used as roof supports. They engaged in farming and adopted terrace farming or agricultural methods designed for the hilly terrain of that area. They obtained their water by cutting cisterns out of bedrock, often within a room of the house.

About 1125 BCE another wave of newcomers arrived at Ai and established the second Iron Age I village. The newcomers not only adapted and remodeled the facilities but also expanded the size of the village. One of the most noticeable features of this period is the numerous silo granaries built throughout the village, on the cobblestone streets as well as in buildings of the preceding periods. This reflects the agricultural base of the community and the extensive use of terrace farming techniques.

In the absence of any Late Bronze ruins at Ai, Joseph Callaway proposed that the conquest of Ai described in Joshua 7–8 is best associated with newcomers who arrived and took control of the site ca. 1125 BCE. According to the biblical account, when Joshua and the Israelites initially approached the site, they were soundly defeated by the citizens of Ai (Josh 7). After confronting the sin of Achan and regrouping, they were successful in capturing the site (Josh 8). For some, this account does not answer the question of the conquest of Ai. They propose that the real Ai has not yet been located and still awaits discovery. Others have proposed that the stories in Joshua 7–8 are etiological and lack historical value, or that the story of the conquest of Ai is really the story of the conquest of Bethel. For Callaway the archaeological finds helped not only to illuminate the conquest of the site itself but also to fix the time it took place as 1125 BCE, approximately one hundred years later than many scholars have maintained. Regardless of the continuing debate concerning Ai and the conquest, the archaeological remains excavated at the site have yielded valuable insights concerning the Early Bronze city and the Iron Age I agricultural village.

Perhaps most intriguing among the artifacts discovered by Judith Marquet-Krause are the cultic remains from the Iron Age village including an Iron Age sanctuary and a pottery offering stand. While the sanctuary was designed like the other domestic buildings at the site and while some might prefer to label it a household shrine rather than an Iron Age sanctuary, its cultic use is certainly implied by the pottery offering stand as well as a ritual bowl that may have been used with the pottery offering stand, the figurine of an ox and the figurine of a small animal. The pottery offering stand resembles a large storage jar with some forty openings or windows giving it the appearance a house. Five lion's paws are located on the exterior of the stand extending outward from the base. The offering stand and its motifs seem to reflect local Canaanite influence as well as north Syria and Anatolia. In addition to the cultic remains discovered at Ai, the Ai-Raddana excavations directed by Joseph Callaway recovered a libation bowl in the ruins of the village at Raddana, which is of the same period as the Iron Age village at Ai. Only a portion of the libation bowl was found, but originally it had eighteen looped handles around it. The inner part of the bowl was designed with a conduit tube around the upper rim of the bowl. Libation offerings were poured into the tube on one side, flowed through the tube to the opposite side of the bowl, and exited the tube into the bowl through two spouts that look like the heads of either a lion or a bull.

Raddana Bowl

The cultic remains at the site provide valuable information about the cultic practices of the Iron Age Israelite village. The design of the pottery offering stand and its motifs, as well as other artifacts, reflects cultic influence from north Syria and the local Canaanite population. The cylindrical pottery stand with its windows suggests that the stand was recognized and revered by those who used it as the house of God, a localized house of God or miniature temple. The lion's paws extending from the base of the stand were designed with flat fingerlike projections, a lion-paw design commonly found in the cultic remains in temples in north Syria. And the small animal figurine found in the offering stand, which was probably that of a mouse but was identified by Judith Marquet-Krause as a marten, was a cultic symbol that would have had definite implications in a grain-producing community. Mice and other forms of pestilence would be a constant threat, and this cultic symbol would most likely be associated with a deity like Resheph, the god of plagues and pestilence. The cultic remains from the Iron Age village at Ai seem to reflect the cultic practices of ancient Israel as described in the book of Judges: "And the people of Israel did what was evil in the sight of the LORD, forgetting the LORD their God, and serving the Baals and the Asheroth" (Judg 3:7).

Bibliography: AHARONI, Y., *The Archaeology of the Land of Israel* (Philadelphia: Westminster, 1978); BLAIKLOCK, E. M., "Ai," *NIDBA,* 14; CALLAWAY, J. A., "Ai," *ABD,* 1:125–30; idem, "Ai," *NEAEHL,* ed. Ephraim Stern (New York: Simon & Schuster,

1993) 39–45; idem, "Ai," *IDBSup*, 14–16; COHEN, A., "Ai," *IDB*, 1:72–73; COOLEY, R. E., "Ai," *OEANE*, 1:32–33; DRINKARD, J. F., "Ai," *HBD*, 18; FINKELSTEIN, J., "Ai," *The Archaeology of the Israelite Settlement* (Jerusalem: Israel Exploration Society, 1988) 69–72; FINLEY, H. E., "Ai," *BEB*, 1:45–46; HARRISON, R. K., "Ai," *ISBE*, 1:81–84; HUCKABY, G. C., "Ai," *HolBD*, 29–30; MATTINGLY, G. L., "Ai," *MDB*, 18; MILLARD, A. R., "Ai," *NBD*², 22–23; SCHOVILLE, K. N., "Ai," *BAF*, 277–83.

ASHKELON   27

Harbor City of the Canaanites and Philistines

Along with Ashdod, Ekron, Gaza, and Gath, Ashkelon was one of the cities that formed the Philistine pentapolis, league of five city-states with which the Israelites encountered conflict. While perhaps the leading city of this league was Gath, located geographically like a hub of a wheel with the other four arranged in a semicircular fashion to the west, Ashkelon had features that contributed uniquely to this federation.

Located on the Mediterranean coast, a distinction held by none of the other Philistine cities, Ashkelon had characteristics and natural resources that contributed to its settlement, growth, and development over a history that spanned from the Neolithic period (fifth millennium BCE) down to the Mamluk period (thirteenth century CE). Of the local features that formed the city's economic base, the fertile soil, the fresh water provided by underground prehistoric water channels, and its location on the Mediterranean coast were perhaps the most important. Fertile soil and fresh water provided the essentials for habitation, and its position on the Via Maris, the coastal plain highway that was a part of the international route connecting Egypt and Mesopotamia, contributed to Ashkelon's status as a major center of trade. Consequently, during the course of its history, Ashkelon enjoyed an economy based on agriculture and land and sea trade. As an agricultural center, Ashkelon was a source of cultivated cereal crops such as wheat and barley, as well as other commodities including dates, onions and vegetables, and the tropical oriental shrub, henna. Today, the name Ashkelon, also spelled Ascalon, survives in the name scallion, a type of onion found in modern-day vegetable markets.

References to Ashkelon occur in both biblical and extrabiblical literature. According to the Bible, Ashkelon was one of the five major cities that comprised the Philistine city-state system (Josh 13:3; 1 Sam

6:4, 17). Though the site was located in the territory allotted to Judah, it remained unconquered (Judg 1:18). During the period of the Judges, Samson went to Ashkelon in a rage of anger and killed thirty men following his betrayal in the riddle episode (Judg 14:19). In an attempt to divert the wrath of Yahweh, the God of Israel, Ashkelon along with the other cities of the Philistine pentatopolis returned a guilt offering with the ark of the covenant (1 Sam 6:17). The city is also mentioned in the elegy David chanted for Saul and Jonathan (2 Sam 1:20), who were killed in battle against the Philistines (1 Sam 31). References to Ashkelon also appear in the prophetic literature: Amos condemns Ashkelon, Ashdod, and Ekron for their apparent involvement in slave trade with Gaza (Amos 1:6–8); and the prophets Jeremiah, Zephaniah, and Zechariah speak of the impending doom of the city (Jer 25:20; 47:5–7; Zeph 2:4–7; Zech 9:5).

The important role Ashkelon played in history and the status the city enjoyed are highlighted further by references to it in other ancient Near Eastern texts. For instance, Ashkelon is mentioned in the Egyptian Execration texts, which date to the nineteenth and eighteenth centuries BCE. Such references indicate that it was an important city already during the Middle Bronze Age, the period of the Patriarchs. References to the site also appear in the Amarna letters, which reveal that it was a vassal city-state of Egypt during the Late Bronze Age. The correspondence included several letters written by the city-state king of Ashkelon, Widya, who promised his support of the Egyptian king by providing Egypt with commodities such as oil, grain, bread, beer, and cattle; however, in another letter Abdi-Heba, the city-state king of Jerusalem, accused Ashkelon's ruler of supporting the Habiru who were responsible for putting the land of Canaan in a state of turmoil. A relief at Karnak, which dates to the time of the Egyptian ruler Merneptah, and the Merneptah stele both reflect Ashkelon's attempt to break away from Egyptian domination near the end of the thirteenth century BCE. The Karnak relief portrays Egyptian troops besieging the city. The Merneptah stele perhaps refers to the event on the relief when it states, "carried off is Ashkelon." (Incidentally, the stele inscription constitutes the earliest reference to Israel outside the Bible.) The city is also mentioned in other ancient Near Eastern texts including an inscription on an ivory plaque discovered in excavations at Megiddo, an Assyrian inscription describing Tiglath-pileser III's campaign against cities in Syria-Palestine, an Assyrian inscription that provides details of Sennacherib's attack on Jerusalem, and a Babylonian inscription describing Esarhaddon's military campaign against Syria-Palestine.

The earliest excavations of Ashkelon were sponsored by the Palestine Exploration Fund and directed by John Garstang, 1920–1922. The most recent fieldwork, the Leon Levy Expedition under the direction of Lawrence Stager, began in 1985 and continues to the present. These excavations have provided valuable information concerning Ashkelon's historical profile and its major features.

Evidence of the earliest settlement of the site comes from the Neolithic Age in the form of round huts, silos, and tools made of bones and flint. The Neolithic village was located on the Mediterranean shore. During the Early Bronze Age, Ashkelon already began to profit from its location. As a major seaport of the Canaanites, it was located on the shipping route that ran from Egypt up along the coast to Byblos. Considering also that an international trade route connecting Egypt and Mesopotamia passed through Ashkelon, it is evident how the city became a center of trade and exchange, a type of way station for donkey caravans.

While a break in occupation at the site occurs following the Early Bronze Age, it was resettled during the Middle Bronze Age. This new city was fortified with a massive earthen embankment or rampart. The embankment, made of packed earth with a surface of mud bricks and field stone, was about thirty meters thick at its base, about fifteen meters high, and had an exterior sloping surface with a pitch or incline of about thirty-five degrees. This protective barrier functioned as the city's fortification during most of its history. One of the most unique discoveries from the Middle Bronze city was a sanctuary built into the stone surface embankment near the entrance of the city. The sanctuary contained a silver calf and a cylindrical pottery model of a temple or cultic shrine in which the calf was found. Apparently, such objects were used in the worship of the god Baal. Other evidence from this period, including pottery and an Assyrian cylinder seal, indicates that Ashkelon was one of the largest cities in Canaan at that time, an important seaport and center of trade and exchange. It was this Middle Bronze city to which the Egyptian Execration texts made reference. But in spite of its status and impressive fortification system, Ashkelon was destroyed around 1550 BCE.

While excavations at the site have failed to provide a clear picture of Ashkelon during the Late Bronze Age, information from the Amarna Letters, the relief of the city under siege by the Egyptians found in the temple at Karnak, and the Merneptah inscription all suggest that Ashkelon was under Egyptian control at this time. Though evidence from this period is meager, the discovery of burials has provided new insight concerning interment customs at Ashkelon during the Late Bronze Age. The graves featured the deceased entombed in a vault lined with mud bricks, and the bodies were accompanied by the essentials for the hereafter, including food offerings of animals, such as sheep, goats, and birds.

During the period known as Iron Age I, major changes took place at Ashkelon. With the arrival of the Philistines, the city was expanded to about 150 acres and was refortified. The monochrome and later bichrome pottery was decorated with spirals and geometric designs and motifs characteristic of the Philistine pottery of that era. The discovery of cylindrical pottery loom weights suggests that weaving played a significant role in the Iron Age Philistine city. And the discovery of swine bones reflects the role pigs played in animal production, a feature of the Philistine community not found in Israelite communities of that time. Throughout this period, the city was a major seaport.

Among the discoveries from the Iron Age II period were different types of Phoenician pottery suggesting strong Phoenician influence, and a number of different kinds of fish indicating the role fishing played in the economy of Ashkelon. The city was captured by the Assyrian king Tiglath-pileser III about 732 BCE and was destroyed by the Babylonian king Nebuchadnezzar around 604 BCE. As with the citizens of Judah and Jerusalem, the Babylonians deported people from Ashkelon to Babylonia.

With the rise of Persia and the demise of the Babylonian empire, the history of Ashkelon took a new turn. The Persian period at Ashkelon is well attested in the thick deposits discovered at the site. During this time the city witnessed the construction of large buildings made of ashlar stones and mud bricks. The presence of warehouses reflects Ashkelon's role as an important seaport. Of the discoveries from this period, that of a massive dog cemetery is most unusual; indeed, it is the largest known cemetery of its kind in the ancient world. The burial site included the remains or partial remains of more than eight hundred dogs, and each grave followed a special pattern with the dog placed on its side, the legs flexed up close to its body, and the tail tucked around its back legs. The special care exhibited in the burials suggests the animals were considered sacred and were perhaps part of a healing cult that had ties to the Phoenician culture. The discovery of Phoenician inscriptions as well as other artifacts suggests that the Phoenician culture was predominant at Ashkelon during the Persian period. About 300 BCE, the city was destroyed, marking the end of the Persian period site.

Discoveries at Ashkelon from the Hellenistic period include apartment villas and a colonnade that apparently led to a theater. During the Roman and Byzantine periods, Ashkelon functioned again as a major seaport of the eastern Mediterranean. While the discovery of a marble seat and a circular depression with steps indicates the presence of a Greco-Roman theater, evidence of the theater is limited since the stones of the complex were robbed during later periods and used in other building projects. In addition to the theater, excavations revealed remains of a large facility 110 meters long and thirty-five meters wide. The structure was designed with a rectangular central courtyard surrounded by twenty-four columns that functioned most likely as a forum. Accompanying the forum was a basilica which, like the forum, probably dated to the third century CE. Pillars that were a part of an apse located on the south side of the forum were decorated with a variety of deities including Nike, Isis and Horus, Aphrodite, Hermes, and Pan. Other artifacts discovered from the Roman city include a first-century CE bone token perhaps used as a theater ticket, and lead and marble coffins. Historically, Ashkelon holds the distinction of being the city from which Herod's family came. According to Josephus, some 2500 Jews were slaughtered in Ashkelon during the early stages of the Jewish-Roman War (*War* 2.477). During the Byzantine period Ashkelon was equipped with a bathhouse constructed on the site of the apartment villas. The cosmopolitan flair of the city, the result of ties with other communities around the Mediterranean, is evident in the discovery of numerous amphorae from throughout the Mediterranean, Aegean, and Black Sea areas. Excavations have also revealed church and synagogue remains that date to the Byzantine period. By the mid sixth century CE Ashkelon became an important center of Christianity and the location of the seat of a bishop.

With the arrival of the Muslims during the seventh century, Ashkelon became a Muslim city; however, Christians and Jews continued to live there. The fortifications of the city were rebuilt once again during the Fatimid period (ca. 975–1171 CE). Excavations have recovered the remains of houses each designed with a courtyard in which a garden and pool were located. The city was captured by the Crusaders from the Fatimids in 1153 CE, but it fell to Saladin in 1187. The history of the site finally came to an end in 1270 as the city was destroyed by the Mamluks.

Bibliography: AVI-YONAH, M., and Y. Eph'al, "Ashkelon," *EAEHL,* 1:121–30; CRAWFORD, T. G., "Ashkelon," *MDB,* 69; ESSE, D. L., "Ashkelon," *ABD,* 1:487–90; KNIGHT, G. W., "Ashkelon," *HolBD,* 112; PREWITT, J. F., "Ashkelon," *ISBE,* 1:318–19; REID, S. B., "Ashkelon," *HBD,* 75; SCHLOEN, D., "Ashkelon," *OEANE,* 1:220–23; STAGER, L. E., "Ashkelon," *NEAEHL,* 1:103–12; idem, *Ashkelon Discovered* (Washington, D.C.: Biblical Archaeological Society, 1991); idem, "When Canaanites and Philistines Ruled Ashkelon," *BAR* 17 (2, 1991) 24–37, 40–43; idem, "Why Were Hundreds of Dogs Buried at Ashkelon?" *BAR* 17 (2, 1991) 26–42; STINESPRING, W. F., "Ashkelon," *IDB,* 1:252–54; WHITE, W. Jr., "Ashkelon," *ZPEB,* 1:336.

Traditional Southern Boundary of Ancient Israel

Beersheba marked the traditional southern boundary of ancient Israel, just as Dan indicated the northern boundary. But Beersheba was much more than a geographical marker or road sign in OT times. It carried a rich tradition and history. There Abraham made an important covenant concerning a well and water rights. Throughout Israel's history Beersheba served as an important district capital or headquarters. It may also have been a border sanctuary.

Site of ancient Beersheba

Ancient Beersheba is identified with Tell es-Saba, commonly called Tell Beer-sheba, the mound of ruins located approximately three miles east of the modern city of Beersheba. The site was geographically significant for several reasons. Beersheba was located in a basinlike area that formed a boundary between the Judean hill country to the north and the Negeb, a desert area to the south. Rainfall amounts at Beersheba average ten to twelve inches annually, but drop to as little as two inches annually south of Beersheba in the Negeb. Consequently, Beersheba was an important border site between the more productive and habitable central hill country of Judah and the extremely arid Negeb region to the south. Although rainfall at Beersheba was limited, the annual winter and spring rains that fell in the fertile basin and on the hills in the region provided enough vegetation to graze sheep and goats during spring and early summer. This resulted in an annual influx of shepherds and herdsmen to the Beersheba region. The area around Beersheba, often called the Beersheba valley, was a major junction. The basin was formed by the convergence of two wadis from the east, one from the direction of Hebron and the other from the direction of Arad, Hormah, and the Arabah. After converging at Beersheba, the wadi continued westward forming the Wadi Besor that moved eventually in a northwesterly direction to the Mediterranean Sea. But wadi beds, which are stream beds carrying water during the rainy season, have a greater significance. During the dry season the wadi beds were used as highways by merchants and caravans. In addition to the wadis, the major north-south route of the central hill country passed through Beersheba. Thus Beersheba was located at the crossroads of the major highways and trade routes in the south.

In view of these unique geographical features, it is not surprising that Beersheba was an important biblical site reaching back to the patriarchal period. According to the Bible, the site was given the name Beersheba, meaning "the well of seven," or "well of the oath." Two stories relate to the naming of this site. The meaning "well of the oath" appears to be the result of a covenant established between Abimelech, king of Gerar, and Abraham, who was a semi-nomadic sojourner (Gen 21:22–34). Designed to resolve a dispute over a well, the covenant was sealed by seven ewe lambs that Abraham gave to Abimelech (Gen 21:27–32). This covenant-making ritual involving a well and the water rights demonstrates the important role wells played in this semi-arid region on the northern edge of the Negeb. In another incident, Isaac has a similar experience with Abimelech over water rights (Gen 26:17–33) in which the dispute was also resolved through a covenant (Gen 26:28–29).

Isaac named the new well his servants dug for him *Shibah*, "seven," and consequently the name of the place was Beersheba (Gen 26:32–33). The religious significance of the site already during the patriarchal period is perhaps reflected in the fact that Abraham planted a tamarisk tree in Beersheba at the conclusion of the covenant and called upon the name of El Olam, meaning "God Everlasting," the divine name associated with worship in the area of Beersheba (Gen 21:33–34). The patriarchal narratives further inform us that Hagar "wandered in the wilderness of Beersheba" following her expulsion from Abraham's household (Gen 21:14), that Beersheba was one of the sites at which Abraham lived (Gen 22:19), that it was from Beersheba that Jacob fled from his brother (Gen 28:10), and that it was at Beersheba that Jacob had a vision as he departed for Egypt (Gen 46:1–5).

Following the conquest Beersheba was allotted to the tribe of Simeon (Josh 19:2) but became a part of the territory of Judah (Josh 15:2). Because of its unique location Beersheba was identified perhaps quite early as the border town in the south marking the extent of Israel's territory that ran "from Dan to Beersheba" (Judg 20:1). Beersheba's identity in this capacity became well established and continued throughout the united monarchy and through the divided monarchy. Its role as the southern border town of both the united kingdom and kingdom of Judah is reiterated through history and is mentioned in conjunction with the reigns of Saul (2 Sam 3:10), David (2 Sam 24:2), Solomon (1 Kgs 4:25), Jehoshaphat (2 Chron 19:4), Hezekiah (2 Chron 30:5), and Josiah (2 Kgs 23:8).

As a result of its location on the southern border, Beersheba became a major administrative center, religious center, and border fortress. Early in its history Beersheba apparently was a local administrative center for the region, the so-called Negeb of Judah. For that reason, Samuel appointed his sons, Joel and Abijah, as judges in Beersheba (1 Sam 8:1–2).

Later, David had Joab conduct a census in the southern part of Judah from the regional center in Beersheba (2 Sam 24:1, 7). Both the Bible and archaeological discoveries at the site reflect Beersheba's role as a religious center. Beersheba apparently had a sanctuary similar to the border sanctuaries at Dan and Bethel in the northern kingdom. The worship center at Beersheba was criticized by Amos (Amos 5:5; 8:14), and it was perhaps among those targeted in the reform of Josiah (2 Kgs 23:8).

Excavations at the site have uncovered the rampart, walls, and gateways that were necessary for a border fortress. During the postexilic period Beersheba was among the sites in Judah that were resettled (Neh 11:27). Archaeological exploration of the ancient site was initiated in recent times with soundings conducted at the site in 1962 and a full-scale excavation beginning in 1969. The excavations, directed by Yohanan Aharoni, were sponsored by the Institute of Archaeology, Tel Aviv University.

Excavations at other sites in the area of Beersheba indicate that the earliest occupation of the region dates to the Chalcolithic period. Among the discoveries from that period are a copper metal working industry at Tell Abu Matar. But while excavations at other sites in the vicinity have produced discoveries from the Chalcolithic period, the Aharoni excavations at Beersheba determined that the city itself was founded in the twelfth or eleventh century BCE. Among the important discoveries at the site are the fortifications of the city, private dwellings, a governor's palace, and a well.

During the premonarchic period, the earliest occupation of the site, a village was established. The village may have been an administrative center during the period of the judges, as the account of Samuel's sons would indicate. A fortified city was built at the site during the tenth century BCE, the period of the monarchy. The new city, which covered only three acres, was built on a large, artificially constructed rampart or base approximately twenty-three feet high.

The fortified city went through several occupational levels, each of which experienced destruction. The earliest fortification was probably built by Solomon and consisted of a solid mud-brick wall approximately thirteen feet thick and a gateway. It was surrounded by a glacis (a plastered slope) and a moat. The city was destroyed by fire perhaps in the late tenth century and rebuilt using the original brick wall and gateway. The destruction may have occurred when Shishak, king of Egypt, invaded Judah. After the second destruction, the solid brick wall was replaced by a casemate wall, a double wall with compartments between the sides. King Uzziah probably built the new casemate wall, which stood until it was destroyed in 701 BCE, probably at the hand of Sennacherib, king of Assyria. Following this destruction the ruins of the city were apparently used as a squatters' site, the evidence of which comprises the final phase, stratum I. The fortified city of Beersheba with its earthen rampart base and massive wall on top was apparently a part of a line of border fortresses, including Arad, at the southern edge of Judah.

Of special interest is the city plan, a plan that is characteristic of the royal fortified cities built by the Israelites. The most prominent feature of the plan is the street that encircled the city. The street which begins and ends at the city gate encircled the city at an equal distance inside the city wall. The street was lined with houses on both sides; those on the outside of the street were built against the city wall. Two other streets led from the gate to the center of the city, the highest part of the tell, where public buildings and a sanctuary perhaps stood. The massive city gate (forty-five by fifty-five feet) was designed with chambers, typical of that period. The city was also equipped with a series of long rectangular buildings immediately to the right of the gate. These were divided into three sections by two rows of stone pillars. The function of these buildings is still debated. They may have been used for different purposes, probably the storage of supplies and perhaps stable areas. Private dwellings were also discovered at Beersheba. The dwellings were of the typical four-room house design, comprised of a broad room and three long rooms divided by two rows of pillars.

The most unusual discovery at Beersheba was a large horned altar made of ashlar stones (square, hewn stones). This altar, to be distinguished from the small horned altars usually found in excavations, had been dismantled and its stones reused to repair the walls of the storehouse complex. Along with the other stones of the altar were four, each designed as a horn, that formed the corners of the altar. The altar was perhaps a part of the worship center at Beersheba to which Amos referred (Amos 5:5; 8:14). It was probably dismantled during the reform of Hezekiah (2 Kgs 18:22), a reform designed to remove outlying worship centers and once again centralize worship in Jerusalem. Other cult objects found in the excavations at Beersheba include small clay incense altars, figurines, and kernos or zoomorphic vessels, the latter designed as a circular tubelike object on which animals or birds are perched. An Iron Age crater bearing the Hebrew inscription *qdš* "holy" was obviously used in sacred rituals in the sanctuary. Many of the cult objects found at the Beersheba sanctuary reflect the foreign influences that were criticized by Amos.

Other important discoveries at the site include the so-called governor's palace, a large complex comprised of a large living area and a public area; a large water system similar to those at Megiddo and Hazor with a flight of stairs that leads to a water shaft; and a deep well near the city gate that may come from the patriarchal period.

Bibliography: AHARONI, Y., "Beersheba, Tel," *EAEHL,* 1:160–68; idem, "Excavations at Tel Beer-sheba," *BA* 35 (1972) 111–27; idem, *The Archaeology of the Land of Israel* (Philadelphia: Westminster, 1978); BAILEY, L. R., "Beersheba," *MDB,* 93; BLAIKLOCK, E. M., "Beersheba," *NIDBA,* 94–95; BOYD, B., "Beer-sheba," *IDBSup,* 93–95; COGAN, M., "Beer-sheba," *HBD,* 101; COHEN, S., "Beer-sheba," *IDB,* 1:375–76; FINKELSTEIN, I., "Beersheba Valley," *The Archaeology of the Israelite Settlement* (Jerusalem: Israel Exploration Society, 1988) 37–47; FREDRICKS, D. C., "Beer-Sheba," *HolBD,* 161–63; GATES, J. F., "Beersheba," *NIDB,* 131–32; GOPHNA, R., "Beersheba," *EAEHL,* 1:153–59; HERZOG, Z., "Beersheba," *OEANE,* 1:287–91; idem, "Beer-Sheba of the Patriarchs," *BAR* 6 (6, 1980) 12–28; idem, "Tel Beer-sheba," *NEAEHL,* 1:167–73; MANOR, D. W., "Beer-sheba," *ABD,* 1:641–45; MARTIN, W. J. and A. R. Millard, "Beersheba," *NBD*[2], 128; RAINEY, A. F., "Beer-sheba," *ISBE,* 1:448–51; idem, "Beersheba," *ZPEB,* 1:507–9; SCHOVILLE, K. N., "Beer-sheba," *BAF,* 315–21; VOS, H. F., "Beersheba," *BEB,* 1:274.

City at the Crossroads

The limited number of references in the OT to Bethshan might cause one to conclude that it was an unimportant city. But such was not the case. Bethshan was a major Canaanite city during much of the OT period; in fact this cosmopolitan city has artifacts not only from the local Canaanite culture but also from Egypt, Anatolia, north Syria, and Mesopotamia.

Bethshan is mentioned in ancient Egyptian texts as well. The city is listed among those taken by Pharaoh Thutmose III during his annual campaign to Syria-Palestine in 1468 BCE. About a century later the name appears in one of the Amarna letters. The city-state king of Jerusalem, Abdi-Heba, informed the Egyptian pharaoh, Akhenaton, that a military garrison from Gath-Carmel had been stationed at Bethshan. The name Bethshan also appears in a model letter, Papyrus Anastasi I, used as a writing assignment for young scribes who copied it as a part of their instruction. The letter, which dates to the latter part of the Nineteenth Dynasty, provides information about cities and lands that were a part of the Egyptian empire at that time.

Of the references to Bethshan (also spelled Beth-Shean) in the OT, two seem to be especially important and informative concerning the role of the city in OT history. According to the account of the conquest in the book of Judges, "Bethshean and its villages" (Judg 1:27) were among the major Canaanite cities in the territory of Manasseh not taken in the conquest, though the site was listed as a part of the territory allotted to Manasseh (Josh 17:11). Also of special interest is the reference to Bethshan in connection with the death of Saul. At that time the city of Bethshan was in the hands of the Philistines and was the site to which the Philistines took Saul's body and his armor (1 Sam 31:8–10). The Bible and archaeological research make it quite clear that Bethshan did not come under Israelite control until the time of David or Solomon.

Though the origin and background of the name Bethshan are unknown, the name itself could hold the key to understanding the site. Bethshan means "House of Shan," or "Temple of Shan." Thus the city was apparently named after a god named Shan or Shean, perhaps a serpent deity similar to Sahan, the serpent deity of the ancient Sumerians. Like Bethel, meaning "House of El," and Bethanath, meaning "House of Anath," Bethshan must have been an important center of worship. This conclusion is confirmed by the discovery of five or six major temple complexes, numerous offering stands, dedicatory inscriptions that mention several different deities, and numerous other cult objects. Known as Beisan, the modern town (population 15,000) retains the ancient name. The mound of the ancient city is adjacent to the modern town and is named Tell el-Husn.

Of all the factors that contributed to Bethshan's role as an important city of ancient Palestine, its location must have been most vital. Bethshan was situated on a promontory located at the junction of two important valleys—the Jordan valley and the Jezreel valley. The Jordan valley, which ran north and south, provided a major corridor for a north-south trade route immediately west of the Jordan. The Jezreel valley, an east-west valley, connected with the Esdraelon plain and provided the corridor through which a major trade route moved westward connecting the route in the Jordan valley with the Via Maris on the coast. Consequently, Bethshan was located at the junction where the coastal plain route joined a major inland route, a junction that witnessed the travel of traffic and merchants from all points of the ancient Near East. The important role this trade route played in biblical history is reflected in the story of the death of Saul on Mount Gilboa (1 Sam 31). During the time of Samuel and Saul the Philistines had penetrated the central hill country and apparently controlled the route. In an attempt to regain control of the major highway, Saul moved northward with his army and engaged in battle with the Philistines on Mount Gilboa. He and his forces were utterly defeated, Saul and three of his sons losing their lives (1 Sam 31:6). Located approximately four miles west of the Jordan River and fifteen miles south of the Sea of Galilee, Bethshan was also situated near one of the major fords in the Jordan, which provided a connecting route with the King's Highway, the major north-south route in the Transjordan. Its position as an inland city situated at a major junction of international trade routes must have had a definite bearing on the community's economy.

Other factors that contributed to the importance of the site were the water supply provided by the Jalud River and the fertile soil of the Jezreel valley. The Jalud River, located on the north side of Bethshan, was a perennial river that flowed through the Jezreel valley eastward and emptied into the Jordan River. Its water supply was a major asset to the area. The Jezreel valley with its fertile soil, in essence a broad fertile plain, made the area one of most productive agricultural regions in the land. Consequently, the local economy was based on agriculture.

One final feature that contributed to the site's strategic importance was the size of the mound on which OT Bethshan was situated. The mound, which has a present height of three hundred feet, provided a natural defense system with its steep surrounding incline and a visual command of the surrounding area. This mound, the highest in Palestine, is still approximately 350 feet below sea level.

Remains of a Middle Bronze temple at Bethshan

Excavations at the site conducted by the University of Pennsylvania Museum began in 1921. They were directed by C. S. Fisher (1921–23), Alan Rowe (1925–28), and G. M. Fitzgerald (1930, 1931, 1933). The excavations resulted in the discovery of eighteen occupational layers ranging from the Chalcolithic period, levels XVIII–XVI, to the Byzantine and Arab periods, levels II and I. During the Hellenistic, Roman, and Byzantine periods the city moved from the tell to the valley south of the tell. The new city named Scythopolis was a part of the cities of the Decapolis mentioned in the NT. Today the lower city is being excavated and reconstructed under the direction of the Department of Antiquities of the state of Israel.

Incense stand

The history of the site of Bethshan probably goes back to the pottery Neolithic period of the fifth millennium BCE. Pottery from that period, similar to the pottery of Jericho some forty-five miles to the south, has been found at Bethshan. The earliest occupational level dates to the Chalcolithic period of the fourth millennium BCE. Occupation of the site continued on into the Early and Middle Bronze ages when Bethshan became an important Canaanite town. Remains from this time include private dwellings, public buildings, and streets, though the city at that time did not have a defense wall.

The most significant period in Bethshan's history came during the Late Bronze and Early Iron Age periods. During the Late Bronze Age Bethshan became a major fortified Canaanite city and a center of religion under Egyptian control. Discoveries of the Late Bronze and Iron Age city revealed the city wall and gateway and several temples with accompanying cultic artifacts. While Egyptian control of the site lasted throughout the Late Bronze Age and into the Early Iron Age (which are contained in level IX to level V), it was apparently replaced by Philistine control during the eleventh century BCE (level V), and later by Israelite possession of the site (level IV). Though information is limited, Bethshean is listed among the cities in the tax district of Baana (1 Kgs 4:12) during the reign of Solomon. The Israelite city at Bethshan (level IV) was destroyed, perhaps by Shishak (1 Kgs 14:25), king of Egypt. The site was not occupied again until the Hellenistic period (level III), when it was named Scythopolis.

The temples and their artifacts have been of special interest because they reflect Canaanite worship practices and the deities worshiped at Bethshan. The large temple complex of level IX was apparently dedicated to the god Mekal. It included several altars, the remains of a young bull that had been sacrificed, a sacred standing stone dedicated to the god "Mekal, the lord of Bethshan," and a stone panel depicting a lion and a dog fighting. Mekal is featured with a beard, a tall conical headdress and two gazelle horns projecting from his forehead.

The temple of levels VII and VI was comprised of one main court with two antechambers and altars. A stone panel from the level VII phase of the temple featured a goddess with two horns, who may be the wife of Mekal. A small basalt stele from the level VI phase of the temple was dedicated to "Antit lady of heaven and mistress of all the gods." Two additional temples were found in level V, a southern temple and a northern temple. The two temples dedicated to Resheph and Antit are perhaps the temples of Dagon and Ashteroth mentioned in the account of Saul's death (1 Chron 10:10; 1 Sam 31:10). Numerous pottery offering stands were also found among the ruins of the level V temples.

Of the artifacts found in the temple ruins, those of the pottery offering stands are among the most unique. The offering stands were designed in two basic shapes, cylindrical stands and house-shaped stands. The cylindrical stands had a bell-shaped base with two handles and numerous triangular-shaped windows cut in the wall of the stand. The stands were apparently designed with windows in order that the stand would have a houselike appearance. The stands were decorated further with reliefs of doves and serpents. The house-shaped stands were square and were designed to have the appearance of a two- or three-story house.

Anthropoid coffin from Bethshan

The house-shaped stands had windows and doors as well as other decorations including serpents, doves, lions, and humanlike figurines apparently representing deities. The offering stands were most likely used in a variety of Canaanite fertility rituals. Evidence from stelae, inscriptions, clay figurines, and other artifacts suggests that Canaanite worship at Bethshan was influenced by gods and religious practices from other areas including Egypt, Anatolia and north Syria, and Mesopotamia. Among the gods worshiped at Bethshan were Mekal, Resheph, Baal, Antit, Anath, Astarte, Dagon, and Ashteroth.

Also of interest are the anthropoid clay coffins used in burials and discovered in the nearby cemetery at Bethshan. The coffins, not usually found in burials in Palestine, have the appearance of a mummy and are designed with a removable lid. The lid, decorated with features that probably belong to the person inside, resembles the upper part of a human body including the face, arms, and headdress. The coffins, discovered in Philistine burials at other sites, apparently reflect the presence of the Philistines or Sea Peoples at the site.

Bibliography: COLE, D., "Beth-shean," *HolBD,* 173–75; DRINKARD, J. F., "Beth-shan," *HBD,* 108–9; ELWELL, W. A., "Beth-shan, Beth-shean," *BEB,* 1:291–92; FITZGERALD, G. M., "Beth-shean," *Archaeology and Old Testament Study,* ed. D. Winton Thomas (Oxford: Clarendon, 1967) 185–96; FRY, V., "Beth-shan," *MDB,* 98–99; HAMILTON, R. W., "Beth-Shan," *IDB,* 1:397–401; HARRISON, R. K., "Beth Shan, Beth Shean," *NIDBA,* 100; HOUSTON, J. M., "Beth-shean," *ZPEB,* 1:543–45; KEMPINSKI, A., F. James, N. Tzori, and D. Bahat, "Beth-shean," *EAEHL,* 1:207–29; MAZAR, A., "Beth-Shean," *OEANE,* 1:305–9; idem, "Beth-Shean (Tel Beth-Shean and the Northern Cemetery)," *NEAEHL,* 1:214–23; MCGOVERN, P. E., "Beth-shan," *ABD,* 1:693–96; MITCHELL, T. C., "Bethshean, Bethshan," *NBD*[2], 135–36; PRAUSNITZ, M. W., "Beth-shan," *IDBSup,* 97–98; RAINEY, A. F., "Beth-Shean," *ISBE,* 1:475–78; ROSS, A. M., "Beth Shan, Beth Shean," *NIDB,* 144–45; SCHOVILLE, K. N., "Beth-shan," *BAF,* 329–35; SHANKS, H., "Glorious Beth-Shean," *BAR* 16 (4, 1990) 16–31; THOMPSON, J. A., "Beth-shan," *BW,* 143–45.

DAN    30

Traditional Northern Boundary of Ancient Israel

Dan marked the traditional northern boundary of Israel in OT times just as Beersheba marked Israel's southern boundary. Like its counterpart in the south, Dan was much more than just a geographical marker. It was an important site with its own unique history of development. Woven throughout the history of the site was the role it played as a major center of worship, beginning in the Canaanite period (i.e., the Middle or Early Bronze Age) and continuing through the Israelite period (with interruption) to the Hellenistic and Roman periods. Information from the Bible and archaeological research indicates that the site of Dan served a variety of functions during its history including border sanctuary, border fortress, and center of trade.

According to the Bible the city became a part of Israelite territory following its conquest by the tribe of Dan (Judg 18). Prior to that, the city was a major Canaanite stronghold named Laish (Judg 18:7) or Leshem (Josh 19:47). Following the conquest, during which the city was burned with fire (Judg 18:27), the Danites rebuilt the city and named it Dan (Judg 18:28–29).

The site of Laish was selected by a search team (Judg 18:2, 7). The team was apparently deployed because the tribe had difficulty finding and securing a permanent homeland (Josh 19:40–47; Judg 1:34; 18:1). Both the site and its location had features that made it attractive for settlement. These features are quite obvious even today. The site of Dan, presently known as Tell el-Qadi, which means "Mound of the judge," or simply as Tell Dan, is a large quadrangular-shaped mound seventy feet high and covering an area of about fifty acres. It is located in a fertile region at the southern base of Mount Hermon. Located twenty-five miles north of the Sea of Galilee, the site is situated at one of the major sources of the Jordan River, the Nahr Leddan, and overlooks the fertile Huleh valley to the south. The Nahr Leddan, a major spring of the Mount Hermon range, provided the site with a perennial supply of fresh water, and the fertile valley provided valuable land for agriculture. Consequently, the area from ancient times to the present has been used for the production of grain, fruit, and vegetables.

The site was located at the intersection of two major routes. One, the east-west route, extended from the Phoenician city-state of Tyre on the coast to inland Damascus, which was the caravan and trade center in southern Syria on the route connecting the lands of the Fertile Crescent. The second was the north-south route that came from Hazor and moved northward through the Beth-rehob valley (Judg 18:28), the pass that separated the Lebanon Mountains on the west from Mount Hermon on the east. Located at this important crossroads, the site occupied a strategic position that provided both advantages and challenges to the population that controlled it.

The important role the site played in ancient history is demonstrated in biblical literature as well as other ancient Near Eastern sources. It is mentioned in the Execration Texts and the records of Thutmose III, both of which reflect the selection and exploitation of valuable and strategic city-states in Palestine and Syria by the Egyptians during the Middle Bronze and Late Bronze ages. Its involvement in the international trade market is reflected in the Mari tablets, which contain information about the city's purchase of tin from Mari.

In the Bible, Dan is mentioned many times. It was to the area of Dan that Abraham pursued the kings who had taken Lot captive (Gen 14:14). During the tribal period the city was conquered by the tribe of Dan and became their home (Judg 18). During the rule of the united monarchy "from Dan to Beersheba" (Judg 20:1; 1 Sam 3:20; 2 Sam 3:10; 17:11; 24:2; 1 Kgs 4:25), Dan became the traditional northern boundary. Following the death of Solomon in 922 BCE and the division of the kingdom, Jeroboam I established Dan and Bethel as border sanctuaries of the northern kingdom (1 Kgs 12:29). Because of Dan's location on the northern border of Israelite territory, it functioned as a border fortress and was always subject to attack by Israel's neighbors to the north, the Syrians. The site apparently witnessed frequent skirmishes and was conquered by the Syrians during the reign of the Syrian king Benhadad (1 Kgs 15:20). It was recaptured during the reign of Jeroboam II (2 Kgs

14:25). With the fall of Samaria and the northern kingdom in 722 BCE, Dan became a part of the Assyrian empire.

Continuing excavations that began in 1966 at Tell Dan under the direction of Avraham Biran have provided valuable information concerning the history of the site. We may assume that Dan was initially settled during the pottery Neolithic period, since remains of that period, though questionable, have been found. By the middle of the third millennium BCE, the Early Bronze Age, Dan was already an important city with an estimated population of eight to ten thousand people. During the early part of the Middle Bronze Age (1900–1700 BCE) the city, then Canaanite, was fortified with a massive earthen rampart that surrounded it and a mud-brick arched gateway flanked by two towers. A large tomb from the Late Bronze Age was found to contain the remains of some forty-five men, women, and children. The accompanying funerary objects included Mycenean and Cypriote pottery, silver and

Bronze Age city wall at Tel Dan

gold jewelry, ivory cosmetic boxes, and numerous bronze arrowheads and swords. They reflect the wealth and international relations of the Canaanite city during that period. While the archaeological evidence for the early part of Iron Age I is somewhat imprecise, the conquest of the city by the Danites took place perhaps during the mid-twelfth century (ca. 1150 BCE), about when the city was destroyed and a change took place in the material culture at the site. The most significant features of the Israelite period are a major city gateway and wall discovered on the south side of the tell and a sacred area or high place discovered on the northwest part of the tell, both dating to the ninth century BCE (Iron Age II), a time that seems to fit the era of Jeroboam I who established Dan and Bethel as border sanctuaries of the northern kingdom (1 Kgs 12:26–31). During the Israelite period, the sacred area apparently went through three different building phases, the first attributed to Jeroboam I, the second to Ahab, and the third to Jeroboam II. Following the Israelite period the site continued to be occupied, though perhaps with some interruption, and the sacred area at Dan continued to be used through the Hellenistic and Roman periods. An inscription in both Greek and Aramaic from the Hellenistic period contains the vow a worshiper named Zoilos made to the "god who is in Dan." The inscription is significant for two reasons: it identifies the site by name, thus assuring current scholars that Tell el-Qadi is ancient Dan; and it further reflects the lengthy period through which the sacred area of Dan was used.

Iron Age gate at Tel Dan

Of the discoveries at Tell Dan two in particular help illuminate something of the character of the ancient site—the fortifications and the sacred area or high place. The fortifications from both the Middle Bronze Age and Iron Age II reflect the role that the city of Dan played as a major fortified city. The Middle Bronze fortification of the Canaanite city of Laish consisted of a massive rampart wall that surrounded the city and a gateway. The rampart wall, 175 feet wide at the base and sixty feet high, was comprised of a sizable stone core with a sloping earthen rampart on each side. The Middle Bronze fortification also included a large mud-brick arched gateway. The arch, which remains intact, was flanked by two towers preserved to a height of nearly twenty feet. The Iron Age fortification dating to the late tenth century BCE (generally associated with Jeroboam I) consisted of a wall approximately twelve feet thick and city gate, the only one of its kind found in Palestine. The gateway built at the base of the Middle Bronze rampart measured ninety-five by fifty feet and was comprised of two main towers and four guard rooms. One of the unique features of the gate is a paved area with decorated column bases, perhaps an area that originally had a canopy under which the king sat on special occasions. A stone bench some fifteen feet long, also located at the gate, may have been used by the elders of the city.

Of all the functions the city of Dan had in ancient times, its role as a center of worship, high place, or cult center has to be one of the most interesting. According to the archaeological evidence at the site, the so-called sacred area functioned as such as far back as the Early Bronze Age and continued in use perhaps with some interruptions in the Hellenistic and Roman periods.

In the Bible two stories shed light on the religious practices at Dan during the Israelite period: the story of the Danite conquest of the site (Judg 18) and the story of the establishment of Dan and Bethel as border sanctuaries by Jeroboam I (1 Kgs 12:28–33). According to Judges 18 the Danites who conquered the site established their own cultic worship at the site as they set up a graven image (Judg 18:30; also 18:14–20) and appointed their own priesthood, the head of which was Jonathan, the grandson of Moses (Judg 18:30). This practice supposedly continued "as long as the house of God was at Shiloh" (Judg 18:31). The Bible informs us further that Jeroboam I established a calf or bull sanctuary at Dan and declared, "Behold your gods, O Israel" (1 Kgs 12:29) and that "he also made houses on high places, and appointed priests from among all the people, who were not of the Levites" (1 Kgs 12:31).

The discovery of the sacred area in the northwest part of the city of Dan has provided valuable insight for the biblical stories. The sacred area was in essence a large open-air worship area covering one-half acre. The central feature was a large high place or bamah; this large stone platform was sixty feet long and sixty feet wide, with a flight of stairs twenty-seven feet long and twenty-six feet wide. The platform was probably built in the latter part of the tenth century by Jeroboam I and went through two additional building phases that are attributed to Ahab and Jeroboam II. It was most likely used for a variety of offerings and sacrifices. Also found in the sacred area were the remains of incense stands and burners, figurines, the bones of small animals like sheep and goats, and a horned altar, all of which reflect the rituals performed in the sacred area. The bilingual inscription dedicated to the god of Dan that was mentioned earlier indicates that the sacred area continued to be used in the Hellenistic and Roman periods.

In 1993, the site of Dan yielded exciting evidence in the form of an inscription that makes reference to the "house of David." The inscription appears to be that of a victory stele, perhaps of an Aramean king interested in posting a record of his victory over the kingdoms of Israel and Judah at the site of Dan. The discovery is important because it is the first inscriptional evidence that makes reference to the "house of David." The excitement of the discovery was enhanced in 1994 when additional fragments of the inscription were found.

Bibliography: BIRAN, A., *Biblical Dan* (Jerusalem: Israel Exploration Society, 1994); idem, "Dan," *NEAEHL*, 1:323–32; idem, "Dan (City)," *IDBSup*, 205; idem, "Dan (Place)," *ABD*, 2:12–17; idem, "Dan, Tel," *EAEHL*, 1:313–21; idem, "Tel Dan," *BA* 37 (1974) 26–51; idem, "Tel Dan," *BA* 43 (1980) 168–82; idem, "The Discovery of the Middle Bronze Gate at Dan," *BA* 44 (1981) 139–44; BRUCE, F. F., "Dan," *NBD²*, 262; COLE, D., "Dan," *HolBD*, 332–34; EWING, W., and J. F. Prewitt, "Dan," *ISBE*, 1:856; FINKELSTEIN, I., "Dan," *The Archaeology of the Israelite Settlement* (Jerusalem: Israel Exploration Society, 1988) 102–3; ILAN, D., "Dan," *OEANE*, 2:107–12; JENNINGS, J. E., "Dan," *NIDBA*, 148–49; LAPP, N. L., "Dan," *HBD*, 203–4; LAUGHLIN, J. C. H., "Dan, Tell," *MDB*, 194–95; idem, "The Remarkable Discovery at Tel Dan," *BAR* 7 (5, 1981) 20–37; SCHOVILLE, K. N., "Dan," *BAF*, 347–53; SHANKS, H., ed. " 'David' Found at Dan," *BAR* 20 (2, 1994) 26–39; VAN BEEK, G. W., "Dan (2)," *IDB*, 1:759–60; WHITE, W., Jr., "Dan (city)," *ZPEB*, 2:10–11.

EKRON 🏺   31

Site of a Major Olive Oil Complex in the Ancient Near East

While literary accounts are often the only means by which we can reconstruct portraits of cities in biblical times, their usefulness is often limited because of the brevity of the information in the accounts. Such was the case with Ekron, one of the cities of the Philistines in southwest Palestine in the area of Philistia. The important character of this biblical city began to emerge in the 1980s when excavations unearthed not only a Philistine city but also one of the largest industrial complexes in the ancient Near East.

The site of ancient Ekron, known today as Tell Miqne or Khirbet el-Muqanna, is located on the Wadi Timnah twenty-five miles west of Jerusalem and ten miles inland from the Mediterranean coast. It was one of the cities of the Philistine pentapolis, a city-state system comprised of five cities (1 Sam 6:17; Josh 13:3), the other four being Ashdod, Ashkelon, Gaza, and Gath. Ekron, the northernmost of the five, along with Gaza, Ashkelon, and Ashdod, seemed to form part of an outer circle around and to the west of Gath, which conceivably served as the hub of the pentapolis. The location of the site had a definite bearing on the development of life and culture of the inhabitants of Ekron. Located near the eastern edge of the coastal plain and the western edge of the shephelah, Ekron had both economic and political consequence. The cereal crops that grew well in this area played an important part in its economy. But Ekron's location near the border between the Philistines and Israelites also meant that the city was subject to border skirmishes between the two groups. The site was also near important travel routes: one turned inland from the coastal plain highway and moved northeastward from Ashdod toward Gezer, and another was the Sorek valley, which was a major corridor that carried the inland route from the coastal plain eastward toward Jerusalem.

Ekron is mentioned in a number of passages in the OT. In Joshua it is identified as one of the cities in the land that was not taken in the conquest. While it is listed among the towns allotted to both Judah (Josh 15:20, 45–46) and Dan (Josh 19:40, 43), it was perhaps a part of Judah's territory for a time during the period of the settlement (Judg 1:18) before falling ultimately to the Philistines. During the period of the Judges, Ekron certainly emerged as an important Philistine city. It was one of three cities to which the Philistines took the Ark of the Covenant (1 Sam 5:10) after they had captured it in the battle of Ebenezer. Though the Israelites perhaps gained control of Ekron at some point during the period of the Judges (1 Sam 7:14), the site may have been retaken by the Philistines shortly thereafter because it was to "the gates of Ekron" that the Philistines fled following David's defeat of Goliath (1 Sam 17:52). According to the Bible, Ekron was a center for the worship of the god Baalzebub (2 Kgs 1:2, 3, 16). It was the city to which Ahaziah, king of Israel, sent messengers to inquire about his illness (2 Kgs 1:2). Ekron is also mentioned in the prophetic literature, where it is denounced along with the other Philistine city-states (Amos 1:8; Jer 25:20; Zeph 2:4; Zech 9:5–7).

Ekron is also mentioned in ancient Egyptian and Assyrian records. In the annals of Shishak, Ekron is listed among the sites Shishak took during his invasion of Palestine (1 Kgs 14:25). It is also mentioned in the Assyrian account of Sennacherib's invasion of Palestine in 701 BCE, in which a rather lengthy discussion of Ekron's role in the anti-Assyrian rebellion is included. During the invasion Ekron was captured, and the anti-Assyrian rebels and officials behind the uprising were killed and their bodies hung on poles around the perimeter of the city. Other citizens of the city involved in the rebellion were taken as prisoners of war. Sennacherib restored Ekron to its pro-Assyrian position by reinstating Padi as the king of Ekron. Padi had been taken captive by Hezekiah, king of Judah, who was also involved in the rebellion against Assyria. Ekron is also mentioned in the accounts of Sargon II, Esarhaddon, and Ashurbanipal. Prior to the attack by Sennacherib, the city had been assaulted by Sargon II for a similar rebellion in 712 BCE. The assault is depicted in relief form on a panel in the palace of Sargon II in Khorsabad. During the reign of Esarhaddon and Ashurbanipal, Ekron paid tribute to the Assyrians. While the fate of the city during the Babylonian period is unknown, it may have been destroyed by

Nebuchadnezzar, since the Babylonian Chronicle describes his assault on one of the cities in Philistia. According to Josephus, during the Hellenistic period Alexander Balas, the Syrian ruler, gave Ekron to Jonathan, the Hasmonean, as a reward for Jonathan's loyalty to Balas (*Ant.* 13.102; also 1 Macc 10:89). In the fourth-century CE *Onomasticon* by Eusebius, Ekron is described as "a very large village of the Jews" (11.9–10). It is also mentioned in the accounts of the crusades of Baldwin I from ca. 1100 CE.

Unlike many biblical sites, Ekron has been discovered in very recent times. The site's discovery is attributed to the efforts of two men, Natan Aidlin of the Kibbutz Revadim, who first discovered the site, and Joseph Naveh of the Israeli Department of Antiquities, who surveyed the site in 1957 and confirmed the identification. A major excavation began in 1984 and has continued to the present. The excavation project is directed by Trude Dothan of the Hebrew University and Sy Gitin of the Albright Institute of Archaeological Research.

Located along the Wadi Timnah, Tell Miqne (the site of ancient Ekron) is in some ways unusual. The site covers fifty acres and is comprised of a ten-acre upper city and a forty-acre lower city. The rectangular-shaped upper city is located on the north side of the square lower city. But while the tell covers an area of fifty acres, it rises to a height of only twenty-two feet. Consequently the tell has a low profile and is almost indistinguishable from the surrounding area, explaining why the site was discovered only recently.

Excavations at Ekron have provided new insight concerning the history of the ancient city. Apparently the settlement of the site began in the fourth millennium BCE during the Chalcolithic period and continued through the Early Bronze, Middle Bronze, and Late Bronze periods, though information concerning the early periods is still limited. The current excavations have identified nine distinct occupational levels. The earliest city is from the Late Bronze era. It is in stratum IX and bears evidence of having had an industrial area that was destroyed by fire during the fifteenth or fourteenth century BCE. A second Late Bronze city, stratum VIII, was apparently built at the site during the fourteenth or thirteenth century BCE. The remains of the Late Bronze city have produced evidence of Canaanite culture and international ties that the site had with the Aegean area and Anatolia. The Late Bronze city came to an end late in the thirteenth century BCE.

Remains of a cult center at Ekron

During Iron Age I Ekron was apparently occupied by the Sea Peoples (stratum VII) and the Philistines (stratum VI). This conclusion is based primarily on pottery analysis, especially the absence of imported Mycenean and Cypriote pottery and the appearance of locally made Mycenean pottery in stratum VII, and the appearance of Philistine bichrome pottery in stratum VI. The occupational phases of the site during Iron Age I include stratum VII, which dates to the first third of the twelfth century BCE; stratum VI, to the last two-thirds of the twelfth century BCE; stratum V, to the eleventh century BCE; and stratum IV, to the late eleventh to early tenth century BCE.

The Iron Age I city at Ekron was fortified with a mud-brick wall some ten feet thick that apparently enclosed the entire fifty-acre tell, both the lower and upper cities. In addition to the wall the city's fortification included a massive gateway with attached side rooms. The upper city had a large industrial area comprised of kilns, both square and horseshoe-shaped. Evidence from the area suggests that the industrial area was the site of a large pottery-making industry. The upper city also contained a shrine or cultic center consisting of a building with four rooms and a stone pillar base. Discoveries in the cult center include a pit containing the shoulder blade of a cow, clay Ashdoda-like figures, kernos vessels (cultic libation vessels), and a lion-headed rhyton. The presence of the Philistines is evident in the bichrome ware found at the site. The pottery, decorated with red and black geometric designs, highly stylized birds and fish, is also found at other Philistine sites.

A major discovery in the lower city was that of a building, perhaps a temple or palace-temple, identified as building 351 in stratum V and building 350 in stratum IV. The building was comprised of a large rectangular hall thirty-three feet long and twenty-six feet wide and three chambers to the side of the hall.

Both the architectural features of the building and the artifacts associated with it suggest that it was a temple or worship center in which cultic rituals took place. The middle chamber of the three siderooms contained a mud-brick offering platform or *bamah,* a bench, as well as cultic pottery pieces. Other discoveries in the cultic complex include pieces of a bronze cult stand similar to the bronze lavers in Solomon's temple (1 Kgs 7:27–30); a variety of pottery including a horn-shaped bottle and a Philistine beer jug; an iron knife with an ivory handle; pillar bases in the main hall similar to the Philistine temple found at Tell Qasile; numerous bones of animals and fish; and three large round hearths in the north end of the main hall.

The large Iron Age I Philistine city of Ekron, reflecting influences from the Aegean as well as from Egypt and the local Canaanite population, reached its peak during the eleventh century BCE and was destroyed during the early part of the tenth century BCE. The site, destroyed perhaps by David, diminished considerably in size. The lower city was abandoned, and only the upper city was occupied.

At the beginning of Iron Age II, Ekron was a very small town and continued as such throughout the ninth and eighth centuries BCE. The city was apparently refortified about the mid-tenth century, the time of the united monarchy, by the so-called Ekronites, the inhabitants of the city. The new fortifications consisted of a new mud-brick wall and a large tower. Among the major discoveries at Ekron from this period are those of two *lᵉmelek* jar handles from the late eighth century, apparently the time of Hezekiah, king of Judah. The jar handles, which bear the *lᵉmelek* inscription meaning "belonging to the king," reflect the administrative reforms of that period.

Near the end of the eighth century BCE, Ekron experienced a dramatic change. The city was taken away from Judah and became a part of the Assyrian empire. Both the upper and lower cities were refortified, and the city was expanded even beyond the size of the Philistine city of Iron Age I. The new city was divided into four major zones for fortifications, industry, general residential, and upper class residential.

Olive oil industrial complex at Ekron

The most fascinating feature of the new city was the industrial area, a massive olive oil industry. The industrial area was comprised of rectangular-shaped buildings that included three rooms: a production room, a work and storage room, and an anteroom. The production room included crushing basins and pressing vats, while the work and storage room included jars and kraters used in the separation and storage process. The work room also contained a stone niche with a four-horned altar, apparently a cultic installation used in some type of dedicatory rite or ritual in connection with the industry. Thus far, 103 olive oil producing units have been found at Ekron with a production capacity of one thousand tons (290 thousand gallons) of olive oil annually, making Ekron the largest known olive-oil producing industry in the entire ancient Near Eastern world.

Ekron was destroyed near the end of the seventh century BCE, ca. 603, perhaps in one of Nebuchadnezzar's campaigns. The site was abandoned during the early part of the sixth century BCE and not reoccupied until the Roman period. Very limited occupational evidence has been found at the site from the Roman, Byzantine, and Arab periods.

Bibliography: BORAAS, R. S., "Ekron," *HBD,* 251; CRAWFORD, T. G., "Ekron," *MDB,* 240; DOTHAN, T., "Ekron of the Philistines, Part I: Where They Came From, How They Settled Down and the Place They Worshiped In," *BAR* 16 (1, 1990) 26–36; DOTHAN, T., and S. Gitin, "Ekron," *ABD,* 2:415–22; idem, "Ekron of the Philistines: How They Lived, Worked and Worshiped for Five Hundred Years," *BAR* 16 (1, 1990) 20–25; idem, "Mique, Tel," *OEANE,* 4:30–35; DRINKARD, J. F., Jr., "Ekron," *HolBD,* 404; GITIN, S., "Ekron of the Philistines, Part II: Olive-Oil Suppliers to the World," *BAR* 16 (2, 1990) 32–42, 59; GITIN, S., and Trude Dothan, "The Rise and Fall of Ekron of the Philistines: Recent Excavations at an Urban Border Site," *BA* 50 (1987) 197–222; HARRINGTON, C. E., "Ekron," *NIDB,* 298; LEWIS, J. P., "Ekron, Ekronite," *ZPEB,* 2:259–60; MITCHELL, T. C., "Ekron," *NBD*[2], 312; RAINEY, A. F., "Ekron," *IDBSup,* 255; idem, "Ekron," *ISBE,* 2:47–48; STINESPRING, W. F., "Ekron," *IDB,* 2.69; YAMAUCHI, E., "Ekron," *NIDBA,* 173.

GEZER 🏺   32

Pharaoh's Gift to Solomon

Of all the references made to Gezer in the Bible, certainly one of the most interesting is found in 1 Kings where the Deuteronomic historian states, "And this is the account of the forced labor which King Solomon levied to build . . . Hazor and Megiddo and Gezer" (1 Kgs 9:15). The ancient historian continued, "Pharaoh king of Egypt had gone up and captured Gezer and burned it with fire . . . and had given it as dowry to his daughter, Solomon's wife; so Solomon rebuilt Gezer . . ." (1 Kgs 9:16–17). With these words the ancient historian shared important information about the city: that it was a gift to the Israelite king and that it must have been an important city because it was designated as one of the special royal cities fortified by the king's corvée labor. With the assistance of the biblical accounts, other ancient Near Eastern texts, and archaeological research, Gezer's important role in ancient times has come to light.

Ancient Gezer was located twenty miles west-northwest of Jerusalem at the northern edge of the shephelah, the foothill region of southwest Palestine that lay between the coastal plain on the west and the central hill country on the east. Its location at the edge of the shephelah placed Gezer in a strategic position. The site had a commanding view of the junction of two important highways, the Via Maris that ran through the coastal plain to the west, and the inland route that ran through the valley of Aijalon to the north, which moved eastward from the Via Maris along the coast to Jerusalem. Consequently, control of Gezer had both political and economic benefits. Gezer had other valuable features that provided the essentials for daily life. An adequate water supply was provided by local springs east of the site. Fertile plains supplied cereal crops like wheat and barley, and nearby hillsides were covered by grasslands for grazing sheep and goats.

Gezer is mentioned several times in biblical accounts regarding the conquest. According to Joshua and Judges, Gezer did not become an Israelite city during the period of the conquest and settlement. Joshua and the Israelites defeated Horam, the king of Gezer, as he attempted to provide assistance to the king of Lachish (Josh 10:33; 12:12). The city of Gezer was then allotted to the tribe of Ephraim (Josh 16:10; 1 Chron 7:28) and designated a Levitical city (Josh 21:21; 1 Chron 6:67) but apparently remained in the hands of the Canaanites during the period of the Judges (Josh 16:10; Judg 1:29). After David conquered Jerusalem and established it as his capital (2 Sam 5:6–10), he drove the Philistines back to Gezer (2 Sam 5:25). But Gezer apparently still was not an Israelite city. It was not until the time of Solomon that Gezer came under Israelite control. The city, captured and destroyed by the king of Egypt, was given to Solomon's wife, the daughter of the pharaoh (1 Kgs 3:1) as a dowry. Solomon rebuilt the city and made it one of the royal fortified cities of the kingdom.

Information about Gezer also comes to us from other ancient Near Eastern sources including Egyptian and Assyrian records. For instance, a list in the temple of Amon in Thebes names Gezer among the cities captured by the Egyptian king Thutmose III during what was possibly his first annual campaign into Canaan. According to a stele inscription, the Egyptian pharaoh Thutmose IV apparently visited the city and took captives back to Egypt from Gezer. The Amarna letters indicate that Gezer also played a prominent role in Palestine during the Amarna period. At one point, Milkilu, the city-state king of Gezer, appealed to the Egyptian king Akhenaton for help against the Habiru. But letters from the city-state king of Jerusalem, Abdi-Heba, imply that Milkilu of Gezer established alliances with other city-states in Palestine, a sure sign that his loyalty to the Egyptian king was in question. Gezer is also mentioned in the famous Merneptah stele from the Nineteenth Dynasty. Regarding his exploits in Canaan, Merneptah boldly claimed, "Gezer is seized," and "Israel is laid waste, his seed is no more." Gezer appears in the Karnak inscription where it is listed among the cities in Palestine taken by Shishak during the reign of Rehoboam (1 Kgs 14:25–28; 2 Chron 12:1–9). The Egyptian references are especially important because they provide valuable information about the city during a major part of the OT period, especially the Late Bronze and Iron Age periods. The Egyptians recognized Gezer as an important city in a strategic location and tried to maintain control of it. It was apparently for similar reasons that the Assyrians were interested in Gezer as they attempted during the eighth century BCE under the leadership of Tiglath-pileser III to build an empire that would encompass the lands of the Fertile Crescent. Tiglath-pileser's conquest of the city is recorded in relief form.

While Gezer played an important role in Palestine in biblical times, the rediscovery of the ancient site in modern times dates back to the nineteenth century. The thirty-three acre mound of the ancient city was discovered by C. Claremont-Ganneau in 1871. It was excavated by R. A. S. Macalister from 1902 to 1909 and again by Alan Rowe in 1934. From 1964 to 1974, yet another series of excavations were conducted at the site under the direction of G. Ernest Wright, Joe Seger, and William G. Dever.

Standing stones near Gezer

As a result of the excavations at Gezer (Tell el-Jezer), the historical profile of the site has been outlined. The site was originally settled during the latter part of the Chalcolithic period, perhaps as early as the mid-fourth millennium BCE and continued (with some occupational breaks) to first century CE of the Roman period. During the Chalcolithic period, Gezer was an unfortified village, in essence, a settlement with campsites. Though the size of the community grew during the Early Bronze Age, Gezer still remained an unfortified site. During the Middle Bronze Age an important change took place at Gezer. It became one of the major fortified Canaanite cities in Palestine. The new city was fortified with a formidable wall with towers, a plastered glacis, and a huge three-chambered gateway. Excavations at the site further indicate that among the developments at Gezer during the Late Bronze Age, the city faced some turbulent times. It was destroyed during the fifteenth century BCE at the hands of Thutmose III. Following the destruction the city was enlarged and reinforced with a new defense system. The presence of bichrome ware in occupational levels of the twelfth and eleventh centuries BCE (Early Iron Age I) indicates that Gezer was a Philistine city during at least the early part of Iron Age I. Following the destruction of the Philistine city, apparently at the hands of the Egyptians, the city was occupied and strengthened by the Israelites, presumably during the time of Solomon (1 Kgs 9:15–19). During the Iron Age II period, following its destruction by Shishak, king of Egypt, Gezer never again regained the prestige it had during the Canaanite and Philistine periods. The city was destroyed by both the Assyrians in the eighth century BCE and the Babylonians in the early part of the sixth century, ca. 587 BCE. The site was a minor one during the Persian, Hellenistic, and Roman periods. It was occupied and the city wall and gateway were used once again during the Maccabean period by both Simon (1 Macc 13:43–48) and Jonathan (1 Macc 13:53; 14:34).

Several substantial discoveries were made at Gezer, including the high place, the water system, the Israelite defense system, and the Gezer calendar. The high place was originally discovered by R. A. S. Macalister. It was apparently constructed in the Canaanite city during the Middle Bronze Age. The focal point of the high place was a series of ten stone pillars, some reaching a height of ten feet. The Canaanites apparently used the pillars in cultic rituals.

Ancient Gezer was equipped with a water system similar to those at Megiddo, Hazor, and Gibeon. The water system, which perhaps dates to the Late Bronze Age, was comprised of a large shaft and stepped tunnel that led to a cave in which spring water was found.

Excavations at Gezer have also produced the remains of the Israelite defense system. The defense system, most likely built by Solomon (1 Kgs 9:15–17), was comprised of a casemate wall (a fortified, double wall partitioned into chambers) and a four-chambered gateway similar to those found by excavations at Megiddo and Hazor and mentioned in the account of Solomon's building enterprises (v. 15).

Farming activities in the area of Gezer are reflected in the Gezer calendar discovered at the site by R. A. S. Macalister. The calendar, a small limestone tablet about the size of a human hand, is inscribed in paleo-Hebrew characters and dates to the Israelite period. It outlines agricultural phases for the Israelite farmer during the course of the year. The calendar included: two months of (olive) harvest; two months of planting (grain); two months of late planting; a month of hoeing up flax; a month of harvest of barley; a month of harvest and celebration; two months of vine-tending; a month of summer fruit. The calendar is valuable not only for the information it provides about the agricultural calendar in ancient Israel, but also because of the script in which it was written and the insight it provides about the development of the Hebrew language.

Gezer calendar

Bibliography: BLAIKLOCK, E. M., "Gezer," *NIDBA*, 212; DEVER, W. G., "Excavations at Gezer," *BA* 30 (1967) 47–62; idem, "Further Excavations at Gezer, 1967–71," *BA* 34 (1971) 94–132; idem, "Gezer," *ABD*, 2:998–1003; idem, "Gezer," *EAEHL*, 2:428–43; idem, "Gezer," *HBD*, 343–45; idem, "Gezer," *IDBSup*, 361–63; idem, "Gezer," *MDB*, 328–29; idem, "Gezer," *NEAEHL*, 2:496–506; idem, "Gezer,"

OEANE, 2:396–400; DeVries, C. E., "Gezer," *BEB*, 1:860–61; Garner, G. G., "Gezer," *NBD*[2], 416–18; Hamilton, R. W., "Gezer," *IDB*, 2:388–89; Rainey, A. F., "Gezer," *ISBE*, 2:458–60; idem, "Gezer," *ZPEB*, 2:706–10; Russell, E., "Gezer," *NIDB*, 386–87; Schoville, K. N., "Gezer," *BAF*, 355–61; Young, F. E., "Gezer," *BW*, 254–57.

HAZOR 🏺   33

Leading Canaanite City-State in the North

The biblical description of Hazor in the book of Joshua as the city that "formerly was the head of all those kingdoms" (Josh 11:10) certainly suggests that at one time Hazor was the leading city in northern Palestine. But the biblical description took on new meaning as the site was excavated and the physical remains of the ancient Canaanite city were brought to light. Of all the biblical sites excavated in the land of Palestine, Hazor provides one of the most impressive portraits of a major city in Palestine at the time of the Israelite conquest of Canaan. Archaeological remains at the site demonstrate that Hazor was the leading Canaanite city in the northern area of Galilee during most of the Middle Bronze and Late Bronze periods.

The site of ancient Hazor, Tell el-Qedah, is located approximately five miles southwest of Lake Huleh, fifteen miles south-southwest of Dan, and ten miles north of the Sea of Galilee. Hazor's important role in ancient history was due to its location. First, Hazor was located on the major international trade route that ran from Egypt to Mesopotamia; consequently, it saw the passing of caravans and merchants from Mesopotamia, Syria, and Anatolia from the east and north, and Arabia and Egypt from the south and southwest. Second, it was located at a major junction on the international trade route. For instance, from Hazor one could travel northeast to Damascus and beyond to Mesopotamia or go directly north past the city of Dan through the Beth-rehob valley, the major pass between the Lebanon Mountains on the west and Mount Hermon on the east. Hazor (in some instances perhaps Dan) was the first major city that travelers met coming to Palestine from the north. Not only did caravans and merchants pass by the city, but Hazor served as a major hub for ancient merchants. Consequently, Hazor became an important center of international trade and exchange that had ties with all parts of the ancient Near Eastern world. The city entertained travelers from throughout the Fertile Crescent. It was an internationally known city whose life and culture were shaped by international influences. A third factor that contributed to Hazor's growth and development was the unique topography of its location. Hazor was situated on a large mound that had a commanding view of the international highway. Its position made it possible for the inhabitants of the city to observe traffic approaching the city on the international route from a great distance both from the north and northeast as well as from the southwest. The fourth and final feature that played an important role in the development of Hazor as a major city in Palestine was its location in an agricultural basin. Hazor was located at the southwest edge of the Huleh basin, one of the most fertile and productive agricultural regions in Palestine. The abundant annual rainfall resulted in bumper harvests of grain and fruits as well as lush grazing lands for shepherding and herding. Consequently, agriculture and animal husbandry were major elements of the local economy.

Hazor is mentioned in the Bible and in extrabiblical sources of the ancient Near East. In the Bible, Hazor is described as the major city in the north at the time of the conquest. Joshua tells us that Jabin, the king of Hazor, rallied the kingdoms of the north (Josh 11:1–4), which he headed (Josh 11:10), encamped by the waters of Merom in preparation for the confrontation with the Israelites (Josh 11:5). During a surprise attack he was soundly defeated by the Israelites, who used military tactics that included hamstringing the horses and burning the chariots (Josh 11:6–9). Following the defeat of the Canaanite forces, Joshua and the Israelites took the city of Hazor, killed Jabin, and destroyed the city by fire (Josh 11:10–11). A second encounter between the Israelites and the leaders of Hazor is mentioned in the book of Judges (Judg 4). Hazor was allotted to the tribe of Naphtali (Josh 19:32, 36). As an Israelite city along with Gezer and Megiddo, Hazor was fortified and established as a major royal city by Solomon (1 Kgs 9:15) during the united monarchy. Though Hazor is not mentioned by name, the city was apparently among those attacked by Benhadad, king of Syria, during the reign of Baasha, king of the northern kingdom (1 Kgs 15:20). According to the Bible, Hazor was among the cities captured by Tiglath-pileser III, king of Assyria, during the reign of Pekah, king of Israel (2 Kgs 15:29).

The Bible reflects the role Hazor played as the leading Canaanite center in the north, and extrabiblical sources highlight the city's international significance. Hazor is mentioned in the Execration Texts from Egypt. Dating to the time of the Twelfth Dynasty (the period of the Middle Kingdom in Egypt), these texts contain the names of vassal city-states in Syria-Palestine and list the curses that the Egyptians attempted to inflict upon those who were not loyal to Egypt. References to Hazor found in the Mari tablets indicate that the city was an active caravan center, a major governmental center involved in diplomatic activities with Mesopotamia, and a center of metal trade. Hazor's location on the international trade route and its strategic position in northern Palestine made it a prime target for the imperialistic pharaohs of Egypt. Hazor appears in the lists of cities captured by the Egyptian pharaohs of the Eighteenth and Nineteenth dynasties, including Thutmose III, Amenhotep II, and Seti I. Hazor further appears in the correspondence of the Amarna Age. While Abdi-Tarshi, city-state king of Hazor, wrote to the king of Egypt assuring him of his loyalty, letters from neighboring city-state kings include complaints that Abdi-Tarshi had rebelled against the Egyptian pharaoh, had captured several cities from neighboring city-states and added them to his own territory, and had aligned himself with the Habiru.

Solomonic gate at Hazor

The discovery of the site of ancient Hazor goes back to J. L. Porter in 1875. In 1928 John Garstang conducted soundings and reconfirmed the identity of the site. Major excavations were conducted under the direction of Yigael Yadin in 1955 through 1958 and again in 1968 through 1972. A new series of excavations aimed at clarifying the Early Israelite period are currently under way, under the direction of Amnon-Ben-Tor of the Hebrew University.

Hazor is a large site comprised of two parts, a tell or upper city that covers thirty acres and a large rectangular plateau or lower city on the north side of the tell that encompasses 175 acres. The bottle-shaped upper city rises 120 feet above the surrounding plain and wadi beds, while the lower city attains a height of sixty feet above the surrounding wadis and plain. In ancient times the lower city was fortified by a large earthen rampart, glacis (a plastered slope), and a moat. It is estimated that during its peak, Hazor had a population of perhaps thirty to forty thousand people. The large size of the city and archaeological research at the site indicate that Hazor was the predominant city in Palestine during the Middle Bronze and Late Bronze ages.

Israelite storehouse at Hazor

Excavations at the site sponsored by the Rothschild Foundation and Hebrew University have provided a valuable historical profile of ancient Hazor. Hazor was originally settled sometime during the Early Bronze Age (2900–2600 BCE). The earliest habitation at the site took place on the tell itself, the upper city. During the Middle Bronze Age the city experienced tremendous expansion and the lower city was developed. With the fortification of the lower city and the upper city, Hazor became the largest fortified Canaanite city-state in Palestine during the Middle Bronze Age, a prestigious position it continued to enjoy during the Late Bronze Age. After being destroyed, the fortifications of the city were rebuilt during the Late Bronze Age. The discovery of several Canaanite temples from this period indicates that Hazor was a major Canaanite center of worship during the Late Bronze Age, a worship center with cultic rituals and practices that were shaped by influences from north Syria and Anatolia. Near the end of the Late Bronze Age (latter part of the thirteenth century BCE), Hazor experienced massive destruction, perhaps by Joshua and the Israelites (Josh 11), and the lower city was never again occupied. During Iron Age I, the period of early Israelite occupation, the status of the city changed. No longer the large well-fortified city, Hazor was a simple squatter's site or encampment area or settlement. The semi-nomadic Israelites had no city walls or fortification system and lived in huts or tents. The early Israelite settlement was limited to the area of the upper city or tell. But during the latter part of the Iron Age I period (tenth century BCE), the upper city was buttressed with a casemate wall (a fortified, double wall partitioned into chambers) and a four-chambered city gate. This was apparently the work of King Solomon, who built similar fortifications at Megiddo and Gezer (1 Kgs 9:15). During the Iron Age II period Hazor was an important city of the kingdom of Israel, the northern kingdom. The city experienced further development during the reign of King Ahab with the addition of a large storehouse, a fortified citadel, and a massive water system. The Israelite city was destroyed by Tiglath-pileser III in 732 BCE (2 Kgs 15:29). Following this destruction by the Assyrians, Hazor was never again occupied as a city. The final phases of Hazor's history date to the Assyrian, Persian, and Hellenistic periods from which evidence of fortresses have been found. According to 1 Maccabees (11:63, 67), Jonathan engaged in battle with the forces of Demetrius in the plain of Hazor.

Among the discoveries at Hazor several have special significance. The Middle Bronze fortification system, though rebuilt during the Late Bronze Age, includes a large cyclopean wall (namely, construction using irregular blocks of stone without mortar). It is made of massive stones that are irregular in shape and size, a large earthen rampart with a slick, steep, sloping surface, and a dry moat on the west side of the city, as well as a sizable gateway comprised of three chambers. The Middle Bronze fortifications are especially valuable because they provide important evidence about the city during the period in which Hazor became the predominant Canaanite city in all Palestine.

Equally impressive are Canaanite temples that date for the most part to the Late Bronze Age. These are in the lower Canaanite city that the Israelites apparently conquered (Josh 11:10–14). Temples were discovered at three major sites in the lower city, and the most extensive remains were those found in area H. A series of temples were found one on top of the other. The first temple, comprised of a broad room with a holy niche, was eventually replaced by a temple with three main parts: a porch, a holy place, and a holy of holies, similar to Solomon's temple. The temple was decorated with basalt slabs or orthostats and is often referred to as the orthostat temple. The temple entrance was flanked by two large orthostatic lions. The orthostat temple is similar to those found in north Syria and Anatolia and reflects influences from those regions at Hazor. The holy of holies contained a wide variety of cult vessels, including a basalt incense altar with the engraved emblem of the storm god; a large round basalt basin, perhaps similar to the sea of bronze in Solomon's temple; libation tables or vessels; and numerous other artifacts. A statue of a god standing on the back of a bull perhaps represented the deity worshiped in the temple. Many other cultic installations or artifacts were found in the excavations at Hazor including an incense shovel or ladle with a hand engraved on the bottom side, a drain system in a temple conceivably used for the disposal of blood from animal sacrifices, a one-piece pottery offering stand or incense altar, and clay masks probably used in cultic rituals.

Also impressive are the fortifications of the Solomonic city consisting of the casemate wall and four-chambered gateway to the city with flanking towers. The Iron Age I reinforcements which are similar to those at Megiddo and Gezer help to illuminate the building activities that Solomon carried out by means of corvée labor (1 Kgs 9:15).

One of the most significant discoveries from Iron Age II is the elaborate water system constructed in the upper city by Ahab. The water system, which is similar to others found at sites like Megiddo and Gezer, is comprised of a huge upper shaft with a rock-cut staircase, a sloping tunnel, and a pool room in which the water supply was located.

In addition to the discoveries mentioned above, excavations at the site have produced numerous temples or cult centers, tombs and burials, palaces, public buildings, and residential areas.

While the earlier excavations at Hazor were directed by Yigael Yadin, a new series of excavations have been initiated by Amnon Ben Tor. With the discovery of a palace with a throne room and four clay tablets inscribed in Akkadian cuneiform during the 1996 excavation season, the prospect of finding perhaps one or two archives at the site seems imminent. Information from the tablets, including a reference to Hazor, multiplication tablets apparently used in the instruction of scribes, and a list of goods sent from Hazor to Mari all underline the important status of Hazor during the Middle Bronze Age, the period of the patriarchs.

Bibliography: BEN-TOR, A., "Hazor," *OEANE*, 3:1–5; BORAAS, R. S., "Hazor," *HBD*, 375–76; BRANGENBERG, J., "Hazor," *HolBD*, 615–16; COKER, W. B., "Hazor," *ZPEB*, 3:50–52; DEVER, W. G., "Hazor," *MDB*, 359–60; FINKELSTEIN, I., "Hazor," *The Archaeology of the Israelite Settlement* (Jerusalem: Israel Exploration Society, 1988) 98–101; GOLD, V. R., "Hazor," *IDB*, 2:539–40; HAMILTON, J. M., "Hazor," *ABD*, 3:87–88; HARRISON, R. K., "Hazor," *NIDBA*, 229–30; HUEY, F. B. J., "Hazor," *BEB*, 1:934–35; MITCHELL, T. C., "Hazor," *NBD*[2], 456; SCHOVILLE, K. N., "Hazor," *BAF*, 371–78; YADIN, Y., "Excavations at Hazor," *BA* 19 (1956) 2–11; idem, "Further Light on Biblical Hazor: Results of the Second Season, 1956," *BA* 20 (1957) 34–47; idem, "Hazor," *Archaeology and Old Testament Study*, ed. D. Winton Thomas (Oxford: Clarendon, 1967) 244–63; idem, "Hazor," *EAEHL*, 2:474–95; idem, "Hazor," *IDBSup*, 387–91; idem, "Hazor," *NEAEHL*, 2:594–603; idem, *Hazor: The Rediscovery of a Great Citadel of the Bible* (New York: Random, 1975); idem, "The Fourth Season of Excavations at Hazor," *BA* 22 (1959) 2–20; idem, "The Rise and Fall of Hazor," *Archaeological Discoveries in the Holy Land*, compiled by the Archaeological Institute of America (New York: Bonanza, 1967) 56–66; idem, "The Third Season of Excavations at Hazor," *BA* 21 (1958) 30–47; YOUNGBLOOD, R., "Hazor," *Major Cities of the Biblical World*, ed. R. K. Harrison (Nashville: Nelson, 1985) 119–29.

JERICHO 🏺   34

Citadel of the Neolithic Age

Jericho could be called "the big disappointment of biblical archaeology" because excavations at the site have failed to produce the kind of evidence described in the biblical account of the conquest of Jericho in Joshua 6.

Middle Bronze mud-brick wall

While excavations at Hazor have produced evidence of a massive destruction of the city that may well be that of the Israelite conquest of Hazor (Josh 11), evidence of a massive destruction at Jericho has not been found. Excavations at the two sites demonstrate quite clearly some of the values and limitations of archaeology as it relates to biblical events. In some instances archaeological research provides evidence that seems to illuminate biblical history or events; however, in other instances the archaeological evidence does not support the biblical account. In the final analysis, archaeological evidence is always a silent or a mute kind of evidence. Nothing in the destruction layer at Hazor says "destroyed by the Israelites," though that is certainly a legitimate conclusion. To be sure, the Kenyon excavations at Jericho produced limited evidence of a Late Bronze settlement at the site. But massive erosion by rain and wind removed valuable remains from earlier periods, and so the extent of the Late Bronze settlement is not discernible. But while the evidence from Jericho regarding the period of the conquest may be disappointing, the evidence from earlier periods, especially the Neolithic, Early Bronze, and Middle Bronze ages, has been most valuable.

Neolithic circular stone tower

The site of OT Jericho, Tell es-Sultan, is located in the Jordan valley approximately ten miles north of the Dead Sea and four miles west of the Jordan River. Located near one of the major fords in the Jordan, Jericho was the gateway city to western Palestine from the Transjordan region. Numerous nomadic groups entered the main part of Palestine in ancient times, most likely an important factor in the strategy of the Israelites as they approached the land through the Transjordan.

The two features that may have contributed to the origin of Jericho more than any others were the site's abundant water supply provided by the perennial spring, Ain es-Sultan, located on the east side of the tell, and the tropical climate of the immediate area due to the site's location in the Jordan valley approximately one thousand feet below sea level. These two features combined to make the site of ancient Jericho a tropical oasis, a major factor that contributed to its early stages of development during the Mesolithic period. The oasislike setting and the water from the spring made the area immediately east of the site a garden land that produced fruits and vegetables. Since early times the water from the spring was dispersed through an irrigation system for agricultural purposes. Because Jericho had an abundant growth of date palms, the ancient city was known as "the city of palm trees" (Deut 34:3). The combination of food, water, and a tropical climate is responsible for the fact that Jericho is one of the oldest cities in the world.

Other geographical features of the region also contributed to Jericho's development and importance. Its location in the Jordan valley and its close proximity to the Dead Sea had both economic and political significance for the site. Because the Dead Sea area had its own valuable resources including sulphur, bitumen, and salt, Jericho was involved in both the processing and trading of these resources.

Jericho's location in the Jordan valley near a major ford in the Jordan River also had implications for the site. The city was a gateway from the Transjordan and the plains of Moab to western Palestine, that is, Palestine beyond the Jordan (Num 22:1; 26:3; 31:12; 33:48, 50; 35:1; Deut 32:49; Josh 2:1). It was situated on the major east-west trade route that controlled the flow of traffic from the Transjordan area westward into the central hill country, including the city of Jerusalem located approximately fourteen miles southwest of Jericho, as well as traffic that moved eastward from western Palestine into the Transjordan. Jericho was also located on an important north-south highway that connected the city with Bethshan to the north. Consequently, the possession of Jericho carried with it numerous benefits, including control of the major entrance to western Palestine from the Transjordan, control of the water rights and the oasislike garden land east of the city, and the control of mineral traffic in the Dead Sea area.

The site of Jericho also had hazards. The city was vulnerable to attack and destruction by outside forces, especially from the east. Jericho was also ravaged by the forces of nature. The Jordan valley near the Dead Sea is a region troubled by earthquakes, and the city seems to have been devastated by earthquakes several times during its history. Jericho was occasionally crippled by forces of wind, torrential rains, and massive mud slides, which contributed to erosion and were potentially dangerous in a city that was built primarily of mud brick.

Jericho is mentioned in both the OT and the NT; however, NT Jericho was located approximately one mile south of Tell es-Sultan at the site of Tulul Abu el-Alayiq in the Wadi Qelt. In the OT, Jericho is best known for its role in the Israelite conquest of Canaan. Jericho, the gateway city to western Palestine, was the first city to fall to the Israelites (Josh 6). First, spies were sent on a scouting mission to "go, view the land, especially Jericho" (Josh 2:1), and then the Israelites crossed the Jordan River (Josh 3–4). According to the OT story, they took Jericho in an unusual fashion, by ritually processing around the city for six days (Josh 6:3–14). The campaign came to a climax on the seventh day when "the wall fell down flat" (Josh 6:15–21). Following the conquest of Jericho, Joshua cursed the site (Josh 6:26), and the book of Joshua makes repeated references to the Israelite conquest of the site (Josh 8:2; 9:3; 10:1, 28, 30; 12:9). The site of Jericho is mentioned further in the account of the boundary divisions of the Joseph tribes (Josh 16:1), and was a part of the territory of Benjamin (Josh 8:11–12, 21). A few references are made to Jericho outside of the accounts in the book of Joshua. During the period of the Judges, Jericho, "the city of palms," was apparently in the possession of Eglon, the king of Moab, for a time (Judg 3:12–13). Jericho was the site to which David sent his servants following their humiliation by Hanun, king of Ammon, who shaved off half their beards (2 Sam 10:4–5). During the reign of Ahab, king of the northern kingdom, Hiel of Bethel attempted to rebuild Jericho but in the process lost both his oldest and youngest sons (1 Kgs 16:34), a reminder of Joshua's earlier curse against any who would try to rebuild Jericho (Josh 6:26). Jericho is also mentioned in the accounts regarding Elijah and Elisha (2 Kgs 2). Among the inhabitants of the community were the so-called sons of the prophets (2 Kgs 2:5, 15), and during a brief stay at the site Elisha purified the water of the spring of Jericho with salt (2 Kgs 2:18–22). According to the Chronicler, Judahites taken captive in a war between Syria and Israel on one side and Judah on the other, during the reign of Ahaz, were returned to Jericho (2 Chron 28:5–8, 15). Jericho was also the site at which Zedekiah, king of Judah, was captured by the Babylonians (2 Kgs 25:5). During the postexilic period, 345 "sons of Jericho" returned to Judah from Babylonian captivity and assisted in rebuilding the wall of Jerusalem (Ezra 2:34; Neh 3:2; 7:36).

Though Jericho was an important ancient city, the site itself was relatively small, the tell covering only ten acres and standing seventy feet high. Why the site was named Jericho is really not clear; however, the name was probably derived from the word *yareah* or some derivative meaning moon, month, or new moon, indicating the site had been dedicated to the worship of Yerah, the moon god. This might indicate that among the early inhabitants of the site were those who gave particular attention to the cycles of the moon and the agricultural seasons, all of which they attributed to the moon god. Jericho was excavated by Earnest Sellin and Carl Watzinger in 1907 through 1911, John Garstang in 1929 through 1936, and Kathleen Kenyon in 1952 through 1958. Excavations at Jericho indicate that the earliest occupation at the site took place around 8500 BCE during the Mesolithic period. While the evidence is very limited, the remains of some type of structure have been found near the spring. The structure was apparently that of a sanctuary erected by the Mesolithic hunters who visited the spring.

By far the most valuable discoveries from Jericho come from the Neolithic period, which may be divided into four distinct times— prepottery Neolithic A, prepottery Neolithic B, pottery Neolithic A, and pottery Neolithic B. During the Neolithic period (ca. 8000 BCE), Jericho may have been the earliest city to be fortified in the ancient world. This began during the prepottery Neolithic A period when the inhabitants of the city built round houses constructed of stone for private dwellings. Jericho was protected during this period with an impressive defense system. There was a large stone wall twenty feet high surrounded by a moat twenty-seven feet wide and nine feet deep. The east side of the city wall was equipped with a circular stone tower thirty feet high and twenty-eight feet in diameter.

After a gap in occupation following the prepottery Neolithic A period, a group arrived at Jericho marking the beginning of the prepottery Neolithic B period. The new inhabitants, who apparently came from Anatolia, built rectangular mud-brick houses. During this period Jericho was an agricultural community. Perhaps the most unusual feature of the prepottery Neolithic B community was its burial practices. The deceased were buried under the floors of the houses, and special attention was given to the skulls. Excavations at Jericho have produced several plastered skulls from this period perhaps indicating some type of ancestral cult. Some of the skulls consist of plaster over an actual human skull, while others are completely made of plaster.

Middle Bronze anthropomorphic vase (Collection of the Israel Antiquities Authority, The Israel Museum, Jerusalem)

After another significant break in the occupation at the site, Jericho was settled by new occupants who introduced pottery to the site. The new community, probably semi-nomadic, seemed to be more primitive than the preceding one. The people lived in small huts in contrast to the fine rectangular dwellings of the preceding period. The pottery that was introduced at this time was of a poor quality. The appearance of permanently fixed houses constructed of mud bricks and new pottery types characterized the pottery Neolithic B period.

After yet another gap in occupation the Proto-urban period began at Jericho about 3400 BCE. The most unique feature of the Proto-urban period pertains once again to the burial practices of the community.

During this period burials were made in rock-cut tombs with some tombs containing the remains of several hundred individuals. The Proto-urban burials were accompanied by vast collections of pottery.

During the Early Bronze Age (ca. 3100 BCE), Jericho became an urban center with a large mud-brick city wall. Excavations at the site indicate the town wall went through seventeen successive stages, the last of which was destroyed by fire ca. 2300 BCE. During this period Jericho was a thriving urban center. The Early Bronze city was destroyed by nomadic invaders identified by Kenyon as the Amorites who used the site as a campsite. Eventually the newcomers built poorly constructed houses on the site.

During the Middle Bronze Age, Jericho once again became a major fortified urban center in Palestine. According to Kathleen Kenyon, the new prosperous urban center was built by Canaanites arriving from the area of north Syria. The newcomers constructed a new mud-brick city wall on a rampart with a glacis, or steep sloping embankment. The burials from the Middle Bronze Age have been especially valuable because the artifacts in the tombs were things used for daily living. Burial during the Middle Bronze Age was in family tombs that were cut out of rocks. The deceased individual was buried with his or her own possessions that they had used in daily life and that would be essential in the afterlife. The array of possessions generally included tables, beds, stools, combs, beads, mats, baskets, textiles, and food. The city was destroyed about 1500 BCE most likely by the Egyptians.

Unfortunately the remains of the Late Bronze city are very limited. Excavations to this point have produced scant evidence of the Late Bronze occupation; much of the evidence of the period has probably been lost to massive erosion. Though Jericho experienced limited occupation during some succeeding periods, the city was never again fortified. Evidence of buildings from the seventh century BCE has been found on the site. Apparently the city experienced some rebuilding during the eighth and seventh centuries BCE. Jericho's final destruction presumably came at the hands of the Babylonians in the sixth century BCE. During the NT period the city of Jericho was rebuilt at a new location in the Wadi Qelt about a mile south of the OT city.

Bibliography: BARTLETT, J. R., Jericho (Grand Rapids: Eerdmans, 1982); BIMSON, J. J., Redating the Exodus and Conquest (Sheffield: Almond Press, 1981); BRISCO, T. V.,

"Ancient Jericho," *BI* (Fall 1990) 40–49; CALLAWAY, J. A., "Jericho (Old Testament)," *BW*, 305–9; COUGHENOUR, R. A., "Jericho," *ISBE*, 2:992–96; DEVER, W. G., "Jericho," *MDB*, 438–40; DUMBRELL, W. J., "Jericho," *Major Cities of the Biblical World*, ed. R. K. Harrison (Nashville: Nelson, 1985) 131–38; ELWELL, W. A., "Jericho," *BEB*, 1:1118–20; GRAYBILL, J. B., "Jericho," *NIDB*, 509–12; HOLLAND, T. A., "Jericho," *ABD*, 3:723–37; idem, "Jericho," *OEANE*, 3:220–24; JAMIESON, H., "Jericho," *ZPEB*, 3:451–55; JOINES, K., "Jericho," *HolBD*, 759–64; KELSO, J. L., "Jericho," *IDB*, 2:835–39; KENYON, K. M., "Jericho," *Archaeology and Old Testament Study*, ed. D. Winton Thomas (Oxford: Clarendon, 1967) 264–75; idem, "Jericho," *EAEHL*, 2:550–64; idem, "Jericho," *NEAEHL*, 2:674–81; idem, "Jericho: Oldest Walled Town," *Archaeological Discoveries in the Holy Land*, compiled by the Archaeological Institute of America (New York: Bonanza, 1967) 19–28; KITCHEN, K. A., "Jericho," *NBD²*, 563–65; LANDES, G. M., "Jericho," *IDBSup*, 472–73; SCHOVILLE, K. N., "Jericho," *BAF*, 391–99; THOMPSON, J. A., "Jericho," *NIDBA*, 258–61; TOOMBS, L. E., "Jericho," *HBD*, 458–61; WOOD, B. G., "Did the Israelites Conquer Jericho? A New Look at the Archaeological Evidence," *BAR* 16 (2, 1990) 44–58.

Citadel of Government and Religion in Ancient Israel

Of all the religious and political centers in Palestine in OT times, not one surpasses the importance and lasting significance of Jerusalem. Today Jews offer prayers at the wailing wall as they have for centuries, Moslems visit the Dome of the Rock Mosque, the traditional site where Abraham brought Isaac to offer him as a sacrifice, and Christians flock to the Church of the Holy Sepulchre and other sites associated with the life and ministry of Jesus of Nazareth. Certainly Jerusalem has a longstanding tradition as an important religious and political center that goes back even to the time of Abraham. After defeating the coalition of

View of the Ophel Ridge and Kidron Valley

kings that had captured Lot and his family (Gen 14), Abraham worshiped God near Jerusalem (called Salem).

David set Jerusalem's course of history as the center of religion and government when he captured the city from the Jebusites (2 Sam 5:6–10), built a palace for himself (2 Sam 5:11), made Jerusalem the royal center of ancient Israel, transferred the ark of the covenant and the tent of meeting to Jerusalem (2 Sam 6:12–19), and made Jerusalem the center of worship in ancient Israel. And what David initiated, Solomon firmly established with the building of the temple (1 Kgs 6–8).

Jerusalem is located in the central hill country thirty-five miles east of the Mediterranean Sea and fifteen miles west of the Dead Sea. The city is almost due west of the upper end of the Dead Sea and is approximately 2500 feet above sea level. The site of the ancient city resembles a rectangular-shaped plateau and was basically comprised of an eastern ridge and a western ridge or plateau. The two ridges were separated by a north-south valley known as the Tyropoeon valley or cheesemakers valley. The L-shaped Hinnom valley marked the western and southern limits of the city, and the Kidron valley marked the eastern limit of the city.

The eastern ridge of the ancient city outlined by the Kidron valley on the east and Tyropoeon valley on the west was actually comprised of three hills or sections—the southernmost part of the ridge, known as Ophel or the city of David, was a spur or a very narrow ridge with steep inclines on both the east and the west; the broader flat area immediately north of Ophel was known as the temple mount; and the area directly north of the temple mount was known as Bezetha or the new city. The ridge outlined by the Hinnom valley on the west and the Tyropoeon valley on the east was comprised of two hills commonly known as the southwestern hill and northwestern hill. The original settlement of Jerusalem took place on the southeastern hill known as Ophel. During the OT period the temple mount and the southwestern hill were developed. The northernmost part of both the eastern ridge and western ridge was not developed until the Roman period.

The oldest part of Jerusalem, the Ophel ridge, was originally settled because the site had two vital features: a water supply and an easily defensible position. Water was supplied by two springs located on the east side of Ophel in the Kidron valley. The two springs, which are referred to in the OT, were known as the Gihon spring (1 Kgs 1:33, 38) and the En-rogel spring (2 Sam 17:17). Steep slopes on the east and west made the site easily defensible. The southeastern hill was a narrow pointed ridge with sheer inclines on the east, the Kidron valley, and on the west, the Tyropoeon valley. With the addition of a wall around the slopes, Ophel became almost impregnable.

Another feature that contributed to Jerusalem's growth and development was its location near the junction of two important routes in the area: the north-south route of the central hill country that traveled through Hebron, Jerusalem, and Shechem, and on to Bethshan; and the east-west route that moved from Jericho and Jerusalem through the valley of Aijalon to the coastal plain highway. Though these routes were secondary compared to major routes like the Via Maris, they were valuable thoroughfares that contributed to Jerusalem's development as a major commercial center. The routes made the city accessible from almost any direction.

Herodian Jerusalem

The city was commonly called Jerusalem or Yerusalem. While scholars disagree on the precise meaning of the name, Jerusalem most likely meant "city of peace," "city of salem or shalem," or "foundation of Shalem." The city originally was recognized as "the center of Shalem," a Canaanite deity. According to Genesis 14:18 the city was called Salem or Shalem during the patriarchal period. Some speculate that the name Salem in Genesis is to be seen in the light of a similar term in the Ugaritic texts in which it is associated with the birth of the twin Canaanite deities, Shahar and Shalem, the morning star and the evening star.

Jerusalem was also called by other names. The biblical writers used the name Jebus (Josh 18:28; Judg 19:10; 1 Chron 11:4) in reference to Jerusalem. This name, though it rarely appears in the biblical texts, referred to the old city of Jerusalem that was inhabited by the Jebusites, a Canaanite group, during the period of the Judges. Following David's conquest of Jerusalem, the city was known as the city of David (2 Sam 5:9). His palace and royal headquarters were located in the city. The old city of Jerusalem was also called Zion or stronghold of Zion (2 Sam 5:7). This designation seems to have been used synonymously for the city of David. Two other names referred to Jerusalem or some part of it. Moriah (Gen 22:2; 2 Chron 3:1) is where Abraham was prepared to offer his son Isaac as a sacrifice and where Solomon built the temple. Ariel (Isa 29) means "altar" or "altar hearth," a title that perhaps underscored the idea that Jerusalem was the site at which the altar of Yahweh was located.

The name Jerusalem or some form of it is found in other ancient Near Eastern texts. The earliest appearance of the name Jerusalem, Rushalimum, is found in the Execration Texts (Twelfth Dynasty). The texts, which were written on pottery bowls or figurines, contained curses and the names of Egyptian vassal city-states in Palestine and Syria. The curses were released against any city-state that did not remain loyal to Egypt. While the Execration texts date to the nineteenth century BCE, the name Shalem appears in the Ebla tablets from the twenty-fourth century BCE. The name Urusalim is also found in the Amarna letters in Egypt from the fourteenth century BCE. In the letters, Abdi-Heba, the city-state king of Jerusalem, appeals to the Egyptian king for assistance against the Habiru. The name also appears in the Assyrian texts of Sennacherib's account of his attack on Jerusalem and the cities of Judah at the end of the eighth century BCE.

Of all the cities of the biblical world, none have experienced more exploration and archaeological investigation than Jerusalem. One of the earliest such projects was conducted by Charles Warren in 1867. Warren, who was sponsored by the newly established Palestine Exploration Fund of Great Britain, used the shaft and tunneling techniques to study the walls on the southeast corner of the temple enclosure. Though his methods fail to match the scientific methods used by archaeologists today, his investigation marks the beginning of the modern exploration of ancient Jerusalem. Since the days of Charles Warren, Jerusalem has been investigated and excavated by a host of others including Charles Wilson, E. R. Conder, C. Clermont-Ganneau, F. J. Bliss and A. C. Dickie, L. H. Vincent, R. A. S. Macalister and J. G. Duncan, J. W. Crowfoot, Kathleen Kenyon, Benjamin Mazar, N. Avigad, M. Broshi, and Yigael Shiloh, as well as others. Jerusalem has seen explorers and archaeologists come and go for nearly 150 years, yet it is very difficult to recover the ancient city because the site has been occupied continuously from ancient times to the present. Ancient Jerusalem is buried beneath the present-day city. One other factor further complicates the exploration of Jerusalem. Because parts of the ancient city are recognized as sacred, archaeological investigation of some areas is prohibited.

While archaeological research has been restricted, excavations in and around Jerusalem have added greatly to the Bible and extrabiblical sources in providing a historical profile of the city. Flint implements found in the valley of Rephaim southwest of Jerusalem reflect human habitation in the area during the Paleolithic and Mesolithic periods, but the settlement of Jerusalem itself took place much later, probably during the Chalcolithic or Early Bronze periods. According to information provided through archaeological research, the earliest settlement was located on Ophel, the southeastern hill of the old city. During the Early Bronze Age the old city became a more permanent settlement. Although the inhabitants of the site built houses on Ophel, the Early Bronze city apparently did not have a city wall. It was during the Middle Bronze Age, the period of the Canaanite city, that Jerusalem (the Ophel ridge) became a walled and flourishing city. The wall, built ca. 1900 to 1800 BCE, was eight feet thick. Remains of the Canaanite-Jebusite wall, located about two-thirds of the way down the eastern slope of the Ophel ridge in the Kidron valley, were perhaps those of the city of Melchizedek in Genesis 14, the same basic city and city wall captured by David at a later date (2 Sam 5:6–9). The wall, which seems to have encompassed the Ophel ridge, continued in use for one thousand years. During that period, both the Middle Bronze and Late Bronze ages, the city of Jerusalem covered about eleven acres.

Two of the most interesting features of the Canaanite-Jebusite city of the Middle and Late Bronze ages were the city's terraces and water system. Excavations on the east side of the Ophel ridge have discovered the remains of a massive system of terraces comprised of retaining and revetment walls filled with rubble. The terraces were apparently built by the Canaanite-Jebusite citizens of the city in order to utilize the steep sloping incline for building purposes. The terraces enabled the inhabitants of the city to build houses on the hillside, an utterly impossible task without the flat surface of the terraces. It is quite likely that references in the OT to the Millo (2 Sam 5:9), which means "fill," actually pertain to the terraces on the east side of Ophel.

The genius of the early inhabitants of the city is also reflected in the city's water system. Because the city's water supply, the Gihon spring, was located outside the city wall at the base of the hillside, the citizens designed a water system to give them access to the water from inside the city wall. The water system was comprised of a long stepped passage or tunnel and a vertical shaft. The stepped tunnel, ninety-two feet long, was cut through solid bedrock and ended at the shaft, which was forty feet deep. By going through the tunnel to the water shaft and dipping water from the spring below, the inhabitants of the city could secure water during times of warfare without being exposed to the enemy. While the Bible speaks of Melchizedek, king of Salem, who would have been a city-state king during the Middle Bronze Age, the Amarna texts include letters from Abdi-Heba, a city-state king of the Late Bronze city.

According to the Bible, Adoni-zedek was king of Jerusalem at the time of the conquest (Josh 10:1). But while Joshua and the Israelites defeated Adoni-zedek and the Amorite coalition of kings (Josh 10:1–27), and even though the forces of Jerusalem were apparently defeated at some point during the period of the Judges (Judg 1:8), the Jebusites, the inhabitants of Jerusalem during the period of the conquest and settlement, continued to occupy the city (Josh 15:63) until the time of David.

It was not until about 1000 BCE that the city of Jerusalem, called Jebus after its inhabitants, the Jebusites, fell into Israelite hands. David, who had been anointed king over the house of Judah (2 Sam 2:4) and Israel (2 Sam 5:3), apparently recognized the potential of the site. First, the city was located in neutral territory between the tribes of the north and the tribes of the south. The site's neutrality would tend to prevent tribal jealousies that might arise with other sites. The site was easily defended, had an adequate water supply, and was located at an important crossroads in the central hill country. According to 2 Samuel 5:6–8, David took the city of Jerusalem by means of the water shaft, perhaps by having Joab scale it; however, the precise meaning of the passage is still open to debate. David carried out several building projects in the new capital. He built a palace for himself in the city (2 Sam 5:9, 11), repaired the walls of the city as well as the Millo, those terraces on the east side of the city (2 Sam 5:9; 1 Chron 11:8), and brought the ark of the covenant and the tent of meeting to Jerusalem (2 Sam 6:12–19).

While David started the centralizing process by making Jerusalem both the royal center and center of worship, Solomon completed the task of making Jerusalem the royal capital. He carried out an extensive building program that included extending the city wall, building the temple, and constructing his palace and other royal quarters (1 Kgs 9:15). While the city during David's reign was limited to the southeastern hill (i.e., the Ophel ridge), the city was expanded northward during the reign of Solomon to include Mount Moriah (2 Chron 3:1), the area immediately north of the old city, commonly known as the temple mount. The new addition not only increased the size of the city from eleven to thirty-two acres, but also provided additional space for building the temple. Of all of Solomon's building projects, the temple was perhaps the most important (1 Kgs 6–7). The temple had three basic parts: the porch or vestibule, the holy place, and the holy of holies. It was approximately one hundred feet long, thirty-five feet wide, and fifty feet high. The temple was part of a larger building program that included the House of the Forest of Lebanon (1 Kgs 7:2), the Hall of Pillars (1 Kgs 7:6), the Hall of the Throne (1 Kgs 7:7), Solomon's own palace (1 Kgs 7:8), and a hall for Pharaoh's daughter (1 Kgs 7:8). The Bible seems to describe the temple as part of a royal sanctuary, a complex in which the sanctuary and the royal quarters were intimately interwoven.

During Solomon's reign Jerusalem took on yet another dimension. Solomon's foreign policy program established the city as a major cosmopolitan center of trade. Solomon's extensive trading activity included the operation of a fleet of ships in the Red Sea (1 Kgs 9:26–28); the taxation of merchants and caravans that passed through the land (1 Kgs 10:14–15); the operation of the so-called fleet of ships of Tarshish (1 Kgs 10:22); involvement in the horse and chariot trade market (1 Kgs 10:28–29); as well as extensive commodities trade with Hiram, the king of Tyre (1 Kgs 5:10–12). Although Jerusalem became a thriving cosmopolitan center and the center of government and religion during the reign of Solomon, the material remains of that period have never been recovered.

During the period of the divided monarchy, Jerusalem was the capital of the southern kingdom, the kingdom of Judah, and the city was expanded to include at least a part of the western hill. The remains of houses and a city wall indicate that the expansion took place perhaps during the eighth century BCE. The city's history was also interspersed with periods of conflict. For instance, during the reign of Rehoboam, Shishak, the king of Egypt, invaded Judah and apparently took a heavy tribute from Jerusalem itself (1 Kgs 14:25–28).

According to the Bible, Jerusalem was also refortified at times. The Chronicler reports that Uzziah improved the defenses of Jerusalem by building towers at strategic locations along the city wall (2 Chron 26:9) and equipping the city with new devices of warfare (2 Chron 26:15). Hezekiah made additional improvements in preparation for the assault on Judah by the Assyrian king Sennacherib in 701 BCE. Hezekiah reportedly built towers along the existing city wall, built yet another wall outside the existing wall, and repaired the Millo (2 Chron 32:5). The additional wall mentioned in the account was built on the north side of the existing city wall. A part of the wall and an accompanying tower have been recovered in recent excavations.

One of Hezekiah's major achievements was the construction of another water system, commonly called Hezekiah's tunnel or the Siloam tunnel (2 Kgs 20:22; 2 Chron 32:3). The new water system, undertaken in response to the crisis of 701 BCE, was actually a tunnel 1,731 feet long, cut through the bedrock of the old city of Ophel. The tunnel conveyed water from Gihon spring to the pool of Siloam located inside the city wall on the southwest side. The Siloam inscription, discovered on the wall inside the tunnel, describes the tunneling process. Though Jerusalem itself was spared in the crisis of 701 BCE, forty-six of the fortified cities of Judah were destroyed (2 Kgs 18:13). According to an Assyrian account of the confrontation, Sennacherib's forces apparently encircled the city of Jerusalem, and Hezekiah is described as being "like a bird in a cage."

Remains of a seventh-century BCE Israelite house

While Jerusalem felt Assyrian imperialism in Syria and Palestine during the eighth and seventh centuries BCE, the latter part of the seventh century and the early part of the sixth century BCE brought a new threat posed by the Babylonian empire. The first major blow to Jerusalem at the hands of the Babylonians came in 597 BCE when Babylonian forces invaded Judah, besieged Jerusalem, and carried Jehoiachin and the royal family into captivity. The decisive blow came in 587 BCE when Nebuchadnezzar and his forces, responding to a rebellion led by Zedekiah, attacked the city of Jerusalem and destroyed it (2 Kgs 25:8–10). Evidence of this massive destruction of the city has been found in excavations in both the western city and the Ophel ridge.

During the period of the exile, Jerusalem lay in ruin. But with the arrival of the Persian period in 539 BCE, it entered a period of restoration. The edict of Cyrus, king of Persia, in 538 BCE marked a new day for Jerusalem. In that year Zerubbabel organized a group, returned to the city of Jerusalem from exile in Babylonia, and began rebuilding the temple (Ezra 3:8–13). With the prompting of the prophets Haggai and Zechariah (Ezra 5:1–2), the temple was completed in 515 BCE (Ezra 6:13–15). At yet a later date, the mid-fifth century BCE, the walls of the city of Jerusalem were rebuilt under the leadership of Nehemiah (Neh 2–3). The walls were completed in fifty-two days (Neh 6:15).

In 332 BCE, Alexander the Great arrived in Jerusalem. The Hellenistic period that followed saw much turmoil. When Alexander the Great died in 323 BCE, Jerusalem became a part of the kingdom of the Egyptian Ptolemies. The city was often caught in the struggle that existed between the Ptolemies and the Seleucids, the ruling family in Syria. In 198 BCE with the arrival of Antiochus III, Jerusalem became a part of the Seleucid kingdom. The darkest hour in Jerusalem's history came during the era of Antiochus Epiphanes, the Seleucid ruler who defamed the holy city, especially the temple area, and built the Acra, a fortified garrison for soldiers in the city of Jerusalem. The Maccabean revolt in 167 BCE led to a new day for the city of Jerusalem. In 165 BCE the temple was recaptured and rededicated, providing religious liberty for the citizens of Jerusalem. In 142 BCE the Acra was destroyed, resulting in political freedom and the establishment of an independent Jewish state, the Hasmonean kingdom. But freedom from foreign oppression came to an end in 64 BCE when Pompey made Palestine a part of the Roman Empire.

Bibliography: AMIRAN, R., "Jerusalem," *IDBSup*, 475–77; AP-THOMAS, D. R., "Jerusalem," *Archaeology and Old Testament Study*, ed. D. Winton Thomas (Oxford: Clarendon, 1967) 277–95; AULD, A. G., and M. Steiner, *Jerusalem, Volume 1: From the Bronze Age to the Maccabees* (Macon, Georgia: Mercer University Press, 1996); AVIGAD, N., *Discovering Jerusalem* (Nashville: Nelson, 1980); idem, "Jerusalem (The Tombs in Jerusalem)," *EAEHL*, 2:627–41; BAHAT, D., "Jerusalem," *OEANE*, 3:224–38; BAHAT, D., with C. T. Rubinstein, *The Illustrated Atlas of Jerusalem* (New York: Simon & Schuster, 1990); BAR-YOSEF, O., "Jerusalem (The Site in the Valley of Raphaim)," *EAEHL*, 2:579–80; BASKIN, J. R., "Jerusalem," *HolBD*, 765–73; BURROWS, M., "Jerusalem," *IDB*, 2:843–66; CALLAWAY, J. A., "Jerusalem," *BW*, 309–23; DRINKARD, J. F., Jr., "Jerusalem," *MDB*, 441–43; ELWELL, W. A., "Jerusalem," *BEB*, 2:1123–35; HARRISON, R. K., "Jerusalem, Old Testament," *NIDBA*, 265–70; KENYON, K. M., *Digging Up Jerusalem* (New York: Praeger, 1974); idem, *Jerusalem: Excavating 3000 Years of History* (New York: McGraw-Hill, 1967); KENYON, K., and M. Avi–Yonah, "Jerusalem (History of the Excavations)," *EAEHL*, 2:591–97;

KING, P. J., "Jerusalem," *ABD*, 3:747–66; LaSOR, W. S., "Jerusalem," *ISBE*, 2:998–1032; MARE, W. H., *The Archaeology of the Jerusalem Area* (Grand Rapids: Baker, 1987); MAZAR, B., "Jerusalem (Jerusalem in the Biblical Period)," *EAEHL*, 2:580–91; idem, "Jerusalem (The Early Periods and the First Temple Period)," *NEAEHL*, 2:698–701; idem, "Jerusalem in the Biblical Period," *Jerusalem Revealed*, ed. Y. Yadin (Jerusalem: The Israel Exploration Society in Cooperation with "Shikmona" Publishing Company, 1975) 1–8; PAYNE, D. F., "Jerusalem," *NBD*[2], 566–72; PAYNE, J. B., "Jerusalem," *ZPEB*, 3:459–95; SCHEIN, B. E., "Jerusalem," *HBD*, 463–73; SCHOVILLE, K. N., "Jerusalem," *BAF*, 401–17; SHANKS, H., *Jerusalem: An Archaeological Autobiography* (New York: Random House, 1995); SHILOH, Y., "Jerusalem (Tables of Major Archaeological Activities in Jerusalem since 1863)," *EAEHL*, 2:642–47; idem, "Jerusalem (Topography and Excavation Results)," *NEAEHL*, 2:701–712; SMITH, W. M., "Jerusalem," *NIDB*, 514–22; WILKINSON, J., "Jerusalem," *Major Cities of the Biblical World*, ed. R. K. Harrison (Nashville: Nelson, 1985) 139–55.

Strategic Center in the Shephelah

Lachish was a defense center second in importance only to Jerusalem itself during the history of the kingdom of Judah. Its importance is asserted by several sources: the Bible; the excavation and restoration of the defense system at Lachish; the discovery of the Lachish letters containing information on the role Lachish played as a major defense center; and Assyrian records both in inscriptions and in relief form. The Bible mentions that Rehoboam fortified the site (2 Chron 11:9), that it was one of the last of the cities to be taken by Sennacherib in the Assyrian campaign of 701 BCE (2 Chron 32:9), and that it was one of the last of the fortified cities of Judah to fall to the Babylonians (Jer 34:7). Information from the Lachish letters and the Assyrian relief depicting Sennacherib's conquest of the city provide additional substance to these clues.

The location of Lachish, its features, and the ingenuity of its inhabitants contributed to make it a strategic defense center. Lachish was located in the shephelah midway between Jerusalem, which lay about thirty miles northeast of Lachish, and Gaza, some twenty-five miles west-southwest of Lachish. It lay on one of the major routes to Jerusalem from the coastal plain, especially the plain of Philistia. Consequently, Lachish was in a position to guard the pass and monitor groups from the west and southwest seeking entrance to the cities of Judah in the central hill country.

The role of Lachish as a major watch and defense center guarding the highway leading inland was due to its size as well as its location. The site, known today as Tell ed-Duweir, is a large rectangular-shaped mound. The upper part of the tell has a surface covering eighteen acres, while the base covers thirty acres. Because the massive tell reached a height of approximately 150 feet, the occupants of ancient Lachish had a commanding view of the valley below. Today nearly half of the site's height is formed of the imposing defense system the Israelites built over the earlier defense systems of the Canaanite city of the Middle and Late Bronze ages.

Massive remains of Israelite fortification at Lachish

Lachish is mentioned in both the OT and other ancient Near Eastern sources. In the Bible it appears first in Joshua 10 which describes the battle between Joshua and the Israelites and the Amorite city-state kings of the south. According to the biblical account, the city-state king of Lachish at the time was Japhia (Josh 10:3), who along with the other kings of the confederation was defeated and executed (Josh 10:16–27). Following the execution, Lachish, as well as the other sites of the confederation, was conquered and destroyed by the Israelites (Josh 10:31–32). Lachish was allotted to the tribe of Judah (Josh 15:39). It is not mentioned again in biblical history until the reign of Rehoboam, the son of Solomon. During his reign Lachish was fortified along with other cities in Judah and became a major defense center of the southern kingdom (2 Chron 11:5–10), second only to Jerusalem. The new defense program apparently involved strengthening the fortifications of the city and equipping it with supplies of food, oil, and wine as well as weapons such as shields and spears (2 Chron 11:11–12). Lachish was also the site at which Amaziah, king of Judah, was killed as he tried to take sanctuary in the city following a conspiracy in Jerusalem (2 Kgs 14:17–19; 2 Chron 25:26–28). One of the most important events in the history of Lachish was the encounter the city had with Sennacherib, king of Assyria, who in 701 BCE moved into Judah and destroyed forty-six of Judah's fortified centers (2 Kgs 18:13), including the city of Lachish (2 Chron 32:9). According to Jeremiah, Lachish was one of the last of the Judean cities to be conquered and destroyed by the Babylonians (Jer 34:7). The biblical reference to Lachish informs us that the site was among those in Judah resettled during the postexilic period (Neh 11:30).

Lachish is mentioned in extrabiblical sources, including records of the commercial activities of the city-state of Ebla that date to ca. 2400 BCE. In the Amarna letters from Egypt Lachish is accused of assisting the Habiru by providing them with supplies of food and oil. The name "Lachish" appears in an Assyrian inscription accompanied by bas-reliefs depicting Sennacherib's conquest of the city in 701 BCE. The reliefs, found in the palace of Sennacherib in Nineveh, portray the Assyrian siege of the city as well as a procession in which spoil from the city is presented to Sennacherib.

Some of the most valuable insights about the history of ancient Lachish come from archaeological excavations conducted at the site during this century. The earliest excavations began in 1932 under the direction of J. L. Starkey and continued until 1938 when Starkey's murder ended the expedition. Additional excavations were undertaken at the site for two brief seasons in 1966 and 1968 under the direction of Y. Aharoni, who attempted to clarify the function of the so-called solar shrine. One of the most comprehensive excavation projects at Lachish began in 1973 under the direction of David Ussishkin. The new series of continuing excavations sponsored by Tel Aviv University and the Israel Exploration Society have attempted not only to clarify the chronology of the site but also to reconstruct the Israelite fortification at Lachish.

Archaeological investigation of the area demonstrates that the region around Lachish has been inhabited since the Paleolithic period; however, the site itself was not settled until a later period of time, perhaps during the Neolithic Age. During the latter part of the Chalcolithic period and the early part of the Early Bronze Age, a troglodyte (cave-dwelling) community existed in the area. The inhabitants took shelter in the caves of the surrounding hills. By the latter part of the Early Bronze Age, the inhabitants had moved out of the caves to the site of the present tell, and the caves were used as graves.

Little is known about settlements at Lachish prior to the Middle Bronze Age. During that period (ca. 1700 BCE) the site was fortified with a brick wall about one hundred feet above the surrounding valley. In addition to the brick wall, fortifications included a glacis or a plastered slope, and a moat or fosse around the base of the mound, a fortification system commonly associated with the Hyksos. Egyptian influence at Lachish during the Middle Bronze Age is seen in the scarabs (seals in the form of a beetle) found at the site. A palace or a palace-citadel was built within the city itself; however, following the expulsion of the Hyksos from Egypt, the defense system fell into disuse and gradually deteriorated.

Lachish became an important Canaanite city-state during the Late Bronze Age partly due to Egyptian influence in the area. One of the most interesting features of the Late Bronze city was the construction of a temple in the moat or fosse at the base of the tell. The temple commonly called the "fosse temple" was enlarged twice during its history. While the Late Bronze city was protected somewhat by the Middle Bronze glacis, it had no city wall. The Canaanite city of the Late Bronze Age was destroyed ca. 1200 BCE, most likely by Joshua and the Israelites.

Lachish was not occupied again until the tenth century BCE perhaps during the reign of David, but little is known about the early Israelite settlement at Lachish. Apparently the site was refortified during the reign of Rehoboam, and Lachish was well on its way to becoming a royal fortified Judean defense center, second to Jerusalem in importance. One of the most impressive features of the new city was a palace-fort that went through three building stages, often referred to as palace A, palace B, and palace C, corresponding to levels V, IV, and III of the ancient city. The palace-fort that was built on a huge podium made of stone walls filled with rubble, perhaps yet another millo, was eventually a massive structure roughly 250 feet long by 115 feet wide. In addition to the palace-fort the royal fortified city was equipped with government storehouses similar to those found at Beersheba and Megiddo, indicating that Lachish functioned as a major administrative center in the southern kingdom. The storehouses were perhaps used for the storage of items like "food, oil, and wine" (2 Chron 11:11) as well as other goods.

The most impressive feature of the city was the fortification, the building of which apparently began during the reign of Rehoboam. The city was enclosed in a massive brick wall some twenty feet thick. An additional wall was built midway down the slope to act as a revetment or barrier to help retain the glacis and prevent its deterioration. One final feature of the fortification was the massive city gateway located on the west side of the city. The gate complex was comprised of an inner gate with six chambers, similar to but larger than those at Megiddo, Hazor, and Gezer, an outer gate, and a roadway leading up to the gates themselves.

Lachish letter

One final feature of the royal Judean fortress was a large shaft dug in the surface on the east side of the mound. The shaft, approximately seventy-five feet square and nearly eighty feet deep, was most likely designed as a water shaft or reservoir. The water-shaft project may have been similar in purpose to Hezekiah's tunnel in Jerusalem that was designed to provide water for the community due to the impending threat posed by Sennacherib in 701 BCE. While the purpose and circumstances of the shaft are not clearly discerned, the fate of the city certainly is. In 701 BCE Sennacherib attacked the city. Using a siege ramp built by the Assyrians on the southwest corner of the tell, he conquered the city's massive fortifications and destroyed it. Consequently, the royal Judean defense center and store city that stood for perhaps two hundred years came to an end and stood abandoned.

The city was rebuilt following the decline of the Assyrian empire. A new city wall and gate complex made it once again a major Judean fortification and defense center. But the period of resurgence was not to last. Nebuchadnezzar destroyed the city in 587 BCE, and it never again equaled its magnitude of the Judean period.

Among the unique discoveries found in excavations at Lachish are the so-called Lachish letters that date to the destruction of Lachish at the hands of the Babylonians under Nebuchadnezzar. The twenty-one letters, eighteen of which were discovered in a guardroom in the city gate, include correspondence between two military officials. Yoash was a military commander stationed in Lachish, and Hoshiah was stationed in an outlying garrison. Their letters reflect the deteriorating circumstances in the southern kingdom as the war nears an end. Letter four is especially informative; it states that while the watchman in the outlying garrison continues to watch for fire signals from Lachish, he no longer sees those of Azekah. This indicates that Azekah, one of the last of the cities to be conquered by the Babylonians (Jer 34:7), has fallen. Following the destruction of Lachish by the Babylonians, the site was not occupied for more than a century. A palace consisting of a courtyard surrounded by rooms was built during the fifth century BCE on the ruins of the podium of the earlier palace. A small sanctuary commonly called a solar temple was built on the site during the Hellenistic period. The history of ancient Lachish came to an end ca. 150 BCE when the site was destroyed and finally abandoned.

In addition to the Lachish letters, excavations have produced other discoveries that are of special interest including the so-called fosse temple, the Canaanite temple from the late Bronze Age built in the city's moat. The temple was built about 1550 BCE and went through two additional building phases ca. 1450 and 1350. The temple was designed with several features that were used in offerings and other cultic rituals, including benches on which offerings were received, an altar with a hearth, numerous pottery bowls, and pits in which the bones of birds, fish, sheep, and goats were found. These bones are of special interest because they are those of the right forelegs of sheep and goats, the part of the animal prescribed as the priestly portion of the peace offerings in the Levitical law (Lev 7:32). Additional features of the temple complex included niches or compartments in which the pottery vessels were apparently stored, and ovens outside the temple proper, perhaps used for other types of offerings. While the structure and its contents include features that tend to imply a cultic context, some propose that the fosse temple was a potter's workshop rather than a temple.

Another building of special interest is the so-called solar shrine briefly mentioned above, which was originally discovered by James Starkey. More recent excavations at the site under the direction of Y. Aharoni have identified the facility as a Jewish temple from the Hellenistic period. The temple was similar in design to the Arad temple from the preexilic period, having two chambers and a courtyard, a design similar to that of Solomon's temple, which included a porch or vestibule, a holy place, and a holy of holies.

Bibliography: AHARONI, Y., and D. Ussishkin, "Lachish," *EAEHL,* 3:735–53; BOYD, B., "Lachish," *IDBSup,* 526; CRESSON, B. C., "Lachish," *HolBD,* 856; DAHLBERG, B. T., "Lachish," *IDB,* 3:53–57; DAVEY, C. J., "Lachish," *NBD*^{2}, 669–70; DIVITO, R. A., "Lachish Letters," *ABD,* 4:126–28; ELWELL, W. A., "Lachish Letters," *BEB,* 2:1297–98; GOLD, V. R., and K. N. Schoville, "Lachish," *ISBE,* 3:55–58; GUINAN, M. D., "Lachish Letters," *ISBE,* 3:58–60; KING, P. J., "Lachish," *HBD,* 537–42; LAUGHLIN, J. C. H., "Lachish," *MDB,* 495–96; PARDEE, D., "Lachish Inscriptions," *OEANE,* 3:323–24; PAYNE, J. B., "Lachish," *NIDB,* 576–78; PEARSON, A. T., "Lachish," *BW,* 343–49; SCHOVILLE, K. N., "Lachish," *BAF,* 419–28; THOMPSON, J. A., "Lachish," *NIDBA,* 283–84; idem, "Lachish," *ZPEB,* 3:850–58; idem, "Lachish Letters," *NIDBA,* 284; TUFNELL, O., "Lachish," *Archaeology and Old Testament Study,* ed. D. Winton Thomas (Oxford: Clarendon, 1967) 296–308; USSISHKIN, D., "Lachish," *ABD,* 4:114–26; idem, "Lachish," *OEANE,* 3:317–23; idem, "Restoring the Great Gate at Lachish," *BAR* 14 (2, 1988) 42–47; idem, "Lachish," *NEAEHL,* 3:897–911; VOS, H. F., "Lachish," *BEB,* 2:1296–97.

City of Many Battles

Megiddo was one of the most consequential cities in Palestine during the OT period. Originally a city of the Canaanites, Megiddo became a major Israelite administrative center during the first millennium BCE. Though the chronology of ancient Megiddo remains somewhat imprecise and open to debate, and though some features of the ancient city continue to encourage discussion and debate, the importance of the city itself is unquestioned. The central role the city played in OT times is reflected in the features of the site brought to light through archaeological research: twenty occupational levels dating from the Chalcolithic period to the Persian period; massive Early Bronze walls; a multichambered Middle Bronze gateway; a sacred area with a variety of features including a huge altar or high place and temples; the Solomonic fortifications, storehouses, a gigantic grain silo; a community water system; and numerous destruction levels. To these features may be added a wide array of artifacts, many of which reflect international influences at the site, influences that came from throughout the ancient Near Eastern world including Egypt, Anatolia, the Aegean, north Syria, and Mesopotamia. Megiddo was much more than a citadel of the Canaanite and Israelite cultures; it was a major cosmopolitan center on the international highway connecting the lands of the Fertile Crescent. Megiddo was located at a strategic site in northern Palestine on a spur of the Mount Carmel mountain range. The city had a commanding view of the Wadi Arah, the major pass through the Carmel range located on the south and east sides of the mound, and the Esdraelon plain, a vast sweeping plain located on the east and north sides of the mound to which the pass led. The location was significant because the major highway connecting the Fertile Crescent to Egypt and Mesopotamia passed through the Wadi Arah and the Esdraelon plain. Thus the city of

Megiddo could exercise control over the international highway. During its lengthy history Megiddo witnessed many battles, often international in scope, fought in the vast Esdraelon plain in full view of the city. Three other noteworthy routes passed by Megiddo. The first was another international route that traveled from Megiddo along the north side of the Carmel range to Acco and along the coast to Tyre and Sidon and beyond; the second was a regional highway connecting Megiddo with other major sites of the central hill country including Shechem, Jerusalem, and Hebron; the third passed eastward from Megiddo through the Esdraelon plain and valley of Jezreel to the city of Bethshan. The site's location carried geopolitical implications.

Other important features contributed to the site's growth and development, including a water supply and fertile farm land. The city's water supply came from a spring in a small cave near the base of the mound. The site was also adjacent to one of the most fertile agricultural breadbaskets in Palestine, the Esdraelon plain. It provided food and grain for the entire region as well as for export purposes. Clearly the site of Megiddo made it one of the key cities in Palestine in OT times.

Megiddo is mentioned in both the Bible and other ancient Near Eastern sources. Megiddo is mentioned in the accounts of the conquest and settlement in the books of Joshua and Judges. According to the book of Joshua, Megiddo was one of the sites taken by Joshua and the Israelites in the territory west of the Jordan River (Josh 12:21), and Megiddo and its villages were allotted to the tribe of Manasseh (Josh 17:11). The book of Judges indicates that while the site was in the territory of Manasseh, the inhabitants of Megiddo were not driven out but continued to live there (Judg 1:27). According to the Song of Deborah in the book of Judges it was at Taanach, by the "waters of Megiddo" that the Israelites defeated the Canaanite kings of the north (Judg 5:19). Based on the biblical accounts and archaeological evidence we may reasonably assume that Megiddo did not become an Israelite city until the period of the united monarchy, perhaps during the reign of David or Solomon.

During the reign of Solomon, Megiddo became one of the administrative centers of the kingdom (1 Kgs 4:7, 12), and like Hazor and Gezer, one of the royal fortified cities (1 Kgs 9:15). Ahaziah, king of Judah, died at Megiddo following an encounter with Jehu (2 Kgs 9:27). Josiah was killed there as he attempted to intercept Neco, the king of Egypt, who was on his way to assist the Assyrians in their final confrontation with the Babylonians (2 Kgs 23:29–30). During the course of its history the site of Megiddo had witnessed so many battles that it came to occupy a special place in apocalyptic literature. The "plain of Megiddo" was associated with death and mourning (Zech 12:11), and Megiddo itself is referred to in the book of Revelation as Armageddon, meaning "Mount Megiddo," the site of history's final confrontation of forces (Rev 16:16).

Extrabiblical sources also reflect the important role played by ancient Megiddo in international affairs. Egyptian sources from the reign of Thutmose III inform us that during the period of the Eighteenth Dynasty in 1468 BCE, Megiddo underwent a seven-month siege as the Egyptian king attempted to lay hold of this important Canaanite city-state and bring it under Egyptian control once again. The significance of the site for the Egyptians is reflected in their lengthy account of the battle and the list of the booty Thutmose transported from Megiddo to Egypt, including prisoners of war, hands (apparently used to count those killed in battle), horses, cows, goats, and sheep, to name a few.

Megiddo is also mentioned in the Amarna letters from the fourteenth century BCE. During the Amarna period Megiddo was caught in the state of chaos and revolution that prevailed in Canaan as Egyptian domination in the area slipped. Biridiya, the city-state king or prince of Megiddo, complained to the Egyptian pharaoh about the encroachment of Labayu, the city-state king of Shechem, who was seeking to enlarge his territory. Characteristic of many of the city-state kings of that period, Biridiya requested assistance in face of this threat and assured the Egyptian king of his loyalty to Egypt. Megiddo is also listed in the annals of the Egyptian king, Shishak, among the cities Shishak conquered in his campaign to Palestine, though it does not appear in the biblical account of the campaign (1 Kgs 14:25–28).

Megiddo also appears in the Assyrian record of the campaigns of Tiglath-pileser III to Syria-Palestine. According to the Assyrian account Tiglath-pileser III captured Megiddo in 732 BCE and established his provincial headquarters in that city.

In addition to the literary sources mentioned above, excavations at the site bring yet another dimension to the portrait of ancient Megiddo. The site of ancient Megiddo, modern Tell el-Mutesellim, is a large mound approximately seventy feet high but reaching a height of about two hundred feet above the plain to the east and northeast. The summit of the tell covers about fifteen acres, the total mound about thirty-five acres. The site was originally excavated by G. Schumacher from 1903 to 1905. A major excavation project was initiated by the Oriental Institute of the University of Chicago in 1925. This project excavated the site layer by layer down to bedrock and continued until 1939. It was directed by C. S. Fisher, P. L. O. Guy, and G. Loud. Y. Yadin conducted excavations at the site between 1960 and 1971 in order to clarify the stratigraphy of the Early Iron Age. The most recent excavations at the site have been conducted by David Ussishkin and Israel Finkelstein.

Though flint tools and bone material seem to reflect activity at the site dating to the prepottery Neolithic period, the oldest settlement at the site apparently occurred during the Chalcolithic period. During the Chalcolithic period Megiddo was the home of an agricultural community whose members gathered grain with flint sickles and domesticated animals. The people of the site lived in mud-brick houses, used rock-cut pits for storage, and had ovens and pottery for daily usage. There is some indication that the Chalcolithic population may have used olive presses to produce olive oil.

Massive Early Bronze altar at Megiddo

During the Early Bronze Age (ca. 3000–2000 BCE) Megiddo became a major urban center. Several impressive developments took place including the establishment of a sacred area and the fortification of the city. The sacred area, located in the eastern part of the town, was initially established with the construction of a temple. Typical of the Early Bronze temples in Palestine, the temple was rectangular in shape with the entrance located in one of the long walls rather than at the end. The temple had an altar adjacent to the entrance on the back wall and a paved courtyard. Later in the Early Bronze Age, the sacred area was equipped with a massive round altar, approximately twenty-five feet in diameter and four and one-half feet high. The altar was enclosed by a wall. Steps built into the east side of the altar led to the top. A large quantity of animal bones were found in the debris around the altar, apparently the bones of animals sacrificed at the high place. During the later part of the Early Bronze Age, three additional temples were built in the sacred area. The three temples, all of the broad-house type with entrances in the long wall of the south side, were equipped with altars. The city was fortified during the early part of the Early Bronze Age. The largest wall found at Megiddo is twenty-five feet thick and sixteen feet high. Megiddo was destroyed during the latter part of the third millennium BCE, and the Early Bronze city came to an end. During the century or two that followed, commonly called the Intermediate Early Bronze/Middle Bronze period, Megiddo was apparently no more than a small and limited villagelike community.

Following a period of decline near the end of the Early Bronze Age and the beginning of the Middle Bronze Age, Megiddo once again became a thriving city. During the early part of the Middle Bronze Age, Megiddo must have been under Egyptian control and was fortified with a new mud-brick city wall and gate. Around 1750 BCE the city was refortified with a new city wall made of stone, a large earthen rampart or glacis, and a multichambered city gate: a fortification system characteristic of the Hyksos period. A large earthen ramp led up to the gateway. It was during the Middle Bronze Age that the city spread from the citadel or the upper city to the lower city. The city experienced tremendous growth and prosperity. Domestic buildings including houses and large structures, apparently the first in a series of palaces, were discovered from this period. The palaces were located near the gateway of the city. The large round altar continued to be used, and additional temples were built in the sacred area. While the Egyptians lost control of Megiddo during the Hyksos period, Egyptian control of

Canaanite Megiddo apparently returned with the expulsion of the Hyksos around the beginning of the Late Bronze Age. Evidence of Egypt's heavy hand in the area is seen in the account of the seven-month siege of the city by Thutmose III mentioned earlier. In spite of the fact that the city was destroyed by Thutmose III, Megiddo

Solomonic gate

moved into one of its most prosperous periods. Excavations indicate that the palace area was expanded and that it was a citadel of rich treasures including jewelry, beads, gold, and some two hundred ivory carvings or plaques, treasures hidden under the floor of the palace. A new large fortified temple, often called the "fortress temple," was built in the sacred area over some of the earlier shrines. Also of special interest from the Late Bronze city are a number of cultic items including pottery offering stands and figurines or bronze images of gods and goddesses such as Resheph and Astarte. These reflect Hittite and Hurrian influence from north Syria and Anatolia. During the Amarna period Egyptian control of Megiddo was apparently quite limited. A clay tablet of the Gilgamesh Epic (the Babylonian flood account), found by a shepherd near the gate of the city, apparently belonged to the Late Bronze city of Megiddo.

The Late Bronze city experienced a violent destruction near the end of the Late Bronze Age and the beginning of the Iron Age, perhaps ca. 1150 BCE. Just who was responsible for the destruction is not clear; however, it was probably the Israelites, Egyptians, or perhaps the Philistines. The Iron Age city that followed was poorly built. The presence of Philistine pottery indicates a Philistine presence or town at Megiddo until the end of the eleventh century when the site was destroyed again, perhaps by David.

Grain silo from the time of Jeroboam II

The new occupation of the site was marked by poorly built structures and a general period of decline in the material culture of the site, which may have been the beginning of the Israelite occupation of Megiddo during the early monarchy. During the era that followed Megiddo was once again transformed into a major fortified city, apparently by Solomon. During the mid-tenth century BCE Megiddo was fortified with a massive six-chambered gate and casemate wall (a double wall partitioned into chambers), a fortification similar to those built by Solomon at Gezer and Hazor (1 Kgs 9:15). Solomon apparently rebuilt the city, making it one of the royal administrative centers in the north. Contemporary with the Solomonic fortifications were two major buildings usually designated palaces, most likely royal quarters, one located in the southern part of the city and one in the north. Also associated with the Israelite city were numerous cult objects including horned altars, cylindrical pottery offering stands, and bronze stands as well as a variety of other objects including pottery bowls and figurines. The cult objects were found in the rooms of the houses or royal dwellings, implying that they were used in the rituals of household shrines (Judg 17:4–5). Near the end of the tenth century BCE, Megiddo became a part of the northern kingdom and the Solomonic city was at least partially destroyed, most likely by Shishak.

The city was rebuilt once again during the Omride dynasty. The city was refortified with a new city wall designed with offsets and insets, a feature that provided added protection for the citizens of Megiddo. The new wall was presumably built by King Ahab, who also equipped the city with a massive complex originally designated "Solomon's stables" but more recently labeled storehouses, and a large grain silo. The construction of the city's water system has also been associated with Ahab's reign, though it was originally identified with the Canaanites of the Late Bronze period. The water system was comprised of two major parts, a massive shaft and a tunnel, and afforded protected access to the city's water supply in a cave near the base of the mound. The occupation of Megiddo continued until the city was destroyed by the Assyrians in 732 BCE.

During the period that followed, Megiddo was apparently an unfortified Assyrian provincial center that was destroyed, perhaps by Pharaoh Neco, in 609 BCE. The city continued to exist, though unprotected, into the Persian period when it was finally abandoned in 350 BCE.

Bibliography: AHARONI, Y., and Y. Shiloh, "Megiddo," *NEAEHL*, 3:1003–24; AHARONI, Y., and Y. Yadin, "Megiddo," *EAEHL*, 3:830–56; CHAPMAN, B. C., "Megiddo," *NIDBA*, 308–9; DAVIES, G. I., *Megiddo* (Grand Rapids: Eerdmans, 1986); DEVRIES, C. E., "Megiddo, Megiddon," *NIDB*, 637–38; FREDERICKS, D. C., "Megiddo," *HolBD*, 941–43; LAMON, R. S., *The Megiddo Water System* (Chicago: University of Chicago Press, 1935); LAMON, R. S., and G. M. Shipton, *Megiddo I* (Chicago: University of Chicago Press, 1939); LAPP, N. L., "Megiddo," *HBD*, 620–24; LAUGHLIN, J. C. H., "Megiddo," *MDB*, 564–65; LOUD, G., *The Megiddo Ivories* (Chicago: University of Chicago Press, 1939); MAY, H. G., *Material Remains of the Megiddo Cult* (Chicago: University of Chicago Press, 1935); MITCHELL, T. C., "Megiddo," *NBD²*, 757–59; RAINEY, A. F., "Megiddo," *ISBE*, 3:309–11; idem, "Megiddo," *ZPEB*, 4:164–76;

SCHOFIELD, J. N., "Megiddo," *Archaeology and Old Testament Study*, ed. D. Winton Thomas (Oxford: Clarendon, 1967) 309–28; SCHOVILLE, K. N., "Megiddo," *BAF*, 439–45; USSISHKIN, D., "Megiddo," ABD, 4:666–79; idem, "Megiddo," *OEANE*, 3:460–69; VAN BEEK, G. W., "Megiddo," *IDB*, 3:335–42; VOS, H. F., "Megiddo, Megiddon," *BEB*, 2:1431–32; YADIN, Y., "Megiddo," *IDBSup*, 583–85; idem, "Megiddo of the Kings of Israel," *BA* 33 (1970) 66–96.

SAMARIA 🏺   38

Capital of the Northern Kingdom

Samaria was the northern kingdom's answer to its need for a capital. But while the establishment of Samaria solved one problem, it seemed to give rise to a host of others. Even as the new capital helped to bring stability and focus to the kingdom, its founding seemed to mark the beginning of a class system, and in the end Samaria became a citadel of wealth and affluence, the home of the rich upper class, the landed aristocracy.

While the origin of most biblical cities is hidden in antiquity, the Bible provides a brief account of the founding of the city of Samaria. It was founded by Omri, king of the northern kingdom and first of the Omride dynasty (1 Kgs 16:23–24). Perhaps more than anything else, the establishment of Samaria reflects the genius of Omri in dealing with one of the most critical problems in the north—the need for a permanently fixed capital. From the beginning of the northern kingdom in 922 BCE until the reign of Omri, several sites had served as the capital of the northern tribes, including Shechem (1 Kgs 12:25), Penuel (1 Kgs 12:25), and Tirzah (1 Kgs 14:17). The movement of the capital from one location to another reflects several problems that were prominent in the north, including the problem of tribal jealousies, the antimonarchial feelings of the people of the north, and the general political instability that prevailed in the northern kingdom. Against this backdrop the founding of Samaria takes on real significance. Omri, one of the most powerful and stable kings in the north, established a new capital in a new location, a hill on which a fortified city had never stood, and built Samaria, the city that served as the capital of the northern kingdom until it fell in 722 BCE. According to the Bible, Omri bought the hill of Samaria from Shemer for two talents of silver, fortified the site, and named it Samaria after Shemer (1 Kgs 16:24).

But the selection of the site was important for other reasons. It was neutral and free of previous tribal jealousies. It was easily fortified because of its relationship to the immediate area. Samaria is situated on a hill in a basinlike formation that cuts across the highlands of the central hill country forty miles north of Jerusalem and twenty-five miles east of the Mediterranean Sea. Because the hill rises some three hundred feet above the valley floor that surrounds it on the north, west, and south, the site was easily fortified and defended.

Casemate wall from Samaria

The hill of Samaria had two other important benefits. First, it was located along major trade routes that moved through central Palestine. It lay along the major north-south highway that extended through the central hill country that led to Dothan, Megiddo, and the Esdraelon plain in the north and Jerusalem as well as other important sites in the south. Its position on the major east-west highway provided access to the coastal plain and Mediterranean Sea on the west, and Shechem and the Jordan valley on the east. Second, the hill of Samaria was situated in a fertile agricultural basin. The local economy's strong agricultural base was built on the cultivation of cereal crops like wheat and barley, and the production of wine and olive oil from the numerous vineyards and olive orchards in the area. While Omri's decision to build a new capital at the new location seemed to solve permanently the problem of a capital, the new capital seemed to set in motion yet another problem, the development of a class system. The new capital was located in a sense on two hills, an upper hill or acropolis, and a lower hill or slope. With the royal quarters set apart to themselves on the upper hill, the acropolis, the king and those of the royal court could shut themselves off from the people and the prophets. A class system developed with a wealthy upper class, the landed aristocracy on the one hand, and a poor lower class, the workers and serfs, on the other. Samaria became a citadel of wealth and affluence, and the growing class system ate away like a cancer at the core of the nation and in the end contributed to its decline and fall. We learn about this situation in 1 Kings 21, but we are especially informed about it by the eighth-century prophets Amos and Hosea. The prophets became the conscience of the nation and were instrumental in exposing the atrocities that were produced by the class system.

Samaria is mentioned frequently in the OT, particularly in 1 and 2 Kings and the prophets. While Omri apparently began to build Samaria (1 Kgs 16:24), it was continued by his son Ahab. According to the Bible, Ahab built at least two important structures in the capital city: an ivory house (1 Kgs 22:39; probably an elaborately decorated palace for himself) and a sanctuary equipped with an altar dedicated to the worship of Baal (1 Kgs 16:32). Since Omri's son Ahab married Ethbaal's (the king of the Sidonians, 1 Kgs 16:31) daughter Jezebel, we may assume that Omri initiated a foreign policy that included a marriage alliance with the Phoenicians. Assyrian texts that refer to Israel as "the house of Omri" also imply that Omri had an alliance with the Assyrians. This was most likely an attempt by Omri to neutralize any threat from the Syrians to the north. The alliance with the Phoenicians opened the door to cultural exchange between the two nations. Consequently, during the reign of Omri and Ahab life and culture in Samaria were shaped and influenced by the Phoenician culture. This may explain the construction of the Baal sanctuary (1 Kgs 16:32) and the "four hundred and fifty prophets of Baal and the four hundred prophets of Asherah" who ate at Jezebel's table (1 Kgs 18:19), in essence a government-supported missionary program. During Ahab's reign, the city of Samaria was besieged by the Syrian king, Benhadad (1 Kgs 20:1ff.). While Ahab initially defeated the Syrian king (1 Kgs 20:16–21), a later confrontation between the two proved fatal for Ahab (1 Kgs 22:29–37). His body was returned to Samaria, where it was buried (1 Kgs 22:37), and Ahab's blood-covered chariot was washed in the pool of Samaria (1 Kgs 22:38), conceivably a pool in the courtyard of the royal palace. Samaria was also the scene of the death of Ahab's son, Ahaziah (1 Kgs 22:51), who died after he fell through the lattice of a window on the second floor of the palace (2 Kgs 1:2–17). During the reign of Ahab's son Jehoram, Samaria was again besieged by the Syrians under Benhadad (2 Kgs 6:24ff). Jehu, the commander of the army (2 Kgs 9:1–37), led a successful coup and then exterminated the entire house and royal court of Ahab in Samaria (2 Kgs 10:1–17), thus bringing to an end the Omride dynasty.

During the reign of Jehu, the kingdom of Israel and its capital Samaria entered a period of rapid decline. While Omri established alliances and trade relations with countries like Phoenicia and Assyria and expanded the borders of the northern kingdom into areas of the Transjordan like the land of Moab, Jehu allowed these alliances to be destroyed and lost the territory in the Transjordan. Israel's weakened state was due primarily to the loss of its top officials (2 Kgs 10:11). Consequently, the nation had little power to withstand aggression by neighbors such as Hazael, the king of Damascus (2 Kgs 10:32–33). Jehu became a vassal of Shalmaneser III, the king of Assyria. His vassalage is recorded and portrayed on one of the panels of the black obelisk of Shalmaneser III.

The first half of the eighth century brought a time of unprecedented prosperity and expansion in Samaria and the northern kingdom under Jeroboam II (2 Kgs 14:23–29). But the wealth was concentrated in the hands of a small minority, the landed aristocracy. Consequently, Israel and its capital Samaria faced great social problems resulting from the oppression of the poor by the wealthy landowners, conditions reflected in the preaching of the prophet Amos (Amos 2:6–8; 3:9–10, 15; 4:1–3; 5:10–13; 6:4–6).

The forty-one-year reign of Jeroboam II in essence constituted the Indian summer of Israel's history. Jeroboam II extended the borders of the northern kingdom to their greatest extent (2 Kgs 14:25), apparently modeling his kingship on Solomon, and the nation and its capital enjoyed a period of unequaled prosperity. During the twenty-five-year period that followed, a period reflected in preaching of Hosea, the nation experienced rapid decline and in the end fell. The decline and fall was due to a state of political anarchy that characterized the kingdom and was reflected in the rapid turnover in leadership— Zechariah, the son of Jeroboam reigned for six months and was killed by Shallum (2 Kgs 15:8–12); Shallum was killed by Menahem (2 Kgs 15:13–16); Pekahiah, the son of Menahem, was liquidated by Pekah (2 Kgs 15:23–26); and Pekah was killed in a conspiracy led by Hoshea (2 Kgs 15:27–31). Weakened by internal strife and political anarchy, the kingdom of Israel and its capital Samaria fell to the Assyrians in 722 BCE. While the attack on Samaria was initiated by Shalmaneser V (2 Kgs 17:1–6), according to Assyrian records, the Assyrian king Sargon II was responsible for its final fall and destruction.

Sargon deported 27,290 people, according to the Sargon cylinder. Samaria and its territory were repopulated by people from other places including Babylon, Cuthah, Avva, Hamath, and Sepharvaim (2 Kgs 17:24), and Samaria became the Assyrian provincial capital. Apparently the city continued to function as an administrative center during the Babylonian and Persian periods.

The prophets criticized Samaria for its many social ills and its religious practices—the oppression and exploitation of the poor (Amos 2:6–7; 4:1; 6:1–7); the perpetuation of a corrupt court system (Amos 5:10–12); arrogance and pride (Isa 9:9); and an irrelevant and idolatrous religion (Amos 4:4–5; Isa 10:10–11; Ezek 23:1–10; Mic 1:6–7).

The history and portrait of ancient Samaria have also been enhanced by ancient Assyrian records, including the annals of Tiglath-pileser III, Shalmaneser III, and Sargon II. Archaeological excavations at the site add their own unique dimension to the life and history of Samaria. Samaria has been the site of several archaeological excavations including those directed by G. A. Reisner and C. S. Fisher (1908–10), J. W. Crowfoot (1931–35), E. L. Sukenik and K. M. Kenyon (1965–67), and J. B. Hennessey (1968). While excavations at the site have produced valuable discoveries, they have also encountered some major problems. Because ancient Samaria was repeatedly rebuilt, and the foundations for new buildings were dug down into the ruins of the preceding period, the remains of many of the structures from earlier periods have been severely damaged and in some cases entirely removed. The problem is complicated even more by the building practices of the

Israelites. The Israelites built with stone, and many of the stones from the buildings of earlier periods were salvaged and reused, consequently removing the kind of evidence archaeologists attempt to recover. In spite of these problems, however, important discoveries have been made at Samaria.

Excavations at the site have found evidence of some occupation in the area during the Early Bronze Age, but the earliest city built at the site dates to the ninth century BCE, the time of Omri and Ahab. Six occupational levels have been identified as Israelite with levels I and II belonging to the time of Omri and Ahab. During that period the acropolis was fortified and turned into a royal citadel.

The new capital was fortified by Omri with an outer wall and an inner wall. Omri equipped the new royal citadel with a palace as well as other buildings. The palace area, enclosed in a wall, encompassed an area nearly three hundred by six hundred feet. A pool discovered near the north wall may be the pool of Samaria mentioned in the Bible (1 Kgs 22:38).

During the reign of Ahab building activities continued and the city was enlarged. Omri's fortification walls were replaced by a casemate wall (a double wall partitioned into chambers), the palace was enlarged to nearly eighty by ninety feet, and a large storehouse was built. Over two hundred ivory plaques or panels were found around the palace storehouse and near the casemate wall. The ivory fragments are of special interest because of the biblical references to the ivory house built by Ahab (2 Kgs 22:39) and the beds of ivory mentioned by Amos (Amos 6:4). The ivory panels, many of which were designed with Egyptian and Syrian motifs, were apparently used as inlays in furniture and reflect the wealth and affluence of the city. During the reign of Ahab the city continued to enlarge to the east, the lower city.

The earlier city of Samaria survived its periodic destruction by rebuilding. The city of level III reflects a time of material decline and is generally assigned to Jehu and his successors. During the following period of Jeroboam II in the eighth century (levels IV, V, and VI), building activities once again resumed in Samaria. The palace was repaired, and the city's fortifications were strengthened. Some of the ivories come from this period, as do sixty-five ostraca discovered in the storehouse. The ostraca, inscriptions written on pieces of broken pottery, were receipts for the shipment of olive oil and wine produced in the royal olive orchards and vineyards and shipped to the royal court. They reflect a major source of the wealth of the period.

The city was destroyed in 722 BCE, and levels VII, VIII, and IX furnished only a small collection from the Assyrian, Babylonian, and Persian periods. The subsequent Hellenistic period also left little behind. In 332 BCE Samaria fell to Alexander the Great, and the city was heavily refortified with walls and towers. In 107 BCE the city was destroyed by John Hyrcanus, the Hasmonean. In 63 BCE Samaria, along with other cities in Palestine, fell into the hands of the Romans. During the Roman period it was rebuilt and became one of the grand cities of Palestine during the NT period. Herod the Great renamed it Sebaste after Augustus, who gave the city to him.

Bibliography: ACKROYD, P. R., "Samaria," *Archaeology and Old Testament Study,* ed. D. Winton Thomas (Oxford: Clarendon, 1967) 343–54; ARMERDING, C. E., "Samaria," *NIDBA,* 394–96; AVIGAD, N., "Samaria," *EAEHL,* 4:1032–50; idem, "Samaria (City)," *NEAEHL,* 4:1300–310; BLAIKLOCK, E. M., "Samaria," *NIDB,* 887–90; DAR, S., "Samaria (Archaeological Survey of the Region)," *ABD,* 5:926–31; DEVRIES, L. F., "Samaria," *BI* (Winter 1989) 10–15; HENNESSY, J. B., "Samaria," *IDBSup,* 771–72; KAUFMAN, I. T., "Samaria (Samaria Ostraca)," *ABD,* 5:921–26; KELSO, J., "Samaria, City of," *ZPEB,* 5:232–40; POTTS, D. R., "Samaria," *HolBD,* 1224–25; PRICE, J. D., "Samaria," *Major Cities of the Biblical World,* ed. R. K. Harrison (Nashville: Nelson, 1985) 223–33; PURVIS, J. D., "Samaria," *HBD,* 895–96; idem, "Samaria (Samaria the City)," *ABD,* 5:914–21; RAINEY, A. F., "Samaria," *BEB,* 2:1885–86; ROWELL, E., "Samaria," *MDB,* 788–89; SCHOVILLE, K. N., "Samaria," *BAF,* 465–72; TAPPY, R., "Samaria," *OEANE,* 4:463–67; VAN BEEK, G. W., "Samaria," *IDB,* 4:182–88; VAN SELMS, A., "Samaria," *ISBE,* 4:295–98; WISEMAN, D. J., "Samaria," NBD^2, 1060–62; WRIGHT, G. E., "Samaria," *BA* 22 (1959) 67–78.

City of Altars, Sacred Pillars, Trees, and Temples

Shechem is perhaps best described as a community of sacred places and traditions. It was one of the major religious and political centers in ancient Israel. During the united monarchy Shechem was second only to Jerusalem as a major religious and political center. While religion and politics often play important roles in the life and development of a community, at Shechem they were an essential part of the character of the community itself. The Bible, extrabiblical sources, and archaeological discoveries confirm ancient Shechem of the Canaanite, Israelite, and Samaritan periods as a city of altars, sacred pillars and trees, temples, covenants, covenant renewal, and political confirmation ceremonies. The Bible tells us that Abraham (Gen 12:6–7) and Jacob (Gen 33:18–20) built altars at Shechem or in the vicinity of the site. It was the place where Joshua reviewed the words of the law (Josh 8:30–35, esp. 33) and delivered his farewell address (Josh 24); there Abimelech attempted to become king (Judg 9); Rehoboam sought confirmation for his kingship (1 Kgs 12:1–20); and Jeroboam I built the first capital of the northern kingdom (1 Kgs 12:25).

Ancient Shechem, the modern Tell Balatah, is located at a strategic position in the central hill country thirty to thirty-five miles north of Jerusalem. Situated at the east end of the pass between Mount Ebal and Mount Gerizim, it was a place where several trade routes converged. Shechem controlled the major north-south highway through the central hill country that led to Megiddo in the north and Jerusalem and Hebron in the south, and the east-west highway that moved westward from Shechem to Samaria and on to the coastal plain highway.

In addition to its location on the major highways of central Palestine, the site had two other important features that contributed to its growth and development: a spring at the southeast corner of the mound that provided the water supply for the community and a fertile valley east of the city that provided valuable farmland. While many of the cities of Palestine were located on prominent mounds or ridges, Shechem was situated on the lower slope or shoulder of Mount Ebal, a small rise that offered little natural defense. Consequently, extensive fortifications were required to protect the site. The city's location on the shoulder of Mount Ebal was perhaps the means by which the city got the name Shechem, which in Hebrew means "shoulder."

One final feature of the location that was an integral part of ancient Shechem and its story is the presence of the two mountains that flanked the site—Mount Ebal (elevation 3,000 feet) to the north-northwest and Mount Gerizim (elevation 2,900 feet) to the south-southwest—and the role they played in the history of Shechem and its people. The two mountains were significant in their sacred character. Joshua and the Israelites built an altar on Mount Ebal and offered burnt offerings (Josh 8:30–32; Deut 27:1–8). The ritual, a covenant renewal ceremony, was witnessed by all of Israel with half the people standing in front of Mount Gerizim and half in front of Mount Ebal (Josh 8:33–35; Deut 27:11–14). The Samaritans revered Mount Ebal as the mountain of God, as opposed to Mount Zion in Jerusalem, and built a Samaritan temple at Mount Gerizim. The Samaritan tradition that identified Mount Ebal as the mountain of God is reflected in the statement of the Samaritan woman in the Gospel of John (John 4:19–20). During the biblical period one of the mountains was perhaps recognized as the "navel (center)" of the land (Judg 9:37). The four to five hundred Samaritans who still live in the area today observe their Day of Atonement and its rituals on Mount Gerizim much as they did in biblical times.

Shechem is mentioned frequently in the OT. It was an important worship site during the patriarchal period. It was Shechem that Abraham first visited when he arrived in Canaan (Gen 12:6–7). There by the oak of Moreh, Abraham built an altar. The site commemorated the promise, "to your descendants I will give this land" (v. 7), and like the other places where Abraham built altars, Shechem became one of the sites where the patriarch worshiped. Jacob visited the site after returning to the land of Canaan following his sojourn in upper Mesopotamia. At Shechem, Jacob purchased a piece of land and, like Abraham, erected an altar there (Gen 33:18–20). Shechem was the site at which Dinah, the daughter of Jacob, was molested by Shechem (Gen

34), the prince of the city and its territory (Gen 34:2). While the incident led to a covenant between Jacob's family and the local inhabitants (Gen 34:8–24), in the end it resulted in an attack on the city in which Shechem and his father Hamor were killed (Gen 34:25–26) and the city was plundered (Gen 34:27–29). Under the oak at Shechem Jacob buried the foreign gods (Gen 35:4) and to Shechem Joseph went in search of his brothers (Gen 37:12–14). Following the exodus, Joseph's body was returned from Egypt and buried at Shechem in the plot his father Jacob had purchased long before (Josh 24:32).

Shechem played an important role in the conquest and settlement. Since Shechem is not mentioned among the cities that were taken in the conquest, we may assume that it passed into Israelite hands peacefully. The site was obviously involved in the covenant renewal ceremony described in Joshua 8. The ceremony involved constructing an altar on Mount Ebal, presenting offerings and sacrifices, and reading the words of the Law (Josh 8:30–35). On the basis of the biblical references, we may assume that Shechem was the site at which covenant renewal ceremonies such as this one and the one described in Joshua's farewell address were periodically conducted (Josh 24:1–28). Following Joshua's address his words were written in the book of the Law of God, and the event was commemorated by erecting a stone "under the oak in the sanctuary of the Lord" (Josh 24:26–27). Shechem is listed as one of the cities of refuge (Josh 20:7) and is included among the Levitical cities (Josh 21:20–21).

The story of Abimelech in Judges 9 demonstrates the status that Shechem had already achieved as a religious and political center during the period of the Judges. Although this period is described as one in which "there was no king in Israel; every man did what was right in his own eyes" (Judg 17:6; 21:25; also see 18:1; 19:1), Shechem was the site of the first attempt at a kingship. Abimelech, the son of Gideon by a concubine from Shechem (Judg 8:29–31), became the self-appointed king. While Abimelech initially rallied the support of the people of Shechem (Judg 9:1–6), including "his mother's kinsmen" (9:1) and "all the citizens of Shechem" (9:2), after three years the citizens of the city revolted against him (Judg 9:22–41). Abimelech retaliated by destroying the city (9:42–45) and the sacred area (9:46–49). The sacred area was apparently comprised of the temple, referred to as "the house of Baal-berith" (v. 4), the "Beth-millo" (v. 6), the "Tower of Shechem" (v. 46), "the house of El-berith" (v. 46), and a sacred oak and pillar (9:6).

Shechem's importance as a political center is reflected in the account of the division of the nation in 1 Kings 12. Shechem is not mentioned in accounts of the united monarchy. When Solomon died in 922 BCE, his son Rehoboam went to Shechem to be crowned king (1 Kgs 12:1). We may assume that Rehoboam had already been anointed king in Jerusalem and that he appeared in Shechem, the major political center in the north, for a confirmation ceremony, a stamp of approval from the people of the north. The role Shechem played in the episode reflects the fact that by that time the nation was already polarized into two groups, the more promonarchial people of the south and the more antimonarchial tribes of the north. Dissatisfied with Rehoboam's response (12:12–15) to the people's request (12:3–5), the people of the north rejected the Davidic dynasty of Jerusalem (12:16). They rallied around Jeroboam (12:2), formerly the head of Solomon's corvée labor task force in Jerusalem (1 Kgs 11:26–28), and made him king over the newly-formed northern kingdom (1 Kgs 12:20). Shechem became the first capital of the northern kingdom (12:25).

Shechem is mentioned in extrabiblical sources, particularly those from Egypt, that date from the period of the Twelfth Dynasty. That era, the period of the Middle Kingdom, was one of the high points in Egyptian history. Sesostris III, who may have been the most powerful king of the entire period, captured Shechem. The city is also mentioned in the Execration texts, which refer to the vassal city-states in Syria-Palestine over which the Egyptians attempted to maintain control. The appearance of the name in the Amarna letters indicates that Shechem was a powerful troublemaking city-state during the Amarna period (fourteenth century BCE). From the Amarna letters we learn that Labayu, the king of Shechem, encroached upon the territory of surrounding city-states in order to enlarge his own territory in spite of the fact that he had assured the Egyptian king of his loyalty to Egypt.

The site itself has furnished important information. While the tell is relatively small, encompassing only ten to twelve acres, excavations during this century have discovered significant remains of this influential religious and political citadel of the north. Excavations were conducted at the site by German archaeologists under the direction of E. Sellin between 1913 and 1934, and by an American team under the direction of G. E. Wright, E. F. Campbell, and L. E. Tombs from 1956 to 1973.

The earliest occupation at the site dates back to a village that existed during the Chalcolithic period (ca. 4000 BCE). The first significant settlement at the site occurred during the Middle Bronze Age, the patriarchal period (ca. 1900–1800 BCE), when the biblical city of Shechem was founded. During the Middle Bronze Age Shechem became one of the major city-states in Palestine. Two important developments took place at the site during that period: the site was heavily fortified and the sacred area of Shechem was established. While the earliest Middle Bronze Age city had little or nothing in regard to fortifications, beginning ca. 1800 BCE or shortly thereafter the city was fortified with a substantial defense system. The new defense system, characteristic of the so-called Hyksos period, was comprised of a huge sloping embankment or glacis, and a mud-brick wall with a stone foundation. The massive glacis encircling the site was some eighty feet wide and twenty feet high and added significant protection to a site otherwise characterized by a low profile. During the latter part of the Middle Bronze Age the earlier fortifications were replaced by a large cyclopean wall constructed of massive, irregular stones. The new defense system had multichambered gateways located on the east and north sides of the city.

One of the most important features of the Middle Bronze Age city was the sacred area built on the acropolis. Originally the sacred precinct was enclosed by a wall and comprised a temple complex, or perhaps a palace-temple complex—a complex of rooms and courtyards sur-rounding a central courtyard in which stood the sacred pillars. During the latter part of the Middle Bronze Age, the temple complex of the earlier period was filled in, forming a large rectangular podium, and a massive rectangular-shaped fortress temple was constructed on the podium of fill. The new temple, with walls seventeen feet thick, obviously doubled as a defensive structure. The fortress temple built on the podium fill was equipped with sacred stones including pillars, standing stones, and slabs. The Middle Bronze Age city and its fortress temple were destroyed about 1550 BCE, most likely by the Egyptians.

Following its destruction and an occupational gap of about a century, the city of Shechem was reoccupied and rebuilt. Fortifications from the preceding era were apparently used during the Late Bronze Age. The fortress temple was rebuilt, though on a smaller scale. It was apparently the fortress temple of this period to which Judges 9 refers. During the course of its history the temple had several names: the house of Baal-berith, meaning the house of the lord of the covenant (9:4); Beth-millo, meaning the house of the fill (9:6), probably a reference to the massive fill constructed podium on which the temple was built; the Tower of Shechem (9:46), probably a title inspired by the tower of the temple; and "the house of El-berith," meaning the house of god of the covenant (9:46). One feature of special interest in the Late Bronze ruins is the absence of a destruction layer at the end of the Late Bronze Age. This means that the Late Bronze city continued on into the Iron Age, which fits the biblical materials that do not mention Shechem among those sites taken in the conquest. The city was destroyed during the twelfth century BCE, probably by Abimelech (Judg 9:42–49), and the temple was never rebuilt.

After standing unoccupied for a century, the site was rebuilt during the period of the divided monarchy. The fortification towers at the east gate were reworked, apparently by Jeroboam I, who built a capital at Shechem during the early part of his reign (1 Kgs 12:25). After the capital was moved from Shechem to other sites and eventually to its permanent location at Samaria, Shechem continued to function as a significant center in the north. During the ninth and eighth centuries BCE some of the city's fortification walls were rebuilt, and a large granary was constructed on the site of the former fortress temple. Shechem became a major provincial center of the northern kingdom where taxes in the form of grain were collected in the community's granary/warehouse. It prospered during the eighth century and had many of the typical Israelite four-room houses. But the citadel of the northern kingdom came to an end ca. 722 BCE when the city was destroyed by the Assyrians. The site was reoccupied during the Assyrian period but was abandoned during much of the fifth and fourth centuries BCE. Shechem was rebuilt once again during the latter part of the Persian period (ca. 350 BCE). During the period that followed, from ca. 350 to 107 BCE, Shechem enjoyed its final phase of prosperity as the capital and religious center of the Samaritans. The new city was for the Samaritans what Jerusalem was for the Jews. Excavations at the site have recovered evidence of the houses and fortifications that were a part of the Samaritan citadel. The Samaritan temple was located on one of the spurs of Mount Gerizim overlooking the city. The remains of the temple were found during the 1960s in excavations at the site of Tell er-Ros just south of the city. But while the city of Shechem prospered during much of the third and second centuries BCE, the tide turned during the latter part of the second century BCE as the land of Samaria and its capital experienced hostility from the Hasmonean state to the south. The conflict between the two religious rivals culminated in 107 BCE, when John Hyrcanus, the Hasmonean ruler, destroyed Shechem so thoroughly that it would never rise again. During the Roman period two important building projects took place: the emperor Vespasian built a new city on a location to the west of the ruins of Shechem and named it Neapolis, "new city"; and the emperor Hadrian built a temple for Zeus over the remains of the Samaritan temple on Mount Gerizim.

Bibliography: ANDERSEN, H. G., "Shechem," *ZPEB,* 5:381–85; CAMPBELL, E. F., "Shechem (City)," *IDBSup,* 821–22; idem, "Shechem (Tell Balatah)," *NEAEHL,* 4:1345–54; DEVER, W. G., "Shechem," *MDB,* 816–17; DeVRIES, C. E., "Shechem," *NIDB,* 927–29; ELWELL, W. A., "Shechem," *BEB,* 2:1941–43; FINKELSTEIN, I., "Shechem," *The Archaeology of the Israelite Settlement* (Jerusalem: Israel Exploration Society, 1988) 81–82; HUMMEL, H., "Shechem (Tell Balata)," *BW,* 518–22; MURRELL, R., "Shechem," *HolBD,* 1258–59; REED, W. L., "Shechem (City)," *IDB,* 4:313–15; ROSS, J. F., and L. E. Toombs, *Six Campaigns at Biblical Shechem,* compiled by the Archaeological Institute of America (New York: Bonanza, 1967) 119–28; SCHOVILLE, K. N., "Shechem," *BAF,* 473–80; SEGER, J. D., "Shechem," *OEANE,* 5:19–23; THOMPSON, J. A., "Shechem," *NIDBA,* 410–11; idem, "Shechem," *NBD²,* 1099–1101; TOOMBS, L. E., "Shechem," *ABD,* 5:1174–86; idem, "Shechem," *HBD,* 935–37; WRIGHT, G. E., "Shechem," *Archaeology and Old Testament Study,* ed. D. Winton Thomas (Oxford: Clarendon, 1967) 355–70; idem, "Shechem," *EAEHL,* 4:1083–94; idem, *Shechem* (New York: McGraw-Hill, 1965); WRIGHT, G. E., and E. F. Campbell, "Shechem," *ISBE,* 4:458–62.

Part II

CITIES OF THE
NEW TESTAMENT
WORLD

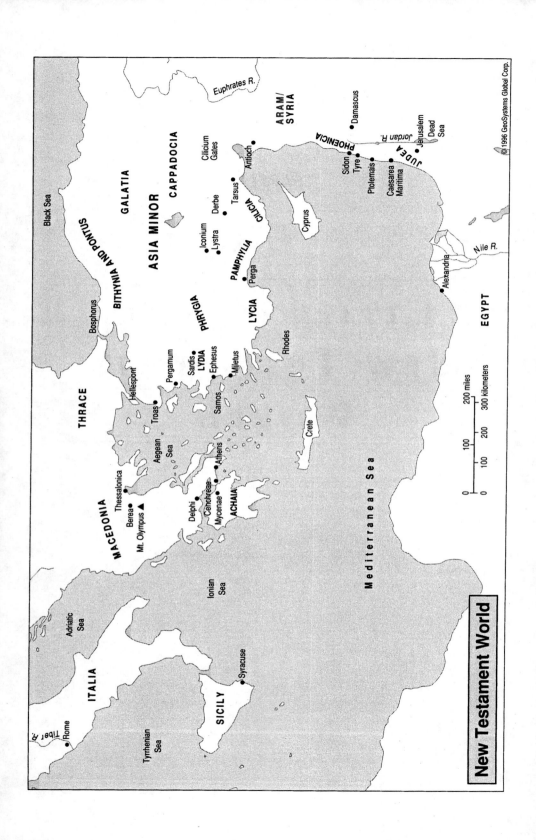

New Testament World

© 1996 GeoSystems Global Corp.

Unit 1

CITIES OF
PALESTINE

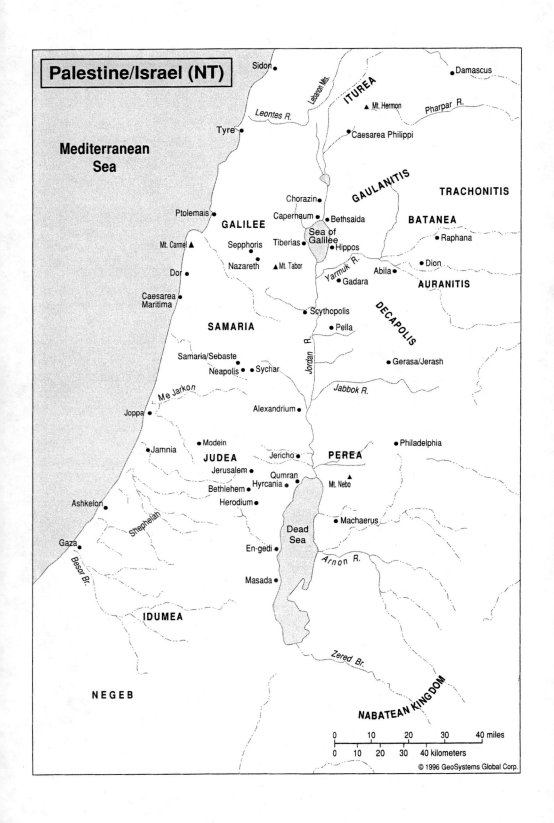

Palestine/Israel (NT)

Mediterranean
Sea

Sidon

Damascus

ITUREA

Lebanon Mts.

Leontes R.

Mt. Hermon

Pharpar R.

Tyre

Caesarea Philippi

GAULANITIS

TRACHONITIS

Chorazin

Ptolemais

Capernaum • Bethsaida

BATANEA

GALILEE

Sea of
Galilee

Raphana

Mt. Carmel ▲

Sepphoris

Tiberias

Hippos

Nazareth ▲ Mt. Tabor

Dion

Dor

Yarmuk R.

Abila

AURANITIS

Gadara

Caesarea
Maritima

Scythopolis

DECAPOLIS

SAMARIA

Pella

Samaria/Sebaste

Gerasa/Jerash

Neapolis • Sychar

Jordan R.

Me Jarkon

Jabbok R.

Joppa

Alexandrium

Modein

Philadelphia

Jamnia

JUDEA

Jericho

PEREA

Jerusalem

Qumran

Bethlehem Hycania

Mt. Nebo

Ashkelon

Herodium

Machaerus

Shephelah

Dead
Sea

Gaza

En-gedi

Arnon R.

Masada

IDUMEA

Zered Br.

NEGEB

NABATEAN KINGDOM

| 0 | 10 | 20 | 30 | 40 miles |

| 0 | 10 | 20 | 30 | 40 kilometers |

© 1996 GeoSystems Global Corp.

Land Bridge between East and West

No land has ever been shaped by a broader array of forces than biblical Palestine. Those forces include the forces of nature that shaped the physical features of the land and the cultural, religious, sociopolitical, and military forces that shaped the history of the land and in many places provided the material remains which provide us with windows into the past.

The land of Palestine had its own distinctive physical features. While Palestine is small—about forty miles wide in the north, sixty miles wide in the south, and 200 miles long—it is a land with a variety of physical features. It can be divided into five areas: the coastal plain, the narrow rolling plain along the Mediterranean coast; the shephelah, a narrow pie-shaped band of foothills located between the coastal plain and the central hill country in southwest Palestine; the central hill country, the highland and hilly area that runs throughout the length of the land west of the Jordan River; the Jordan River valley, a significant rift in the earth's crust that reaches a depth of 1,295 feet below sea level at the Dead Sea; and the Transjordan, the highland area east of the Jordan valley.

Due to its location along the major international highway connecting the lands of the Fertile Crescent from Mesopotamia on the east to Egypt on the west, Palestine in OT times witnessed migrations, business traffic, the imperialism of world powers, and the devastation brought by armies. During that period it was the homeland of Canaanites, Israelites, Philistines, Moabites, Edomites, and Ammonites. It saw the migration of such groups as the Amorites and the Habiru. The land was used for political purposes by the Egyptians, the Assyrians, and the Babylonians. And while nature left its own distinctive mark upon the land, the people who lived there left their own distinctive mark by populating Palestine's first major cities or tells with Canaanites, Israelites, and Philistines. Among the important cities of the OT period were Ai, Beersheba, Bethshan, Dan, Ekron, Gezer, Hazor, Jericho, Jerusalem, Lachish, Megiddo, Samaria, and Shechem.

Palestine of the NT period must be seen against the background of major political changes that occurred during the Babylonian, Persian, Greek, and Roman periods. The dramatic chain of events began to unfold with the arrival of the Babylonians near the end of the seventh and the beginning of the sixth centuries BCE. While Nebuchadnezzar and his forces posed a major threat to Judah and its cities as early as 605 BCE and 597 BCE and had already deported citizens to Babylonia during earlier visits, the final blow came in 587 BCE as the Babylonian king destroyed the city of Jerusalem and its temple, the center of worship and symbol of God's presence. During the period that followed, life in Palestine was marked by hopelessness, despair, and extreme pessimism. The land of Judah lay in ruins, its cities were destroyed, and its leadership and wealthy citizens had been deported to Babylonia. Only the poor of the land were left to fend for themselves. To make matters worse, the land was hit by a series of famines that resulted in massive starvation. The situation was so grave that nursing children's tongues stuck to the roofs of their mouths and little children were in the streets begging for food (Lam 4:4).

But the most debilitating experience of all was the destruction of Jerusalem and the temple. Believed by the people to be the impregnable citadel of Yahweh God, Jerusalem and its temple had been a constant reminder of the divine presence. But now the holy city lay in ruins. It resembled a widow in mourning (Lam 1:1).

Many of the exiles living in Babylonia also experienced trying circumstances. Yet it was during the Babylonian and Persian periods that the birth of a new religious institution took place. Meeting together for informal worship that included reading the Law, praying, and singing psalms, the exiled people began to lay the foundation for the synagogue, the institution that became the center of worship and study of the law in local communities throughout Palestine during the NT period.

Following a period of decline, the Babylonian empire fell to Cyrus the king of Persia in 539 BCE, and Palestine, like the rest of the lands of the Fertile Crescent, came under Persian control. The edict of Cyrus in

538 BCE allowed the exiles in Babylonia to return to their homeland, rebuild it, and once again practice their own cultural and religious traditions. Though several thousand apparently returned to Palestine between 539/38 BCE and 450/440 BCE, the precise number is not known. What the returnees found upon their homecoming was most discouraging. The cities of the central hill country of Judah and the shephelah lay in ruins, and the land was marked by extreme poverty. Two major schisms developed during that era, one between the returnees and the people who had remained in the homeland, the so-called people of the land, and the second between the Jews and their Samaritan neighbors to the north. Nevertheless, under the leadership of Zerubbabel (Ezra 3:1–6:22) and with additional encouragement from the prophets Haggai (Hag 1:1–15) and Zechariah (Zech 8:9–10), the temple in Jerusalem was rebuilt and finally dedicated in 515 BCE. The walls of Jerusalem were rebuilt in fifty-two days (Neh 3:1–4:6; 6:15) with the encouragement of Nehemiah during the fifth century BCE.

When Alexander the Great arrived in 332 BCE, Palestine came under the control of not only the Macedonian ruler but also a whole new cultural base, the Greek or Hellenistic culture from the west. Although Alexander died in 323 BCE, Hellenistic influence continued through the period of the Ptolemies and Seleucids, the successors of Alexander in Egypt and Syria. Palestine belonged to the kingdom of the Egyptian Ptolemies between 321 and 198 BCE, but it came under Seleucid control in 198 BCE. During the Seleucid period, particularly during the rule of Antiochus Epiphanes, Hellenism was forced upon the Jews in and around Jerusalem as the Seleucid king attempted to mold and solidify his empire. He erected a garrison, the Acra, in Jerusalem, made the worship of the Olympian god Zeus as well as other Greek gods and goddesses mandatory, and prohibited traditional Jewish worship. This pressure caused extreme unrest in Jerusalem.

The unrest resulted in a major revolt in 167 BCE that began the Maccabean era. In 165 BCE Jews regained religious liberty as Judas the Maccabee recaptured and rededicated the temple. Political independence came in the year 142 BCE, when Simon and his Jewish forces destroyed the Acra. The newly-formed Jewish state was a source of great hope, but it was not without problems. There was internal strife between groups such as the Sadducees and Pharisees and external conflict with the Samaritans to the north. John Hyrcanus and his forces destroyed the

Samaritan temple on Mount Gerizim and conquered Samaria, Edom, and Moab, making them a part of the Jewish state. The independent Jewish state came to an end in 63 BCE when Pompey conquered Syria and Palestine for Rome. Roman control of the land continued until ca. 330 CE; consequently, Palestine was a part of the vast Roman Empire during the NT period.

While Palestine was a relatively small land compared to the vast Roman Empire that encircled the Mediterranean Sea, the Romans realized its political value. Located at the eastern extreme of Roman imperial holdings, Palestine was an important gateway to the lands around and beyond it—Egypt to the south, Syria to the north, and Mesopotamia to the east. It was a land bridge traversed by the major highways that connected it with everything to the east and to the west.

Intent on maintaining good relations with the local population, the Roman government attempted to appoint local citizens to provincial administrative posts. In ca. 55 BCE Antipater, an Idumean and friend of both Pompey and the Roman statesman Julius Caesar, was appointed the local administrator or procurator of Judea. A highly capable administrator, Antipater was responsible for the administrative affairs of most of the land of Palestine. Because good relations prevailed between Antipater's family and Rome, Antipater was succeeded by his son Herod who was appointed the king of Judea by the Roman Senate in 44 BCE. While Herod the Great did not begin to rule his kingdom until 37 BCE, the Herodian dynasty introduced a new and important chapter in the history of Palestine. Herod's kingdom ultimately included: the regions of Idumea, Judea, Samaria, and Galilee (west of the Jordan); Perea (east of the Jordan); and the five districts of Gaulanitis, Auranitis, Batanea, Trachonitis, and Iturea (in the northern Transjordan east and northeast of the Sea of Galilee).

Though Herod was basically a good administrator, at least during the early part of his reign, his most notable contribution was to the landscape of Palestine. Many of the cities of the OT era had been destroyed by the Babylonians and Assyrians, and Herod, an advocate of Greco-Roman culture, implemented building enterprises throughout the land. Palestine was refurbished with a host of new cities, often built at old sites, that boldly displayed the architectural features of the Greco-Roman world. Consequently, during the NT period Palestine bore the distinctive mark of Herod the Great in the form of the masonryof the cities and fortress/retreat centers. Among Herod's most notable building projects were those at Jerusalem and its temple area, Caesarea on the Sea, Samaria (which he renamed Sebaste), Jericho, and the fortified retreat centers of Herodium, Machaerus, Masada, and Alexandrium. At Herod's death in 4 BCE, his kingdom was divided among his sons: Archelaus became the ethnarch of Judea, Samaria, and Idumea; Antipas became the tetrarch of Galilee and Perea; and Philip became the tetrarch of the five districts in the upper Transjordan east and northeast of the Sea of Galilee. Because of unrest and riots, Archelaus was removed from office in 6 CE by the emperor Augustus, and a procurator system was reestablished in the area. One of the most notable procurators was Pontius Pilate, who is mentioned in the NT. Philip continued to rule until his death in 34 CE, and Antipas ruled Galilee until 39 CE. The Herod most frequently referred to in the gospels is Herod Antipas, the tetrarch of Galilee. The Herodian dynasty ended with Herod Agrippa II (son of Herod Agrippa I and great-grandson of Herod the Great), before whom Paul appeared (Acts 26:1–32).

During the NT period Palestine was comprised of several smaller territories, including Idumea, Judea, Samaria, and Galilee, west of the Jordan; Perea, east of the Jordan; the districts of Gaulanitis, Auranitis, Batanea, Trachonitis, and Iturea in the upper Transjordan east and north of the Sea of Galilee; the Decapolis, a district of ten independent city-states, all but one of which were located east of the Jordan; and Nabatea, the homeland of the Nabateans located east, south, and southwest of the Dead Sea.

Bibliography: ADAMS, J. M., "Herodian Palestine," *Biblical Backgrounds,* revised by Joseph A. Callaway (Nashville: Broadman, 1965) 143–67; AHARONI, Y., and M. Avi-Yonah, *The Macmillan Bible Atlas* (New York: Macmillan, 1968); BALY, D., "New Testament Palestine," *Basic Biblical Geography* (Philadelphia: Fortress, 1987); BALY, D., and A. D. Tushingham, *Atlas of the Biblical World* (New York: World, 1971); BEITZEL, B. J., *The Moody Atlas of Bible Lands* (Chicago: Moody, 1985); BLAIKLOCK, E. M., "Palestine," *NIDB,* 742–48; BRUCE, F. F., "Palestine, Administration of (Roman)," *ABD,* 5:96–99; DEVRIES, C. E., "Palestine," *BEB,* 2:1598–1605; FINEGAN, J., *The Archaeology of the New Testament* (Princeton: Princeton University Press, 1969); FRANK, H. T., *Hammond's Atlas of the Bible Lands* (Maplewood: Hammond, 1984); idem, "Jesus," *Discovering the Biblical World,* rev. ed.; ed. James F. Strange (Maplewood: Hammond, 1988) 199–215; idem, "The Roman East and Herod the Great," *Discovering the*

Biblical World, rev. ed.; ed. James F. Strange (Maplewood: Hammond, 1988) 164–78; GRAF, D. F., "Palestine: Palestine in the Persian through the Roman Periods," *OEANE*, 4:222–28; GROH, D. E., "Palestine: Palestine in the Byzantine Period," *OEANE*, 4:228–32; HOPKINS, D. C., "Palestine, Geography of," *MDB*, 637–42; HOUSTON, J. M., "Palestine," *NBD*², 865–71; KENYON, K. M., "From the Exile to Herod the Great," *The Bible and Recent Archaeology*, rev. ed.; ed. P. R. S. Moorey (Atlanta: John Knox, 1987) 139–60; idem, "New Testament Palestine," *The Bible and Recent Archaeology*, rev. ed.; ed. P. R. S. Moorey (Atlanta: John Knox, 1987) 161–83; KING, P. J., "Palestine," *HBD*, 740–46; LASOR, W. S., "Palestine," *ISBE*, 3:632–49; MAY, H. G., "Palestine in New Testament Times, A.D. 6–70," *Oxford Bible Atlas*, 3d ed.; ed. John Day (New York: Oxford University Press, 1984) 86–87; idem, "Palestine Under the Herods (c. 40 B.C. to A.D. 6)," *Oxford Bible Atlas*, 3d ed.; ed. John Day (New York: Oxford University Press, 1984) 84–85; idem, "The Hellenistic Period," *Oxford Bible Atlas*, 3d ed.; ed. John Day (New York: Oxford University Press, 1984) 82–83; McCOWN, C. C., "Palestine, Geography of," *IDB*, 3:626–39; PATERSON, J. H., "Palestine," *ZPEB*, 4:564–86; PRITCHARD, J. B., *The Harper Atlas of the Bible* (New York: Harper & Row, 1987); RASMUSSEN, C. G., *NIV Atlas of the Bible* (Grand Rapids: Zondervan, 1989); ROGERSON, J., *Atlas of the Bible* (New York: Facts On File Publications, 1985); ROSEN-AYALON, M., "Palestine: Palestine in the Islamic Period," 4:233–34; STRANGE, J. F., "Palestine, Archaeology of (New Testament Period)," *ABD*, 5:116–19; THOMPSON, J. A., "Archaeology and the New Testament," *The Bible and Archaeology*, 3d ed. (Grand Rapids: Eerdmans, 1982) 307–437; idem, "The Days of Herod the Great," *The Bible and Archaeology*, 3d ed. (Grand Rapids: Eerdmans, 1982) 288–306; TRAMMEL, T., "Palestine," *HolBD*, 1063–69; WRIGHT, G. E., "Palestine in the Time of Christ," *Biblical Archaeology* (Philadelphia: Westminster, 1962) 221–47; YAMAUCHI, E., *Harper's World of the New Testament* (San Francisco: Harper & Row, 1981).

Site of Jesus' Birth

The prophet Micah demonstrated prophetic insight about the cities of his day that played an important part in shaping the destiny of Bethlehem. As a poor country boy from the peasant village of Moresheth in Judah, Micah was critical of big cities and their evils. He proclaimed,

> What is the transgression of Jacob?
>   Is it not Samaria?
> And what is the sin of the house of
>   Judah?
>   Is it not Jerusalem? (Mic 1:5b)

Terraced olive orchards

And as if he were championing the cause of the underdog, Micah continued,

> But you, O Bethlehem Ephrathah,
>> who are little to be among the
>>> clans of Judah,
> from you shall come forth for me
>> one who is to be ruler in Israel,
> whose origin is from of old,
>> from ancient days. (Mic 5:2)

Herodium, palace fortress of Herod the Great

Micah's prophetic declaration about Bethlehem, along with the accounts of Jesus' birth (Matt 2:1, 5–6; Luke 2:4) in the NT, indelibly etched Bethlehem in biblical history. The remains of ancient Bethlehem most certainly lie under the surface of the modern town of fifteen thousand people, beyond the reach of archaeologists.

Bethlehem is located in the Judean hill country about five miles south of Jerusalem. It has an elevation of about twenty-five hundred feet above sea level and lies on a spur of the central north-south ridge that runs through Palestine. The ancient town occupied a strategic position. To the east was the Judean desert, the extremely rugged and arid band of land on the west bank of the Dead Sea that often provided sanctuary for rebels and dissident groups. To the west was the fertile Judean hill country that provided tillable slopes and valleys for the cultivation of cereal crops, vineyards, and olive and fig orchards, as well as grazing land for sheep and goats. Consequently, there were economic and political implications to Bethlehem's surroundings. Agriculture and shepherding were always an important part of the economy of Bethlehem, and control of the site provided protection for the Judean interior to the west. Bethlehem was adjacent to the major north-south highway, the major inland route that traveled through the central hill country connecting the towns and cities of that region with the international trade routes.

There has never been a major excavation of the material remains of Bethlehem; the exploration of the site has been limited to surveys and minor investigations. The surveys indicate the site was occupied as early as prehistoric times. We may assume that during the OT period Bethlehem was an important Canaanite town that in time became Israelite. At one point the site or perhaps the territory in which it was located was named Ephrath or Ephrathah (Gen 35:19; 48:7; Ruth 1:2; Mic 5:2).

The precise origin of the name "Bethlehem" is not clear. It is generally interpreted as meaning "house of bread" but it may have once had some religious connotation similar to the name "Bethel," which meant "house of El" or "house of God." Rivalry between Jerusalem and Bethlehem during the Canaanite period may be reflected in the Amarna letters, in a letter from the city-state king of Jerusalem complaining about Bit Lahmi (Bethlehem) because it aligned itself with the Habiru, a stateless, homeless nomadic people that had entered Palestine.

Bethlehem appears in several accounts in the OT. It was the site of the burial of Rachel (Gen 35:19; 48:7), the home of the young Levite and the concubine mentioned in Judges 19–20, and the setting for the story of Ruth (Ruth 1:1–2, 19–22; 2:4; 4:11). But Bethlehem's greatest claim to fame during the OT period came through its association with David the king of Israel. Bethlehem was David's hometown (1 Sam 17:12) and the site at which he was anointed (1 Sam 16:1–13), and it is mentioned in other accounts about his life (1 Sam 16:14–22; 17:15; 20:6, 28). Its role as a strategic military site in the hill country of Judah is reflected in the accounts of its Philistine occupation during the reign of David (2 Sam

23:14–16) and its fortification during the reign of Rehoboam (2 Chron 11:5–6). But while Bethlehem was perhaps a significant town of key military importance during the period of the united monarchy and the early part of the divided monarchy, the town declined and by the eighth century BCE was unimportant (Mic 5:2). During the Babylonian period, Bethlehem is mentioned as a place where Judean refugees stayed as they escaped to Egypt (Jer 41:17). The Bible further informs us that during the Persian period some one hundred citizens of Bethlehem were among those who returned from Babylonia to the homeland (Ezra 2:21; Neh 7:26).

Herod's pool at the base of the Herodium

But Bethlehem's greatest claim to biblical history is found in the accounts of Jesus' birth. It was in Bethlehem that Jesus was born (Matt 2:1, Luke 2:4–7; John 7:42), and the wise men (Matt 2:1–12) and shepherds (Luke 2:8–20) visited him. While the accounts provide little information about Bethlehem itself and though no archaeological remains have been found, we may assume that during the first century CE, Bethlehem was a small village whose citizens were engaged in the same sort of agriculture, shepherding, and herding as their forebears of the OT period.

During the NT era, Bethlehem, like the rest of Judea, was under Roman domination and under the direct control of Herod the Great and his successors, either Archelaus, his son, or one of the procurators. And as if to provide a constant reminder of his presence in the area, Herod the Great constructed a palace-fortress, Herodium, four miles southeast of Bethlehem and in clear view of the town. Though no archaeological remains from the time of Christ have been found, interest at Bethlehem has centered around the Church of the Nativity, the cave beneath the church, and the traditions associated with that site.

While the Gospels of Matthew and Luke refer to Bethlehem as the place of the birth, the tradition that Jesus was born in a cave is mentioned in the writings of the early church father Justin Martyr, who lived during the second century CE. The tradition about the cave was also noted by the early church father Origen (ca. 248 CE) who apparently had visited the site on one of his many trips to Palestine. According to Jerome, who resided in Bethlehem during the latter part of the fourth century CE, the site of the cave had been desecrated by the Roman emperor Hadrian ca. 130 CE. In an attempt to halt the veneration of the site and to destroy the Christian faith, Hadrian planted a sacred grove over the cave and dedicated it to the Babylonian vegetation deity Tammuz.

During the reign of Constantine the obvious desecration of the site came to an end. The new emperor, the first to embrace the Christian faith, constructed a large basilica-style church over the cave (ca. 325 CE) to commemorate the place of Jesus' birth. It was dedicated by Helena, the mother of Constantine (ca. 327 CE). Since its original construction, the site of the church has had an interesting history. Though the church was destroyed during a revolt by the Samaritans ca. 529 CE, it was rebuilt and enlarged shortly thereafter by Emperor Justinian I and still stands as the Church of the Nativity. The church was spared destruction during the Persian invasion of the land in 614 CE because of the mosaic of the Magi that portrays them in Persian attire. Excavations conducted in 1934 by William Harvey, though limited in scope, discovered the plan of the church built by Constantine. One of the most interesting features of the Church of the Nativity is the architecture of the entrance which is exposed and above the ground. The entrance features three architectural styles or modifications—the long horizontal lintel that remains from the original Justinian church, the arch that was added during the

Crusader period, and the small entrance added even later to keep horses out of the structure.

In addition to the Church of the Nativity, the traditional site of the shepherds' field (though a couple of different options are possible) is located east of the town. Bethlehem is also recognized as the burial site of Jerome, the early church father who lived in a cave adjacent to the Cave of the Nativity (ca. 385 CE) and stayed there until his death. During that time he completed the translation of the Bible into common Latin. The translation, known as the Vulgate, became the official translation for the church. A statue of Jerome, located in the courtyard of the Church of the Nativity, commemorates his life and contributions.

Bibliography: ANDERSEN, H. G., "Bethlehem, Bethlehemite," *ZPEB*, 1:538–40; AVI-YONAH, M., "Bethlehem," *EAEHL*, 1:198–206; BALY, D., "Bethlehem," *HBD*, 106–7; CAZELLES, H., "Bethlehem," *ABD*, 1:712–15; FINEGAN, J., "Bethlehem," *The Archaeology of the New Testament* (Princeton: Princeton University Press, 1969) 18–26; HARRISON, R. K., "Bethlehem," *NIDBA*, 99–100; HENNESSY, J. B., "Bethlehem," *IDBSup*, 97; HOUSTON, J. M., "Bethlehem," *BEB*, 1:289–90; JUNG, K. G., "Bethlehem," *ISBE*, 1:472–74; KNIGHT, G. W., "Bethlehem," *HolBD*, 171–72; LAUGHLIN, J. C. H., "Bethlehem," *MDB*, 100–101; MANOR, D. W., "Bethlehem," *OEANE*, 1:302; McCREADY, W. O., "Bethlehem," *Major Cities of the Biblical World*, ed. R. K. Harrison (Nashville: Nelson, 1985) 58–62; McRAY, J., "Bethlehem," *Archaeology and the New Testament* (Grand Rapids: Baker, 1991) 156–57; PAYNE, D. F., "Bethlehem," *NBD*[2], 134–35; STEKELIS, M., M. Avi–Yonah, and V. Tzaferis, "Bethlehem," *NEAEHL*, 1:203–10; STEPHENS, W. H., "Bethlehem," *Where Jesus Walked* (Nashville: Broadman, 1981) 12–19; VAN BEEK, G. W., "Bethlehem," *IDB*, 1:394–95.

CAESAREA MARITIMA 42

Seaport Gateway to Herod's Kingdom

Caesarea was Palestine's major seaport during the NT period, but it was much more than just a harbor on the coast. It was a port city that demonstrated the architectural ambitions of Herod the Great. It was the gateway to his kingdom of Palestine, which showcased his embrace of Greco-Roman culture through ambitious building enterprises. Caesarea was sixty-five miles northwest of Jerusalem, on the coast between the cities of Joppa to the south and Dor to the north.

Ruins of Herod's Tower

In addition to designing it as the gateway to the kingdom, Herod the Great had several important reasons for constructing the seaport city. Because it had been given to Herod by the emperor Caesar Augustus, the new city was named Caesarea Maritima. Herod also tried to win favor with the people of Palestine through his building projects. Caesarea was designed and constructed to maintain good favor with the Gentile world, and Herod built the temple in Jerusalem as an attempt to appease and gain the support of the Jewish people who populated much of his kingdom.

Another reason for building at Caesarea was that Herod needed a major seaport to achieve his goals for the kingdom, and Caesarea was suitable. It was on a major shipping route in the Mediterranean Sea that traveled from Alexandria, along the coast of Palestine, Phoenicia, and Syria, ultimately to Athens and Rome. Located on a stretch of coast that often proved hazardous during stormy weather, the well-protected port of Caesarea had the potential to become an important stop on the route. Caesarea also commended itself as a port because, being on a shipping route that connected vital ports in the Mediterranean, it was a suitable location for Herod to bring into his kingdom the materials necessary for his other projects and to collect revenue to pay for those materials.

The site had yet other features that were valuable for Herod's purposes. It was located in a region of fertile soil that produced cereal grains and fruits. Caesarea had the potential to become an important center for land trade, since it was located along the international trade route that linked Egypt and Mesopotamia.

No major city had been built at the location previously. In the fourth century BCE, Strato I, the king of Sidon, erected a tower or lighthouse and provided a fortified anchorage on the coast for the ships traveling the shipping route along the eastern end of the Mediterranean Sea. The small Phoenician community that developed at "Strato's Tower" achieved some status as a commercial center. During the Maccabean period Alexander Jannaeus captured the site from Zoilus, a local ruler, and the Jewish population at the site grew. In 63 CE Jewish control of the site ended as Pompey acquired the site, and Strato's Tower became a part of the Roman province of Syria. Following the battle of Actium (31 BCE), in which Octavian defeated the forces of Mark Antony and Cleopatra, Octavian, who became known as Caesar Augustus, gave the site to Herod the Great.

Herod's city was constructed between 22 BCE and 10 BCE and covered 165 acres. It was comprised of two parts, a man-made harbor and a Roman city. Following Herod's death in 4 BCE the city became a part of the territory awarded to his son Archelaus. Because of unrest during his reign, Archelaus was replaced by a Roman procurator in 6 CE. During the period that followed Caesarea Maritima enjoyed a new status. It became the Roman capital of the province of Palestine, especially the territories of Judea and Samaria, and it was expanded beyond the city wall of the original Herodian city. Caesarea was the major headquarters for the procurators, one of whom was Pontius Pilate, as well as the site where the Roman legions were stationed. During that period Caesarea's Jewish population grew significantly.

As the first century continued to unfold, the community experienced unrest caused by tension between the Jewish community and the Roman rulers. Riots and disturbances occurred under the procurators Felix and Festus. But in 66 CE, during the era of the procurator Florus, the synagogue in Caesarea was desecrated, and a full-scale revolt broke out. The revolt resulted in the slaughter of twenty thousand Jews and marked the beginning of a long and bloody war that would spread to other areas. The Jewish-Roman War of 66–72 CE left an indelible mark on Jewish history. Caesarea continued to play an important part in that war. It served as home base for the Roman generals Vespasian, Titus, and Silva, and the Roman legions that fought in Jerusalem and other places. It was at Caesarea that Vespasian was elevated from army general to emperor. In appreciation for the city's support, Vespasian elevated Caesarea to the rank of Roman colony, making it the leading city of Palestine. Caesarea played an important role as the home base for Roman forces during the Second Jewish Revolt (132–135 CE).

During the third and fourth centuries CE Caesarea became an important center of early Christianity and a center of Jewish learning. Caesarea was home to the early church father Origen, following his move from Alexandria in Egypt. During his years in Caesarea, Origen taught in the famous catechetical school of Christian learning using his famous *Hexapla*, a parallel text of the OT. He also established a major library at the school. Caesarea became home to Eusebius who during his years in the city wrote his *Ecclesiastical History* and the *Onomasticon*, an important work on the geography of Palestine. From 313 to 340 CE Eusebius served as bishop of the city. A Jewish rabbinic school established in the city was, according to tradition, responsible for the development of part of the Babylonian Talmud.

During the Byzantine period the inner part of Caesarea was refortified with a wall in response to approaching Moslem forces, who nonetheless succeeded in capturing the city in 640 CE. In 1101 the city was captured by Baldwin I and the forces of the first Crusade. During the period that followed the city was refortified with a crusader fortification wall and a moat. In 1291 crusader rule came to an end as the site was recaptured and destroyed by the Moslems.

Among the most valuable resources for the study of Caesarea Maritima have been the accounts and descriptions provided by the Jewish historian, Josephus (*Ant.* 15.331–41; *War* 1.408–14). In recent times Caesarea Maritima has undergone a series of archaeological expeditions intended to clarify some of the major features of the city and the harbor. From 1959 to 1961 the Roman theater was excavated by an Italian team under the direction of Antonio Frova. In 1960 the Herodian harbor was investigated by the Link underwater exploration team. But the most extensive archaeological investigation began with the Joint Expedition of Caesarea Maritima project in 1971 under the direction of Robert Bull. The multiseason program introduced the use of computer analysis of artifacts and investigated numerous features of the ancient city including the city plan and streets, the hippodrome, the warehouse or vault area, the mithraeum (the sanctuary of Mithra), the sewer system, and others.

Among the most intriguing features excavated at Caesarea Maritima was the seaport constructed by Herod the Great. Josephus suggested that the harbor was as large as Piraeus, the harbor at Athens, and that it was most likely the largest harbor in the Mediterranean Sea at the time. Archaeological exploration of the harbor at Caesarea confirms that it was equal to and perhaps even larger than Piraeus. The seaport was designed to provide a protected harbor for the merchant ships within. It was comprised of a major wall or breakwater that extended westward from the coast and curved northward, protecting the south and west sides of the port area. A second sea mole (barrier or breakwater) extended outward from the coast forming the north wall of the port. A sixty-foot opening on the northwest corner of the port where the two walls approached each other provided the entrance to the port within. This entrance was flanked on both sides by three colossal statues. Both of the two major walls that formed the perimeter of the port were constructed of stones and hydraulic concrete, a type of concrete that hardened under water. According to Josephus the stones, measuring up to fifty feet long, ten to eighteen feet wide, and nine feet deep, were lowered into 120 feet of water. Underwater exploration confirmed stones of these dimensions and found some that were even larger. The harbor was designed with a sluice system to prevent the silting of the harbor floor.

Equally impressive are the remains of the city. The Herodian city was built around the harbor on the coast immediately east of it. It was enclosed in a semicircular wall that extended from the sea on the south side of the harbor around to the sea on the north side of the harbor. The 165-acre city had a theater, an amphitheater, a hippodrome, a temple dedicated to Augustus, storerooms, palaces, public buildings, a residential area, a sewer system, and an aqueduct that supplied the city with water.

Ancient theater

The original city built by Herod the Great was apparently designed with a street plan typical of Roman cities of that day. It was laid out with streets running parallel to each other both north and south and east and west, forming a grid of squares. The main street or thoroughfare in the city was the Cardo, a north-south street that lay midway between the harbor on the west and the city wall on the east.

The design and grid apparently remained the same during the Late Roman and Byzantine periods.

Caesarea Maritima was also constructed with a city sewer system. The sewer system was comprised of a series of underground passages constructed beneath the surface. Excavations have uncovered manholelike openings in the paved streets of the city that were connected with the subterranean passages some ten feet below. The passages below were vaultlike arches constructed of brick. The subterranean passages were flushed by the sea. Because the underground passages are clogged with silt, archaeological exploration of the sewer system has been extremely limited.

Inscription with name of Pontius Pilate, the Roman prefect of Judea

One of the largest structures at Caesarea Maritima was the theater, located on the south side of the city just outside the city wall. It was constructed of large stones, typical of those used by the masons employed by Herod the Great, and had three parts—the large semicircular stepped seating area, the stage area, and a semicircular arena behind the stage where gladiatorial fights were held. It is approximately three hundred feet in diameter. It had a seating capacity of about four thousand people. The theater has been restored and is once again used for performances and concerts. The acoustic quality of the theater is such that the ping of a dime dropped in the center of the performance area can be heard clearly by those seated in the top row of the theater. An inscription discovered in the process of excavating the theater has been of special interest to students of the Bible because it refers to "Pontius Pilate, Prefect of Judea," the Roman procurator mentioned in the accounts of Jesus' trial.

Aqueduct near Ceasarea Maritima

The city also had a large hippodrome that may date to the second century CE. Located on the east side of the city, the hippodrome was 1500 feet long and 250 feet wide. With a seating capacity of about thirty-eight thousand people, the hippodrome was used especially for chariot races. Among the discoveries in the hippodrome was a massive stone column used as a *taraxippos*, a "horse frightener." The *taraxippos* was a highly polished stone that had a reflecting quality similar to that of a mirror. The stone was designed to excite the race horses through the reflection of their images.

Excavations at Caesarea Maritima also unearthed a large number of massive stone vaults eighty to ninety feet long and fifteen to sixteen feet wide. The upper part of the chambers formed an arch for a roof. The chambers along the shore south of the harbor were a part of a large complex of more than one hundred such vaults. The large number of amphora fragments, including handles, suggests that the vaults were used for storage, probably for the city and for the harbor. They also may have garrisoned troops.

Among the discoveries in the warehouse area was a vault that had been converted into a mithraeum perhaps sometime during the third century CE. The mithraeum, a sanctuary dedicated to the worship of the god Mithra, was adorned with scenes from the life of Mithra painted on the plaster walls of the chamber and an altar at the end of the vault. An opening in the roof of the vault was so positioned that a stream of light from the sun beamed down on the altar at midday on June 21 at the time of the summer solstice. While Mithra, the god of light and truth, was originally a Persian god, the worship of Mithra was popular among Roman soldiers. It included a ritual sacrifice in which Mithra slew a sacred bull. During the Roman and Byzantine periods the cult maintained its popularity and became a strong rival to Christianity. The paintings and a white marble medallion found in the chamber portray Mithra in the ritual sacrifice of slaying the sacred bull.

Perhaps the greatest engineering feat at Caesarea Maritima was the design and construction of the water system comprised of two aqueducts. The high-level aqueduct in its earliest phase was most likely built by Herod the Great and was a water channel supported by arches running seven miles northward from Caesarea Maritima to Mount Carmel. The aqueduct was fed by a six-mile tunnel cut through bedrock that conveyed the water from a collecting point in Samaria, ten miles east of Caesarea, to the upper end of the aqueduct at Mount Carmel.

Current excavations at Caesarea Maritima are revealing yet another significant feature of the Herodian city, the temple of Augustus and the expansive platform on which it was constructed. Located east of the harbor and facing the harbor to the west, this was an impressive complex designed to meet and greet those who entered the city through the magnificent seaport.

Caesarea is mentioned in several passages in the NT, particularly in the book of Acts. Philip preached here (Acts 8:40); Cornelius, the Roman centurion converted through the ministry of Peter, lived here (Acts 10:1–11:18); Herod Agrippa I, grandson of Herod the Great, had a residence here (Acts 12:19); Paul used its port (Acts 9:30; 18:22; 21:8);

and Paul was imprisoned (Acts 23:23–26:32) and tried before Felix (Acts 24), Festus (Acts 25:1–12), and Herod Agrippa II (Acts 26) in Caesarea.

Bibliography: BLAIKLOCK, E. M., "Caesarea," *NIDBA,* 111; idem, "Caesarea," *ZPEB,* 1:680–81; BULL, R. J., "Caesarea," *IDBSup,* 120; idem, "Caesarea Maritima: The Search for Herod's City," *BAR* 8 (3, 1982) 24–40; CRISLER, J., "Caesarea World Monument," *BAR* 8 (3, 1982) 41; EWING, W., and R. K. Harrison, "Caesarea," *ISBE,* 1:567–69; FINEGAN, J., "Caesarea," *The Archaeology of the New Testament* (Princeton: Princeton University Press, 1969) 70–80; idem, "Caesarea," *The Archaeology of the New Testament: The Mediterranean World of the Early Christian Apostles* (Boulder: Westview, 1981) 184–91; HARRISON, R. K., "Caesarea," *NBD²,* 155–56; HOHLFELDER, R. L., "Caesarea," *ABD,* 1:798–803; idem, "Caesarea: Beneath the Sea," *BAR* 8 (3, 1982) 42–47; idem, "Herod the Great's City on the Sea," *National Geographic* 171 (2, 1987) 260–79; HOLUM, K. G., "Caesarea," *OEANE,* 1:399–404; HOLUM, K. G., A. Raban, A. Negev, A. Frova, M. Avi–Yonah, L. I. Levine, and E. Netzer, "Caesarea," *NEAEHL,* 1:270–91; KNIGHT, G. W., "Caesarea," *HolBD,* 218–19; McRAY, J., "Caesarea Maritima," *Archaeology and the New Testament* (Grand Rapids: Baker, 1991) 139–45; MILNE, M. K., "Caesarea," *HBD,* 148; NEGEV, A., A. Frova, and M. Avi–Yonah, "Caesarea," *EAEHL,* 1:270–85; PELLET, D. C., "Caesarea," *IDB,* 1:479–80; SCHOVILLE, K. N., "Caesarea," *BAF,* 337–45; SPENCER, A. B., "Caesarea Maritima," *Major Cities of the Biblical World,* ed. R. K. Harrison (Nashville: Nelson, 1985) 63–71; STRANGE, J. F., "Caesarea," *Best of the Illustrator: The Journeys of Paul,* ed. Michael J. Mitchell (Nashville: The Sunday School Board of the Southern Baptist Convention, 1990) 79–84; TRAMMELL, T., "Caesarea Maritima," *BI* (Spring 1989) 38–48; VARDAMAN, J., "Caesarea," *MDB,* 125.

Capital of Herod Philip

Even though Caesarea Philippi is mentioned only twice in the NT and its ruins remain mostly hidden, the city requires study for at least two reasons. First, it was the largest and most important city in extreme northern Palestine during the NT period. It was the capital of the tetrarch Herod Philip, the son of Herod the Great, who inherited the five districts of Gaulanitis, Trachonitis, Batanea, Auranitis, and Iturea from his father's kingdom. Second, excavations are currently under way to bring the material remains of the site to light for the first time.

Banias, NT Caesarea Philippi, is located two miles east of the OT site of Dan, twenty-five miles north of the Sea of Galilee and forty miles southwest of the city of Damascus. It is one of the most unique settings in northern Palestine. It is 1150 feet above sea level, ten miles southwest of Mount Hermon, which rises to a height of 9200 feet and provides Caesarea Philippi with an abundant supply of water. Clear cool water from the melting snow on Mount Hermon forms a spring that leads to the Nahr Banias, one of the major sources of the Jordan River. The presence of water made this site hospitable for human habitation and inspired the ancient inhabitants to dedicate the cave from which the spring came to the gods they associated with the water's source.

Caesarea Philippi's location also had strategic value militarily. Located on the southwestern slope of the Mount Hermon range, the city had a commanding view of the fertile plain below to the southwest, from which travelers or armies would approach. The site was also close to the major highways in the area. It was on a secondary east-west route midway between the major international highway to the east that ran through Damascus and the north-south highway to the west that ran through the Beth-rehob valley, which was the major pass between the Lebanon Mountains and Mount Hermon. The east-west highway on which the city was located provided access to the Mediterranean coast thirty miles to the west. Consequently, Caesarea Philippi had access to the major international highway that traveled eastward to Mesopotamia, the highway that moved northward to Syria, and the highway that ran westward to the coast and on to Egypt to the south.

Caesarea Philippi is only one of several names the site has had during its history. Though definitive evidence is lacking, during the OT period the site may have been known as "Baalgad," a site "in the valley of Lebanon below Mount Hermon" (Josh 11:17), or Baalhermon (Judg 3:3). The earliest name clearly identified with the site in historical records is the name "Panias" or "Paneas," the name used for the site during the Greek period as a result of its association with the worship of the god Pan. During the Roman period, Herod the Great built a temple at the site, and Herod Philip founded the first city there at about 2 BCE. The city was named Caesarea in honor of the emperor Caesar Augustus, and in order to distinguish the site from the one on the coast, Philip added his name, hence Caesarea Philippi. Herod Agrippa II rebuilt the city, at which time it became one of the most magnificent cities of the ancient world. The new refurbished city was renamed Neronias, in an attempt to win the favor and support of the emperor Nero. Of all the names that have been used during the history of the site, Panias has been the most enduring. After the NT era, the name Panias again came into use. During the Arab period the name was modified to Banias, the name it carries today.

The various names attached to the site are a reflection of its history. When the site was first settled is not clear; however, the site's abundant supply of water makes it safe to assume that some kind of settlement developed quite early. The archaeological history of Banias will be clarified as excavations proceed, but excavations at the site of Dan have revealed evidence of occupation as early as the fourth millennium BCE. It is likely that during the OT period the site was occupied by the Canaanites and, because of the spring and the abundant vegetation in the area, became a major center for the worship of Baal, the Canaanite god of fertility. During the remainder of the OT period we may assume that the site was a part of the territory of Dan, the united kingdom, and the northern kingdom.

An important phase of the history of the site began during the Greek period, following the conquest of the area by Alexander the Great during the latter part of the fourth century BCE. It was during that era that the site became a major center of worship for the god Pan, and was

renamed Panias, and the community as a whole began to be shaped by
the Greek culture. Apparently the community's focal point was the cave
and the spring that constituted the cultic area for the worship of the
impish Pan. Numerous niches were carved in the bluff around the cave,
and according to a Greek inscription below one of the niches, the site
was dedicated "to Pan and the nymphs." The worship of Pan, the god of
fields and forests, sheep and goats, and shepherds, was most likely
inspired by the rich vegetation of grass and woods that surrounded the
spring that supplied fresh water for the flocks. Pan was featured with a
human upper half and the lower half of a goat. The bearded head of the
Greek god usually had horns and sometimes the ears of a goat. One of
the most significant events to take place at the site of Panias during the
Greek period occurred in 198 BCE when Seleucid forces defeated the
Ptolemies and gained control of Palestine. According to Josephus, Jewish
control of the site was secured when Alexander Jannaeus gained
control of the Golan of which the site was a part (*Ant.* 13.397). Jewish
control ended in 63 BCE with the arrival of Pompey.

Cave of Pan at Ceasarea Philippi

Panias probably experienced little change with the introduction of the
Roman period. It continued as a center of the Greco-Roman culture and
maintained the worship of Pan. In 20 BCE the emperor Augustus gave the

site and the territory around it to Herod the Great who in turn erected a temple dedicated to Augustus. Following Herod's death in 4 BCE, the site became a part of the tetrarchy of Herod Philip. Significant changes apparently took place during Philip's reign. Philip founded a city at the site and named it Caesarea Philippi. The founding of the city signaled a change in the role of the site. While the site had functioned primarily as a worship center, with the construction of the new city, the site also became an important political center. The city became Philip's residence and the capital of his territory. Later, Caesarea Philippi became a part of the territory of Herod Agrippa II, was rebuilt, and was renamed Neronias. According to Josephus the city figured into the activities of the Jewish-Roman War of 66–70 CE (*War* 3.443–44; 7.23–24). Vespasian and Titus rested their troops here, and Titus spent considerable time here following the war. During his stay in the city Titus sponsored gladiatorial fights in which he disposed of large numbers of Jewish prisoners. Following the NT era, the city of Caesarea Philippi, whose name reverted to Panias, continued to be an important city in northern Palestine during the latter part of the Roman period and throughout the Byzantine period. During the eleventh and twelfth centuries the crusaders occupied the site and built a fort on the ruins of the city. The remains of the fort are still visible today.

Until recently Banias has been basically untouched by modern archaeologists, but a major excavation program is currently under way at the site. The project is sponsored by the Nature Reserves Authority, the Israel Antiquities Authority, and a consortium of American colleges and universities. It hopes to bring to light as much as two hundred acres of the ancient city. The discoveries of a Roman basilica, Roman arches and sidewalk, and crusader arches and walls thus far provide a preview of what is to come. A most exciting discovery came at the end of the 1993 season, with the unearthing of a first-century CE Roman building, perhaps an asclepium, a medical center and healing complex, or a palace. This discovery was followed by yet another during the 1994 season, when the column-lined Roman cardo (or main street) of the city was uncovered.

Caesarea Philippi is mentioned in Matthew and Mark as one of the areas to which Jesus traveled with his disciples (Matt 16:13–20; Mark 8:27–30) and the place where Simon Peter made the famous declaration, "you are the Christ, the Son of the living God" (Matt 16:16). During Jesus' ministry Caesarea Philippi was a prestigious center of the Greco-Roman culture, the royal center of Herod Philip, and the capital of his domain. The biblical references to "the district of Caesarea Philippi" (Matt 16:13) and "the villages of Caesarea Philippi" (Mark 8:27), reflect the city's status as the capital of Philip's territory. Eusebius observed a bronze statue of Jesus that had been erected in the city at the house of a lady who had been healed of a hemorrhage (*Hist. eccl.* 7.18).

Remains of a basilica at Caesarea Philippi

Bibliography: ADAMS, J. M., *Biblical Backgrounds*, rev. Joseph A. Callaway (Nashville: Broadman, 1965; see esp. 71, 146 and 149); BASKIN, J. R., "Caesarea Philippi," *MDB*, 125; BLAIKLOCK, E. M., "Caesarea Philippi," *NIDBA*, 111–12; idem, "Caesarea Philippi," *ZPEB*, 1:682–83; EDWARDS, W. T., "Caesarea Philippi," *HolBD*, 219–20; EWING, W., and R. K. Harrison, "Caesarea Philippi," *ISBE*, 1:569; HUCKABY, G. C., "Caesarea Philippi," *BI* (Summer 1988) 14–17; KUTSKO, J. "Caesarea Philippi," *ABD*, 1:803; MA'OZ, Z. U., "Banias," *NEAEHL*, 1:136–43; McRAY, J., "Caesarea Philippi," *Archaeology and the New Testament* (Grand Rapids: Baker, 1991) 171–73; MILNE, M. K., "Caesarea Philippi," *HBD*, 148–49; PAYNE, D. F., "Caesarea Philippi," *NBD*[2], 156; PELLETT, D. C., "Caesarea Philippi," *IDB*, 1:480; THOMPSON, J. A., *The Bible and Archaeology*, 3d ed. (Grand Rapids: Eerdmans, 1982; see esp. 310–11, 365–66); TZAFERIS, V., "Banias," *OEANE*, 1:270–71.

CAPERNAUM 44

Home Base of Jesus' Galilean Ministry

Jesus made Caperaum his home base during much of his public ministry. Capernaum was one of the most important cities in the region of Galilee. It was a major commercial and population center on the northwest shore of the Sea of Galilee, at the present-day site of Tell Hum. Thirteen miles long and eight miles wide, the Sea of Galilee provided Capernaum with one of its most successful industries, fishing. There were also support industries such as tying and repairing nets and building and repairing fishing boats; one of these boats has been excavated on the west side of the Sea of Galilee and is currently in the Yigal Allon Museum at Kibbutz Ginnosaur, Israel. Capernaum was equally blessed by particularly fertile soil. An agricultural industry thrived around the perimeter of the lake in places such as the plain of Gennesaret. An abundant annual rainfall and a warm climate favored the cultivation of a variety of crops, particularly olives, dates, and citrus fruit. Hills to the north provided the black basalt stone that was used in the construction of domestic and public buildings such as houses and synagogues.

In addition to its fishing and farming industries, Capernaum played an important role in commerce. Located on the international trade route that traveled from Egypt through Palestine onward to Syria and Mesopotamia, Capernaum saw the movement of caravans from Damascus and points to the east to trade centers on the Mediterranean Sea to the west. It was located just inside the eastern border of Galilee, the territory of Herod Antipas, some two and one-half miles west of the Jordan and the tetrarchy of Herod Philip that lay to the east of the Jordan. It became a port of entry and customs station for the Roman government and a major center of trade and commerce in Galilee. Its role in that capacity is reflected in the story of the call of Levi/Matthew (Matt 9:9), the tax collector who became a disciple of Jesus. Capernaum's status as a major center of the Roman government in Palestine is also indicated by the presence of the Roman military. Apparently a garrison of troops and official military personnel were stationed at the city (Matt 8:5; Luke 7:2). From our present understanding of the site, we may assume that during the first century CE, Capernaum was both one of the major cities of Galilee and one of the most important cities around the perimeter of the Sea of Galilee.

Mosaic of first-century CE fishing boat

Capernaum is mentioned in the NT, Josephus, rabbinic literature, some of the church fathers, and the accounts of Christian pilgrims who visited the land of Palestine. Capernaum is mentioned in all four gospels. According to the Synoptics, a major part of Jesus' public ministry took place in the territory of Galilee (Matt 4:12, Mark 1:14; Luke 4:14). Jesus apparently moved from his hometown of Nazareth in southern Galilee to Capernaum, the hometown of Peter and Andrew, and James and John, and made it his base of operation (Matt 4:13; Mark 2:1). It was at Capernaum that he called his first disciples (Matt 4:18–22); he taught and healed in the synagogue (Mark 1:21); he performed miracles of healing in private homes, including the healing of Simon Peter's mother-in-law (Mark 1:29–31, 32–34; 2:1–12); he called Matthew/Levi (Mark 2:13–17); he healed the centurion's servant (Matt 8:5–13); and did much more (Matt 17:24–27; Mark 9:33–50; John 4:46–54; 6:16–21, 22–40, 41–59). But in spite of the fact that it was his home and the site of important events in his ministry, Capernaum was condemned along with Chorazin to the northwest and Bethsaida to the east (Matt 11:20–24; Luke 10:13–15).

Among extrabiblical references to Capernaum (Josephus mentions being taken there after being injured by a horse in *Life* 72.403), those made by Christian pilgrims are of special interest. For instance, references are made to the special buildings at the site, especially the synagogue and the house, or house of Peter, by such people as Aetheria, a nun who visited the site in 385 CE, Theodosius, who visited the site in 530 CE, and the so-called Anonymous of Piacenza, who visited the site in 570 CE. While the buildings they saw were not first-century CE facilities, they were special points of interest in the community with which traditions had been associated. Although traditions and stories about a site cannot be taken at face value, they often provide valuable insight into the original site.

During the past century and a half the site of ancient Capernaum (the Greek name for the Hebrew *kepar-nahum,* meaning "the village of Nahum") has been explored by several excavation teams. Though two sites, Khirbet Minyeh and Tell Hum, were originally considered as possible candidates for the NT city, Tell Hum has been recognized as the most likely location following exploration of the site by Charles Wilson in 1865. Since then numerous developments have taken place in the exploration of the site. In 1894 the western part of the site, where the synagogue is located, was purchased by the Franciscans, an order of the Roman Catholic Church, who covered the ruins to preserve them. The eastern sector of the site was purchased by the Greek Orthodox Church. Heinrich Kohl and Carl Watzinger excavated the synagogue in 1905. Father Gaudence Orfali continued the work in the 1920s; he partially reconstructed the synagogue and excavated in the area of the church. Father Virgilio Corbo resumed excavations in the area of the synagogue in 1968, and Vassilios Tzaferis began excavating the eastern sector of the site owned by the Greek Orthodox Church in 1978, especially exploring the period when Palestine was invaded by Moslem forces during the seventh and eighth centuries CE.

While the history of the site is still somewhat imprecise and awaits further investigation, excavations that have taken place during the past century have helped to identify some of the important highlights of that history. Though the evidence for Capernaum's early history is limited, the site was apparently first established during the first century BCE, the early part of the Roman period. How quickly the site grew is difficult to determine; however, we may assume that its growth was rapid and that by the first century CE the city had become one of the most important towns in the area of the Sea of Galilee and the entire Galilee region. Archaeological data indicate that the site developed in two stages: the earlier stage, that of the early town, is located in the western sector corresponding to the Franciscan portion of the site; the latter stage, or later town, is located in the eastern sector corresponding to the Greek Orthodox sector of the site. The presence of the synagogue and octagonal church indicates that during its early history Capernaum had a thriving Jewish community. With the passing of time, the city became a center of early Christianity. During the early part of the seventh century CE, the

Bas-relief of the ark of the covenant

early town (western sector) came to an end and a completely new town with an entirely new city plan was constructed to the east. The destruction of the early city and construction of the new city may have resulted from the Persian invasion of Palestine in 614 CE and the subsequent invasion and recovery of the land by Byzantine forces in 629 CE. During the eighth century the destiny of the city changed. The new city constructed in the eastern sector experienced a violent destruction by earthquake in 748 CE, and the city of Capernaum came to an end, with only a small village existing on the site for the next two centuries. The site was finally abandoned during the tenth century CE. It was never again resettled, although primitive stone fishing huts were built during the Middle Ages.

Excavations at Capernaum have also brought to light the remains of the Capernaum synagogue, the house church, domestic houses, the waterfront jetty, the Roman bath, and a hoard of 282 gold coins. The synagogue at Capernaum has been of special interest because of the NT references that Jesus taught there (Mark 1:21) and because the facility was originally built for the Jewish community at Capernaum by a Roman centurion (Luke 7:1–5). It was initially believed that the synagogue at the site was the one mentioned in the NT. But later excavations have demonstrated that the white limestone building that has been partially restored at the site dates to the second or third century CE and perhaps as late as the fifth century. While the white limestone synagogue dates to a later period, it is nonetheless impressive and represents the strong Jewish community at Capernaum. The synagogue, located in the Franciscan sector, was an elaborately decorated structure sixty-five feet long and two stories high. The basilica-type structure was designed with three entrance doors, rows of columns topped with Corinthian capitols, and a colonnaded courtyard on the east side. Among its decorations were carvings of the ark of the covenant and the menorah in relief form.

In excavations that began in 1968, archaeologists found evidence of yet another massive building beneath the white limestone structure. The earlier structure is constructed of native black basalt with a black basalt cobblestone floor that dates to the first century. This synagogue may or may not be the one referred to in the NT.

Equally impressive and interesting are the discoveries of the octagonal church and what appears to be a house church beneath it, which has been interpreted by some as the site of the house of Peter. The original structure on the site, located to the south of the synagogue, seems to be a domestic dwelling or a common house of the first century. At some point very early in its history the house received special attention and by the second century was apparently used as a place of worship. The floors and the walls of the structure were repeatedly plastered and refinished and the walls were decorated with graffiti that included Christian symbols and names. During the fourth century the structure was enlarged, but the focal point continued to be the original room or house at the center. During the following century the earlier structures were destroyed, and a new octagonal church was constructed on the site. This Byzantine church was designed with two concentric octagonal walls and a mosaic floor decorated with flowers and a peacock. The site of the church is commonly referred to as the house of

Remains of a synagogue at Capernaum

Peter because several accounts detailing the travels of early Christian pilgrims make reference to a building in Capernaum by that name. While that identification is still open to debate, it is apparent that the building had special meaning to the early Christian community in Capernaum and that it was a special meeting place or house church for that community.

The remains of first-century houses have also been found in excavations at Capernaum. The walls of the houses were constructed of unworked black basalt stone. The cracks and crevices between the unworked stones were filled in with smaller stones and pebbles rather than mortar. Likewise the floors were paved with black basalt stone. The roofs were most likely made of wooden beams covered with straw thatch and perhaps mud. The general house plan was comprised of several rooms located around an open central courtyard. The central role of fishing in the community is reflected in the discovery of fishhooks in the floors of the houses.

The city was also equipped at some point with a seawall, a jettylike wall, wharf, or harbor along the waterfront. The wall, some two meters thick, was built of basalt stone. The wall not only provided a barrier between the lake and the community, but with parallel walls extending from the shore into the water, the waterfront construction perhaps provided docking facilities for fishing boats.

One of the most unique discoveries in the recent excavations in the new city in the eastern sector was a collection of 282 gold coins. The coins, deposited under a stone slab in the floor of a large building, were Ummayad dinars, apparently hidden under the stone slab during the Moslem period of the mid-seventh to mid-eighth centuries CE.

Two more discoveries that reflect something of the culture or cultural influences at Capernaum deserve mention. The first is a Roman-style bathhouse constructed near the lake during the first or second centuries CE. This bathhouse reflects the influence of the Roman culture in Capernaum. The second is a structure with pools or ponds obviously designed for the storage of fish. This building was most likely a fish market.

Bibliography: ADAMS, J. M., "Capernaum," *Biblical Backgrounds,* rev. Joseph A. Callaway (Nashville: Broadman, 1965) 165; ARCHER, G. L., "Capernaum," *ZPEB,* 1:746–48; AVIGAD, N., "Capernaum," *EAEHL,* 1:286–90; BARABAS, S., "Capernaum," *NIDB,* 192–93; CORBO, V. C., "Capernaum," *ABD,* 1:866–69; FINEGAN, J., "Capernaum," *Where Jesus Walked,* ed. William H. Stephens (Nashville: Broadman, 1981) 56–62; FINEGAN, J., "Galilee," *The Archaeology of the New Testament* (Princeton: Princeton University Press, 1969) 43–60, esp. 50–56; HARRIS, B. F., and E. M. Blaiklock, "Capernaum," *NIDBA,* 118–19; HORN, S. H., "Capernaum," *BW,* 162–64; JOINER, E. E., "Capernaum," *MDB,* 135; KANE, J. P., "Capernaum," *NBD²,* 177–78; KNIGHT, G. W., "Capernaum," *HolBD,* 230–32; LEA, T. D., "Peter's House in Capernaum," *BI* (Winter 1984) 72–75; LOFFREDA, S., "Capernaum," *OEANE,* 1:416–19; LOFFREDA, S., and V. Tzaferis, "Capernaum," *NEAEHL,* 1:291–96; McRAY, J., "Capernaum," *Archaeology and the New Testament* (Grand Rapids: Baker, 1991) 162–66; MILLER, C. H., "Capernaum," *HBD,* 154–55; MOUNCE, R. H., "Capernaum," *ISBE,* 1:609–10; PELLETT, D. C., "Capernaum," *IDB,* 1:532–34; ROGERSON, J., "Capernaum," *Atlas of the Bible* (New York: Facts On File Publications, 1985) 138–41; SANDERSON, J. E., "Capernaum," *Major Cities of the Biblical World,* ed. R. K. Harrison (Nashville: Nelson, 1985) 72–82; STRANGE, J. F., "Capernaum," *IDBSup,* 140–41; TZAFERIS, V., "New Archaeological Evidence on Ancient Capernaum," *BA* 46 (1983) 198–204; WILSON, J., "Capernaum," *Discovering the Bible,* ed. Tim Dowley (Grand Rapids: Eerdmans, 1986) 86.

GERASA/JERASH 45

An Important Greco-Roman Center on the King's Highway

As a city of the Decapolis, Gerasa was an important commercial, political, and religious center in the Transjordan area. Although the NT does not mention the city by name, the gospels do contain references to the region in which the city was located. For instance, among the multitudes that followed Jesus were those from "the Decapolis . . . and . . . beyond the Jordan" (Matt 4:25). It is quite possible that some of the Greeks who sought him out (John 12:20–21) were from the Decapolis, an area that was heavily populated by people of Greek background. Jesus healed a demoniac (Mark 5:1–20; Luke 8:26–39) or demoniacs (Matt 8:28–34) whom he met when he entered "the country of the Gerasenes" (Mark 5:1; Luke 8:26) or "the country of the Gadarenes" (Matt 8:28). While "the country of the Gerasenes" perhaps refers to the region in which Gerasa was located, we may assume that Gerasa was not the city referred to in the account because of its distance from the Sea of Galilee. Rather, the miracle took place at a location near the shore, such as the site of Kursi, which appears to fit the setting of the account.

Ancient Gerasa is located at the modern site of Jerash thirty-five miles southeast of the Sea of Galilee, twenty miles east of the Jordan River, and twenty-five miles north of the city of Amman. At an elevation of two thousand feet above sea level, Gerasa became a prominent city of the Transjordan because of geographical features, the site's relationship to other important cities in the area, and the sociopolitical climate of that time. Situated among the rolling hills of Gilead in the Chrysorrhoas valley, a tributary of the Jabbok River, the area of Gerasa produced cereal crops, grapes, and olives. Midway between the cities of Pella and Philadelphia, Gerasa was on the Roman highway that by either major or secondary routes connected all of the cities of the Decapolis. Located along the major north-south highway that ran through the Transjordan commonly referred to as the King's Highway, Gerasa also had international ties. The city had access to the international trade route that led to the rest of the world, Arabia to the south and Syria and other lands to the north.

Gerasa was located in the area known as the Decapolis. According to tradition the Decapolis was a league of ten cities that originated during the Hellenistic period. The ten cities of the Decapolis were Philadelphia, Gerasa, Pella, Scythopolis, Gadara, Abila, Hippos, Dion, Kanatha, and Damascus. While the cities of the Decapolis were the product of Alexander's influence in the area, Damascus, Scythopolis (OT Bethshan), and Philadelphia (OT Rabbath-Ammon) were in existence before the Macedonians arrived. Nevertheless, during the Greek period, the cities of the Decapolis took on a new character. They were either built or rebuilt on new foundations using Greek or Greco-Roman building techniques and became citadels of Greek culture in the foreign territory of Palestine.

The history of Gerasa seems to go back to the Early Iron Age, though some evidence of habitation dates to the Stone Age. But a new chapter in the history of the site began to unfold during the latter part of the fourth century BCE with the arrival of Alexander the Great, who supposedly founded the NT city. We may assume that the Greek city of Gerasa came into existence shortly after his arrival. During the third century BCE Gerasa was under the control of the Ptolemies of Egypt. With the arrival of Antiochus IV, however, Gerasa became a part of the Seleucid empire of Syria and was both reestablished and renamed. The new title "Antioch on the Chrysorrhoas," combined "Antioch," the name of the Seleucid provincial capital in north Syria, and "Chrysorrhoas," the name of the tributary on which the city was located. That the site bore the name "Antioch" reflects its high status during the Seleucid period. Seleucid control of the site came to an end in 82 BCE as Alexander Janneus captured the city of Gerasa and incorporated it into the Jewish state, but Jewish rule was short-lived. With the arrival of Pompey in 63 BCE, Gerasa became a part of the Roman Empire. The city apparently functioned as a regional capital. As one of the ten city-states of the Decapolis, Gerasa enjoyed the privilege of self-rule, being subject only to the Roman governor of Syria. Because of its position and self-governing status and the cultural and political climate that prevailed, the city of Gerasa flourished during the Roman period. The city was rebuilt in 65 CE on an even grander scale than before. The building process began in the first century CE and continued on into the second and third centuries when temples, theaters, and other public facilities were added. During that period Gerasa engaged in trade relations with Arabia to the south and other lands of the ancient east to the north and east. It became one of the chief cities of the Roman Empire in that area. In 129 CE the city was visited by the emperor Hadrian himself, and a new entrance, the triumphal arch, was constructed to commemorate the visit. The city reached its highest stage of development between 100 and 200 CE and today remains one of the best preserved Greco-Roman ruins of that era. The city reached its peak near the end of the second century with the construction of the temple of Artemis. It experienced a period of decline during the first part of the third century but apparently revived during the latter part of the third century under the Roman emperor Diocletian. By the fourth century the city had become an important center of Christianity; the remains of some thirteen churches have been discovered at the site. The city continued in that role until the Muslim conquest in 635 CE. The ultimate blow came in 747 when the city was destroyed by an earthquake. Limited settlement continued until the site was totally abandoned in the twelfth century.

Twentieth-century excavations of the remains of ancient Gerasa were initiated in 1925, when a joint project was sponsored by the Department of Antiquities, the British School of Archaeology, Yale University, and the American Schools of Oriental Research. Under the direction of John Garstang and others, one of the best-preserved Greco-Roman cities in the Near East was recovered. The excavations at the site have revealed both the city plan and the individual features of ancient Gerasa including the city wall, the colonnaded way and street plan with drainage system, the city's forum, the temple of Artemis, the temple of Zeus, the south theater, the north theater, two Roman bath complexes, the triumphal arch, the hippodrome, and the remains of thirteen churches.

The city had a defense system comprised of a city wall some ten feet thick that surrounded the entire city, the circumference of which was two and one-half miles. The wall was fortified with towers interspersed along its course and with as many as eight gateways. The major gates were the south gate, the north gate, the southwest gate, and the northwest gate. The primary approach to the city was from the south through the triumphal arch some fifteen hundred feet south of the city wall and south gate. The hippodrome was located along the west side of the triple arch and approach to the city.

South gate of the city wall

The forum was located inside the city wall at the main entrance just inside the south gate. The forum, the meeting place for business transactions as well as other activities, was a paved semicircular area enclosed by fifty-six columns.

The colonnaded way, the main street or boulevard of the city, ran from the forum on the south side of the city to the north gate. Paved with limestone blocks that still bear the grooves of wear from chariot wheels, the north-south thoroughfare was lined on each side by columns. There were two major intersections along its course; the intersections formed two side streets that intersected the main boulevard at right angles. The two intersecting streets led to the southwest gate and northwest gate located in the wall on the west side of the city.

Though the city had several temples, there were two major temples of the Greco-Roman period: the temple of Zeus, dedicated to the supreme god of the Greco-Roman period, was near the south gate, while the temple of Artemis, the goddess of hunting and wild animals, was at the midpoint of the west side of the colonnaded way. Since the temple of Artemis, some fifteen hundred feet long from east to west, occupies the most prominent position, we may assume that Artemis was the principal deity and protector of Gerasa.

Columned forum at Gerasa

In addition to the temples, the Greco-Roman city had two major theaters. The south theater was next to the temple of Zeus near the south gate, and the north theater was on the north side of the temple of Artemis. The South Theater, similar in design to other theaters of the first century CE, had thirty-two rows of seats that accommodated approximately five thousand spectators.

Additional features of the Greco-Roman city include fountains at intervals along the colonnaded thoroughfare, and the east bath and west bath situated on each side of the Chrysorrhoas tributary that bisects the eastern sector.

The ruins of thirteen churches in the city reflect the important role Gerasa played as a major center in early Christianity. Several of the churches have been excavated, including the Church of St. Theodore, the Church of Genesius, the Church of Procapius, the Church of St. Peter and Paul, and the Church of St. Cosmas, St. John, and St. George. Some of the churches were constructed on the site of a temple of a preceding era. One church replaced a synagogue.

Bibliography: ADAMS, J. M., "Gerasa," *Biblical Backgrounds,* rev. Joseph A. Callaway (Nashville: Broadman, 1965) 156–60; APPLEBAUM, S., "Gerasa," *EAEHL,* 2:417–28; APPLEBAUM, S., and A. Segal, "Gerasa," *NEAEHL,* 2:470–79; AUBIN, M. M., "Jerash," *OEANE,* 3:215–19; BLAIKLOCK, E. M., "Gerasa," *NIDBA,* 210–11; BUCK-WALTER, H. D., "Gerasa, Gerasene, Gergesa, Gergesene," *BEB,* 1:857–58; CLARK, K. W., "Gerasa," *IDB,* 2:382–84; DEYOUNG, J. C., "Gerasa, Gerasenes," *ZPEB,* 2:698–701; FINEGAN, J., "Decapolis," *The Archaeology of the New Testament* (Princeton: Princeton University Press, 1969) 61–70; McRAY, J., "Gerasenes," *ABD,* 2:991–92; MITCHELL, T. C., "Gerasa," *NBD²,* 414–15; PERKINS, P., "Gerasa," *HBD,* 340; PFIEFFER, C. F., "Gerasa, Jerash," *BW,* 252–54; SCHOVILLE, K. N., "Jerash," *BAF,* 491–94; STATON, C. P., Jr., "Gerasa," *MDB,* 326; VOS, H. F., "Gerasa," *ISBE,* 2:447–48.

Winter Palace of Herod the Great

Ancient sites occasionally moved from one location to another during the course of their history. Such was the case with Jericho during the course of biblical history. Jericho of the OT period was located at the present-day site of Tell es-Sultan, while Jericho of the NT period was located one mile south on the Wadi Qelt at the site of Tulul Abu el-Alayiq.

These two locations occupied an oasis ten miles north of the Dead Sea, four miles west of the Jordan River, and nearly one thousand feet below sea level. From earliest times water, good soil, and tropical conditions created a garden land. In addition to the fertile alluvial base of soil, the oasis also had valuable freshwater springs; Ain es-Sultan was the primary spring, and the waters of Ain Duk and Ain Nueima were channeled through aqueducts. Ain es-Sultan, or Elisha's spring, produces more than a thousand gallons of water per hour. Here the earliest settlement was established. Ain Duk and Ain Nueima provided water for the later city. From early on the oasis was one of Palestine's most valuable agricultural basins, known for the production of vegetables and fruits, especially date palms. Because of the numerous date palm groves, OT Jericho was known as "the city of palm trees" (Deut 34:3). Jericho was also well known as a source of balsam that was acquired from the balsam groves in the area and used as a cure for a variety of medical problems and as a base for perfumes.

A feature that further enhanced the value of the site of ancient Jericho was its relationship to the major trade routes in the area. The oasis was located both near a major ford in the Jordan River and on the major highways of the lower Jordan valley. Its close proximity to the Jordan ford made it a gateway to Palestine west of the Jordan. From this gateway city routes moved to other sites in western Palestine, to the south, the north, or the west. Consequently, Jericho became a prominent city on the east-west highway that connected the ancient cities of Rabbath-Ammon, the capital of the Ammonites, and Jerusalem, the capital of Israel. During the NT period the east-west route traveled from Philadelphia, the southernmost city of the Decapolis, formerly Rabbath-Ammon, across the Jordan, through Jericho and on westward to Jerusalem and beyond to Joppa and the coastal plain highway on the Mediterranean coast.

Ancient Jericho began at Tell es-Sultan during the Mesolithic period, when a small Natufian community settled just above the spring, Ain es-Sultan. During the following Neolithic period the city became one of the largest fortified sites in the ancient Near East. The Chalcolithic period saw only limited occupation, but important developments took place during the Early Bronze and Middle Bronze Ages, when Jericho became one of the important urban centers of Palestine. The remains of the Late Bronze city, the city reported to have been captured by Joshua and the Israelites, have been seriously eroded. There is some evidence that the site was reoccupied by the Israelites during the period that followed. We may assume that Jericho was abandoned after the Babylonians destroyed it in the early part of the sixth century BCE, but the site may have been briefly occupied as a district headquarters during the Persian period. For all practical purposes the site of OT Jericho was never again occupied.

During the Hellenistic and Roman periods a new Jericho developed at a new location. One mile south of the OT city, on the Wadi Qelt, the new Jericho, sometimes referred to as "NT Jericho" or "Herodian Jericho," was originally designed and constructed by the Hasmonean kings of Judea as a royal center. The new city became the eastern capital or winter retreat of Herod the Great, who added his own touch through the construction of a massive palace complex. The new city flourished from approximately 105 BCE to 70 CE, when it was captured by Roman forces.

References to Jericho, its history, and features of its surrounding area appear in ancient historical sources such as the writings of the Jewish historian Josephus, the Greek geographer Strabo, 1 Maccabees of the Apocrypha or Deuterocanon, and the NT. Both Josephus (*Ant.* 14.54; *War* 4.468) and Strabo (*Geography* 16.763) refer to the date palm and balsam groves that provided a lucrative economy for the city. According to the book of First Maccabees, Simon the Maccabee was killed at Jericho (1 Macc 16:14–16). Strabo further informs us that the Roman general Pompey visited Jericho in 63 BCE on his sweep through Palestine and captured Threx and Taurus, two fortifications at the entrance to Jericho that protected the Hasmonean city. Apparently, Vespasian visited Jericho in 68 CE and established a garrison at the site. Whether he destroyed the city is not really clear. After NT Jericho came to an end following the war, the site may have been maintained as a garrison for soldiers.

While the NT reveals nothing about the city itself, it does provide several references to the ministry of Jesus in or near Jericho. Jesus' baptism in the Jordan River (Matt 3:15–17) and the temptation in the wilderness (Matt 4:1–11) must have been close to Jericho. Jericho was where Jesus healed blind Bartimaeus (Mark 10:46–52) and encountered Zacchaeus, the wealthy tax collector (Luke 19:1–10). The highway "going down from Jerusalem to Jericho," was the setting for the story of the Good Samaritan (Luke 10:30).

In recent years important features of NT Jericho have come to light through excavations at the site of Tulul Abu el Alayiq on the Wadi Qelt, marked by two artificially constructed mounds north and south of the wadi. Excavations conducted by James Kelso (1950), James Pritchard (1951), and Ehud Netzer (1973–79) have uncovered the remains of both the royal palace complex of the Hasmonean kings who were initially responsible for the construction of the new city and the winter palace complex of Herod the Great who continued the building process at Jericho.

It was originally believed that Herod the Great was responsible for the founding of the new city. But recent excavations have demonstrated that the Hasmonean rulers (the line of kings who ruled Judea from 142 to 63 BCE) near the end of the second century BCE must be credited with the ingenious move. The new building enterprise was initiated during the reign of John Hyrcanus (135/34–104 BCE) or Alexander Jannaeus (104–76 BCE) and was located on the mound north of the Wadi Qelt. The new royal citadel was a palace complex for the Hasmonean kings and covered three acres with a large palace, a double swimming pool, ritual baths, and aqueducts that brought water to the palace complex area from the springs Ain Duk and Ain Nueima. The palace, located on top of the mound, was a large structure 170 feet long and 155 feet wide. Constructed of mud brick, it had two stories and was comprised of a large central court surrounded by rooms. The palace walls were finished with plaster and decorated with frescoes. The large double swimming pool northeast of the palace was 105 feet long and sixty feet wide, with open promenades around it and a roof supported by columns. Water was conveyed to the pools through aqueducts. A number of ritual baths were also found in the area. The baths were designed to accommodate the high priests who were members of the Hasmonean family. Other features of the Hasmonean complex included a pavilion or reception hall south of the pool, a long colonnade north of the pool, and a storage hall east of the pool.

The excavations also unearthed a number of coins. While most of the coins date to the time of Alexander Jannaeus, twenty coins found in the swimming pool are from the reign of Mattathias Antigonius, the last of the Hasmonean rulers. Herod the Great defeated Antigonius at Jericho in 37 BCE, but Jericho was not his until 31 BCE, when Augustus awarded it to him after Augustus defeated Antony at the battle of Actium.

Like the Hasmonean rulers who preceded him, Herod the Great realized the value of Jericho. The tropical climate of the valley, the agricultural and consequently economic wealth of the oasis, the water supply of the springs of the Wadi Qelt, and the proximity to Jerusalem some thirteen miles southwest, led Herod to construct his winter palace there. The Herodian city had three major palace areas.

Herod's first palace complex was located south of the Wadi Qelt. Originally believed to be a gymnasium, the rectangular building was 290 feet long and 150 feet wide. It had a large central court, a large hall, and other living facilities; at one time it apparently served as the major residential palace for Herod. Later Herod built a second palace. It was constructed on an artificial platform on the north mound, north of the Wadi Qelt, over the remains of the Hasmonean palace. This villa included the residential palace itself on the mound, nearby servant's quarters, and the renovated Hasmonean pools, where Herod most likely had his brother-in-law and Aristobulus drowned.

Herod's third and major building enterprise was the recreational complex that straddled the Wadi Qelt, three structures to the south of the wadi and one to the north. The complex covered some seven acres along 975 feet of the wadi. To the south was a large building constructed

on an artificial mound, a large pool, and a sunken garden. To the north
was the so-called north wing of the palace. Though the function of the
large building is uncertain, it was clearly a part of the wadi-front project
because a stairway led from it down to the sunken garden and pool
below. The exotic sunken garden, approximately 490 feet long, was
designed with a grand facade that formed the back wall of the garden.
The garden had elaborate colonnaded ends. The pool, at the east end of
the sunken garden, was three hundred feet long and 130 feet wide. The
north wing of the palace complex was comprised of large colonnaded
courtyards, two major halls, an elaborate Roman bath, as well as a
number of additional rooms. The largest of the halls, ninety-five feet by
sixty feet, was apparently used for receptions or other festive occasions.
One of the most impressive features of the north wing was the Roman
bath equipped with a large round *frigidarium*, a cold bath, a *tepidarium*,
a warm bath, and a *caldarium*, a hot bath. Similar to building
enterprises at other locations, the Herodian facilities at Jericho exhibited
the influence of Roman building techniques. This is particularly evident
in the brickwork of the buildings. Square-faced stones were set in
mortar at a forty-five degree angle, that is, diagonally, giving the
finished surface of the wall a netlike appearance, a building technique
known as *opus reticulatum*.

It is now fairly certain that the Herodian city also had a hippodrome
and a theater. While excavations at the site have uncovered the
Hasmonean and Herodian palace complexes, the major part of the NT
Jericho located most likely beneath the present-day town remains
unexcavated. That the city had a wealthy Jewish populace is indicated by
the discovery of an elaborately decorated first-century Jewish tomb that
was used for family burials for three generations and produced
some thirty-two inscriptions.

Bibliography: ALDEN, R. L., "Jericho," *BEB*, 2:1118–20; BARTLETT, J. R., "Jericho
Under the Hasmoneans and the Herods," *Jericho* (Grand Rapids: Eerdmans, 1982)
115–25; COLLINS, A. O., "New Testament Jericho," *Where Jesus Walked,* ed. William
A. Stephens (Nashville: Broadman, 1981) 135–41; COUGHENOUR, R. A., "Jericho
(Hasmonean and Herodian Jericho)," *ISBE*, 2:995–96; DEVER, W. G., "Jericho,"
MDB, 438–40; DRUMBRELL, W. J., "Jericho," *Major Cities of the Biblical World,* ed.
R. K. Harrison (Nashville: Nelson, 1985) 130–38; FINEGAN, J., "Jericho," *The Ar-
chaeology of the New Testament* (Princeton: Princeton University Press, 1969)
81–88; FOERSTER, G., and G. Bacchi, "Jericho (Jericho from the Persian to the
Byzantine Periods)," *EAEHL*, 2:564–65; idem, "Jericho (The Chalcolithic Settle-

ment at Tulul Abu El-Alaiq)," *EAEHL*, 2:571–74; GRAYBILL, J. B., "Jericho," *NIDB*, 509–12; HACHLILI, R., "Herodian Jericho," *OEANE*, 3:16–18; JAMEISON, H., "Jericho," *ZPEB*, 3:451–55; JOINES, K., "Jericho," *HolBD*, 759–64; KELSO, J. L., "Jericho," *IDB*, 2:835–39; idem, "Jericho (New Testament)," *BW*, 303–5; KITCHEN, K. A., "Jericho," *NBD*², 563–65; McRAY, J., "Jericho," *Archaeology and the New Testament* (Grand Rapids: Baker, 1991) 133–36; NETZER, E., "Jericho (Roman Jericho–Tulul Abu el-Alayiq)," *ABD*, 3:737–39; idem, "Jericho (Tulul Abu el-Alaiq Exploration)," *EAEHL*, 2:565–70; idem, "The Winter Palaces of the Judean Kings at Jericho at the End of the Second Temple Period," *BASOR* 228 (1977) 1–13; NETZER, E., G. Foerster, and R. Hachlili, "Jericho (Hellenistic to the Early Arab Periods)," *NEAEHL*, 2:681–97; NETZER, E., and Eric M. Meyers, "Preliminary Report on the Joint Jericho Excavation Project," *BASOR* 228 (1977) 15–27; THOMPSON, J. A., "Jericho," *NIDBA*, 258–61; TOOMBS, L. E., "Jericho," *HBD*, 458–61.

Herod's Showplace of Greco-Roman Building Techniques

Jerusalem had a long and eventful history prior to the NT period. But a new and dramatic chapter in that history began to unfold near the end of the first century BCE and the beginning of the first century CE. The new era began with grand projects by the master builder Herod the Great. It ended with the destruction of Jerusalem in 70 CE and the complete realignment and rebuilding of the city on a new Roman plan in 135 CE. This was a deliberate attempt by the Emperor Hadrian to destroy the threat of the Jewish culture and faith that tended to be marked by zealotism and revolt and was often associated with the city, especially the temple area.

Jerusalem is located approximately fifteen miles west of the upper end of the Dead Sea and thirty-five miles east of the Mediterranean Sea (see OT Jerusalem). During the NT period the city was comprised of two hills, the eastern ridge on which the earliest OT city had been located and the western hill to which the city expanded during the latter part of the OT period. The eastern ridge was separated from the western hill by the Tyropoeon or cheesemakers valley. The city was outlined by the Kidron valley on the east and the Hinnom valley on the south and southwest.

There is evidence of human habitation around Jerusalem as early as the Paleolithic and Mesolithic periods, but settlement did not take place until the earliest houses were built on the southeastern hill, the Ophel ridge, in the Early Bronze Age. During the Middle Bronze Age, Jerusalem became a major walled city on the southeastern hill, using the Gihon spring as its water supply. It was this city, occupied by a Canaanite/Jebusite population, that David eventually conquered and established as the capital of all the tribes of the nation Israel. During the reign of Solomon, the eleven-acre city was expanded to the north. The newly-enlarged city encompassed some thirty-two acres and included a temple and temple area that became the focal point the city.

With the division of Israel in 922 BCE, Jerusalem became the capital of the kingdom of Judah, and it was enlarged to the western hill. Both the Bible and archaeology bear some evidence of attempts at fortifying the city such as those introduced by Uzziah and Hezekiah. The city, with its holy temple, was revered as the impregnable citadel of Yahweh. But the dreams vanished during the early sixth century BCE when Jerusalem was destroyed by the Babylonians and its leading citizens were exiled to the land of Babylonia.

Plaza area south of the Temple enclosure

During the centuries following the Babylonian period Jerusalem was controlled successively by the Persians, the Greeks, the Ptolemies, and the Seleucids. The city's temple (Ezra 3:8–13; 5:1–2; 6:13–15) and city wall (Neh 2–3; 6:15) were rebuilt during the Persian period. Archaeological evidence shows that the refurbished city was limited to the Ophel ridge. The temple area with a new city wall was located farther up the side of the Ophel ridge than that of the Canaanite/Jebusite city of the Middle Bronze and Late Bronze ages.

In 332 BCE Jerusalem became part of Alexander the Great's empire and consequently fell under the influence of the Hellenistic culture that prevailed throughout the Mediterranean world. We may assume that the size of the city remained approximately the same as during the Persian rule. Following Alexander's death, Jerusalem came under the control of the Ptolemies of Egypt until 198 BCE, when Antiochus III made Palestine part of the Seleucid kingdom. During the reign of his successor, Antiochus IV (known also as Antiochus Epiphanes), Jerusalem entered one of its darkest periods. Intent on uniting his kingdom, Antiochus set in motion a plan to Hellenize all lands under his domain. That decision carried drastic implications for Jerusalemites. Antiochus forbade worship according to the Law of Moses, including the practice of circumcision, the observance of the Sabbath, and the reading of the Pentateuch. He erected altars dedicated to Greek gods throughout the city and constructed an altar to the Olympian god Zeus in the Jewish temple area. He constructed gymnasiums and instituted Greek games played in the nude, so as to embarrass young Jewish males who had been circumcised. He built the Acra, a garrison for troops, whose presence would help ensure the success of the Hellenization program. Finally, in December of 168 BCE, he offered a hog on the altar of burnt offerings as an act of spite aimed at the Jewish people and their faith.

The Seleucid oppression removed any semblance of religious and political tolerance or freedom. The atrocities committed by Antiochus Epiphanes were intolerable. They constituted nothing less than deliberate and blatant defilement of the holy city and the faith of its citizens. Some Jews were tolerant of Hellenism and others embraced it, but the majority of the citizens were enraged and primed for action. In 167 BCE an elderly priest named Mattathias, who lived in the small town of Modein, killed the king's servant rather than follow the king's orders to offer a Greek sacrifice. The Maccabean revolt followed, led by Mattathias's sons, and paved the way for a new day in the history of Jerusalem. Under the leadership of Judas called Maccabeus, the temple was reclaimed and in December, 165 BCE was cleansed and rededicated. The celebration, referred to in the Gospel of John as the Feast of Dedication (John 10:22), continues today and is known as Hanukkah. While the Jews regained religious liberty at that time, they were unable to reestablish their political independence. Political freedom was finally achieved by Judas's brother, Simon. On May 23, 142 BCE Simon and his forces took the Acra, the last of the Seleucid/Syrian garrisons in Jerusalem. Jerusalem became the center of a new independent Jewish state that existed from 142 BCE to 63 BCE. During that period, the Hasmonean period, Jerusalem again experienced a time of growth. The rulers of the Hasmonean dynasty expanded the city to include a new palace on the western hill.

With the arrival of Pompey in 63 BCE, the Hasmonean state came to an end and Jerusalem became a part of the Roman world. However, the influence of the Greek culture that had been so prevalent in the Mediterranean continued along with new elements of influence from Rome. Rome was content with basically relying on the local community in matters of government and administration of the province. Local governments managed their own affairs, and local courts made decisions concerning local cases. Rome attempted to appoint someone from the province as a type of local administrator. For Palestine that person was Antipater, an Idumean and very capable administrator who was appointed over Palestine by Julius Caesar. Antipater's son Herod was appointed governor of Galilee, and his son Phasael was appointed administrator of Jerusalem. Following the death of Julius Caesar, Herod was appointed king of Judea by the Roman Senate in 44 BCE. In 37 BCE, Herod gained control of the major part of the land of Palestine, including Jerusalem.

The reign of Herod brought about a new day for the city of Jerusalem and the land of Palestine, marked by some of the greatest building enterprises in their history. Jerusalem served as Herod's primary residence and administrative center. Incorporating building techniques from Rome and the Greco-Roman world in general, Herod pursued substantial building projects in the city of Jerusalem, Caesarea on the coast, Samaria, and Jericho, as well as the fortified retreats of Herodium, Machaerus, Masada, Hyrcania, and Alexandrium.

Upon Herod's death in 4 BCE his kingdom was divided among his successor sons: Philip, Antipas, and Archelaus. Jerusalem was a part of the territory allotted to Archelaus, the ethnarch of Judea, Samaria, and Idumea. Plagued by riots and unrest, the reign of Archelaus was short-lived. Emperor Augustus removed him from office in 6 CE and replaced him with a procurator, a type of provincial administrator who was directly responsible to the emperor.

The period of the procurators of Jerusalem and Judea was significant for at least two reasons. First, it was a time of growing unrest due to mounting tensions between the Jews and the Romans. The problem was brought about by the procurators themselves, who became increasingly hostile toward the Jews, often acting with deliberate violence and cruelty. Second, the official residence of the procurator was moved from Jerusalem to Caesarea on the coast, the great harbor city and gateway to Palestine built by Herod the Great. In Jerusalem, the procurator apparently made his headquarters at either the tower of Antonia, a palace/fortress on the northwest corner of Herod's temple enclosure, or the palace of Herod the Great on the western hill. Tensions erupted during the time of the procurator Gessius Florus. In 64 CE Roman troops went on a rampage in the city of Jerusalem. About the same time trouble was also brewing in Caesarea on the coast. The synagogue at Caesarea was desecrated and twenty thousand Jews were killed in the battle that followed. The massacre marked the beginning of the Jewish-Roman war, 66–70 CE.

The war was extremely costly for the city of Jerusalem. The Roman general Vespasian was originally sent to Jerusalem in 68 CE to end the war, but he was recalled in 69 CE to become the emperor of Rome. The task of ending the conflict was passed to his son Titus. Surrounding the city with four Roman legions, Titus launched his attack during the spring of 70 CE. He attacked the city from the north, and his forces broke through the third north wall as well as the second north wall and proceeded into the city. In the end the Roman forces took both the tower of Antonia and the temple in which the Jews had made their last stand. The city and its temple were destroyed. The destruction of Jerusalem was commemorated in Rome with the construction of the Triumphal Arch of Titus, which bears the relief of a victorious procession of Roman soldiers carrying a candlestand that had been taken from the temple.

Following the war Jerusalem lay in ruins and for the most part was not rebuilt. Jews and Christians who survived the conflict fled to other areas. The town of Jamnia, near the coast, became a center of rabbinic study. But the Jewish-Roman conflict was not over. Rebellions continued, and relations between the Jews and Romans became more volatile, culminating in the eruption of the Bar Kochba revolt (132–35 CE). Intent on squelching the problem once and for all, Emperor Hadrian visited Judea, initiated a new program of suppressing the Jewish people, and razed the city of Jerusalem. Upon the leveled ruins Hadrian built an entirely new city that he named Aelia Capitolina. The new city was completely realigned and built according to Roman city plans typical of that day. There was one main street running north and south and a second main street running east and west. It is likely that the Byzantine Cardo, the main north-south street from the Byzantine period, discovered in recent times in the Old City, actually follows the main north-south street of the Roman city. Aelia Capitolina also had a forum, temples dedicated to the worship of Jupiter and Venus, a theater, hippodrome, and Roman baths. Jews were restricted from Aelia Capitolina until the fourth century CE.

During the Byzantine period yet another new chapter was written in the history of Jerusalem. When Constantine became emperor, Christianity became the religion of the empire. He attempted to relocate and identify the many special sites in Jerusalem and throughout the land. Constantine's special emissary for the mission was his mother, Helena. The holy sites were often marked by means of the construction of a building or special structure such as the Church of the Holy Sepulchre, which was originally constructed under the direction of Helena as the shrine commemorating the site of the tomb of Jesus. Unfortunately the location and identification of holy places by Helena were not based on reliable methods. During this period Jews were still restricted from Jerusalem except on the Ninth of Ab, when they were admitted to the city in order to mourn and bewail its destruction by the Romans.

Jerusalem has played a notable role in world history in times subsequent to the NT and Byzantine periods, including the early Arab or Moslem period, the Crusader period, the Ayyubid period, the Mamluk period, the Ottoman-Turk period, and the period of the British Mandate. Modern Israel proclaimed Jerusalem its capital in 1950. Its continuing role as one of the most important religious centers in the world is reflected in the thousands of Christian, Jewish, and Islamic pilgrims who visit it annually.

While the NT period is only one among many in the history of Jerusalem, it has always been of special interest to students of the Bible. They examine the role it played in the historical development of that era, the major physical features that comprised the city in NT times, and the special places mentioned in the NT in relationship to the life of Jesus and the early church. However, the recovery of the ruins of NT Jerusalem has been complicated for several reasons. One substantial problem confronting archaeologists is that the city has always been inhabited; the present-day area of the Old City is so closely built up that even limited excavations are difficult at best. In some places the remains of the city from biblical times lie beneath forty feet of rubble. Jerusalem has been destroyed and rebuilt many times; major changes took place even during the first centuries CE. The city of the NT period was built by Herod the Great. It was enlarged by Herod Agrippa (ca. 40–44 CE). In 70 CE the Romans destroyed many parts of the city, but the basic city plan did not change. In 135 CE the city experienced an unmitigated destruction at the hands of Hadrian, and it was completely redesigned with a Roman city plan.

However, many features of the NT city have come to light through archaeology, the Bible, other historical sources such as Josephus, and tradition. One of the most important features of the NT city is that it became a showplace of Greco-Roman culture through the building projects of Herod the Great. Herod had three major objectives in mind as he initiated his building program in Jerusalem: to build a palace for himself; to improve the fortifications of the city through the construction of walls and towers; and to build a temple for the Jews.

Herod carried out two major fortification projects in the city, one in the temple area and the second on the western hill or upper city. The first, the tower of Antonia (named for Mark Antony, Herod's friend), was constructed on the northwest corner of the temple enclosure area. The fortification may have included facilities that served as his early palace but was designed primarily as a garrison for soldiers. The structure was equipped with four towers, one on each corner, and living quarters for approximately five hundred soldiers. The major function of Antonia was twofold—to keep watch over the temple area as a precaution against uprisings and to have a reserve of soldiers nearby in case a disturbance did take place. The temple courtyard could be flooded with soldiers in a matter of minutes.

The second major fortification project was actually a part of a larger project that included the construction of a new palace. This fortification was comprised of three towers: Mariamne, Phasael, and Hippicus. Herod named the towers after one of his wives, a brother, and a friend, respectively. The towers were a part of the city wall on the western hill and were located at the point where the first north wall and the wall on the west side of the city met, the site of the citadel in the Old City today. A part of the tower of Phasael forms the lower part of the tower of

David. Herod's palace, a large rectangular complex of buildings with a large pool and courtyard, was located south of the towers. The new palace complex on the western hill apparently replaced the earlier one in Antonia. The palace was decorated with marblelike panels similar to those found in the city of Pompeii, a technique Herod used in other building projects such as the one at Masada. Herod also extended the city northward by constructing a wall on the north side of the city. The wall, referred to as the second north wall, extended from the tower of Antonia to the first north wall near the Gennath gate.

The remains of two sets of arches from the Herodian period have also been found. The arches, named Robinson's arch and Wilson's arch after the individuals who discovered them, were located on the west side of the temple enclosure wall and served different functions. Excavations directed by Benjamin Mazar indicate that Robinson's arch, located on the southwest corner of the temple enclosure, was part of a monumental stairway and platform. This stairway provided access to the temple enclosure from the street below, a major north-south thoroughfare that ran along the west side of the temple enclosure through the Tyropoeon valley that separated the eastern hill or lower city from the western hill or upper city. Wilson's arch located to the north was apparently a part of a series of freestanding arches or a viaduct that extended from the temple mount westward over the valley to the upper city.

But Herod's most ambitious and most impressive building project in Jerusalem was the temple, a project designed to placate his Jewish opponents. The temple project was comprised of two parts, the temple platform with its enclosure wall and the temple itself. Herod doubled the size of the temple area and constructed a massive platform with an accompanying wall around all four sides. The huge platform was somewhat rectangular and the walls were erected of large stones, some as large as forty to forty-five feet long, and ten feet wide and deep. Though sections of the upper part of the wall have been rebuilt, the Herodian masonry is still visible today in the lower part of the wall. The southeast corner of the temple enclosure wall extends some sixty feet above the present ground level and seventy-five feet below the surface. The impressive height of the southeast corner towering above the Kidron valley below has prompted some to suggest that the southeast corner was the "pinnacle of the temple" mentioned in the NT (Matt 4:5; Luke 4:9). A portion of the western wall, known as the wailing wall, has been immortalized by orthodox Jews who through the centuries have established the tradition of visiting the wall to pray and bewail the capture of Jerusalem by the Romans (68–70 CE).

The approach to the temple area was from the south. It was comprised of a large plaza, massive stone steps leading up to the south enclosure wall, and two sets of gates. The gates, known as the Hulda gates, provided access to a vaulted passage or stairway leading up to the temple area inside through a double gate to the west and a triple gate to the east.

But of all the components of the temple project, the temple itself must have been the most spectacular. According to the Gospel of John, it took some forty-six years to construct. Unfortunately, due to the thorough destruction of the city by the Romans, nothing of the temple itself survives. Fragments of two warning inscriptions were probably located originally along the wall delimiting the court of the Gentiles.

Other points of interest in Jerusalem include those mentioned in the gospels. According to the Gospel of John the pool of Bethesda was the scene of one of Jesus' miracles (John 5:1–18). The pool, described as being near the Sheep Gate, was north of the temple area where the Church of Saint Anne is at present. There seem to have been twin pools with a walkway between.

According to tradition, both the upper room (Mark 14:15) and the house of Caiaphas, the high priest (Matt 26:3) were located on the southwestern hill near the tomb of David; however, the authenticity of the two sites is open to question. The garden of Gethsemane (Matt 26:36) was located on the Mount of Olives (Luke 22:39) east of the Kidron valley. Since Gethsemane means "oil press," we may assume that olive oil was produced from the olive trees in the area. Today both the Franciscan garden next to the Church of All Nations and the Russian garden farther up the Mount of Olives claim to be the garden of Gethsemane.

The Gospel of John also mentions that Jesus appeared before Pilate in the praetorium (John 18:28). Since the official residence of the procurator was in Caesarea on the coast, his headquarters in Jerusalem were located either at the palace of Herod on the western hill or at the tower of Antonia. The tower of Antonia is thought to be the more likely of the two sites.

The Via Dolorosa with the fourteen stations of the cross is always of interest to the Christian pilgrim visiting the Old City, but the route Jesus took to the site of the crucifixion cannot be determined with any certainty. In fact, the NT provides no hint concerning the location of the way.

Two sites have been proposed for the crucifixion and the burial, including Gordon's Calvary, the garden tomb, and the Church of the Holy Sepulchre. Archaeological evidence and tradition favor the site of the Church of the Holy Sepulchre. The garden tomb has features that indicate it was produced in the Byzantine period rather than the Roman period. Excavations in the area of the Church of the Holy Sepulchre indicate that the site was located outside the wall of the city during the NT period and that it was the site of a quarry, a setting compatible with the story. Further, the Church of the Holy Sepulchre has the support of tradition. Constantine had a basilica constructed on the site (ca. 335 CE) because of the prevailing tradition of that day. Excavations at the Church of the Holy Sepulchre have confirmed that it was erected over the remains of Constantine's church.

To be sure, Jerusalem was the most important city of the Jewish people during the first century, with some population estimates running as high as fifty thousand people. While Herod turned the city into a showplace of Greco-Roman culture, some citizens contributed to the city's beauty through elaborate private dwellings that have been excavated on the western hill. The wealthy citizens who lived here had an overview of the temple mount to the east.

Two recent archaeological discoveries have been of special interest to students of the Bible. A first-century tomb discovered at Givat ha-Mivtar includes the remains of a man who died by crucifixion. Another first-century burial that was unearthed contained many ossuaries, one of which bears the remains of several members of the family of Caiaphas. This may well be the Caiaphas who was the high priest during the trial of Jesus of Nazareth.

Bibliography: ADAMS, J. M., "New Testament Jerusalem," *Biblical Backgrounds,* rev. Joseph A. Callaway (Nashville: Broadman, 1965) 168–79; AMIRAN, R., and Y. Israeli, "Jerusalem," *IDBSup,* 475–77; AVIGAD, N., *Discovering Jerusalem* (Nashville: Nelson, 1983); idem, "Jerusalem (The Tombs in Jerusalem)," *EAEHL,* 2:627–41; AVIGAD, N., H. Geva, and M. Avi–Yonah, "Jerusalem (The Second Temple Period; The Roman Period; The Byzantine Period)," *NEAEHL,* 2:717–85; AVI-YONAH, M., "Jerusalem (Jerusalem in the Second Temple Period)," *EAEHL,* 2:599–627; BAHAT,

D., "Jerusalem," *OEANE*, 3:224–38; BAHAT, D., with C. T. Rubinstein, *The Illustrated Atlas of Jerusalem* (New York: Simon & Schuster, 1990); BASKIN, J. R., "Jerusalem," *HolBD*, 765–73; BURROWS, M., "Jerusalem," *IDB*, 2:843–66; BEITZEL, B. J., "Jerusalem," *BEB*, 2:1123–35; CALLAWAY, J. A., "Jerusalem," *BW*, 309–23; DRINKARD, J. F., Jr., "Jerusalem," *MDB*, 441–43; FINEGAN, J., "Jerusalem," *The Archaeology of the New Testament* (Princeton: Princeton University Press, 1969) 109–17; KENYON, K. M., *Digging Up Jerusalem* (New York: Praeger, 1974); idem, *Jerusalem: Excavating 3000 Years of History* (New York: McGraw-Hill, 1967); KING, P. J., "Jerusalem," *ABD*, 3:747–66; LaSOR, W. S., "Jerusalem," *ISBE*, 2:998–1032; MACKOWSKI, R. M., *Jerusalem: City of Jesus* (Grand Rapids: Eerdmans, 1980); MARE, W. H., "Jerusalem, New Testament," *NIDBA*, 261–65; idem, *The Archaeology of the Jerusalem Area* (Grand Rapids: Baker, 1987); McRAY, J., "Herodian Jerusalem," *Archaeology and the New Testament* (Grand Rapids: Baker, 1991) 91–127; PAYNE, D. F., "Jerusalem," *NBD*[2], 566–72; PAYNE, J. B., "Jerusalem," *ZPEB*, 3:459–95; SCHEIN, B. E., "Jerusalem," *HBD*, 463–73; SCHOVILLE, K. N., "Jerusalem," *BAF*, 401–17; SHANKS, H., *Jerusalem: An Archaeological Autobiography* (New York: Random House, 1995); SMITH, W. M., "Jerusalem," *NIDB*, 514–22; STEPHENS, W. H., "Jerusalem," *Where Jesus Walked*, ed. William H. Stephens (Nashville: Broadman, 1981) 95–117; THOMPSON, J. A., "The Jerusalem That Jesus Knew," *The Bible and Archaeology*, 3d ed. (Grand Rapids: Eerdmans, 1982) 345–63; WILKINSON, J., "Jerusalem," *Major Cities of the Biblical World*, ed. R. K. Harrison (Nashville: Nelson, 1985) 139–55; idem, *The Jerusalem Jesus Knew* (Nashville: Nelson, 1978); YADIN, Y., ed. *Jerusalem Revealed* (Jerusalem: The Israel Exploration Society in Cooperation with "Shikmona" Publishing Company, 1975).

MASADA 🏺 48

*Fortified Retreat and Recreation Center of Herod
the Great*

Masada was one of several fortified retreat centers Herod constructed
to provide a citadel or refuge during times of danger. The centers were
also designed as retreats, providing recreation, pleasure, and relaxation.
Other fortified retreats were located at Machaerus, Herodium, Hyrcania,
and Alexandrium, but Masada was probably the most significant. The
features of the site itself provided the ultimate in natural defense.

Masada played a distinguished role in the Jewish-Roman War (66–70
CE). Here the Zealot rebels made their last stand against the Romans and
ultimately fell. While their victory over Jerusalem in 70 CE assured the
Romans of victory, that victory was not clinched until 73 CE. The Zealot
rebels and their families who held out at Masada chose to commit
suicide rather than be captured by the Romans.

Masada's role in history was due in large part to its geography.
Masada was located across from the Lisan (the projection of land off the
east bank of the Dead Sea) and was thirty-five miles south-southeast of
the city of Jerusalem on the rugged terrain of the west bank of the Dead
Sea. It was a natural fortress, an isolated mountain thirteen hundred
feet high with a twenty-acre plateau on top. Separated from the
wilderness of Judea to the west by a huge wadi, the small mountainlike
formation is surrounded on all sides by extremely steep inclines and
sheer cliffs, giving it a shape like a ship, with the plateau resembling an
upper deck.

Though Masada is not mentioned in the Bible, the history of the site
and the story of the dramatic events that took place there have come to
light through two major sources: the accounts of Josephus, the Jewish
historian from the first century CE; and archaeological research conducted

at the site between 1963 and 1965 under the direction of Yigael Yadin. The Yadin excavations, in which thousands of volunteers from around the world participated, have helped to clarify the history of Masada. Evidence of occupation in the area dates back as far as the Chalcolthic period, but buildings were not constructed until the reign of Herod the Great. Based on archaeological research, Masada's history can be divided into five periods: (1) the occupation of the Hasmoneans, starting in the time of Alexander Jannaeus ca. 105 BCE; (2) the occupation by Herod the Great, beginning ca. 40 BCE; the establishment of a Roman garrison, from ca. 6 CE until 66 CE; (3) the entrenchment of the Jewish Zealots from 66 CE until 73 CE; (4) the return of a Roman garrison from 73 CE until shortly after the end of the first century; and (5) the Byzantine period of the fifth and sixth centuries during which the site was occupied by Christian monks. The two most noteworthy periods in Masada's history are the occupations by Herod the Great and the Jewish freedom fighters.

View of Masada plateau

Coins excavated at the site indicate that Masada was apparently used as a fortress or protective refuge by the Hasmoneans, who did not construct any buildings.

Masada was granted to Herod the Great about 40 BCE. Herod had been appointed king of Judea by the Roman Senate, but he nevertheless faced several threats, including lingering resistance from the Hasmoneans as well as attack from the forces of Cleopatra, queen of Egypt. For all practical purposes Herod had to conquer the territories granted to him by the Senate. When Herod traveled to Rome to finalize his appointment, he left his family at Masada for safekeeping. By 37 BCE he had gained control of his territory. Because defense was always a major concern, Herod equipped the natural mountain fortress of Masada with a defense system, living facilities, administrative buildings, and recreational facilities. The majority of all buildings ever built at Masada were constructed during this era (ca. 35–34 BCE).

Herod's storeroom complex

Two events precipitated the end of the Herodian period at Masada—the death of Herod the Great in 4 BCE and the removal of his son and successor, Archelaus, by the Roman government in 6 CE. A procurator was appointed to replace Archelaus, and Roman control of the land was all the more obvious. A Roman garrison was stationed at the site until 66 CE, the year that Jewish rebels captured the site from the Romans. During the years that followed (ca. 66–73 CE), Masada was a citadel of refuge for the Jewish Zealots who modified the buildings of the Herodian period to meet their own needs and erected new facilities designed for the practice of their faith and the rituals associated with it. After Masada fell in 73 CE, the site was reoccupied by a Roman garrison. The Romans abandoned the site in the early part of the second century CE.

Masada apparently remained unoccupied for several centuries. During the fifth century CE, Christian monks established a small monastic community at the site and built a small church of Byzantine style. This era, which continued on into the sixth century, was the last time Masada was inhabited.

Among the archaeological discoveries at Masada the vital ones belong to either the Herodian period or the period of Zealot occupation. The Herodian installations at the site include a protective wall with towers and gates, an extensive water system, a northern palace or three-tier villa, a large western palace and administrative center, storerooms, and an elaborate Roman bath.

While the steep inclines and cliffs surrounding Mount Masada provided a unique natural defense, Herod the Great attempted to enhance the security of the site by surrounding the plateau on top with a large casemate wall (a fortified, double wall partitioned into chambers). The wall was equipped with some thirty watchtowers, apparently designed as observation points from which the area around the mountain could be observed. The two major approaches leading to the top of Masada were kept under especially watchful eyes. The snake path was a winding and zigzagging path on the east side of the mountain, and the approach from the west was for the most part covered up by the earthen ramp the Romans built to take the site from the Jewish Zealots. In addition to the towers, the casemate wall had several gates at key points including the east gate that provided entrance from the snake path; the northwest gate or water gate that provided access to the cisterns in that area; the west gate that provided entrance from the western approach to the site; and the south gate or cistern gate that provided access to the cisterns.

Other than defense, perhaps the most pressing need was for a water supply. Since the mountain had no water supply of its own, Herod designed an elaborate water system comprised of a series of cisterns along the northwest edge of the mountain, a series of cisterns along the southeast edge of the mountain, as well as cisterns on top of the mountain. These cisterns received water either from the wadis to the west and south of Masada or from collecting systems on top of the plateau of the mountain itself.

Of all of the building projects at Masada, the northern palace is the most impressive. Designed as a three-tier villa, the northern palace projected from the north end of the mountain like a massive stairway. Designed with columns, plastered walls painted to appear like marble, and beautiful frescoes, the lavishly equipped and decorated villa reflects building techniques similar to those found at the site of Herculaneum and Pompeii near the city of Rome.

Ritual bath at Masada

Two other sizable facilities Herod constructed near the northern palace were a storage complex and a Roman bath. The storage complex was comprised of long narrow storerooms sixty-five feet long and twelve feet wide, while some were even larger. The storage facilities kept food and supplies for Herod's family and administrative personnel. The Roman bath, designed for recreation and pleasure, was composed of four units: an *apoditerium,* or a disrobing room; a *tepidarium,* or tepid pool room; a *caldarium,* or hot pool room; and a *frigidarium,* or cold pool room.

The western palace was by far the largest of the living complexes at the site. It was the administrative center of Herodian Masada and was comprised of four parts including living quarters and a throne room, additional large storerooms, service area and work quarters, and an administrative wing. Herodian Masada also had smaller palaces or living facilities apparently occupied by members of Herod's family or important officials of Herod's court.

Zealot freedom fighters modified Herod's facilities when they occupied the site. They converted the opulent facilities into survival quarters. The chambers in the casemate wall encircling the plateau were converted into dwellings for the Zealots and their families. The northern palace became a military center and warehouse for large supplies of weapons. The western palace was apparently converted into an administrative center.

The only major new structures installed by the Zealots were two ritual baths and a synagogue. The synagogue was constructed along the northwest section of the wall. The synagogue had four rows of stone benches along three walls. Other important discoveries from the Zealot period include fragments of OT scrolls and some seven hundred ostraca with Hebrew and Aramaic inscriptions. Among the ostraca were eleven sherds, each inscribed with a name. Yadin has suggested that they may have been the lots used in the casting procedure in which men from the community were selected to assist in the suicide ritual.

While the Zealots and their families, some 960 people in all, prepared for the worst, the Roman general Flavius Silva surrounded the mountain with five thousand soldiers and established camps at its base; the outlines of several of these are still visible today from the plateau above. Silva's intent was to force the Zealots to surrender by cutting off food and water supplies, but in this he was thwarted. Determined to end the humiliating experience of waiting out the Zealots, the Roman general constructed an earthen ramp on the west side of the mountain as a way to gain entrance to the rebel camp above. However, the Zealots were determined to die rather than be taken prisoner by the Romans. The evening before Silva's conquest the Zealots set their own plan in motion. After burning the facilities on top of the mountain, the Zealots and their families selected ten men to assist the families in taking the lives of their members. After the killing was completed, the ten men gathered, selected one from the group to kill the other nine, and the last committed suicide.

Masada still stands today: a massive monument, a commemorative marker, a massive tombstone if you will, etched in the terrain of the land as a lasting memorial to the Zealots who took their stand against the Romans. The writings of Josephus bear the literary witness to the event (*War* 7.304–406); they are based on testimony from two women and five children who survived the mass suicide by hiding in one of the cisterns.

Bibliography: BLAIKLOCK, E. M., "Masada," *NIDBA*, 302–3; FOERSTER, G., "Masada," *ZPEB*, 4:112–14; FRIEND, G. W., and S. Fine, "Masada," *OEANE*, 3:428–30; FUNK, R. W., "Masada," *IDB*, 3:293–94; LASOR, W. S., "Masada," *BEB*, 2:1412–14; idem, "Masada," *ISBE*, 3:273–76; LEWIS, J. D., "Masada," *MDB*, 556–57; McRAY, J., "Masada," *Archaeology and the New Testament* (Grand Rapids: Baker, 1991) 136–39; NETZER, E., "Masada," *ABD*, 4:586–87; idem, "Masada," *NEAEHL*, 3:973–85; PEARLMAN, M., *The Zealots of Masada* (New York: Scribner & Sons, 1967); SCHOVILLE, K. N., "Masada," *BAF*, 429–38; YADIN, Y., "Masada," *EAEHL*, 3:793–816; idem, "Masada," *IDBSup*, 577–80; idem, "Masada: A Zealot Fortress," *Archaeological Discoveries in the Holy Land,* compiled by the Archaeological Institute of America (New York: Bonanza, 1967) 169–74; idem, *Masada: Herod's Fortress and the Zealots' Last Stand* (London: Sphere, 1973).

Religious Commune of the Essenes

Near the end of the second century BCE, north of Masada, the Essenes instituted a religious commune at what is known today as Khirbet Qumran. The discoveries at Qumran and Masada provide insight into the real value of the west bank of the Dead Sea and Judean wilderness for those seeking refuge in ancient times. Though rainfall was extremely limited, the rugged terrain of the Dead Sea's west bank and the Judean wilderness with its craggy cliffs, deep ravines and wadis, isolated plateaus, and sporadic caves provided sanctuary for numerous groups during biblical times.

The site of Qumran, not a city but the material remains of a commune, is on the northwest side of the Dead Sea. It may have been the communal headquarters of the Essenes, one of three major sects of Judaism during the first century BCE and the first century CE. Qumran was isolated in one of the most desolate parts of the country. It was nine miles south of Jericho, thirteen miles east of Jerusalem, some thirty miles north of Masada and about a mile west of the major north-south route that ran along the west side of the Dead Sea.

Forsaken as it was, this site held many attractions for those seeking asylum and isolation. Situated along the Wadi Qumran that extended southwestward into the Judean wilderness, the site of Qumran was located on a small plateau. The plateau was set off from the rugged terrain in the background by the Wadi Qumran to the south, deep ravines to the west and north, and the coastal plain of the Dead Sea to the east. Since the plateau stood approximately 150 feet above the plain, the inhabitants of the site had a clear view of the north-south route that traveled along the shore of the Dead Sea. The ravines to the south, west, and north provided a protective barrier from those directions, and the rugged terrain to the west, with its cliffs, crevices, and small cavities and caves, was difficult to travel for those unfamiliar with the terrain.

The site had one feature essential for living, a water supply. While the plateau itself did not have a natural water supply, water could be transported to the site from springs located to the south, the largest known as Ain Feshka. Some water was available from the seasonal rainfall. While it consisted of only four to six inches, it fell during a very limited period of time and consequently in larger volumes than if scattered throughout the year. Also, the ravines and wadis of the area collected and channeled the water naturally. By capturing the water as it came cascading through the ravines, inhabitants could store large volumes of water in cisterns and pools for use during the rest of the year.

Cave 4 at Qumran

The discovery of Qumran actually goes back to the winter of 1946–47. The Dead Sea Scrolls and the caves in which they had been stored were discovered before the site of Qumran itself. The discovery was made by local Bedouin boys who were tending their flocks in the area. Having lost one of the animals from the flock, the three young Bedouins of the Ta'amireh Bedouin tribe began to search for the missing animal in the rugged terrain of the area. Tossing a rock into one of the caves, Muhammad edh-Dhib, one of the three, heard something that sounded like pottery breaking. Because evening was near, they did not enter the cave at that time. When they returned a day or two later, the young Bedouins discovered decaying leather scrolls and pottery containers with caps in which the scrolls had been stored. Taking specimens of their finds with them, they continued on with their flocks for about a week before returning to the home camp. There the scrolls were placed in a guffa, a type of rubber bucket, and were hung on a pole in the camp where they stayed for another month. The scrolls eventually made their way to Bethlehem where they were placed in the hands of a shoe cobbler turned antiquities dealer named Kando. Due to Kando's efforts the scrolls, as well as additional scrolls that came in later, found their way into the hands of Professor E. L. Sukenik of the Hebrew University and Archbishop Samuel of the St. Mark's Monastery.

Cistern and aqueduct system at Qumran

After the first cave was discovered in the spring of 1947, a search for more caves was undertaken in the area. While the details of the events that transpired between 1947 and 1952 are complicated at best, the search eventually resulted in the discovery of eleven scroll-bearing caves in the Wadi Qumran area, all within two miles of the site of

Khirbet Qumran. Among the scrolls were several different types of manuscripts including biblical manuscripts, copies of books of the OT, many of which were fragmentary; commentaries on OT books; sectarian writings, particularly writings that pertain to the community at Qumran itself; apocryphal writings, books that belong to the apocryphal class of literature; and finally, writings that might be best classified as miscellaneous.

While the discovery of the caves and their excavations initially resulted in the discovery of the ancient manuscripts, commonly known as the Dead Sea Scrolls, the work in the caves was important for yet another reason. It created renewed interest in the ruins on the plateau to the east at the site of Khirbet Qumran and ultimately led to the excavation of the site. Archaeologists had been aware of the ruins for some time, but the discovery of the scrolls indicated a possible association between the two. Excavations began at the site of Khirbet Qumran in 1951 under the direction of Roland de Vaux and continued until 1956. The excavations provided information that confirmed the link between the site and the discoveries in the caves. They also shed light on the community that produced the scrolls.

Through the excavations at Khirbet Qumran the historical profile of the site has been defined, and the major periods of occupation have been outlined. The earliest building activities at Qumran date to the eighth and seventh centuries BCE, when an Iron Age II Israelite fortress was constructed. The fortress was perhaps a part of the building enterprise of King Uzziah who attempted to strengthen the defense system of Judah by constructing "towers in the wilderness" (2 Chron 26:10).

The more significant occupation began during the second century BCE, following several centuries of abandonment. Though different schemes may be used to outline the history of the site at this point, three major phases of occupation seem to emerge. Phase I, the original settlement of the site, began about 135 BCE, the time of John Hyrcanus, and continued until ca. 31 BCE. During the early part of the phase, which coincides roughly with the reign of John Hyrcanus, buildings were constructed on existing foundations from the earlier period. Around 105 BCE, the beginning of the reign of Alexander Jannaeus, the site was enlarged and extensive building activities took place. This was when the major components of the Qumran community were built. The site was abandoned ca. 31 BCE for two reasons. First, there was an earthquake in 31 BCE, and the site experienced severe damage such as is seen in the stairway of the large pool. Second, the Essene inhabitants found a friend in Herod the Great, who shared their bitter hatred for the Hasmoneans. Phase II began ca. 4 BCE, about the time Archelaus came to the throne, and continued until about 68 CE. During this period the site of Qumran was again resettled, and the facilities at the site that had been damaged by the earthquake were rebuilt. It was most likely near the end of this period that the inhabitants of Qumran deposited the scrolls in the caves, presumably for safekeeping in light of the threat posed by the Jewish-Roman War and the massive Roman military presence in the land. Phase II ended ca. 68 CE when the site was destroyed by the Romans, who left their arrowheads behind in the ruins.

Scriptorium at Qumran

Phase III began ca. 68 CE when Qumran became home to a Roman garrison. The Roman occupation continued through the duration of the war and perhaps well beyond. During that period Roman soldiers used the buildings at Qumran and adapted them for their own purposes. Following the Roman occupation, Qumran was empty for a number of years until Jewish rebels briefly sought refuge there during the second

Jewish revolt of 132–35 CE. Near the end of the revolt the site of Qumran was completely destroyed and was never again inhabited.

The archaeological evidence from the Qumran project may be divided into three major categories: the evidence of the scrolls and the caves; the evidence of the community and its facilities at Khirbet Qumran; and the evidence from Ain Feshka, a part of the larger Qumran community located about two miles south of Khirbet Qumran.

Of the seven scrolls first discovered, four became a part of the St. Mark's Monastery collection and three became a part of the Hebrew University collection. Following the Six Day War of 1967 all were finally housed in the Shrine of the Book at the Israel Museum in Jerusalem. The St. Mark's Monastery collection included a complete Isaiah scroll; the *Manual of Discipline,* which contains the rules and guidelines by which the inhabitants of the community lived; the Habakkuk commentary, which includes two of the three chapters of Habakkuk; and the Lamech scroll or *Genesis Apocryphon,* a commentary on key figures in the book of Genesis. The Hebrew University collection included an incomplete Isaiah scroll; the *Book of the Wars of the Sons of Light and the Sons of Darkness,* and the scroll of thanksgiving psalms. In addition to the original seven, fragments of other books were discovered in cave one including those of the book of Daniel. Other writings discovered include the *Temple Scroll,* the longest of the scrolls with a length of some twenty-eight feet, which contains instructions pertaining to religious matters including offerings and sacrifices; the *Copper Scroll,* actually a two-scroll work that details a long list of hidden treasures; as well as some forty thousand other fragments of books of the OT, apocryphal texts, or sectarian documents. The only OT book not represented among the fragments is the book of Esther.

The major facilities of the community, with the exception of dwellings, were located on the plateau at the site of Khirbet Qumran. The community was designed as a self-contained community. It included three entrances with a large fortified tower located at the main entrance; a kitchen; storage rooms and pantry facilities equipped with several hundred pottery vessels; work rooms; a pottery-making installation complete with a kiln; a scriptorium equipped with benches, tables, and inkwells; an assembly hall; numerous courtyards; a water system comprised of an aqueduct, settling basins, and series of cisterns and pools; and a ritual bath or *mikvah.* All of the basic components of the community essential for living were found at Khirbet Qumran, but the living quarters were not found. The members of the community presumably lived outside the walls of the compound. The community also had three cemeteries located to the east of the community compound. The main cemetery was comprised of over one thousand graves, all of which contained the remains of men. The two smaller cemeteries were secondary burial sites which contained the remains of men, women, and children.

Excavations at Ain Feshka, two miles south of Khirbet Qumran, show that it too was an extension of the Qumran community. These ruins suggest that Ain Feshka parallels the Qumran community in its history of occupation and facilities, only on a smaller scale. Like Qumran, the Ain Feshka settlement had a central complex or building as well as other enclosures. It may have been the agricultural center of the Qumran community, where the animals of the community were kept and cared for. Ain Feshka had a spring and an irrigation system.

One of the most consequential questions concerning the discoveries at Khirbet Qumran is, Who were the people that lived at Qumran? The *Manual of Discipline* indicates that the Qumran community was a monastic or semimonastic community the members of which took vows and committed themselves to a rigidly ascetic lifestyle. It seems most likely that they were the Essenes, mentioned by Josephus as one of the three major sects of Judaism (*War* 2.119). According to Josephus (*Ant.* 13.171) they existed during the time of the Hasmoneans, and the Roman writer Pliny the Elder placed them along the western shore of the Dead Sea (*Natural History* 5.15.73).

Bibliography: BRUCE, F. F., "Qumran," *NIDBA*, 379; idem, "Qumran," *NBD²*, 1004–5; BURROWS, M., *The Dead Sea Scrolls* (New York: Viking, 1955); CARMIGNAC, J., "Qumran," *ISBE*, 4:13–18; COLLINS, J. J., "Essenes," *ABD*, 2:619–26; CROSS, F. M., Jr., "The Scrolls from the Judean Desert," *Archaeological Discoveries in the Holy Land*, compiled by the Archaeological Institute of America (New York: Bonanza, 1967) 157–67; DAVIES, P. R., *Qumran* (Grand Rapids: Eerdmans, 1982); DEVAUX, R., "Qumran, Khirbet—Ein Feshkha," *EAEHL*, 4:978–86; DEVAUX, R., and M. Broshi, "Qumran, Khirbet and 'Ein Feshkha," *NEAEHL*, 4:1235–41; DONCEEL, R., "Qumran," *OEANE*, 4:392–96; ELLIS-SMITH, M. A., "Qumran," *HolBD*, 1159–60; FITZMEYER, J. A., "Scrolls, the Dead Sea," *HBD*, 915–17; FRANK, H. T., "Scrolls from the Wilderness of Judea," *Discovering the Biblical World*, rev. ed.; ed. James F. Strange (Maplewood: Hammond, 1988) 179–97; HAIK, P. S., "Dead Sea Scrolls," *BEB*, 1:595–602; HARRISON, R. K., "Dead Sea Scrolls," *ZPEB*, 2:53–68; LaSOR, W. S.,

"Dead Sea Scrolls," *NIDB*, 260–63; idem, "Dead Sea Scrolls," *BW*, 184–92; MURPHY-O'CONNOR, J., "Qumran, Khirbet," *ABD*, 5:590–94; idem, "Rule of the Community," *OEANE*, 4:443–44; SCHIFFMAN, L. H., *Reclaiming the Dead Sea Scrolls* (Philadelphia: Jewish Publication Society, 1994); SCHOVILLE, K. N., "The Dead Sea Scrolls and Qumran," *BAF*, 447–63; THOMPSON, J. A., "The Religious Community of Qumran," *The Bible and Archaeology*, 3d ed. (Grand Rapids: Eerdmans, 1982) 269–87; TRAFTON, J. L., "Dead Sea Scrolls," *MDB*, 200–203; VERMES, G., "Dead Sea Scrolls," *IDBSup*, 210–19; WISE, M. O., "Dead Sea Scrolls," *OEANE*, 2:118–27; WRIGHT, G. E., "The Essenes," *Biblical Archaeology*, rev. ed. (Philadelphia: Westminster, 1962) 235–38.

SAMARIA-SEBASTE 50

Herod's Chief Building Enterprise in Samaria

Samaria-Sebaste was Herod's chief city and major building enterprise in the hill country of Samaria. While Caesarea Maritima was Herod's
jewel on the coast, his major seaport and gateway to the kingdom for the
vast Mediterranean world to the west, and Jerusalem was Herod's queen
city in Judea, the site of his primary residence and the magnificent
temple for the Jews, Samaria-Sebaste was Herod's major stronghold in
the interior of Samaria. Because of its central location, the city was
rebuilt and reestablished by Herod as a major cosmopolitan center,
dedicated to the emperor Augustus, in which he stationed his mercenary
troops.

Samaria-Sebaste, some forty miles north of Jerusalem and twenty-
five miles east of the Mediterranean Sea, was strategically located in the
hills of Samaria, the territory between Judea and Galilee. The site was
vital for at least three reasons. First, Samaria-Sebaste had a commanding view of the major north-south highway that connected Jerusalem to
the Esdraelon plain, which separated Galilee from Samaria and
through which the major international trade route ran, and the
east-west route tying the ancient site of Shechem, probably the NT city
of Sychar, to the Mediterranean coast. Second, because the site stood
some three hundred feet above the surrounding valleys, it was easily
fortified and defended. Third, the surrounding fertile valleys provided
valuable agricultural resources.

While Samaria is one of the most frequently mentioned cities in the
OT, it appears only three times in the NT (Acts 8:5, 9, 14). This paucity of
NT references reflects the fact that Jesus' ministry was concentrated in
the territory of Galilee and to some degree Judea rather than the
territory of Samaria (Matt 10:5). Nevertheless, the number of references
made to the territory of Samaria (Luke 17:11; John 4:4, 5, 7, 9) and the

Samaritans (Luke 9:52; 10:33; 17:16; John 4:9, 39, 40; 8:48) shows Jesus' acquaintance with the territory and its people.

Though the NT supplies little information about the city of Samaria, the writings of Josephus and archaeological evidence indicate the significance of the city constructed by Herod the Great during the NT period. Herod was undoubtedly influenced by the city's previous history when he decided to rebuild Samaria-Sebaste.

Unlike many major cities of the OT period, Samaria began quite late. Many biblical sites date to the Canaanite period prior to the arrival of the Israelites, but Samaria originated during the Israelite period during the ninth-century BCE reign of Omri, one of the kings of the northern kingdom. Omri founded the city as the capital during the latter part of the northern kingdom's history (1 Kgs 16:24); it remained the capital until the kingdom of Israel fell.

As the capital of Israel, Samaria became a city of wealth and affluence, the citadel of the king and the upper-class landed aristocracy. The prosperity of the kingdom reached its height during the reign of Jeroboam II, as can been seen in the elaborately carved ivory inlays (Amos 6:4) that decorated the furniture of the wealthy class, and the Samarian ostraca recovered from the site. But while the city of Samaria was wealthy, the kingdom of Samaria faced many problems, especially the oppression of the poor by the rich, a situation addressed in the preaching of Amos (Amos 2:6–8; 3:9–10, 15; 4:1–3; 5:10–13; 6:4–7), and a state of political anarchy reflected in the frequent dynastic changes after the reign of Jeroboam II (2 Kgs 15:8–31). Weakened by internal strife and social ills, Samaria fell to the Assyrians in 722 BCE, and the kingdom of Israel came to an end. The city was initially attacked by Shalmaneser (2 Kgs 17:1–6), and according to the Sargon cylinder, an Assyrian inscription that records the event, it was finally captured and destroyed by Sargon II who removed 27,290 of its citizens.

Following its destruction and fall Samaria was rebuilt by Sargon, and the city and its territory were repopulated by people from other areas including "Babylon, Cuthah, Avva, Hamath, and Sepharvaim" (2 Kgs 17:24). Samaria became the capital of the newly established Assyrian province, which the Assyrians named Samaria. Although there is little archaeological evidence, the city of Samaria seems to have served as the provincial capital of the district of Samaria through the Assyrian, Babylonian, and Persian periods.

With the arrival of Alexander the Great, Samaria's history took a new turn. After first supporting Alexander, the Samaritans revolted while he was in Egypt and burned alive his Syrian governor, Andromachos. Alexander then attacked the city in 332 BCE, destroyed it, and annihilated its leaders. Many of its citizens fled to Shechem. Shechem became the leading center of the Samaritans who are referred to in the NT, and Mount Gerizim became the site of the Samaritan temple. With Samaria under his control, Alexander repopulated the city with Greeks and rebuilt it as a Greek *polis* (city) and center of Hellenism. During the period that followed, Samaria was heavily fortified. Its walls were strengthened and equipped with round stone towers forty feet in diameter. Though the site was threatened by war at times, the Hellenistic city of Samaria continued to prosper for approximately two centuries. The discovery of numerous coins, imported pottery, and Rhodian jar handles shows that it participated in international trade and exchange. A temple dedicated to the Egyptian god Isis demonstrates the city's cosmopolitan character. John Hyrcanus, the Hasmonean ruler and high priest, was intent on destroying elements of the Hellenistic culture in the land. He besieged the city of Samaria for nearly a year and in ca. 107 BCE captured and thoroughly destroyed it. Samaria then lay abandoned for some time.

The city was revived during the Roman period following the arrival of Pompey. It became a part of the Roman province of Syria and was extensively rebuilt ca. 57 BCE by Gabinius, the governor. Because of Gabinius' work the citizens of Samaria renamed the city Gabinius and referred to themselves as Gabinians. But it was not until the building projects of Herod the Great that Samaria regained the recognition and acclaim of its Israelite period. Samaria played a critical role in both political and family affairs during the early part of Herod's reign. The citizens of the city gave their support and assistance to Herod as he tried to solidify his grasp on the land. And it was during that early period that Herod left his family at Samaria for a time for safekeeping and protection. Samaria was the setting of his marriage to his wife, Mariamne.

In 30 BCE, the emperor Augustus gave Samaria to Herod, who introduced a building program to establish Samaria as one of his chief cities. The city was enlarged to encompass approximately two hundred acres, was fortified with a new city wall strengthened periodically by circular towers, and was renamed Sebaste after the emperor Augustus. The most imposing feature of the new city was a large temple built on the acropolis and dedicated to Augustus. The temple stood on a large platform with a monumental stairway, a prominent altar in the courtyard approaching the temple, and an impressive statue of the emperor. Additional features of the new city included a large stadium and an aqueduct as well as a number of imposing buildings around the temple. The city was designed as both a showplace and a fortress where Herod housed some six thousand mercenary troops. Sebaste was the city of Jesus' time in which Philip preached (Acts 8:5–17). During the Jewish-Roman War rebel forces burned Sebaste.

Although the fire caused significant damage, the Herodian buildings were eventually restored. During the second and third centuries Samaria-Sebaste enjoyed a new period of prosperity and expansion, and during the reign of the emperor Severus (193–211 CE) it was declared a Roman colony. The city once again witnessed a massive building program, which included the construction of a colonnaded street, a forum, a basilica, a theater, and a temple dedicated to Kore. During the reign of the emperor Constantine an episcopal see was established at Samaria-Sebaste. Samaria-Sebaste also became known as the place of John the Baptist's burial; consequently, a church was erected in the city in his honor. The church was rebuilt during the Crusader period. Today a mosque occupies the revered site in the modern Arab village of Sebastiyeh.

Bibliography: ACKROYD, P. R., "Samaria," *Archaeology and the Old Testament,* ed. D. Winton Thomas (Oxford: Clarendon, 1967) 343–54; ARMERDING, C. E., "Samaria," *NIDBA,* 394–96; AVIGAD, N., "Samaria," *EAEHL,* 4:1032–50; idem, "Samaria," *NEAEHL,* 4:1300–1310; BLAIKLOCK, E. M., "Samaria," *NIDB,* 887–88; ELWELL, W. A., "Samaria," *BEB,* 2:1885–86; HENNESSY, J. B., "Samaria," *IDBSup,* 771–72; KELSO, J., "Samaria, City of," *ZPEB,* 5:232–40; McRAY, J., "Samaria," *Archaeology and the New Testament* (Grand Rapids: Baker, 1991) 145–48; POTTS, D. R., "Samaria, Samaritans," *HolBD,* 1224–25; PRICE, J. D., "Samaria," *Major Cities of the Biblical World* (Nashville: Nelson, 1985) 223–33; PURVIS, J. D., "Samaria, City of," *HBD,* 895–96; idem, "Samaria (Samaria the City)," *ABD,* 5:914–21; ROWELL, E., "Samaria." *MDB,* 788–89; SCHOVILLE, K. N., "Samaria," *BAF,* 465–72; TAPPY, R., "Samaria," *OEANE,* 4:463–67; VAN BEEK, G. W., "Samaria," *IDB,* 4:182–88; VAN SELMS, A., "Samaria," *ISBE,* 4:295–98; WISEMAN, D. J., "Samaria," *NBD*[2], 1060–62.

Hometown of Joachim and Anna, the Parents of Mary

Though Sepphoris is not mentioned in the Bible and the name is unfamiliar to many students of the Bible, nevertheless, Sepphoris was a prominent city of Galilee. During the NT period Sepphoris was the capital of Galilee and the residence of Herod Antipas, son of Herod the Great and tetrarch of Galilee and Perea. According to tradition, Sepphoris held the distinction of being the hometown of Joachim and Anna, the parents of Mary. According to rabbinic sources, Sepphoris was where Rabbi Judah lived as he edited the Mishnah, a pivotal part of the collection of Jewish tradition known as the Talmud. The city was a mixture of Jews, Christians, and Romans. Sepphoris was located on the top of a large hill where it seemed to perch like a bird. Indeed, the name Sepphoris means "bird." Josephus gave the city yet another title, "the ornament of all Galilee" (*Ant.* 18.27), a title that apparently reflected both the ornate physical features and the important status the city acquired during the first century.

Sepphoris is located in lower Galilee about midway between the Mediterranean Sea to the west and the Sea of Galilee to the east. It was situated on an imposing hill about four miles north-northwest of Nazareth, the hometown of Jesus, and had a commanding view of the plain below. Consequently, the site had real value as a fortified city.

The plain around Sepphoris provided additional benefits. The fertile soil of the plain provided an economy at least partially based on agriculture. Sepphoris attained some status as an important commercial center with an economy that benefited from the activities of merchants and traders. Sepphoris was located along an important highway that ran from the city of Ptolemais on the Mediterranean coast some sixteen or seventeen miles to the northwest, through the Turan valley and the city of Sepphoris, on to the city of Tiberias on the Sea of

Galilee. The site had one major drawback; it did not have a natural water supply.

Remains of a monumental building

The Bible does not mention Sepphoris, but information about the city comes to us from several sources including Josephus, rabbinic sources, the early church fathers, and archaeological research. Exploration at the site began as early as 1908, with the investigation of the crusader Church of Saint Anna under the direction of Prosper Viared of France. Further investigation was initiated in 1931 under the direction of Leroy Waterman and S. Yeivin and sponsored by the University of Michigan. The University of Michigan team investigated the Roman theater at Sepphoris, a semicircular facility designed to accommodate four thousand people. E. L. Sukenik engaged in the investigation of burials during the same period. By far the most exhaustive investigation began during the 1980s, initially by James Strange and the University of South Florida in 1982 and 1983, and beginning in 1985 by Eric Meyers, Ehud Netzer, and Carol Meyers, a project cosponsored by Duke University and Hebrew University. As at many other sites, the architectural remains of the ancient city are extremely limited and fragmentary due to the reuse of the materials by later groups.

While the story of Sepphoris includes many unanswered questions, information from the literary sources and archaeological exploration provides a profile of the city's history. Tradition dates the city of Sepphoris back to the times of Joshua, and pottery fragments found at the site tend to confirm some type of activity there during the early part of the OT period. While information about the origin and early beginning of the city is imprecise, pottery fragments from the Persian period allow us to assume that Sepphoris was a city of some note during the Persian period. However, it was during the early Roman period that the city reached its pinnacle.

Sepphoris is not mentioned in historical records until the end of the second century BCE. Josephus notes that the city of Sepphoris was attacked by the ruler Ptolemy Lathyrus during the early part of the reign of the Hasmonean king Alexander Jannaeus, ca. 104 BCE (*Ant.* 13.338). However, Ptolemy's attempt to take the city from the Jewish state was unsuccessful. We may assume that Sepphoris was already an important administrative center in Galilee during much of the Hasmonean period.

With the arrival of Pompey in 64 BCE Sepphoris, like the other cities of Palestine, came under the influence of Rome. Around 55 BCE, Gabinius, the Roman proconsul in Syria, visited Palestine and initiated a program of administrative reorganization. He separated Galilee from Judea and divided the Jewish state into five separate districts with their own council or Sanhedrin. Gabinius located the Sanhedrin for the district of Galilee at Sepphoris.

During the reign of the Roman emperor Julius Caesar appointments were made that would bring the Herods into the city's history. This era extended from Herod the Great to Herod Agrippa II. Julius Caesar appointed an Idumean named Antipater as the local administrative official of Palestine. Antipater appointed Herod, his son, as the local governor of the district of Galilee. Following the death of Antipater, Herod, commonly known as Herod the Great, was appointed king of Judea by the Roman Senate, an appointment that in time was extended to Samaria, Galilee, Perea, and the districts east and northeast of the Sea of Galilee. Although Herod's appointment took place in 44 BCE, he did not become ruler in fact until 37 BCE when he settled numerous clashes with the Parthians who had invaded the land. Josephus writes that Herod took the city of Sepphoris during that period of turmoil in the midst of a snowstorm during the winter of 39–38 BCE (*Ant.* 14.414–17).

Following that victory Sepphoris continued to function as the capital of Galilee. By this time Sepphoris was clearly the leading city of Galilee.

Upon the death of Herod the Great in 4 BCE, his territory was divided among his sons Archelaus, Philip, and Antipas, with Antipas being appointed tetrarch of Galilee and Perea. During that period of transition violence erupted at Sepphoris. The city became the sanctuary of Jewish nationalists who revolted against Rome. According to Josephus (*Ant.* 17.271) the city of Sepphoris was captured by a band of freedom fighters whose leader was named Judas, perhaps the Judas mentioned in Acts 5:37. The freedom fighters, intent on establishing Sepphoris as a major stronghold of their movement, confiscated the available weapons for the inevitable Roman response. Retaliation came at the command of the emperor Augustus who ordered Varus, the Roman governor of Syria, to Palestine to put down the revolts. Varus's strategy was both decisive and cruel. He gathered his forces, moved into Galilee, took the city of Sepphoris, burned it, and enslaved its citizens (Josephus, *Ant.* 17.289). The sacking of Sepphoris marked the beginning of a campaign in which Varus moved throughout the land of Palestine and destroyed city after city. In the process Varus crucified some two thousand rebel fighters.

With Herod Antipas eventually in place as the tetrarch of Galilee and Perea, a new era began for Sepphoris. Herod Antipas rebuilt the city and its defense system and established it as the capital of Galilee. Sepphoris became a magnificent city, according to Josephus, "the ornament of all Galilee." It was comprised of an upper and lower city. The new Herodian city included a new city wall, a palace, a large market place, a theater, synagogues, a colonnaded street, and a residential area with private dwellings. Since Sepphoris was the largest city of Galilee located on the major trade route running from Ptolemais on the coast to Tiberias on the Sea of Galilee, we may assume that it was a thriving commercial center during this period. Eventually Herod Antipas built the city of Tiberias and relocated the capital there. However, Sepphoris continued to be a prominent city of lower Galilee (Josephus, *Ant.* 18.27).

Following the death of Herod Antipas, Sepphoris came under the control of Herod Agrippa I (37–44 CE), followed by a series of procurators including Felix (52–60 CE) and eventually Herod Agrippa II. Under Felix, Sepphoris once again became the capital of Galilee. During the latter part of the first century Sepphoris numbered prominent priestly families among its populace.

Ritual bath

One of the most interesting chapters in the history of Sepphoris was the era of the first revolt, and the role the city played in the Jewish-Roman War of 66–70 CE. As the initial stages of the revolt began to unfold, the rebel forces established Jerusalem as their governmental headquarters and divided the land into seven military districts with a chief commander in charge of operations in each individual district. The commander dispatched to Galilee was a young priest named Joseph who apparently had little or no military training. Later known as Flavius Josephus, the young priest rallied his forces and fortified the city of Sepphoris in preparation for the inevitable attack by the Romans (*War* 3.61). As Vespasian and the Roman forces advanced, the citizens of Sepphoris, a pacifistic people according to Josephus, willingly surrendered or welcomed Vespasian and pledged to support him in the remainder of the campaigns in the country (*War* 3.30–34). Apparently the city remained loyal to the Romans throughout the war. As the war progressed in Judea, Sepphoris was a refuge for those seeking sanctuary. With the fall of Jerusalem and the destruction of the temple in 70 CE, prominent priestly families moved north and settled in lower Galilee, especially Sepphoris and Nazareth.

The precise role Sepphoris played in the second revolt (132–135 CE) is open to debate. While the city became the hometown of many of the refugees following the first revolt (66–70 CE) and strong nationalistic spirit prevailed among some citizens, there is no clear evidence to indicate that the city was instrumental in causing the revolt to erupt. Sometime during the period that followed, the name of the city changed from Sepphoris to Diocaesarea.

During the next two to three centuries Sepphoris became a city with a mixed population that included Jews, Christians, and Romans. Rabbi Judah, also known as "the Prince," lived here and edited the Mishnah, and the great Galilean sanhedrin met here. Sepphoris became a major center of Jewish learning, the home of a Jewish academy. The city was also the home of a sizable Christian community. References to the Christian community appear in the writings of Eusebius during the third century, and by the fifth and sixth centuries Sepphoris had its own bishop. Perhaps the most notable aspect of this period was not simply the evidence of the mixed population, but the evidence that the three different components of the population equally shared in the important religious, political, and economic developments that took place.

Archaeology adds its own unique dimensions to the story of Sepphoris, even though the reuse of building materials by later generations has both disturbed and limited the material remains. Among the discoveries at Sepphoris was the Roman theater, one of the most impressive features of the community. Typical of Roman theaters of that period, the theater at Sepphoris has a semicircular design and was built to accommodate approximately four to five thousand people. The theater was most likely constructed originally by Herod Antipas during the first century CE and perhaps reconstructed during later Roman and Byzantine periods; however, the date of the origin of the theater is still open to debate. In addition to the theater, excavations have recovered the remains of other large public buildings, including a possible fortress, as well as domestic structures, ritual baths, and numerous underground cavities including those used for cisterns.

The underground cavities, both natural and man-made, seem to have been used for a variety of purposes including the storage of water, food, and commodities for daily life. The cavities and the two aqueducts apparently provided the community's water supply. The cavities vary in design; some had a single chamber and others had multiple chambers. One series of cavities was almost as large as a football field.

The most surprising discovery by far was a large third-century building. The building had a large main hall with a large mosaic floor and three side wings. The design of the mosaic suggests that the room was used as a *triclinium,* a dining room, in which the guests reclined around three sides of the room. The focus of the *triclinium* was the mosaic floor itself, which featured a lovely, delicately designed lady, commonly referred to as the Mona Lisa of Galilee. The central panel was surrounded by smaller mosaic panels that featured scenes related to the god Dionysus. The building appears to have been destroyed during the latter part of the fourth century CE by an earthquake.

Bibliography: AVI-YONAH, M., "Sepphoris," *EAEHL,* 4:1051–55; HOEHNER, H. W., "Sepphoris," *Herod Antipas* (Grand Rapids: Zondervan, 1980) 84–91; KENT, D. G., "Sepphoris: Capital of Galilee," *Where Jesus Walked,* ed. William H. Stephens (Nashville: Broadman, 1981) 26–29; McRAY, J., "Sepphoris," *Archaeology and the New Testament* (Grand Rapids: Baker, 1991) 175–78; MEYERS, C. L., and E. M. Meyers, "Sepphoris," *OEANE,* 4:527–36; MEYERS, E. M., E. Netzer, and C. L. Meyers, "Artistry in Stone: The Mosaics of Ancient Sepphoris," *BA* 50 (1987) 223–31; idem, *Sepphoris* (Winona Lake, Ind.: Eisenbrauns, 1992); idem, "Sepphoris: Ornament of all Galilee," *BA* 49 (1986) 4–19; MILNE, M. K., "Sepphoris," *HBD,* 925; SHANKS, H., ed., "Mosaic Masterpiece Dazzles Sepphoris Volunteers," *BAR* 14 (1, 1988) 30–33; STRANGE, J. F., "Sepphoris," *ABD,* 5:1090–93; idem, "Sepphoris," *MDB,* 808; VIVIANO, P., "Sepphoris," *ISBE,* 4:399–400; WEISS, Z., "Sepphoris," *NEAEHL,* 4:1324–28.

TIBERIAS

52

City Founded by Herod Antipas

The city of Tiberias is mentioned only once in the NT (John 6:23), and the gospels never refer to Jesus visiting the city; nevertheless, Tiberias played a central role as one of the major cities of Palestine during the NT period. Tiberias was one of nine cities located around the perimeter of the Sea of Galilee and is the only one still existing today. It was for a time the capital of Galilee that housed the royal quarters of Herod Antipas, tetrarch of Galilee and Perea. Following the NT period, especially during the second century, Tiberias became a major center of Jewish thought and religion, a center of rabbinic study and the site of the completion of the Talmud. Along with Jerusalem, Hebron, and Sepphoris, Tiberias was considered by the Jews to be one of the four sacred cities of the land. The dominance of Tiberias is reflected in the fact that the Sea of Galilee came to be known as the Sea of Tiberias (John 6:1; 21:1).

The city of Tiberias was originally founded by Herod Antipas, tetrarch of Galilee and Perea, and son of Herod the Great. Antipas, who faced opposition and unfriendly surroundings in his capital at Sepphoris, apparently felt the new site had features that made it commendable for the establishment of a new capital city. It was located on the west bank of the Sea of Galilee, approximately sixteen miles east of Sepphoris, thirty-three miles southeast of Ptolemais on the Mediterranean coast, and seventy-five miles north of Jerusalem. It was a more central position in relation to the territories in his tetrarchy, and it was closer to the territory of Perea, the part of his tetrarchy located east of the Jordan River. Tiberius was the place on the west bank of the Sea of Galilee at which all the major international and local highways from the north, south, and west converged.

The new site had additional assets that were related to the topography of the area, the climate, and the sea itself. The topography of the location was certainly ideal. The site that Antipas selected was a band of land approximately one thousand feet wide that ran along the southwest shore of the Sea of Galilee. Higher elevations to the west formed a natural acropolis for the site, which became the setting for the royal quarters. In this position Antipas had a panoramic view of the entire lake and access by boat to the cities around the Sea of Galilee. Level with the Sea of Galilee, Tiberias was 695 feet below sea level. The elevation of the site and the much higher elevation of the plateau to the west combined to create a nearly tropical climate for the city of Tiberias.

Hot springs at Hamat Tiberias

Tiberias also benefited from the unique features of the surrounding area. South of Tiberias lay the village of Ammathus with hot springs mentioned in the writings of Josephus (*Ant.* 18.36). Known today as Hamat Tiberias, this site may be the Hammath mentioned in the book of Joshua (Josh 19:35). Reference to the site by Pliny, the Roman writer who lived during the first century, indicates that the hot baths and their therapeutic value were well known throughout the ancient world (*Natural History* 5.15). To the north of Tiberias, just around the bulge in the lake's shoreline, lay the plain of Gennesaret. Located between the cities of Magdala and Capernaum on the northwest shore of the Sea of Galilee, the plain of Gennesaret was the most fertile and productive agricultural region in Palestine during the NT period. Known as the garden of Palestine, the region was five miles long and a mile wide. It produced a variety of fruits, vegetables, grains, and nuts including figs, grapes, melons, wheat, rice, olives, and walnuts. Equally important was the Sea of Galilee to the east of Tiberias, which supported a thriving fishing industry. The Sea of Galilee, also referred to as the Lake of Gennesaret (Luke 5:1), had an abundant variety of fish. Consequently, the fishing industry became a mainstay in the economy of several lakeside cities, including Capernaum, Magdala, and Tiberias.

While Antipas built the new capital (ca. 18–22 CE), he ran into problems. As construction proceeded, the workers discovered the remains of a necropolis (burial site or cemetery), perhaps the burial site of the city of Hammath mentioned in the OT (Josh 19:35). For Antipas, the discovery had serious repercussions. According to Jewish law the cemetery made the site unclean and consequently off limits for Jewish settlement. In spite of this obstacle, however, Antipas succeeded through force and enticement in populating the city with a mixture of Galilean Jews and Gentiles, both rich and poor. According to Josephus, Antipas offered free houses and land to those willing to reside in Tiberias (*Ant.* 18.38). We may assume that others were attracted to the new capital by its growing status as a major center of government, trade and exchange, as well as industry. Antipas named the new city Tiberias in honor of the Roman emperor Tiberias Caesar (14–37 CE).

Though the history of Tiberias as we have it today is far from complete, several important features of that history can be outlined. Tiberias continued as the capital of Galilee during a series of leaders including Antipas, Herod Agrippa I, the office of the procurator, and Herod Agrippa II (ca. 61 CE). Herod Agrippa II moved the capital of Galilee from Tiberias back to Sepphoris.

While the NT mentions Tiberias only once, Josephus provides valuable information about the city during NT times (e.g., *Life* 12.64; 34.169; 55.283). According to Josephus, Tiberias had a city government similar to that of the Greek city or *polis*. As a type of *polis* the city had some autonomy and could exercise its sovereignty in certain areas such as minting coins and levying taxes. Matters such as these were determined by the city officials, who were made up of an elected leader *(archon)*, a committee of ten, and a larger city council of six hundred.

Like other cities in Palestine, Tiberias had its own dramatic role in the events of the Jewish-Roman War of 66–70 CE. As the Jewish revolt against Rome broke out in Palestine, Tiberias was captured by Josephus and prepared for the inevitable onslaught of Roman troops. The palace of Herod was destroyed, and the defenses of the city were strengthened. According to Josephus's masterful work entitled *The Jewish War* (2.585–646), Tiberias was caught in the middle of a feud between Josephus and John of Gischala, a powerful self-appointed leader. Josephus eventually prevailed in the feud and recovered the city from the local troublemaker. When three Roman legions under Vespasian laid siege to the city of Tiberias in 67 CE, the city opened its gates, and Josephus and his forces surrendered (*War* 3.445–61). Since Tiberias—along with Tarichaea-Magdala, Bethsaida-Julias, and its fourteen villages—had been given to Herod Agrippa II by the Roman emperor Nero prior to the war, and since Josephus and the inhabitants of the city openly surrendered to Vespasian and his forces, the Romans permitted Tiberias to remain under Jewish rule until 100 CE.

Following the second Jewish revolt and the fall of Jerusalem in 135 CE, the Roman emperor Hadrian attempted to erase any Jewish ties the city had by repopulating it with non-Jews. Nevertheless, Tiberias became a major Jewish center of learning during the second century CE. Several developments were responsible for the city's new status. First, the Sanhedrin moved from the city of Sepphoris to Tiberias ca. 150 CE. Tiberias became an important rabbinic center with schools established for the purpose of rabbinic study and learning. Important work on the Mishnah, the Talmud, and the Masoretic Text took place at Tiberias. It was the site at which Rabbi Judah the Prince finalized the compilation of the Mishnah that he had begun in Sepphoris. Rabbi Yohanan, apparently a student of Rabbi Judah and often referred to as the most important contributor to the Palestinian Talmud, established his *Beth Midrash* (house of study) and laid the basic foundation for the Palestinian Talmud, which reached its completion in Tiberias near the end of the fourth century. The Tiberian vowel pointing system was developed, which became a part of the Masoretic Text of the Hebrew Bible. The city's legacy as a consequential Jewish center is also reflected in the key figures who were buried there, including Rabbi Akiba of the second century and Maimonides, the Spanish rabbi and theologian who lived during the twelfth and thirteenth centuries.

Until recent times our knowledge of the physical features of ancient Tiberias has been based on literary sources such as Josephus and Jewish

traditions reflected in the Talmud, augmented by a few isolated
excavations. In the fall of 1990 a large-scale systematic plan was initiated
that will continue for a number of seasons to excavate the ancient city
buried under the modern city dump. At the present time some of the
major features of the community can be identified. For instance, among
the earlier excavations directed by N. Slouschy in 1921 and Moshe
Dothan between 1961 and 1963, the remains of two synagogue
complexes were discovered at Hamat Tiberias. Additional surveys and
excavations have helped to identify features of the city of Tiberias itself.
The outline of the city wall has been traced, and excavations directed by
Gideon Foerster (1973–74) recovered the impressive southern gate
complex comprised of two large round towers. Like most cities during
the Roman period, Tiberias had a Cardo, a major thoroughfare paved
with stone slabs and lined on each side with a colonnaded portico and
shops. While the major part of the lengthy Cardo has not been
excavated, portions of the shops and porticoes of the Cardo's east side
were excavated by Bazalel Rabbani (1954–56). The Rabbani excavations
also discovered the remains of a bathhouse, an expansive building with
columns that most likely functioned as the city marketplace, and a
basilica with an apse. Excavations directed by Ariel Berman in 1978 also
recovered what is apparently one of the thirteen synagogues that the
Talmud describes as being in Tiberias.

While relying on Josephus and awaiting further excavations, we may
assume that the city of Tiberius included a palace, a stadium, a
synagogue, and a citadel on Mount Berenice, a facility that was apparently
incorporated into the city wall. Like many other cities in Palestine, Tiberias
had a water system with an aqueduct and a reservoir. The aqueduct
channeled water from springs approximately ten miles away to a large
reservoir in the city.

Among the most significant discoveries of the current excavations
directed by Yizbar Hirschfeld are the remains of a sizable building
originally built about 200 CE that Hirschfeld speculates was the house of
study of Rabbi Yohanan, the great shaper of the Palestinian Talmud. The
building is located at the base of Mount Berenice and has thick walls, a
large hall with a mosaic floor, and a large rectangular bath, perhaps a
miqvah (a bath used for ritual ablution). The building continued to be
used until the eighth century.

Bibliography: BLAIKLOCK, E. M., "Tiberias," *NIDB,* 1014; idem, "Tiberias," *ZPEB,* 5:745–46; CLARK, K. W., "Tiberias," *IDB,* 4:639–40; EDWARDS, D. R., "Tiberias," *HBD,* 1069–70; FOERSTER, G., "Tiberias," *EAEHL,* 4:1171–76; HARRIS, B. F., and E. M. Blaiklock, "Tiberias," *NIDBA,* 450–51; HIRSCHFELD, Y., "Tiberias," *OEANE,* 5:203–6; idem, "Tiberias: Preview of Coming Attractions," *BAR* 17 (2, 1991) 44–51; HIRSCHFELD, Y., G. Foerster, and F. Vitto, "Tiberias," *NEAEHL,* 4:1464–73; HOEHNER, H. W., "Tiberias," *Herod Antipas* (Grand Rapids: Zondervan, 1980) 91–100; JOINER, E. E., "Tiberias," *MDB,* 917; MCRAY, J., "Tiberias," *Archaeology and the New Testament* (Grand Rapids: Baker, 1991) 178; idem, "Tiberias," *HolBD,* 1345; MOUNCE, R. H., "Tiberias," *ISBE,* 4:846–47; PATERSON, J. H., "Tiberias," *NBD*^{2}, 1198; STRANGE, J. F., "Tiberias," *ABD,* 6:547–49.

Unit 2

CITIES OF THE
ROMAN WORLD

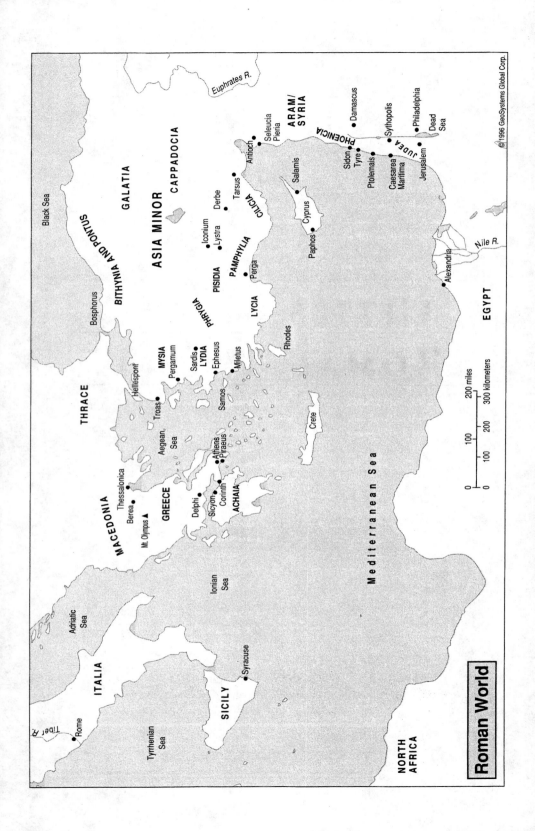

Roman World

© 1996 GeoSystems Global Corp.

Black Sea

Euphrates R.

ARAM/
SYRIA

Damascus

Seleucia
Pieria

PHOENICIA

Scythopolis

Philadelphia

Antioch

Dead
Sea

Sidon
Tyre

JUDEA

GALATIA

CAPPADOCIA

Salamis

Ptolemais

BITHYNIA AND PONTUS

Jerusalem

Caesarea
Maritima

ASIA MINOR

Tarsus

Derbe

CILICIA

Cyprus

Iconium

Lystra

Bosphorus

PAMPHYLIA

PISIDIA

Paphos

PHRYGIA

Perga

Nile R.

THRACE

LYCIA

Alexandria

Hellespont

MYSIA

Rhodes

Pergamum

Sardis

EGYPT

LYDIA

Ephesus

Miletus

Troas

Samos

Aegean
Sea

Athens

Piraeus

Crete

Thessalonica

GREECE

Delphi

Berea

Sicyon

Corinth

Mt. Olympus ▲

ACHAIA

MACEDONIA

Mediterranean Sea

Ionian
Sea

Adriatic
Sea

Syracuse

ITALIA

SICILY

Tyrrhenian
Sea

Rome

Tiber R.

NORTH
AFRICA

0   100   200 miles

0   100   200   300 kilometers

THE ROMAN WORLD   53

Setting for the Spread of the Early Church

Palestine provided the setting for the NT story, but when the writing began, the early Christian church was not confined to Palestine. It quickly spread to the Roman territories and cities around the Mediterranean. Especially noteworthy in the continuing drama were the cities of Damascus and Antioch in Syria, Ephesus in Asia Minor, Athens and Corinth in Achaia (Greece), Rome in Italy, and Alexandria in Egypt.

The Mediterranean world was tied together politically, culturally, and geographically. Politically, the lands and provinces around the Mediterranean Sea were united as a part of the vast Roman Empire. Culturally, the area had a semblance of cohesiveness because of the common base provided by the predominant Greco-Roman culture. And geographically, the lands and provinces of the Roman Empire were centered around the Mediterranean Sea, which provided a means of transportation and trade.

While the historical events of the OT were influenced by the empires of the Egyptians, Assyrians, and Babylonians, the history of the NT period was dominated by the Roman Empire. Though the history of the development of the Roman Empire is complicated and still at many points open to debate, the events of its origin can be traced back to the third century BCE when the Romans began to extend their power and influence beyond their homeland in Italy to other lands around the Mediterranean Sea and other parts of Europe to the north and west, including the island of Sicily and the territory of Spain. During the second century BCE the Romans began their movement eastward, taking the territories of Macedonia and Achaia as well as the city of Carthage, which provided a footing in North Africa. In the years that followed, the Romans held all the lands at the eastern end of the Mediterranean Sea including the territory of Asia Minor, which they took during the latter part of the second century BCE, and the territory of Syria and Judea, which Pompey laid claim to in 64 BCE. After a period of internal turmoil and civil war Augustus defeated Marc Antony and Cleopatra in the battle of Actium in 31 BCE and was decisively established as the sole ruler of the empire. In 27 BCE Augustus officially replaced the republican form of government; the Roman Empire was born, and the Roman Republic died.

Remains of the complex Roman road system

Perhaps the most significant feature of the new empire was the cosmopolitan outlook that prevailed during its early history. The Romans recognized the value of local governments and placed much of the administration of the local Mediterranean provinces in the hands of local administrators. In so doing, the Romans attempted to create an atmosphere of trust in the local provinces.

While it recognized and preserved the local traditions and customs of the provinces, the empire did not sacrifice its unity and its cosmopolitan spirit. Rather, the Romans created a hybrid culture, the "Greco-Roman culture," by adopting the features of Greek culture that they admired and combining them with their own unique contributions. And it was those features of the Greco-Roman culture that provided additional fibers for the fabric of the cosmopolitan spirit. For instance, while many different languages were represented among the peoples of the empire, the Greek language was the language of the empire as a whole. It was the language of trade and commerce.

To those features adopted from the Hellenistic world the Romans added their own—the ideal of *Pax Romana,* "Roman peace." Perhaps more than anything else, this ideal was inspired by the fact that during the reign of the emperor Augustus peace was established throughout the empire. The ideal of *Pax Romana* took on two symbols—the first was the altar of peace, erected along the Tiber River in Rome by the emperor Augustus, and the second was (somewhat ironically) the powerful Roman army with its legions of troops designed to maintain peace throughout the provinces of the empire.

In order to enhance communication and trade among the provinces, the Romans constructed a well-designed system of roads throughout the empire. Travel and communication, trade, and exchange were enhanced even more by the merchant ships that traveled the shipping routes that interlaced the Mediterranean Sea. The merchant ships transported masses of cargo between the leading cities of the empire including the cities of Rome, Carthage in North Africa, Alexandria in Egypt, Caesarea in Palestine, Tyre in Phoenicia, Antioch in Syria, Ephesus in Asia Minor, and Athens and Corinth in Greece.

The Mediterranean world played an influential role in early Christianity. According to the book of Acts the disciples were first called Christians in Antioch of Syria (Acts 11:26), and it was from there that Paul and Barnabas were commissioned and sent out (Acts 13:1–3). Paul's travels took him to numerous provinces, cities, and communities in the Mediterranean area including Salamis and Paphos on Cyprus; Perga, Antioch, Iconium, Lystra, Derbe, Troas, and Ephesus in Asia Minor; Philippi, Thessalonica, and Berea in Macedonia; Athens and Corinth in Greece; and Rome in Italy (Acts 13:4–28; 16:1–21:16; 28:14). At times Paul traveled on highways provided by the Romans, at other times on merchant ships that crossed the Mediterranean (Acts 21:1–6; 27:1–28:14).

The Mediterranean world is also reflected in the Pauline correspondence—the letter to the Romans, First and Second Corinthians, the letter to the Galatians, the letter to the Philippians, the letter to the Colossians, First and Second Thessalonians, all (regardless of theories of authorship) written to early Christian communities in the Mediterranean.

The Mediterranean arena is reflected in other NT writings as well. The author of Hebrews refers to the greetings from those who came from Italy (Heb 13:24). First Peter was addressed "to the exiles of the Dispersion in Pontus, Galatia, Cappadocia, Asia, and Bithynia" (1 Pet 1:1). And the Revelation of John was written to the seven churches in Asia (Rev 1:4).

During the centuries following the NT period the Mediterranean world continued to play an important role in the history of early Christianity. Major centers such as Antioch of Syria, Alexandria in Egypt, Ephesus in Asia, and Rome in Italy, as well as others, were the setting for the development of Christianity and the work of the early church fathers.

Bibliography: ANGUS, S., and A. M. Renwick, "Roman Empire and Christianity," *ISBE,* 4:207–21; BLAIKLOCK, E. M., "Roman Empire," *NIDB,* 867–69; idem, "Roman Empire," *ZPEB,* 5:133–41; FINEGAN, J., *The Archaeology of the New Testament: The Mediterranean World of the Early Christian Apostles* (Boulder: Westview, 1981); GRANT, R. M., "Roman Empire," *IDB,* 4:103–109; HINSON, E. G., "Roman Empire," *MDB,* 769–72; JUDGE, E. A., "Roman Empire," *NBD*[2], 1032–34; KENNEDY, D. L., "Roman Empire," *OEANE,* 4:435–41; MAY, H. G., "The Background of the New Testament: Rome and the East," *Oxford Bible Atlas,* 3d ed.; rev. John Day (New York: Oxford University Press, 1984) 88–89; idem, "The Cradle of Christianity: The Eastern Mediterranean," *Oxford Bible Atlas,* 3d ed.; ed. John Day (New York: Oxford University Press, 1984) 90–91; MCRAY, J., "Rome and the Roman Empire," *HolBD,* 1207–12; PERKINS, P., and P. J. Achtemeier, "Roman Empire," *HBD,* 875–76; PRITCHARD, J. B., ed., *The Harper Atlas of the Bible* (New York: Harper & Row, 1987); SADDINGTON, D. B., "Roman Government, Administration of Cities," *NIDBA,* 388–90; idem, "Roman Government, Administration of Provinces," *NIDBA,* 390–92; WELLS, C. M., "Roman Empire," *ABD,* 5:801–6; WRIGHT, G. E., "The Church in the World," *Biblical Archaeology,* rev. ed. (Philadelphia: Westminster, 1962) 248–76.

Home of the Allegorical Approach to Scripture

Alexandria of Egypt is mentioned only four times in the book of Acts, and the role of the city in the drama of the NT story seems inconsequential based on those references. Nevertheless, Alexandria holds a unique position in the history of the development of early Christianity. First, Alexandria was a leading commercial and cultural center in the Mediterranean world, second only to Rome itself. Second, next to Jerusalem it was the leading center of Hellenistic Judaism. And third, Alexandria, along with Caesarea and Antioch of Syria, was one of the primary sites outside of Palestine that developed into a major center of early Christian learning. It was the home of a major catechetical school characterized by the allegorical approach to the interpretation of Scripture in contrast to the more historical and rational Antiochene approach, which was used in Antioch of Syria.

Antioch was approximately three hundred miles north of Jerusalem in north Syria, and Alexandria was about three hundred miles west-southwest of Jerusalem in north Egypt. Alexandria's location in relationship to the Mediterranean world and Egypt made it an ideal setting for a major cosmopolitan center.

It was founded by Alexander the Great in 331 BCE at the site of Rakotis, a small Egyptian fishing village at the west edge of the Nile River delta on the Mediterranean coast. The original city was designed and planned by Deinocrates, the architect who was also responsible for the design and construction of the temple of Artemis in Ephesus. Over time, the area of Alexandria expanded. The city proper, located on a narrow peninsula and separated from the mainland of Egypt by Lake Mareotis, was protected by Pharos Island, eight-tenths of a mile north of the city, which served as a breakwater for the city. Eventually a causeway, commonly referred to as the heptastadium ("seven stadia"), was added. This served as a connecting link between the city and the island and also divided the bay into two harbors. With this unique coastal formation and harbor facilities, Alexandria was secluded and at the same time proximate to Egypt and the Mediterranean world; it was the ideal setting for a major trade center, military base, and political headquarters for controlling Egypt and the eastern Mediterranean. Alexandria quickly became a vital seaport city on the Mediterranean and a principal citadel of the Greco-Roman culture.

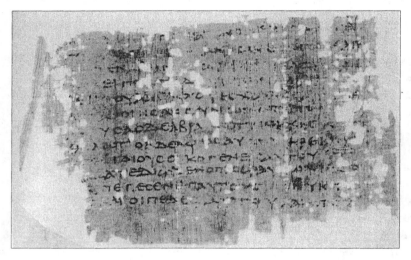

Fragmentary Greek papyrus manuscript containing Gen. 14:12–15
(Beinecke Rare Book and Manuscript Library, Yale University)

Alexandria came under the control of Ptolemy Soter, Ptolemy I, a general in Alexander's army who took control of Egypt following the death of the great conqueror. The Ptolemaic dynasty lasted from the time of Ptolemy I to Cleopatra. During the Ptolemaic period Alexandria became a major seaport and center of the Hellenistic culture.

Alexandria replaced Memphis as the capital of Egypt during the reign of Ptolemy I. Alexandria also became the home of a study and learning complex with a museum and library containing over four hundred thousand volumes, the largest collection of literary works in the ancient world at that time.

The Ptolemaic rulers were responsible for numerous building projects in the city including the lighthouse, the serapeum, and the royal complex. During the reign of either Ptolemy I or Ptolemy II (Ptolemy Philadelphus), the city of Alexandria was connected with the island by means of a causeway, the heptastadium. With the construction of the causeway the city of Alexandria was equipped with three harbors: Lake Mareotis; the west harbor, named Eunostos; and the east harbor, known as the great harbor. While the twin harbors north of the city were located immediately on the Mediterranean Sea, the major shipping harbor was the one located in Lake Mareotis, south of the city. Perhaps the most unique feature of the harbor facilities was the lighthouse Ptolemy II constructed on the island. The lighthouse, named Pharos after the island on which it stood, was known as one of the seven wonders of the world. It was constructed in three different sections with each section having its own unique architectural design. The lowest section was rectangular, the second section was octagonal, and the third section was cylindrical. It stood approximately 450 feet tall. The upper section of the lighthouse was equipped with a beacon designed with bronze mirrors. A flame within was reflected some four to five miles out to sea. One of the most beautiful buildings constructed in the city during the early part of the Ptolemaic period was the serapeum, a temple used for rituals dedicated especially to the god Serapis, a combination of the Egyptian Osiris-Apis. The Ptolemaic rulers also constructed a large royal complex comprised of palaces and overlooking the great harbor. During the Roman period the royal complex was used by Roman governors.

The basic design of Alexandria followed the Greek city plan. The city proper was rectangular in shape and approximately four miles long. It had a main east-west street, the Canopic Way, running the full length of the city with other streets intersecting at right angles. The principal streets of the city were lined with columns.

Ptolemaic rule of Alexandria ended after three centuries. The city as well as the land of Egypt came under Roman control following the battle of Actium in 31 BCE in which Octavian, who later became the emperor Augustus, defeated Cleopatra. Alexandria continued to thrive as a major seaport and cultural center during the early part of the Roman period. As a major cosmopolitan trade center second only to Rome itself, Alexandria imported and exported commodities from throughout the ancient world. Wine, oil, timber, precious stones, fabrics, metals, spices, perfumes, and papyrus all passed through its ports. It was also the major granary for the Roman Empire through the production of cereal crops such as wheat and barley. Among the major exports of the seaport city were wheat and papyrus. During the first century CE Alexandria had a population perhaps as large as one million people. Shortly after the first century the city began to decline. In 641 CE Alexandria was captured by Moslem forces, and the capital of Egypt was moved to Cairo near the junction of the Nile River and the delta. During the centuries that followed, Alexandria's population progressively decreased. The city resurged in more recent times, especially during the nineteenth century. Today the city of Alexandria has a population of approximately two million, and the city again functions as a major seaport of Egypt.

Roman theater in Alexandria

Because of the continuous occupation of the site, archaeological evidence from ancient Alexandria has been extremely limited. However, current understanding of the ancient city is enhanced by literary sources, especially Strabo, the ancient geographer, who spent five years in the city and in his geography describes the city in great detail (*Geography*, book 17); Josephus, the Jewish historian; and Philo, the Jewish philosopher. Among the features identified and described by these authors are the different sectors of the community including the royal sector, the Jewish sector, the Egyptian sector; Rakotis, named after the original community; Pharos, the island and port facilities; the heptastadium or causeway; and the necropolis or community cemetery located west of the city outside the city wall. Also described are the major buildings and outstanding features of the city including the Canopic Way, the lighthouse, the emporium or trade center, the royal palaces, the museum and library, the serapeum dedicated to Serapis, the poseidon dedicated to the sea god, the paneum dedicated to Pan, the caesareum dedicated to Caesar Augustus, the hippodrome, the theater and amphitheater, the stadium, and the Jewish synagogue.

But the ancient literary sources provide more than just information about the major buildings and physical features of the community. They also provide valuable insights into life and culture in Alexandria during the Ptolemaic and Roman periods. With the establishment of the museum and library, Alexandria became the major literary center of the Hellenistic world, a citadel of scientific studies, a major center of research and learning. Early methods of literary studies were employed and the scientific study of mathematics, astronomy, geography, and other disciplines was pursued. At Alexandria new milestones were established—Zenodotus applied early methods of literary criticism to Homer's *Iliad* and *Odyssey*, Eratosthenes calculated the circumference of the earth, Euclid invented geometry, and Aristarchus proposed the rotation of the earth around the sun.

Alexandria was the cosmopolitan center of the Greek culture in the Mediterranean world during the Ptolemaic and early Roman periods. It was the hub of Greek literature and Greek thought. The Greek language was the language of daily life, the language used in trade and exchange. And it was the Greek culture with its many expressions that became the common ground for the cosmopolitan community comprised of a diversity of people including Greeks, Egyptians, and Jews.

For students of the Bible, Alexandria's history at this point is especially important because of the role the city played in shaping Judaism. Alexandria was one of the birthplaces of Hellenistic Judaism. The new form of Judaism developed because of the nature of the community. During the Ptolemaic period Alexandria saw the growth and development of the largest Jewish community in the ancient world outside of Palestine, that is, the largest community of the Diaspora. And because the Greek culture was the prevailing culture in Alexandria, the Jewish community there became a Greek-speaking community, a community whose practices were influenced not only by the Greek language, but also by Greek philosophy and thought. The OT was translated from Hebrew into Greek in order to meet the needs of the Greek-speaking Jewish community there. According to tradition, the new translation, the Septuagint, was produced with the support of the ruler Ptolemy Philadelphus (Ptolemy II). His involvement may have been an attempt not only to meet the religious needs of a major segment of his population but also to provide another means by which Greek influence could permeate a major segment of his population. In addition to the Septuagint, the Jewish community at Alexandria may have produced a number of other writings including the Wisdom of Solomon, 2, 3, and 4 Maccabees, 2 Enoch, and 3 Baruch.

Bust of Ptolemy VI

The amalgamation of Hellenism and Judaism took many different forms; one of its greatest expressions is seen in the life and teachings of Philo, a Jewish scholar/philosopher who was influenced by the Platonic teachings in Hellenism. He attempted to interpret Jewish Scripture, especially the Law and the idea of the divine, in Platonic terms and concepts. Especially important in Philo's interpretation of Scripture was his use of allegorical interpretation. The tension that prevailed between the Hellenistic Jews, such as those in Alexandria, and the Aramaic-speaking Jews of Palestine, is perhaps reflected in the book of Acts, in the dispute with the Hellenists in the early church (Acts 6:1).

Just exactly why the Jewish community in Alexandria grew to the proportions it did is subject to debate, but it was due at least in part to the conditions Jewish families found there. During the time of Alexander, Jewish families enjoyed special rights and privileges that Josephus indicates prevailed to some degree during the Ptolemaic and early Roman periods (*Ant.* 12.8). During the Ptolemaic period the Jewish community had a limited autonomy, and individuals from the Jewish community held important positions in the government. Philo indicates that Jews were involved in trade and commercial activities in the community (*Flaccus* 55–57).

While the Jewish community in Alexandria grew and prospered on the one hand, it experienced times of upheaval and unrest due to the ethnic tensions that prevailed between the Jews and the Greeks. The conflict between the two groups resulted in bloody riots during the time of the Roman governor Flaccus (37–38 CE). The persecution of the Jews of Alexandria during that period provided the inspiration for Philo's two apologetic writings, *Against Flaccus* and *Embassy to Gaius* (Gaius=Caligula, the Roman emperor at the time). The riots and persecution ended during the reign of the Roman emperor Claudius, who in 41 CE stopped the riots and reestablished religious liberty for the Jewish community.

The NT contains limited references to Alexandria and Alexandrians in the book of Acts. Alexandrians were among those who disputed with Stephen (Acts 6:9). Apollos, described as "an eloquent man, well versed in the scriptures," and introduced in the account of Paul's third journey, is identified as "a native of Alexandria" (Acts 18:24). And it was on Alexandrian ships that Paul was transported to Rome (Acts 27:6; 28:11).

While Alexandria played an important role in the history of early Christianity, the means by which Christianity reached Alexandria is not known. According to tradition shared by Eusebius, Mark (the gospel writer) was the first evangelist to visit the city and was responsible for establishing churches there (*Hist. eccl.* 2.16). This tradition cannot be confirmed and is open to serious question, but by the second century

Christianity was well established in the community. The church in Alexandria was on its way to becoming one of the most significant in the Mediterranean world. Like some other early Christians, those in Alexandria faced both the threat of persecution and the challenge of gnosticism. In the midst of this atmosphere Alexandria became a great Christian learning center, the home of the great catechetical school of Christian instruction that produced outstanding early church fathers of the second and third centuries CE, such as Clement and Origen. Perhaps the most noteworthy feature of the Alexandrian school was its allegorical approach to the interpretation of Scripture. For instance, Origen proposed that Scripture had different levels of meaning—the literal meaning and the allegorical or deeper meaning or meanings. Like the work of Philo in the Hellenistic Jewish community, Christian theology in Alexandria was shaped and influenced by Greek philosophy and thought. During the fourth century the church father Athanasius, the bishop of Alexandria, defended the faith against the heretical teachings of Arius and Arianism. Athanasius is especially remembered in the history of Christianity for the Easter festival letter he sent to the churches in the year 367 CE. The letter included a list of twenty-seven books recognized by the Christian community as authoritative. The list is important because it is the first such document to include precisely those books in the NT today.

Bibliography: BAINES, J., and J. Malek, "Alexandria," *Atlas of Ancient Egypt* (New York: Facts on File Publications, 1980) 169; BASSLER, J. M., "Alexandria," *HBD*, 20–21; BLAIKLOCK, E. M., "Alexandria," *ZPEB*, 1:100–103; HUCKABAY, G. C., "Alexandria," *HolBD*, 33–34; MAEHLER, H. G. T., "Alexandria," *Ancient Centres of Egyptian Civilization*, ed. H. S. Smith and Rosalind Hall (Windsor Forest: Kensal, 1983) 87–96; MARE, W. H., "Alexandria," *NIDBA*, 18–20; MOO, D. J., "Alexandria," *Major Cities of the Biblical World*, ed. R. K. Harrison (Nashville: Nelson, 1985) 1–7; PARSONS, M. C., "Ancient Alexandria," *BI* (Spring 1989) 30–34; PEARSON, B. A., "Alexandria," *ABD*, 1:152-57; idem, "Alexandria," *OEANE*, 1:65–69; PORCELLA, B., "Alexandria," *NIDB*, 33–34; RUPPRECHT, A., "Alexandria," *BEB*, 1:51–54; THOMPSON, J. A., "Alexandria," *ISBE*, 1:89–94; WALLS, A. F., "Alexandria," *NBD*[2], 24–25; WILLOUGHBY, H. R., "Alexandria," *IDB*, 1:79–81.

Where Christian Doctrine Was Defended and Debated

Antioch is one of the many cities mentioned in the story of the spread of Christianity in the book of Acts. The site, as it relates both to the Roman world and the developments in the early church and early Christianity, is of major significance. In the broader world Antioch of Syria ranked with Rome and Alexandria—the three major cities of the Greco-Roman world during the NT period. The NT contains only fifteen references to the site, fourteen in the book of Acts and one in Galatians. Antioch of Syria was second only to Jerusalem as a center of early Christianity. Antioch was a commercial center in the Roman Empire. It was a citadel of the Greco-Roman culture, and it became the primary home of Christianity when it moved beyond its Jewish beginnings to the Gentile world.

Antioch was located on the Orontes River in north Syria, fifteen to twenty miles inland from the Mediterranean Sea. Near the bend in the Orontes and at the base of Mount Silpius, the site was three hundred miles north of Jerusalem. While the city of Antioch had not been founded at the time of Alexander, the Macedonian's conquest of the Persian empire to the east had a definite bearing on the status of Syria. Alexander's campaigns into Persia and his conquest of that empire placed Syria at the center of the Hellenistic world, strategically located amid Mesopotamia to the east, Egypt to the south, and the Greek world to the west. Syria-Palestine was a corridor for these regions. The new status of Syria had definite political and economic implications. These factors, as well as others, played a major role in the establishment of Antioch.

Antioch was founded ca. 300 BCE by Seleucus I, one of the generals of Alexander the Great. Seleucus built and named it in honor of his father, Antiochus. It was an attractive site because of its central location in Seleucid territory, its proximity to the larger world, its unique position in regard to land and sea trade, and the local features of the area itself.

The site of Antioch was ideal for commercial activities by both sea and land. Several miles inland, the city was connected to the Mediterranean Sea by the Orontes River. Antioch had its own seaport, Seleucia Pieria, on the coast at the mouth of the Orontes. Commonly known as Seleucia, the city that Seleucus named for himself was originally founded and established as the capital of his territory. As Antioch superseded Seleucia, the latter became the seaport for the new capital at Antioch. Antioch, with its harbor city on the coast, became one of the major seaport cities in the Mediterranean world during the Hellenistic and Roman periods. But Antioch was not only a major center of sea trade. The city was also on the land route connecting Asia Minor and points to the west with Syria, Palestine, and Egypt to the south. Consequently, with a vital port on the Mediterranean Sea, a prime location on the inland highway, and a strategic position, Antioch of Syria became a bustling commercial center in the Greco-Roman world of the NT.

Two other local features enhanced the growth and development of Antioch of Syria—fertile soil and a water supply. Antioch was located in a fertile plain in the bend on the Orontes. The site's water supply was conveyed by aqueduct from natural springs in the lush garden resort area known as Daphne. The resort community was located in the hills along the Orontes, five miles downstream from Antioch. The location of Antioch did have two potential drawbacks, flooding and earthquakes.

With the establishment of Antioch as the capital of the Seleucid kingdom, the city was well on its way to becoming a pivotal political and commercial center and hub of the Greek culture in the eastern Mediterranean. From early in its history Antioch had a mixed population comprised of Greeks, Macedonians, local Syrians, and Jews. Many of these citizens may have been enticed to the area by the benefits Seleucus offered them as retirees of his army. Antioch had several synagogues. During the Seleucid period Antioch went through several stages of expansion. The original core of the city, which was located between the river and Mount Silpius, was expanded not only up the base of the mountain but also to a large island located in the Orontes River. The major building projects that resulted in the enlargement of the city were due largely to the efforts of the Seleucid rulers Antiochus I,

Seleucus II, and Antiochus IV. With the turmoil that prevailed during the latter part of the Seleucid period, the city of Antioch went into a period of decline.

When Pompey arrived in 64 BCE, a new era began to dawn in the history of Antioch. Seleucid rule came to an end, Syria became a Roman province, and Antioch became the capital of the newly-acquired Roman territory. In this position and because of its important geographical location at the eastern end of the Mediterranean, Antioch was equipped as a principal political and commercial center by the Romans. Because of its important political status, Antioch became the military headquarters of Syria, with many reserve troops in residence. The Roman road system enhanced its status as a distinguished commercial center.

Equally important were new physical features added to the city by such prominent Romans as Julius Caesar, Augustus, and Tiberias, as well as contributions made by Herod the Great. Julius Caesar sponsored a number of construction projects including an aqueduct, a public bath, a theater, an amphitheater, and a caesareum, an ornate basilica-like structure that he named for himself and in which he placed a statue of himself. Additional building programs took place during the reign of the emperors Augustus and Tiberias; however, it is difficult to distinguish who was responsible for the new additions. Among the new features of the latter part of the first century BCE and the early part of the first century CE were several temples, a large bathhouse on the island, several bathhouses in the main part of the city on the bank of the Orontes, and the renovation of the theater. One of the most spectacular projects initiated during the reign of Augustus was the construction of a colonnaded street, the main street of the city. According to Josephus, the colonnaded street was constructed by Herod the Great, friend of Augustus and ruler of Palestine (*Ant.* 16.148). The new street, two and one-quarter miles in length, was paved with marble and lined with columns and porticoes, with some thirty-two hundred columns in the porticoes on each side of the street.

Archaeological exploration of the site has been extremely limited due to the fact that the ancient site is for the most part covered up by the modern town, Antakya, Turkey, and since the island in the Orontes is now under water. Nevertheless, based on literary sources such as the writings of Josephus, we may assume that Antioch of Syria as described above must have been one of the most magnificent cities in the entire

Mediterranean during the time of Paul and Barnabas. Luke frequently mentions this city with its mixed population of Gentiles and Jews. For instance, among the seven selected by the church in Jerusalem to care for the needs of the Hellenists was a Jewish proselyte named Nicolaus who came from the city of Antioch (Acts 6:5). It was to Antioch that some of the Jewish believers fled during the persecution that followed the death of Stephen (Acts 11:19). It was in Antioch that the gospel was shared openly and freely with Gentiles (Acts 11:20). The church in Jerusalem sent Barnabas to Antioch because of the magnitude of the developments in that community (Acts 11:22–24). Barnabas and Paul worked an entire year assisting the church in Antioch with its rapid growth (Acts 11:24–26). It was at Antioch that believers were first called Christians (Acts 11:26). Antioch became the home base for Paul's missionary journeys (Acts 13:1–3; 14:26; 15:35–41; 18:22–23). But of all the developments ascribed to Antioch in the history of early Christianity, perhaps the most important was the role the site played in the discussion on how Gentile Christians were to be received (Acts 15:1–21); the policy was first implemented (Acts 15:22–35) in Antioch of Syria.

The history of Antioch is difficult to trace following the NT period, but several features of the city's history can be identified with some clarity. Antioch experienced extensive damage from earthquakes during both the first and second centuries CE. The city was rebuilt after each devastation.

The early church fathers indicate that Antioch continued to be an important center of Christianity. During the second century the Christian community at Antioch encountered two serious problems—the threat of gnosticism and the threat of persecution. With the dawn of the second century a sizable gnostic community that traced its origin back to Simon Magus (Acts 8:9–24) developed at Antioch. Though gnosticism threatened the Christian community and divided it into two camps, Antioch grew in status as a center of Christian theology. One of the most important figures in Antioch's history at that time was the early church father Ignatius. As the bishop of the church at Antioch, Ignatius attempted to lead the Christian community during that difficult period. Due to the imperial persecution that prevailed, Ignatius was transported from Antioch of Syria to Rome, where he died a martyr's death at the hands of the Roman emperor Trajan. The seven letters he wrote to different Christian communities while on his journey from Antioch to Rome provide limited insight concerning the early Christian community of that period.

During the third century Antioch was visited by the early church father Origen and was home to Lucian of Antioch while he did his important critical work on the biblical text. Due to the work of individuals like Lucian, Diodorus, and Chrysostom, Antioch of Syria became a leading center in biblical studies and Christian theology beginning near the end of the third century and continuing through the fourth and fifth centuries. The Antiochene school was especially known for its more historical and rational approach as opposed to the Alexandrian method of interpreting Scripture allegorically. According to information from Chrysostom, the population of Antioch during the fourth century was two hundred thousand, possibly as high as five hundred thousand. Including the population of surrounding communities like Daphne, the population of the greater Antioch area may have been as high as eight hundred thousand.

Two building programs during the later history of Antioch deserve mention. With the establishment of Christianity as the state religion, the emperor Constantine built a large octagonal church on Antioch's island. This great fourth-century edifice was frequently referred to as the Golden Church because of its gold-covered roof. During the mid-sixth century the city was demolished at the hands of the Persians and was subsequently rebuilt by Justinian, the Roman emperor whose interest in restoring Christian sites is manifest at other locations. While Justinian restored the city and refortified it with a new city wall, Antioch of Syria never again regained the status and prestigious position it held during the early Roman period.

From that point Antioch's history was largely determined by the ebb and flow of political events of the region. In 1098 the city was taken by the crusaders, in 1268 by the Mamelukes, and in 1516 by the Turks. Currently the ancient site is occupied by the modern city of Antakya, Turkey, a city with some eighty thousand people.

The site was excavated by Glanville Downey from 1932 to 1939, but the investigation was limited by the modern city that covers much of the ancient remains. In spite of these limitations, archaeological exploration has uncovered a number of the important features of a Roman city, including the remains of walls and fortifications, public buildings, private residences, the theater and amphitheater, the forum, and the circus.

Bibliography: ADAMS, J. M., "Antioch of Syria," *Biblical Backgrounds,* rev. Joseph A. Callaway (Nashville: Broadman, 1965) 198–200; BARABAS, S., "Antioch," *NIDB,* 64–65; BLAIKLOCK, E. M., "Antioch (Syrian)," *NIDBA,* 30; COLEMAN, R. D., "Antioch of Syria," *Best of the Illustrator: The Journeys of Paul* (Nashville: Sunday School Board of the Southern Baptist Convention, 1990) 16–19; DOWNEY, G., "Antioch (Syrian)," *IDB,* 1:145–48; idem, "Antioch (Syrian)," *IDBSup,* 27; idem, "Antioch (Syrian)," *ISBE,* 1:142–43; FINEGAN, J., "Antioch on the Orontes," *The Archaeology of the New Testament: The Mediterranean World of the Early Christian Apostles* (Boulder: Westview, 1981) 63–71; HARRISON, R. K., and C. J. Herner, "Antioch (Syrian)," *NBD*[2], 51–53; JUDGE, E. A., "Antioch in Syria," *ZPEB,* 1:185–89; LONGENECKER, R. N., "Antioch of Syria," *Major Cities of the Biblical World,* ed. R. K. Harrison (Nashville: Nelson, 1985) 8–21; MCRAY, J., "Antioch of Syria," *Archaeology and the New Testament* (Grand Rapids: Baker, 1991) 227–32; MEIER, J. P., "Antioch," *HBD,* 33–34; NORRIS, F. W., "Antioch (Antioch of Syria)," *ABD,* 1:265–69; SMITH, T. C., "Antioch," *MDB,* 34–35; STRANGE, J. F., "Antioch," *HolBD,* 64–65; TATE, G., "Antioch on the Orontes," *OEANE,* 1:144–45; VARDAMAN, J., "Antioch of Syria," *BI* (Fall 1987) 22–26; WRIGHT, G. E., "Antioch in Syria," *Biblical Archaeology,* rev. ed. (Philadelphia: Westminster, 1962) 250–52.

ATHENS 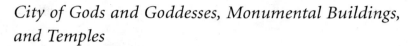 56

City of Gods and Goddesses, Monumental Buildings, and Temples

Athens was a city of gods and goddesses, monumental buildings and temples, sacred precinct and market place; it was a city of philosophy and religion, the arts and government. But perhaps more than anything else, Athens was a city of art and architecture. It was a city of stone, marble, and ivory monuments to its history and culture. Athens reached its height and experienced its golden age several centuries prior to the NT period. But the Greco-Roman city of Paul's day remained a consequential center of learning, a center of philosophy and the arts. The many temples, public buildings, and monuments throughout the city made it a major center of Greco-Roman art and architecture.

Athens was located on Attica, which was a small peninsula in the Aegean, the eastern part of Achaia, ancient Greece. The location had its own unique and awe-inspiring features that must have contributed to the development of the city in ancient times. Those features included the terrain of the land, the weather system of the Aegean and Mediterranean, and the proximity of the sea itself. While the rainfall of the area amounts to only fifteen inches a year, it nevertheless provides moisture adequate for the growth of olive groves and vineyards, fostering the production of olive oil and wine. The clay deposits in the area were especially valuable for the production of pottery, and marble was mined for building materials.

Situated on Attica, where the Aegean and Mediterranean met, Athens enjoyed an excellent location for commercial activities and sea trade as well as naval operations. The city was connected to the sea by Piraeus, the large natural harbor on the coast some five to six miles away. While the city lay several miles inland, the sea itself and the awe-inspiring storms of the region provided the inspiration for the development of Greek mythology. Perhaps equally inspiring was the terrain of the area; the mountains overlooked the fertile plain in which Athens was located, and the massive outcropping of rock, the acropolis, was the focal point of the ancient city.

While the precise details of the origin of the site are hidden in mystery, archaeological discoveries, especially the presence of Neolithic pottery, indicate that the site was founded during the fourth millennium BCE. The earliest settlement at Athens was located on the acropolis. During its early stages, the development of the community seems to have been confined to the acropolis, with a community cemetery or cemeteries northwest of the city in what later became the agora. In the Late Bronze Age was the Mycenean period, named for the culture that prevailed in the Aegean from ca. 1500 to 1100 BCE. During this period the acropolis was fortified with walls whose remains have been found at different points around its perimeter. The inhabitants of the community had strong religious interests and built a sanctuary dedicated to Aphrodite, the Greek goddess of love, on the acropolis. At some point during the Iron Age the community expanded to the northwest, the area previously occupied by the cemetery. The new addition became the location of the agora, the marketplace, which was the main civic center of Athens proper, and the acropolis became the sacred precinct.

During the sixth century BCE Athens, the renowned city of ancient history and sacred city of the goddess Athena, began to emerge. During that period a temple was erected for Apollo; the old bouleuterion, the original council or Senate house of the city, was built; and the first of the temples of Athena, the patron deity of the city, was constructed on the acropolis. Originally under the control of an oppressive aristocracy, during the course of the sixth century the city gradually became a democracy. The establishment of the democratic form of government at Athens was due in large part to two great Athenian statesmen: Solon, the famed lawgiver, who during the early part of the sixth century established a constitution with measures that provided protection for the mistreated in society; and Cleisthenes, who near the end of the sixth century brought about democratic reforms that resulted in a more complete form of democracy. During this period the size of the Senate, the legislative assembly, was increased to five hundred.

While the sixth century saw some promising developments, the course of Athenian history beyond that point was not without problems. Because of the threat of Persian attack during the fifth century, the lower city had to be fortified with an encircling wall and with extensions of the walls from the city to the harbor of Piraeus on the coast. Nevertheless, the city of Athens was destroyed by the Persians. Under the leadership of Themistocles the Athenian navy overpowered and defeated the Persian fleet, and shortly thereafter the city was rebuilt. During the period that followed Athens moved into its golden age. Many of the structures of the sixth century were rebuilt or replaced, and the landscape of the city, including the lower city and the acropolis, saw the construction of new temples, public buildings, and monuments. The new face of Athens was due in large part to the influence of Pericles, and it was during this period that the great classical city of Athens began to emerge. Many buildings were constructed in Athens during this period in the acropolis and in the agora. The Parthenon and the erechtheion were built on the acropolis itself, and the propylaeum was the massive gateway to the acropolis. In the agora there was a new temple of Hephaestus or the Hephaestion, a new bouleuterion or Senate house, the tholos, and numerous stoas, or covered walkways. During this period Athens became not only a showplace of magnificent buildings but also a center for the advancement of the arts including Greek art and architecture, drama, and music. It was renowned for the study of philosophy and science.

While Athens enjoyed a golden age politically and culturally during the fifth century BCE, and though other building projects continued into the Roman period, it began to enter a period of decline during the fourth century. Politically, the city lost its supremacy during the Peloponnesian War, a war between the Athenian empire of Attica and the inhabitants of Peloponnesus, the Spartans, the large Greek province to the west. While the Athenians lost the war to the Spartans, the city continued to be an important cultural center especially in art and learning. A number of construction projects took place in Athens during the latter part of the fourth century, including the dipylon gate, the theater of Dionysus on the southern slope of the acropolis, and the stadium. With the conquest of Greece by Philip of Macedon, Athens became a part of the new Macedonian empire, and a form of democracy was reestablished.

Following the death of Alexander the Great and the breakup of his empire, Athens regained international prominence and became a part of the Achaean league during the third century BCE. During the second and first centuries, it again went into a period of eclipse. The city's role and prestige as the major center of Hellenism was overshadowed by the second-century rise of Alexandria in Egypt. With the arrival of the first century, Rome became the dominant power. In 86 BCE the Roman general Sulla besieged and looted Athens. While the city never again regained political prominence in ancient times, it remained an important center of learning, philosophy and debate, art and architecture. During the Roman period, especially the reigns of Augustus and Hadrian, additional building enterprises were undertaken. Among these were the addition of a Roman agora or forum; a temple of Roma on the acropolis; the odeum or auditorium of Agrippa, the son-in-law of Augustus; the rebuilding of the temple of Ares; and the construction of the temple of Zeus. Following the Roman period, the city continued to decline and during the nineteenth century CE was a small town with a population of only five thousand. During the twentieth century, it experienced rapid growth and mushroomed into a large city with a population well over one-half million. Today Athens is the capital of the modern-day state of Greece and a thriving city and seaport in the Mediterranean and Aegean.

Because of its magnificent works of art and architecture, Athens has attracted the interest of individuals through the ages. Even the account in Acts seems to suggest that Paul toured the city and observed with interest many of its special features (Acts 17:23). One of the most valuable literary sources comes from Pausanias, a Greek geographer, chronicler, and traveler of the second century CE. He provided important descriptions of many buildings and monuments of Athens in his work, *A Description of Greece*. In recent times, especially since the nineteenth century, our understanding of the physical features of ancient Athens has been enhanced through numerous archaeological projects in the city both on the acropolis and in the agora.

Athens had its own unique city plan. During the NT period, it was enclosed by a wall that gave the city a circular appearance. The city was comprised of the acropolis, the agora, and the Areopagus. The acropolis was a spectacular outcropping of stone more than five hundred feet high located in the southern part of the city. During

Athens's golden age the acropolis became the special sacred precinct and visual highlight of the city, the crowning jewel of Athens and of the city's patron deity, Athena. The agora, the lower city, was located north northwest of the acropolis and was in essence the business center, the marketplace, the social and political center of ancient Athens. In Paul's day the agora was comprised of the Greek agora on the west and the Roman forum built during the Roman period on the east. The Areopagus was a marble hill located northwest of the acropolis. Named for Ares, the god of war, the hill was one of the sites at which the council of the city, the Areopagites, met in early times, and was perhaps the site of Paul's appearance before the council (Acts 17:19).

Other important features of the city in Paul's day were the two primary city gates and the city's main thoroughfare. The two gates, the sacred gate and the dipylon or double gate, were located on the northwest side of the city and provided the means by which two roads leading up to the city wall merged into one, the Panathenic Way, the major thoroughfare inside the city wall that moved diagonally through the city. The Panathenic Way, which led from the gate complex to the acropolis, was not only the major thoroughfare for daily traffic; it was also the route used for the annual religious festival honoring the goddess Athena, a festival that included a procession from the gate complex, along the Panathenic Way, to the festival's climax at the Pantheon on the acropolis.

While the city had its own unique design and format, it was the presence of the temples, shrines, public buildings, and monuments of the agora and the acropolis that shaped Athens's character as a city renowned not only for philosophy, science, religion, the arts, and commerce, but also as a showplace of art and architecture. Though the agora brings to mind the community marketplace, the agora in Athens had more than marketplace facilities.

Especially impressive were the many stoas of the agora such as the poikile or painted stoa, the royal stoa, the stoa of Attalus, the stoa of Zeus, and the cluster of stoas including the middle stoa, the east stoa, and the south stoa. Though the stoa had the basic design of a columned walkway with columns on one side and a wall or shops on the other, the function of the structure was quite versatile: it could be used for shops and markets, governmental offices, and public forums. The poikile stoa, for instance, was painted with scenes of important events in the history of Athens, such as the Trojan War and the Persian War, and was the scene of philosophical debates. It was due to the regular meetings at the poikile stoa that the Stoics got their name. The royal stoa was the official headquarters of the ruler of Athens—the king or *archon,* in essence the chief magistrate of the city.

The stoa of Attalus was constructed by Attalus, the king of Pergamum, as a gift to the Athenians during the mid-second century BCE. The stoa ran some 380 feet along the east side of Panathenic Way. It was a two-story structure with Doric columns along the lower level and Ionic columns along the top; these column styles were common in Athens. The marketplace was comprised of a cluster of stoas—the middle stoa, the east stoa, and the south stoa—located in the southern part of the Greek agora. The hub of trade and commerce, the marketplace complex included the largest of Athens's stoas, the middle stoa, which was 450 feet long.

During the Roman period a Roman market or agora was built. The Greek market was located west of the Panathenic Way, and the Roman market was located east of the Panathenic Way. The Roman market or forum was a large rectangular complex with stoas on all four sides, forming a large open courtyard within. The complex measured approximately 365 by 320 feet and had large entrances on the east and west sides. The tower of the winds was located east of the Roman market. The impressive octagonal tower was a large hydraulic clock designed with a number of sundials.

Numerous other buildings and monuments were a part of the agora, the lower city. The odeum was a roofed theater or music hall constructed by Agrippa, the son-in-law of the Roman emperor Augustus. Located in the center of the agora, the odeum, also known as the Agrippeum, seated one thousand spectators. The temple of Ares, dedicated to the god of war, was located in the northern part of the agora near the altar of the twelve gods, dedicated to the Olympian gods. Among the structures of the west side of the agora were the bouleuterion or Senate house; the tholos, a circular building dedicated to Artemis and the meeting place of the prytanes, the city administrators; the metroon, a temple of the mother of the gods, Cybele, which was used as the archives of the city-state and along with the bouleuterion and tholos formed the administrative district of Athens; the temple of Apollo, revered as the father of the Athenians; the temple of Zeus and Athena; the Hephaestion or temple of Hephaestus, the god of the craftsmen; and a large structure that perhaps functioned as the arsenal of the city.

The most visually captivating view in the city was the acropolis and its magnificent structures located to the south of the agora. Towering several hundred feet above the plain and the agora, the acropolis with its brilliant marble structures was a constant reminder of the religious associations of the city. Among the impressive features of the acropolis were the propylaeum, the erechtheion, the Parthenon, and the temple of Athena Nike. Constructed of white marble, the propylaeum was the magnificent massive roomed gateway through which the upper part of the acropolis was approached from the Panathenic Way below. It was through the propylaeum that the procession of the annual festival passed for the climax of the ceremonies on the acropolis. The erechtheion was a relatively small rectangular temple that was sacred to both Athena and Poseidon. While the temple had several rooms commemorating a number of mythological events, the most outstanding feature of the temple was the porch of the maidens, with a roof supported by six stone maidens. The temple of Athena Nike, often referred to as the temple of the Wingless Victory, was a very small but elegant temple that apparently symbolized victory and featured reliefs of the assembly of the gods. By far the most domineering of the structures on the acropolis was the Parthenon, a Doric temple dedicated to Athena. Some 238 feet long and 111 feet wide, the long ledges or steps of the Parthenon were designed with a slight curve instead of a flat or level surface. This slightly curved surface overcame an optical illusion and gave the ledge the appearance of being flat. The roof of the Parthenon was supported by some forty-six Doric columns, thirty-four feet high and six feet in diameter. The panels that surrounded the roof of the Parthenon above the columns were decorated with friezes. The exterior featured mythological scenes of the gods of the Greek pantheon, and the interior depicted the annual procession on the Panathenic Way.

Other important structures at Athens included the theater of Dionysus on the southern slope of the acropolis and the temple of Zeus located southeast of the acropolis.

The NT mentions Athens in regard to Paul's second journey (Acts 17:15–34; 1 Thess 3:1). Paul visited the city after he ran into problems at

Thessalonica and Berea (Acts 17:1–14). While there Paul spoke in the synagogue (Acts 17:17) and in the marketplace, the agora (Acts 17:17); he encountered the Epicurean and Stoic philosophers (Acts 17:18); he defended himself at the Areopagus (Acts 17:19) (the site at which the Areopagites met), which included both the royal stoa and the hill with that name near the acropolis; and he had at least two converts, a woman named Damaris and Dionysius, a member of the council, an Areopagite (Acts 17:34).

Though Paul's visit to Athens was limited, the character of the city is certainly reflected in the brief account in the book of Acts. Above all, it was a city of gods and goddesses, a citadel of Greek religion, the evidence of which can be observed today in the temples, theaters, and other public buildings and relics that remain within modern Athens.

Bibliography: ADAMS, J. M., "Athens," *Biblical Backgrounds,* rev. Joseph A. Callaway (Nashville: Broadman, 1965) 204–8; BLAIKLOCK, E. M., "Athens," *NIDBA,* 80; BRONEER, O., "Athens: City of Idol Worship," *BA* 21 (1958) 1–28; FINEGAN, J., "Athens," *IDB,* 1:307–9; idem, "Athens," *The Archaeology of the New Testament: The Mediterranean World of the Early Christian Apostles* (Boulder: Westview, 1981) 124–42; HALL, D. R., "Athens," *NBD²,* 104; LAIN, G., "Ancient Athens," *BI* (Spring 1989) 24–29; LYON, R. W., "Athens," *BEB,* 1:230–31; MADVIG, D. H., "Athens," *ISBE,* 1:351–52; MARTIN, H. M., Jr., "Athens," *ABD,* 1:513–18; McRAY, J., "Athens," *Archaeology and the New Testament* (Grand Rapids: Baker, 1991) 298–310; NEWPORT, J. P., "Athens," *MDB,* 74; OSBORNE, G. R., "Athens," *Major Cities of the Biblical World,* ed. R. K. Harrison (Nashville: Nelson, 1985) 22–31; PERKINS, P., "Athens," *HBD,* 79–80; RUPPRECHT, A., "Athens," *ZPEB,* 1:403–6; STEPHENS, W. H., "Athens in Paul's Day," *Best of the Illustrator: The Journeys of Paul,* ed. William H. Stephens (Nashville: Sunday School Board of the Southern Baptist Convention, 1990) 28–35; TENNEY, M. C., "Athens," *NIDB,* 108; VANDERPOOL, E., "Athens," *IDBSup,* 78; VOS, H., "Athens," *BW,* 110–18; WRIGHT, G. E., "Athens," *Biblical Archaeology,* rev. ed. (Philadelphia: Westminster, 1962) 260–63.

Shipping Link between Aegean and Adriatic

Athens was a city of gods and goddesses, religion and philosophy, monumental buildings and temples, a showplace of art and architecture. Corinth, though having some features in common with Athens, had its own unique and distinctive character. For the Apostle Paul, Corinth held new and challenging opportunities. Like other sites Paul had visited, Corinth was a bustling commercial center and in that regard a challenging population center. But it was more. It was the major junction between the east and the west, the gateway leading from the Aegean and the eastern Mediterranean to the Adriatic and the vast stretches of the Mediterranean to the west from Italy to Spain. It was a major cosmopolitan center with a diverse population with which Paul could share the gospel. It was the gateway to the west, the springboard from which Paul could launch a series of new journeys. Corinth had the potential to serve as the base of Paul's operations for journeys to Rome and beyond, just as Antioch of Syria had for his journeys to Asia Minor and the Aegean.

Corinth was located in a strategic position on the Peloponnesian peninsula in southern Greece, Achaia, west-southwest of the isthmus, the land bridge that connected the mainland of Greece with the peninsula. Situated on a plateau overlooking the isthmus, with an acropolis (the Acrocorinth) rising 1886 feet to the south, the site had certain features that contributed to its growth and development. First, due to its topography, the site was easily defended and fortified. Second, with its close proximity to the isthmus, Corinth was in a position to control the major east-west trade route that moved from the mainland of Greece to the Peloponnesian peninsula.

As the capital of the Roman province Achaia in Paul's day, Corinth held a strategic position in relation to the Roman world, especially in the world of trade and commerce. It was a major commercial center involved not only in land trade, but also in sea trade. It had two seaports, the port of Cenchreae to the east and the port of Lechaion to the west. These two ports brought shipping operations in the eastern Mediterranean together with those in the western Mediterranean. Treacherous seas made sailing around the Peloponnesian coast to the south dangerous. Thus, ships from the Aegean and eastern Mediterranean docked at the port of Cenchreae in the Saronic Gulf, some six miles east of Corinth, unloaded their cargo, transported it some three miles across the isthmus to the port of Lechaion in the Gulf of Corinth, some two miles north of Corinth, where it was reloaded onto cargo ships that sailed the Adriatic Sea and the western Mediterranean. In some instances smaller crafts were transported across the diolkos, a stone-paved crossover that was designed for this purpose. It connected the Gulf of Saron on the east to the Gulf of Corinth on the west. Consequently, Corinth served as a connecting link and one of the primary trade centers between shipping operations in the east and the west.

Corinth had an economy based on trade and commerce, industry, and agriculture. While the annual rainfall of the region was quite limited, the city benefited from the production of agricultural products in the fertile coastal plain nearby, especially the cultivation of orchards and vineyards. In addition to agriculture, Corinth had at least two thriving industries that produced pottery and bronze metal works that were shipped throughout the Mediterranean.

According to archaeological evidence Corinth had a long and important but interrupted history. It was one of the earliest inhabited sites in Greece. While the city of the biblical period was not founded until the first millennium BCE, the discovery of stone implements and pottery from the Neolithic period indicates that human habitation at the site dates back to at least the fourth millennium BCE. Metal tools discovered in the area reflect occupation during the Early Bronze Age. However, near the end of the Early Bronze Age, the site apparently was destroyed by an invading force and remained unoccupied during much of the second millennium BCE.

Around 1000 BCE a new chapter began to unfold in the city's history. The site was occupied by the Dorian Greeks, and Corinth was founded on the plateau at the base of the acrocorinth. The new city grew to become an important and prosperous city-state. Its influence was reflected in its colonizing, commercial, and industrial activities.

During the eighth century Corinth established colonies at Syracuse, on the island of Sicily, and at Corfu, one of the Ionian islands west of Greece in the Adriatic Sea.

Remains of the Diolcos, the road that carried ships across the Corinthian isthmus

Corinth rose to a new status in the Mediterranean in the seventh and sixth centuries, during the reign of Cypselus and especially his son, Periander. During that period Corinth became a great power and a prosperous commercial and industrial center. The city's new status was due largely to its sea trade in the Mediterranean. By maintaining control of the two ports, Cenchreae in the Saronic Gulf and Lechaion in the Gulf of Corinth, Corinth became the great marketplace and commercial center connecting the Aegean and eastern Mediterranean and the Adriatic and western Mediterranean. To enhance the city's role as the connecting link in the world of sea trade, Periander built the diolkos, the five-foot-wide stone passage for cargo and small crafts to cross the isthmus from one gulf to another. Corinth also became well known for its pottery and famous Corinthian bronze, which were exported through-out the Mediterranean. The acrocorinth was fortified, and during the era that followed walls were built connecting the city of Corinth with the port of Lechaion on the Gulf of Corinth to the north.

Corinth experienced unprecedented growth and prosperity and became the largest city in Greece with a population of perhaps three hundred to four hundred thousand. But Corinth's golden age was not to last. Challenges to Corinth's prominent position and security came in several forms—the rise of Athens, the Peloponnesian wars, and the war of Corinth. But its greatest challenge came during the first century BCE. As the chief city of the Achaian League, Corinth attempted to withstand the advance of Rome, a move that had dire consequences. In 146 BCE, forces under the Roman general Lucius Mummius attacked the city and destroyed it, killing the men and selling the women and children into slavery.

Corinth lay in ruins and was mostly abandoned for the next century. The city was rebuilt and established as a Roman colony in 44 BCE by Julius Caesar. The new Roman city had a mixed population comprised of freedmen from Italy, local Greeks, and others from most of the nations of the ancient world, including Jews. While the new city had a cosmopolitan character, it was nonetheless a Roman city. Latin was the official language, as can be seen in the inscriptions found in the city as well as in the names that appear in the NT; however, Greek must have continued as the language of the marketplace and as the common tongue of many of its citizens. In 27 BCE Corinth was designated the capital of the Roman province Achaia by the Roman emperor Augustus. In the years that followed Corinth thrived as a Roman city and was the recipient of the special attention of many of the emperors including Augustus, Nero, Vespasian, and Hadrian. Imperial interest in the city was often expressed in the form of visits and special building projects. By the end of the first century CE and the beginning of the second century the emperors realized that the city was a leading city of the empire, the connecting link between the Aegean and the Adriatic, and the sponsoring city of the Isthmian games. They had built it into the finest city in Greece.

During the third and fourth centuries the tide of Corinth's fate turned, and the site was repeatedly attacked by Gothic intruders from the north. Finally destroyed in 521 CE, Corinth was rebuilt by Emperor Justinian, and the city continued to function as an important commercial center throughout the Middle Ages. After extensive damage from an earthquake in 1858, the ancient site was abandoned and never rebuilt. During the twentieth century a city was built on a new location near the gulf.

Monolithic columns of the temple of Apollo

Our knowledge of the Roman city Paul visited and the area in which it was located has been enhanced through archaeological research and ancient literary sources. In 1896 excavations were initiated under the directions of the American School of Classical Studies in Athens, and investigation of the ancient site has continued intermittently until the present. Our understanding of the ancient city and its features is enhanced even more by numerous references made by ancient writers, especially Strabo and Pansanius.

Biblical Corinth was a part of an ancient metroplex comprised of the city itself and the acrocorinth and a number of components beyond its walls—the harbors of Cenchreae and Lechaion, the diolkos, and Isthmia and the Isthmian game facilities, all of which Corinth controlled and through which the city gained excessive wealth and international acclaim. Its role as the hub and leading city in the northern Peloponnesus is reflected in the roads radiating out of the city:

the road to Sicyon to the northwest, the road to Philus to the southwest, the road to Tenea to the south, the road to Mycenae to the southeast, the road to Cenchreae to the east, the road to Isthmia to the northeast, and the road to Lechaion to the north. Each road originated at the agora in the center of the city and moved out from there like spokes in a wheel to the city wall, through a gateway, and beyond toward its destination. The city itself was encircled by a six-mile wall. The city of Corinth covered an area of more than two square miles. Two additional walls extended from the north side of the city to the Gulf of Corinth. The two walls, approximately six-tenths of a mile apart, provided a protected corridor for the Lechaion road that connected the Lechaion harbor with the city. While the city proper was located on a plateau, the most obvious topographical feature of ancient Corinth was the acrocorinth at the south edge of the city. The acrocorinth provided the citizens of Corinth with a natural fortification and defense and with a commanding view of the trade routes. But more than anything else, the acrocorinth was known as a sacred mountain. On its summit stood the temple of Aphrodite, the Greek goddess of love and beauty. According to ancient sources the temple personnel included one thousand cultic prostitutes.

The major entrance to the city was from the north; the Lechaion road moved from the Gulf of Corinth and its port southward to the city. As the road entered the city, its width increased to nearly twenty-five feet. It was paved with slabs of limestone and was lined with raised sidewalks with channels for drainage, colonnades, and shops. Beyond the shops to the west was a large rectangular basilica, the great temple of Apollo, the north market, and a theater. The large basilica, often called the north basilica, with chambers at each end, apparently functioned as a large hall. It was divided by two rows of columns and was perhaps used for a variety of public meetings. The temple of Apollo, originally built in the sixth century BCE, was designed with thirty-eight columns, seven of which remain standing today. The peribolos of Apollo and the fountain of Peirene were located east of the thoroughfare. The peribolos was a large courtyard enclosed by columns and dedicated to Apollo whose statue stood in its midst. The fountain of Peirene, a large reservoir with a capacity of more than eighty-one thousand gallons, was fed by natural springs and provided the major source of water for the city.

View of the Acrocorinth from the columns of the temple of Apollo

As the Lechaion road moved southward, it terminated at the propylaeum, a beautiful arched gateway that was the entrance to the agora or forum. Larger than the forum in Rome, the rectangular agora in Corinth was divided into the lower forum to the north and upper forum to the south by a row of shops that ran through the center. The agora was outlined on the north by the north stoa, on the west by a row of shops, on the south by the south stoa, and on the east by the Julian basilica. The south stoa, approximately 525 feet long, was the largest stoa in Greece.

One of the most predominant features of the agora was the *bemah,* a large public speaker's platform located in the midst of the row of the shops that divided the lower forum from the upper forum. The platform was designed with sculptured marble and was surrounded on the back and sides by benches. It was used for public functions such as hearings and the presentation of cases before the magistrate or proconsul and was most likely the place of Paul's appearance before the proconsul Gallio (Acts 18:12–17). Other important facilities near the agora were the bouleuterion, the meeting place of the council, and a series of shops equipped with pits, both of which were located south of the south stoa. The pits in the shops apparently were filled with spring water conveyed to them through underground channels from the fountain of Peirene. Pottery discovered in the area suggests that the shops functioned as restaurants or taverns, and the pits were cooling pits for the wine sold in the establishments. The bouleuterion and the shops were located near the agora's entrance on the south from which the road to the port of Cenchreae departed.

Incription from ancient Corinth

Other important features of the city of Corinth included several small temples at the west end of the agora dedicated to deities such as Apollo, Tyche, Venus, and Hera; the pottery industrial complex about one mile west of the agora; the sanctuary of Demeter and Kore located at the base of the acrocorinth and dedicated to the twin goddesses of fertility; and the Lerna-Asclepeum complex, a healing center in the northwest sector of the city. Dedicated to Asclepius, the god of healing, the complex was comprised of the fountain of Lerna, a sanctuary dedicated to Asclepius, bathing, exercise, and dining facilities, and quarters for patients. The numerous pottery body parts discovered in the area reflect the ritual practices of the clients in which votive offerings were made to Asclepius in the hopes that the physical affliction would be healed. Excavations at the villa near Corinth provide valuable information concerning the design of first-century houses in the area. Early Christians in Corinth met in homes of this sort.

Among the important discoveries at Corinth are several inscriptions from the first and second centuries that provide valuable insight from that period. A Latin inscription found in the area of the shops near the northern entrance of the agora contains the term *macellum,* "market" and is reminiscent of the Greek term Paul used in reference to the "meat market" in the city (1 Cor 10:25). A Greek inscription carved in a block of white marble reads "synagogue of the Hebrews." It was apparently part of the lintel of a building in the area, presumably a synagogue. Although it is from a slightly later period of time, the inscription is a reflection of the Jewish community with which Paul had contact while in Corinth (Acts 18:4). An inscription from the area of the north market is of special interest because it refers to Erastus, the *aedile,* or public official, who was responsible for laying the pavement in that area. We are probably safe in assuming that the Erastus in the inscription is the same Erastus Paul mentions in his letter to the Romans (Rom 16:23), a letter he most likely wrote from Corinth. One additional inscription of importance was found in the area of the *bemah,* the public platform mentioned above. The inscription is of special interest to students of the Bible because it refers to the *rostra,* the Latin equivalent of the Greek *bemah* which appears in the NT text (Acts 18:12), and consequently adds credibility to the identity of the platform as the location to which Paul was taken.

The Isthmian games, held at Isthmia several miles away, were an important part of the life of Corinth. A Corinthian official administered the games. The Isthmian games may have prompted Paul to refer to the challenge faced by athletes as he wrote of the Christian life (1 Cor 9:24–27).

The importance of Paul's ministry in Corinth is reflected in the accounts of his visits in the book of Acts (Acts 18:1–17; 20:2–3) and in his correspondence with the Christians there (1 and 2 Corinthians). He stayed there eighteen months (Acts 18:11), longer than anywhere else, and his correspondence was the most extensive—he wrote at least one or two letters in addition to 1 and 2 Corinthians (1 Cor 5:9; 7:1). It was at Corinth that Paul met Aquila and Priscilla, who like himself were tentmakers (Acts 18:1–3). Presumably all three profited from the traffic in Corinth's thriving agora. Through his ministry there he apparently had a number of converts, both Jews and Greeks, including the ruler of the synagogue (Acts 18:8). Paul's writings reflect the problems the young church at Corinth faced—factions (1 Cor 1:10–17), incest (1 Cor 5:1–5), lawsuits (1 Cor 6:1–8), immorality (1 Cor 6:12–20), marital problems (1 Cor 7:1–9), food offered to idols (1 Cor 8:1–13), the attire of women in worship (1 Cor 11:2–16), the Lord's Supper (1 Cor 11:17–33), spiritual gifts (1 Cor 12–14), and the resurrection (1 Cor 15).

Paul had a significant ministry in Corinth, through both the time he spent there and the letters he wrote to the church of Corinth. But his plans for a series of journeys to Rome and beyond from a new base of operations at Corinth never materialized. In the end Paul had to settle for a letter to Rome instead of a trip there. He returned to Jerusalem to deal with a major problem in the church there. The church was divided over (of all things) the question of unity.

Bibliography: ADAMS, J. M., "Corinth," *Biblical Backgrounds,* rev. Joseph A. Callaway (Nashville: Broadman, 1965) 208–11; BARABAS, S., "Corinth," *NIDB,* 233–35; BLAIK-LOCK, E. M., "Corinth," *NIDBA,* 137–38; BROOKS, J. A., "Corinth," *BI* (Winter 1989) 40–49; DEAN, R. J., "Corinth," *The Best of the Illustrator: The Journeys of Paul,* ed. Mike Mitchell (Nashville: Sunday School Board of the Southern Baptist Convention, 1990) 50–52; FINEGAN, J., "Corinth," *IDB,* 1:682-84; idem, "Corinth," *The Archaeology of the New Testament: The Mediterranean World of the Early Christian Apostles* (Boulder: Westview, 1981) 142–52; FURNISH, V. P., "Corinth in Paul's Time: What Can Archaeology Tell Us?" *BAR* 15 (3, 1988) 14–27; GLAZE, R. E., "Corinth," *HolBD,* 298–301; HARROP, J. H., "Corinth," *NBD*[2], 229; LANE, W. L., "Corinth," *Major Cities of the Biblical World,* ed. R. K. Harrison (Nashville: Nelson, 1985) 83–85; LAUGHLIN, J. C. H., "Corinth," *MDB,* 170–71; MADVIG, D. H., "Corinth," *ISBE,* 1:772–74; MCNEELY, R. I., "Corinth," *BEB,* 1:513–14; MCRAY, J., "Corinth," *Archaeology and the New Testament* (Grand Rapids: Baker, 1991) 311–38; MILLER, C. H., "Corinth," *HBD,* 182–84; MURPHY-O'CONNOR, J., "Corinth," *ABD,* 1:1134–39; idem, *Paul's Corinth: Texts and Archaeology* (Wilmington: Michael Glazier, Jr., 1983); THOMPSON, C. L., "Corinth," *IDBSup,* 179–80; WRIGHT, G. E., "Corinth," *Biblical Archaeology,* rev. ed. (Philadelphia: Westminster, 1962) 263–66.

A City of the Decapolis

Damascus was an important city in the NT world, but it lacked the political prestige it once had known. Nevertheless, the city had a long and eventful history that stretched back to the prehistoric period when it was originally settled. Because the site was located at the junction where international trade routes from Arabia, Egypt, Palestine, Anatolia, north Syria, and Mesopotamia all converged, Damascus became an important international trade center during OT times. Its reputation as a world trade center probably began to develop during the patriarchal period. Near the end of the united monarchy of Israel, Damascus became the capital of a powerful Aramean kingdom, referred to in the Bible as Aram/Syria. That kingdom came to an end in 732 BCE as the Assyrian king Tiglath-pileser III conquered Damascus as well as 119 other towns of the kingdom and made them a part of the Assyrian empire. In biblical times Damascus never again enjoyed its former political prominence.

Events that followed the Assyrian conquest shaped the character of Damascus during the NT period. During the period of Assyrian imperialism Damascus was an Assyrian province under the control of an Assyrian administrator; however, it continued to function as a major trade center. No longer a major political force, Damascus was subject to the changes that came to its world. The city was a provincial center of both the Babylonian and Persian empires, functioning as a major center of trade. Following the conquest of Persia by Alexander the Great, Damascus came under the influence of the Greek culture. Eventually it became a part of the cities of the Decapolis, a league of ten cities organized on the Greek city-state system; however, most of the cities of the Decapolis were located farther south, in the Transjordan, the area east of the Jordan River and the Sea of Galilee.

During the period following the death of Alexander the Great, Damascus was caught in the struggle between the Ptolemies, the rulers of Egypt, and the Seleucids, the rulers of Syria, as each sought control of Palestine and southern Syria. When Seleucids took control of Damascus and its territory about 275 BCE, the status of the city fell. The Seleucids built a new capital in north Syria, named it Antioch, and moved the administrative headquarters to the new location. Damascus was no longer the chief city of Syria.

In 85 BCE Damascus became the capital of an independent Nabatean kingdom under the control of the Nabatean king Aretas III. With Pompey's conquest of Syria in 65 BCE Damascus became a part of the vast Roman Empire. Under Roman policy the city and its territory were for a time presumably under the administrative control of local Nabatean governors such as Aretas IV, the Nabatean king at the time of Paul's conversion experience (Acts 9:2–30; 2 Cor 11:32–33).

What was the status of Damascus during the NT period? Antioch rather than Damascus was the chief city of Syria. However, since Damascus was one of the cities of the Decapolis, we may assume that it, like the other nine cities of the Decapolis, was basically a free city. The cities of the Decapolis enjoyed such privileges as autonomous rule and the coinage of money. Other cities of the Decapolis included Abila, Scythopolis, Hippos, Raphana, Gadara, Pella, Dion, Philadelphia, and Gerasa. Though Damascus, like the other cities of the Decapolis, is not mentioned in the gospels, it is referred to in Acts and the Pauline letters. According to the book of Acts, several synagogues were located in Damascus or its territory (Acts 9:2), indicating a significant Jewish population. The physical features of Damascus during the first century must have reflected the strong Greco-Roman influence in the city. While only limited excavations have been carried out in Damascus, the Greco-Roman character of the city is evident in the discovery of Roman arches, gateways, the remains of a colonnaded street (apparently the street called Straight, Acts 9:11), and the remains of a temple dedicated to the god Jupiter. Eventually Damascus became a center of early Christianity. The physical evidence of the influence of Christianity is perhaps most obvious in the remains of the Church of Saint John the Baptist, which was built by the Roman emperor Theodosius (379–395 CE). The church was constructed over the remains of the temple of Jupiter. It was destroyed in the eighth century.

Bibliography: ADAMS, J. M., "Damascus," *Biblical Backgrounds,* rev. Joseph A. Callaway (Nashville: Broadman, 1965) 152; BORASS, R. S., "Damascus," *HBD,* 203; BOWLING, A., "Damascus," *ZPEB,* 2:7–9; BUTLER, T. C., "Damascus," *HolBD,* 330–32; FINEGAN, J., "Damascus," *The Archaeology of the New Testament* (Boulder: Westview, 1981) 55–63; FREEMAN, J. D., "Damascus," *NIDB,* 248–50; HALDAR, A., "Damascus," *IDB,* 1:757–58; LIVINGSTON, G. H., "Damascus," *Major Cities of the Biblical World,* ed. R. K. Harrison (Nashville: Nelson, 1985) 96–106; MARE, W. H., "Damascus," *NIDBA,* 147–48; McRAY, J., "Damascus," *Archaeology and the New Testament* (Grand Rapids: Baker, 1991) 232–34; idem, "Damascus (The Greco-Roman Period)," *ABD,* 2:7–8; PERKIN, H. W., "Damascus, Damascenes," *BEB,* 1:567–68; PITARD, W. T., *Ancient Damascus* (Winona Lake, Ind.: Eisenbrauns, 1987); idem, "Damascus," *OEANE,* 2:103–6; UNGER, M. F., "Damascus," *ISBE,* 1:852–55; idem, "Damascus," *BW,* 179–84; VARDAMAN, J., "Damascus," *MDB,* 193–94; WISEMAN, D. J., "Damascus," *NBD²,* 260.

Leading Seaport of Asia Minor

Ephesus occupies an important place in the story of early Christianity both because of the position the city held in the Roman world and because of the role it played in the early Christian movement. Like Alexandria in Egypt, Antioch of Syria, Corinth in Greece, and Rome in Italy, Ephesus was one of the major cosmopolitan centers in the Roman world, an important center of the Greco-Roman culture. With the spread of Christianity in the Mediterranean world, Ephesus was the site of a number of important developments. It was a major stop on Paul's missionary journeys (Acts 18:19–21; 19:1–41), and apparently the place where he stayed the longest (Acts 19:10). Ephesus is where tradition says John spent his final years, and where the Third Ecumenical Council met in 431 CE—when Nestorius and Nestorian theology were declared heretical and the Virgin Mary was declared "mother of God."

While Alexandria was the major seaport of Egypt, Caesarea of Palestine, Antioch of Syria, Corinth of Greece, and Rome of Italy, Ephesus was the leading seaport city of Asia during the NT period. Like each of the other centers, Ephesus had its own unique location and setting. For instance, while Corinth was located between the Aegean and the Adriatic seas and functioned as the connecting link between two major worlds in the arena of sea trade—the eastern Mediterranean and western Mediterranean—Ephesus was located on the east side of the Aegean Sea along the southwest coast of Asia. The city was in a prime position not only to function as the major harbor for Asia but also to be a part of a chain of harbors around the eastern Mediterranean for the merchant ships traveling westward. Consequently, Ephesus was a connecting link between Asia, that is the region of Asia Minor, particularly the western part of Asia Minor, and the rest of the Mediterranean world.

Ephesus was located along the southwestern coast of western Asia Minor, a coastline that is very irregular. It was a part of a series of significant cities in western Asia. Miletus and Myrna were on the coast on either side of Ephesus, and Pergamum, Thyatira, Sardis, Philadelphia, Laodicea, and Colossae were located inland. On the coast at the mouth of the Cayster River, between the Hermus River to the north and the Meander River to the south, Ephesus was at a key position for both sea and land trade. While the Cayster valley functioned as a thoroughfare to the interior of western Asia and the cities and major trade routes of that region, the Cayster River emptied into a harborlike formation that provided access to the Aegean Sea. In addition to the highway that traveled inland connecting the Cayster valley with the thoroughfares in the Hermus valley and the Maeander valley to the east, a north-south highway cut through Ephesus tying it with the cities along the coast.

While the setting seemed ideal, it was not without problems. Along with the waters of the Cayster came significant amounts of silt that settled in the harbor and caused it to fill up gradually. While the historian Pliny speaks of the sea at one time washing up to the temple of Diana (*Natural History* 2.201), the geographer Strabo noted that even during the second century BCE King Attalus had to deal with the silting problem and attempted to solve it by restructuring the mouth of the harbor in hopes that a narrower harbor entrance would cause the silt to flush out the harbor, a project that in the end caused a more rapid silting (*Geography* 641). But while ancient Ephesus had to deal repeatedly with the silting problem in the harbor, Ephesus was nevertheless "the largest emporium in Asia." Today the ruins of ancient Ephesus are more than five miles inland due to centuries of silt deposits.

In addition to the Cayster River and the harbor facilities, the site had two small mountain ranges on either side of the major part of the city, Mount Koressos to the southwest and Mount Pion to the northeast. The harbor of the city was located west-northwest of the city. It approached the city through the valley between the two mountains.

According to Strabo, the history of Ephesus extends back to a time when it was inhabited by native Anatolians, Carians, and Lelegians, who lived there during the second millennium BCE. We may assume that even during this early period the site had a cult built around a mother goddess or fertility goddess figure, as did other Anatolian communities during the second millennium.

Near the end of the second millennium BCE a major change took place in the composition of the population of the community. Due to an incursion of people from the west, the site was settled and colonized by Ionian Greeks from the city of Athens, and the city of Ephesus was founded. The new community was comprised mostly of Ionian Greeks with some native Anatolians as well. Apparently the city of Ephesus was founded by Androclus, the son of the king of Athens, who led the Ionian colonists to the new site about 1000 BCE. In a change that reflected the Greek population, the name of the patron deity of the city became Artemis. The Ephesian Artemis was a blend of the Greek Artemis and the old Anatolian goddess of fertility. While the Greek Artemis was worshiped as the huntress, the Ephesian Artemis became a goddess of fertility.

About 560 BCE the city of Ephesus and most of western Asia Minor were conquered by Croesus, the king of Lydia. During that period the city was moved from Mount Pion to the valley to the south and the Artemision, the magnificent temple of Artemis, was constructed. The city of Ephesus became known as the home of the temple of Artemis, a massive sanctuary and cultic complex that was burned, was rebuilt, and survived until its final destruction by the Goths in 262 CE.

Another major change took place at Ephesus in 546 BCE when Croesus was defeated by Cyrus, the king of Persia, and Ephesus came under Persian control. During the latter part of the Persian period the city of Ephesus experienced one of its most disastrous events. The temple of Artemis was destroyed by fire in 356 BCE, the night Alexander was born. In 334 BCE Ephesus was conquered by Alexander the Great, and the city came under Macedonian control. During that period the citizens of Ephesus undertook the rebuilding of the temple of Artemis, a project that was not completed until about 250 BCE. It was rebuilt under the direction of Dinocrates, the master architect responsible for building Alexandria. While Alexander offered to rebuild the temple at his expense, the citizens of Ephesus declined the offer for diplomatic reasons.

Following the death of Alexander, Lysimachus, who was one of Alexander's generals, gained control of much of Asia Minor including Ephesus. During his rule (ca. 301–281 BCE) the city of Ephesus was moved and rebuilt at a higher location. Strabo informs us that the citizens of Ephesus, who were reluctant to move, were persuaded to do so when Lysimachus blocked the city's sewers and drains following a heavy rainstorm, thus flooding the old city (*Geography* 640). The new city, moved to higher ground, apparently included new city walls, whose remnants have been discovered on Mount Pion and Mount Koressos, a new grid of streets, and a new harbor. The city Paul visited during the middle of the first century CE must have been primarily the city designed and built by Lysimachus.

During the greater part of the third century BCE, Ephesus was under Seleucid control. The Seleucid era began in 281 BCE, when Seleucus I defeated Lysimachus and killed him. The city of Ephesus and the part of Asia Minor controlled by Lysimachus were given to Antiochus I, the son of Seleucus I. Seleucid control of Ephesus and Asia Minor ended in 190 BCE, with the Roman defeat of the Seleucid ruler Antiochus III. The city and western Asia Minor belonged to Rome, but the Romans placed the city in the care of the king of Pergamum in appreciation for his military assistance during the conflict with the Seleucids. At the death of Attalus III in 133 BCE, Ephesus came under the direct control of Rome.

During the Roman period Ephesus reached its zenith. While Pergamum was the capital of the province of Asia during the early part of the Roman period, Ephesus was the chief city, the leading seaport, and the gateway to the province. Artemis was the deity of the entire province as well as the city. The status of the city during the era stemmed from the interest that the Roman emperors had in Ephesus and the investment they made in the city. Due to the good relationship that Ephesus enjoyed with Emperor Augustus, the city designated a sector as a sacred precinct dedicated to Rome and Augustus. Later emperors such as Nero and Domitian used Ephesus to advance the concept of the emperor cult; there have been many archaeological discoveries such as the remains of a colossal statue of the emperor Domitian. Ephesus became the capital of the Roman province of Asia during the reign of Emperor Hadrian.

While Ephesus held a prominent position in the Mediterranean during the Roman period, the city went into decline during the Byzantine period. The site was conquered by the Ottoman Turks in 1426. Today the ruins of ancient Ephesus are located near the Turkish town of Selcuk.

The temple of Artemis (the Roman Diana) and its traffic and economic influence dominated Ephesus during the NT period. The temple of Artemis prompted archaeological exploration of the site, beginning in 1863 under the direction of the British archaeologist J. T. Wood. The walls of the temple were discovered in 1869, and a number of additional campaigns have been conducted at the site since then. Today many of the features of ancient Ephesus have come to light through the efforts of archaeologists along with the assistance of ancient sources, especially ancient writers such as Pausanius, Strabo, and Pliny.

Statue of Artemis

The Roman city of Ephesus housed a population of about three hundred thousand. It had a number of important features including a city wall with a grid of streets, the temple of Artemis, a massive theater, the agora, as well as numerous other important structures. The city was apparently enclosed in a five-mile long wall equipped with towers and gates that extended from the south side of the harbor, over Mount Koressos to the east, across the valley to Mount Pion, across Mount Pion and back around to the north side of the harbor. This wall was most likely built by Lysimachus.

Ephesus also had a network of streets that included the Arcadian road, a major colonnaded thoroughfare that extended from the harbor to the theater in the center of the city; Marble street, a marble paved street that connected the theater with the agora; Curetes street, which extended from Marble street eastward through the city to the Magnesian gate in the wall east of the city; and Stadium street, which extended from the north end of Marble street northward past the stadium around to the temple of Artemis. We may assume that Curetes street, Marble street, and Stadium street combined to function as a processional way for religious and community processions that originated on the east side of the city at the Magnesian gate and proceeded through the city on the processional way.

By far the most impressive feature of ancient Ephesus was the temple of Artemis, commonly referred to as the Artemision. The temple of Artemis was recognized as one of the seven wonders of the world. Located on a plain north of Mount Pion, the temple complex was comprised of a platform 418 feet long and 239 feet wide, and the temple proper approximately 340 feet long and 160 feet wide, nearly twice the size of the Parthenon in Athens. This splendid temple had a roof covered with white marble tiles and supported by 127 blue-gray granite columns sixty feet long. The temple complex apparently included a statue of Artemis with a large altar in front of it. Several statues of the Ephesian Artemis have been found in the ruins of the ancient city. The statues feature the goddess with a crown or headdress, a necklace, a fitted skirt decorated with animals, and three rows of egg-shaped objects perhaps representing multiple breasts or eggs, symbols associated with her role as a fertility goddess.

The temple of Artemis was northeast of the city, and the theater was inside the city at the east end of Arcadian or Harbor road. The largest structure in Ephesus, the theater was a semicircular structure nearly five hundred feet in diameter, cut into the western slope of Mount Pion. It had a spectacular view of the city below and the colonnaded Harbor road and harbor to the west. With the seats arranged in three tiers with twenty-two rows of seats to each tier, the theater could accommodate twenty-four thousand people.

At the heart of the commercial activities in Ephesus was the agora, commonly called the commercial agora. Located southwest of the theater on the west side of Marble street, the agora was a large square marketplace, 360 feet square, surrounded on all four sides by stoas and shops. A sundial and water clock were located at the center of the courtyard of the agora.

In addition to the temple of Artemis, the theater, and the commercial agora, Ephesus had numerous other facilities that reflected the social, cultural, religious, and political climate of the city during the Roman period. Some of these were present during the NT period, and others were not constructed until after it. The latter group includes the large state or civic agora, the odeion or bouleuterion, the town hall or prytaeion, the temple of Augustus, the temple of Domitian, the temple of Hadrian, the brothel, the Celsus Library, the stadium, as well as private houses, an aqueduct, and a number of gymnasia, baths, and fountains.

As a major cosmopolitan center of the Hellenistic and Roman cultures, Ephesus is of special interest to students of the Bible because of references to the city in the NT, especially the book of Acts and the Revelation of John.

On the basis of both literary and archaeological evidence, we may assume that Ephesus had a significant Jewish community. The NT refers to the Jewish presence in Ephesus (Acts 19:8), and inscriptions and other artifacts have provided evidence of a Jewish community.

According to Luke's history in the book of Acts, Paul visited Ephesus on both his second (Acts 18:19) and third missionary journeys (Acts 19:1). During his third journey he spent two years in Ephesus (Acts 19:10), spoke in the synagogue (Acts 19:8), performed miracles (Acts 19:11–20), seriously threatened the trade of the silversmiths associated with the temple of Artemis (Acts 19:23–27), and as a result encountered a riot in the theater (Acts 19:28–29).

According to tradition, the Apostle John was living in Ephesus when he was exiled to the island of Patmos during the reign of the Roman emperor Domitian. He later returned to Ephesus where he lived until his death. This tradition about the apostle, which dates back to the second century, was eventually commemorated in the fourth century by a church built northeast of the city, where the apostle had sight of the temple of Artemis, and where he was eventually buried. Emperor Justinian replaced the original church with the Church of Saint John, some 425 feet long.

North of the harbor road is the Church of St. Mary. Though the Church of the Dormition in Jerusalem claims to be the site of Mary's burial, a rival tradition placed Mary in Ephesus during her latter years and claimed that she was buried at Ephesus. The church, a fourth-century double building eight hundred feet long, was the site at which the Third Ecumenical Council met in 431 and declared Mary *Theotokos*, "mother of God."

Bibliography: ADAMS, J. M., "Ephesus," *Biblical Backgrounds*, rev. Joseph A. Callaway (Nashville: Broadman, 1965) 200–203; BAMMER, A., "Ephesus," *OEANE*, 2:252–55; BLAIKLOCK, E. M., "Ephesus," *NIDBA*, 181; idem, "Ephesus," *NIDB*, 315–16; idem, "Ephesus," *ZPEB*, 2:324–32; BLEVINS, J. L., "Ephesus," *BI* (Spring 1991) 2–3, 7–9; idem, "Ephesus," *MDB*, 255–56; BORCHERT, G. L., "Ephesus," *ISBE*, 2:115–17; BOYD, D., "Ephesus," *IDBSup*, 269–71; FINEGAN, J., "Ephesus," *IDB*, 2:114–18; idem, "Ephesus," *The Archaeology of the New Testament: The Mediterranean World of the Early Christian Apostles* (Boulder: Westview, 1981) 155–71; GREEN, E. M. B., and C. J. Hemer, "Ephesus," *NBD*[2], 336–38; McRAY, J., "Ephesus," *Archaeology and the New Testament* (Grand Rapids: Baker, 1991) 250–61; MILLER, C. H., "Ephesus," *HBD*, 270–72; OSTER, R. E., Jr., "Ephesus," *ABD*, 2:542–49; REDDISH, M. G., "Ephesus," *HolBD*, 424–28; TURLINGTON, H. E., "Ephesus," *Best of the Illustrator: The Journeys of Paul*, ed. Michael Mitchell (Nashville: Sunday School Board of the Southern Baptist Convention, 1990) 58–65; VOS, H., "Ephesus," *BW*, 229–31; WRIGHT, G. E., "Ephesus," *Biblical Archaeology*, rev. ed. (Philadelphia: Westminster, 1962) 255–60; YAMAUCHI, E., "Ephesus," *The Archaeology of New Testament Cities in Western Asia Minor* (Grand Rapids: Baker, 1980) 79–114.

ROME 🏺 60

Chief City of the Empire

The prominence of the city of Rome in the NT world, its prestige as the capital of the empire, and the key role the city played in the drama of early Christianity, are all undeniable. As with other cities of the Roman Empire during the NT period e.g., Jerusalem and the cities of Palestine, Antioch of Syria, Athens and Corinth in Greece, Ephesus in Asia, and Alexandria in Egypt, the story of the city of Rome was shaped by many factors, including Rome's geographical location, historical and political developments, the reign of the emperors, and the influence of the Roman and Greek cultures.

Among the factors that had a bearing on the story of Rome was its geographical location. As the capital of the empire, Rome had an ideal location in relationship to the peninsula of Italy and to the provinces of the empire. Situated midway along the west coast of Italy, Rome was like the hub of a wheel, centrally located in the midst of all her territories. Rome had ready access to both the provinces of Europe to the north and the provinces around the Mediterranean Sea to the south. And by maintaining control of the lands at the eastern end of the Mediterranean, Rome had a gateway to the lands to the east of the empire.

While Rome was located midway along the west coast of Italy, the city itself lay approximately fifteen miles inland from the sea. Despite its inland position, Rome had access to the sea by means of the Tiber River, a major stream that collected waters from the interior of Italy in the region north of the city and flowed into the sea along the coast to the west of Rome. Because of its location on the banks of the Tiber River and due to the fact that the Tiber was a navigational stream, Rome became a major seaport city. During the NT period, the Mediterranean Sea provided one of the most valuable means by which Rome engaged in communication and trade with her provinces.

Rome's contact with the provinces was enhanced even more by an extensive road system of major and secondary highways that connected the major cities of the provinces with the capital city itself. Rome's investment in the international highway system, the quality of the highways that were a part of the system, and the golden milestone at the heart of the city all combined to help create the dictum, All roads lead to Rome. The golden milestone, the symbol of the dictum, was erected by Augustus and contained a list of the leading cities of the empire and the distance from each to the capital.

Tradition proposes 753 BCE as the date of the founding of Rome; this date is tied to the legend of Romulus and Remus. Archaeological evidence, however, indicates that the site was first occupied in the second millennium BCE, when a small agricultural village was established at a ford of the Tiber River.

At that time the population of the peninsula was mixed. The central part of the peninsula was occupied by Latins, the northern part by Etruscans, and the southern part by Gruelas. On the basis of limited archaeological evidence, we may assume that while the small Latin village of the early period experienced some growth and development under the leadership of Latin kings, no major developments took place at the site for several hundred years.

A dramatic change began to unfold about 600 BCE when the town fell into the hands of Etruscan kings from the north. By this time the town had become the predominant center of central Italy. The new leadership implemented a major building program in the area of the seven hills of Rome, a program designed to improve and enhance the physical character of the site. The site was surrounded by marshes and swamps, so the initial phase of the project was to drain the swamps between the hills of Rome. Then the Etruscan kings laid the foundation for the city of Rome to become a great urban center. The city was fortified with a city wall. Extensive paving and the erection of large public buildings provided the city with its first major forum. The city of Rome now encompassed seven hills, at the center of which were the Palatine and Capitoline, and became an important commercial, social, political, and religious center, the predominant city-state of central Italy. The Etruscan kings had succeeded in changing the agricultural community into an urban center.

But the achievement of the forceful and dominant Etruscan rule carried a price. In 509 BCE the Latin population, unhappy with the burdens produced by the building projects in Rome and military service, revolted against Etruscan rule and established the Roman Republic. While the new republic was not a democracy as we know it today, it did result in a broader base of representation on the part of the people, both aristocrats and plebeians, and consequently avoided rule by a single figure or office.

By the mid-fourth century BCE the new republic, due to the efforts of the ruling nobles of that period, entered an era marked by unity and the opportunity for expansion. During the next few centuries Rome graduated from the most powerful city-state of central Italy to the dominant force and major cosmopolitan center of the Mediterranean world. Rome's expansion happened in three phases. Phase one was the period of expansion on the peninsula, during which Rome gained control of the city-states to the north and south and welded the peninsula into a unified whole. Phase two was the period of expansion following the fall of Carthage, when Rome gained control of the territories of the western Mediterranean. Phase three was the period of expansion in the eastern Mediterranean, which included Pompey's conquest of Palestine in 63 BCE. Along with its growing influence and new status in the Mediterranean world, the city of Rome experienced significant growth. As a major cosmopolitan center, Rome had a mixed and growing population. The city became a major commercial center and a citadel of wealth. All of this growth led to additional building activities in the city itself. During the period of expansion, especially the latter part of the republic, the city of Rome witnessed a tremendous increase in new temples as well as additional public buildings and housing.

By the beginning of the first century BCE, however, Rome and its republic faced some serious problems. An internal power struggle around the middle of the first century BCE led to the period of the triumvirate, during which control of the Republic was seized by powerful military generals, Pompey, Julius, and Crassus. This coalition of three administrators is commonly referred to as the first triumvirate. With the emergence of Julius Caesar as the most powerful of the three, the resulting civil war, and Caesar's assassination in 44 BCE, the period of the first triumvirate came to a bitter end, and the doom of the republic was certain. In spite of the fate of the first triumvirate, a second triumvirate was established comprised of Mark Antony, Marcus Lepidus, and Octavian. After the battle of Actium in 31 BCE, Octavian emerged not only as the victor over Mark Antony and Cleopatra but also as the one who would decisively shape Rome's future. In spite of problems during the period of the triumvirate, Rome witnessed new building activities that were initiated by Julius Caesar and were continued by Augustus during the period of the empire.

With Octavian the Roman Republic came to an end, and the period of the empire began. Because of the close ties and good working relationship that existed between the Roman senate and Octavian, in 27 BCE the senate bestowed on Octavian the title of Augustus, thus making him the sole ruler, the emperor. While Caesar Augustus was emperor in title, in reality Augustus continued to share the task of governing and administration with the Roman senate, especially with respect to the administration of Roman provinces. With the dawning of the new age and due to the leadership and the efforts of Augustus, the city of Rome and its provinces witnessed many good things politically, socially, and culturally. Perhaps most significant of these benefits was the reign of peace that Augustus established. The peace and resulting political stability enabled Augustus to mount elaborate and extensive building enterprises throughout the empire. No building project of that period was more extensive than what took place in the city of Rome itself. According to his own testimony, Augustus transformed the city of Rome from a city of brick into a city of marble. Augustus not only improved the usefulness and transformed the appearance of many of the existing structures, he also initiated new building projects, including yet another forum, the forum of Augustus, a new senate house, a palace complex on Palatine Hill, the altar of peace, the golden milestone, the rostra or speaker's platform, the temple of Julius Caesar, the temple of Mars, the temple of Apollo, as well as the restoration of some eighty-two temples originally constructed during earlier periods, the Pantheon, the theater of Marcellus, a mausoleum, and others. Because of his many building projects, Augustus left his mark on the city of Rome and on the office of emperor. Emperors following Augustus also wanted to leave memorials as evidence of their influence and greatness. Consequently, the city of Rome saw the construction of additional forums, palaces, theaters, arches, temples, and baths during the first century, especially during the reign of the emperors Tiberias, Caligula, Nero, Vespasian, Titus, and Domitian.

Though the task of recovering first-century Rome has been complicated by the continuous occupation of the site, many of the features of the city from the time of Paul and the early church have been identified through archaeological research and ancient sources. The city, at the heart of which were the seven hills, was reorganized into fourteen districts and 256 precincts by Augustus. Among the major features of the first-century city were the circus maximus, a major recreational complex in the city; the forum, the major religious, social, commercial, and political hub of the city, as well as other forums added by the emperors Augustus, Vespasian, Nerva, and Trajan; and the palace complex of the emperors located on Palatine Hill. Many of the citizens of the city lived in tenement buildings called insulae; shops occupied the ground level of the tenement buildings. Aqueducts, which in Paul's day probably numbered eight, carried water from the Alban hills to the city; there were Roman baths, which in Paul's day numbered perhaps as many as 170; and fountains, which were both beautiful and practical sources of daily water. Other notable sites in Rome were the rostra, from which officials delivered public addresses; the golden milestone, which listed the distance from key cities of the empire to the city of Rome; the Basilica Julia, designed as a facility in which law courts were held; and the Basilica Aemilia, in which business and commercial activities took place. Rome also had the temple of Vesta, the goddess of the living flame of Rome, as well as dozens of other temples; the Pantheon, constructed as a shrine to honor all the gods; and the altar of peace constructed by Augustus as a symbol of the peace that prevailed during his reign. Rome also had a number of noteworthy streets including the Sacred Way, the major street of the forum area, and the Appian Way, the Praenestine Way, the Nomentan Way, and the Flaminian Way, which all led into the city.

While references to Rome in the NT are meager (Acts 2:10; 18:2; 19:21; 23:11; 28:14, 16; Rom 1:7, 15; 2 Tim 1:17), the city played an important background role in the drama of the NT and early Christianity. In 63 BCE Palestine became a Roman province as a result of Pompey's campaign to that region. Consequently, during the NT period Palestine was occupied by the Romans and was a part of the Roman Empire. It was through a combination of local administrators, kings, ethnarchs, tetrarchs, and procurators such as Antipater, Herod the

Great, Herod Archelaus, Herod Antipas, Herod Philip, Herod Agrippa, Pontius Pilate, and others that the Romans provided local leadership in the land of Palestine during NT times. Luke notes that Jesus was born during the reign of Caesar Augustus (Luke 2:1). It was during the reign of the emperor Tiberias Caesar that Jesus' public ministry took place. It was to the cities of the Roman provinces in Asia Minor (Acts 13:1–28), Macedonia (Acts 16:11–17:15), Greece (Acts 17:16–17), and Rome that early Christianity spread (Acts 28:14, 16). Rome permanently changed the face of Palestine during the Jewish-Roman War of 66–70 CE (the destruction of Jerusalem is vividly portrayed in Luke 21:20–24) and the Second Jewish Revolt (132–35 CE). While Rome was one of the cities to which Christianity spread, it also was the citadel of intense persecution during the reign of Domitian, as reflected in the book of Revelation. With the passing of time Rome, along with Alexandria of Egypt and Antioch of Syria, became a major center of Christianity. Today the city and the sites associated with early Christianity are visited by thousands of Christian pilgrims. St. Peter's Basilica and its courts are jammed to overflowing each year on Christmas Eve, Good Friday, and Easter as the events of the birth, crucifixion, and resurrection of the Christ event are celebrated anew.

Bibliography: ADAMS, J. M., "Rome," *Biblical Backgrounds,* rev. Joseph A. Callaway (Nashville: Broadman, 1965) 211–14; BLAIKLOCK, E. M., "Rome," *NIDBA,* 392; idem, "Rome," *NIDB,* 871–73; idem, "Rome," *ZPEB,* 5:162–68; FINEGAN, J., "In Rome," *The Archaeology of the New Testament: The Mediterranean World of the Early Christian Apostles* (Boulder: Westview, 1981) 217–34; FOLEY, R. L., "Rome, Christian Monuments," *IDBSup,* 754–56; GRANT, R. M., "Rome, City of," *IDB,* 4:124–28; HALL, J. F., "Rome," *ABD,* 5:830–34; HINSON, E. G., "Roman Empire," *MDB,* 769–72; JUDGE, E. A., "Rome," *NBD*[2], 1038–40; MCRAY, J., "Rome," *Archaeology and the New Testament* (Grand Rapids: Baker, 1991) 341–50; idem, "Rome and the Roman Empire," *HolBD,* 1207–12; PERKINS, P., "Rome," *HBD,* 880–83; SADDINGTON, D. B., "Rome," *Major Cities of the Biblical World,* ed. R. K. Harrison (Nashville: Nelson, 1985) 208–22; STEPHENS, W. H., "Rome: The Eternal City," *Best of the Illustrator: The Journeys of Paul,* ed. Michael J. Mitchell (Nashville: Sunday School Board of the Southern Baptist Convention, 1990) 85–90; THOMPSON, J. A., "Rome, City of," *BEB,* 2:1868–70; VOS, H., "Rome," *BW,* 484–93; idem, "Rome," *ISBE,* 4:228–36; WRIGHT, G. E., "Rome," *Biblical Archaeology,* rev. ed. (Philadelphia: Westminster, 1962) 266–74.

CHART OF HISTORICAL PERIODS

ARCHAEOLOGICAL PERIODS	EGYPT	ISRAEL	MESOPOTAMIA
Paleolithic (Old Stone Age) prior to 10,000 BCE			
Mesolithic (Middle Stone Age) 10,000–8000 BCE			
Neolithic (New Stone Age) 8000–4000 BCE			
Chalcolithic (Bronze-Stone Age) 4000–3100 BCE			
Early Bronze (or Early Canaanite Age) 3100–2000 BCE			
	Early Dynastic 3000–2700 BCE Dynasties I–II		Early Dynastic Period 2900–2350 BCE
	Old Kingdom 2700–2200 BCE Dynasties III–VI		Akkadian Period 2350–2100 BCE
	First Intermediate 2200–2040 BCE Dynasties (VII–X)		Ur III Period 2100–2000 BCE
Middle Bronze (Middle Canaanite) 2000–1550 BCE	Middle Kingdom 2040–1640 Dynasties XI–XIV	Patriarchal Period	Early Old Babylonian 2000–1800 BCE
			Old Babylonian Period 1800–1600 BCE Hammurabi Age 1792–1750 BCE
	Second Intermediate 1640–1550 BCE Dynasties XV–XVII Hyksos Period	Joseph's Descent	
Late Bronze (Late Canaanite) 1550–1200 BCE	New Kingdom 1550–1070 BCE Dynasties XVIII–XX Amarna Age	Oppression	Middle Babylonian 1600–1000 BCE
		Exodus Conquest	
Iron Age I (Early Israelite) 1200–900 BCE	Late Period 1070–332 BCE Dynasties XXI–XXXI	Period of the Judges United Monarchy	Assyrian Period 1000–626 BCE
Iron Age II (Middle & Late Israelite) 900–600 BCE		Divided Monarchy Fall of Samaria	
			Neo-Babylonian Period 626–539 BCE
Iron Age III 600–300 BCE Babylonian Period 587–539 BCE Persian Period 539–332 BCE		Fall of Jerusalem Exilic Period Post-Exilic Period	Persian Period 539–332 BCE
Hellenistic Period 332–64 BCE			Greek Period 332–200 BCE
Roman Period 64 BCE–324 CE		New Testament Period	
Byzantine Period 324–640 CE			

Maps and Photo Credits

List of Maps

Photo Credits

INDEX OF PLACE NAMES

INDEX OF BIBLICAL AND ANCIENT SOURCES